THE
HANGING
FIGURE

Library of Congress Cataloging-in-Publication Data

Morris, Christopher D.
   The hanging figure : on suspense and the films of Alfred Hitchcock / Christopher D. Morris.
       p.   cm.
   Includes bibliographical references and index.
   ISBN 0-275-97136-8 (alk. paper)
   1. Hitchcock, Alfred, 1899—Criticism and interpretation.   I. Title.
PN1998.3.H38 M67 2002
791.43'0233'092—dc21   2001058948

British Library Cataloguing in Publication Data is available.

Library of Congress Catalog Card Number: 2001058948
ISBN: 0-275-97136-8

First published in 2002

Praeger Publishers, 88 Post Road West, Westport, CT 06881
An imprint of Greenwood Publishing Group, Inc.
www.praeger.com

Printed in the United States of America

The paper used in this book complies with the
Permanent Paper Standard issued by the National
Information Standards Organization (Z39.48–1984).

10 9 8 7 6 5 4 3 2 1

THE HANGING FIGURE

On Suspense and
the Films of Alfred Hitchcock

Christopher D. Morris

Westport, Connecticut
London

Copyright Acknowledgments

The author and publisher gratefully acknowledge permission for use of the following material:

Hitchcock on Hitchcock: Selected Writings and Interviews, edited and translated by Sidney Gottlieb. Copyright © 1955 Sidney Gottlieb. Reprinted with permission of University of California Press, Berkeley, California, and Faber and Faber, Ltd., London.

An excerpt of "The Waste Land" from *Collected Poems 1909–1962* by T.S. Eliot was reprinted with permission of Harcourt, Inc., USA, and Faber and Faber, Ltd., London.

An excerpt was reprinted with permission of Simon & Schuster from *Hitchcock* by Francois Truffaut with the collaboration of Helen G. Scott. Copyright © 1984 by Francois Truffaut; copyright renewed © 1995 by Eva Truffaut, Josephine Truffaut, and Laura Truffaut-Wong.

Suspense: Conceptualizations, Theoretical Analyses, and Empirical Explorations, edited by Peter Vorderer, Hans J. Wulff, and Mike Friedrichsen (Mahwah, NJ: Erlbaum Associates, 1996). A portion was reprinted with permission of Lawrence Erlbaum Associates.

"*Psycho*'s Allegory of Seeing" and "Reading the Birds and *The Birds*" by Christopher Morris originally appeared in *Literature/Film Quarterly* © Salisbury University, Salisbury, Maryland.

"Feminism, Deconstruction, and the Pursuit of the Tenable in *Vertigo*" and "*Easy Virtue*'s Frames" by Christopher Morris originally appeared in *Hitchcock Annual* and portions are reprinted with permission of the publisher.

"The Direction of *North by Northwest*" and "*Torn Curtain*'s Futile Talk" by Christopher Morris appeared in *Cinema Journal* 36:4 (Summer 1997), pp. 43–56, and *Cinema Journal* 39:1 (Fall 1999), pp. 54–73, respectively. Portions reprinted with the permission of the publisher, the University of Texas Press.

"Ro/pe" by Christopher Morris first appeared in *Film Criticism* and a portion is reprinted with permission of the publisher.

Dialogue from *Rope* appears courtesy Universal Studios, Universal City, CA.

Every reasonable effort has been made to trace the owners of copyright materials in this book, but in some instances this has proven impossible. The author and publisher will be glad to receive information leading to more complete acknowledgments in subsequent printings of the book and in the meantime extend their apologies for any omissions.

For Martha

Contents

Illustrations

Acknowledgments

Over the years my intellectual debt to J. Hillis Miller has been substantial. Thomas Leitch gave me valuable feedback as a respondent at conferences. My brother David has been astute and generous in his comments. I've benefitted from discussions with students in my Alfred Hitchcock seminar and with the following colleagues at Norwich University: Dan Lane, Rob McKay, Floyd Stuart, David Ward, and Bill Wick. Ellen Morris, my niece, alerted me to the Egyptian-Canaanite battle scene. For technical assistance I am indebted to Bill Barnard, Bill Estill, Nick Fleming, Darlene Goodrich, and Jason Raposa. Sharon Smith provided excellent secretarial assistance, and Tammy Hunt, the interlibrary loan librarian at Norwich, worked tirelessly on my behalf. Verbena Pastor, David Ward, Fran Chevalier and my brother Michael gave me crucial help with translations. I thank Mark Tompkins and Kristen Eberhard for excellent work as copy editor and production editor, respectively. For subsidies of the costs of permissions and reproductions, I am grateful to the Faculty Development Committee of Norwich University and to Andrew Knauf, Head of the Humanities Division.

Several chapters appeared in preliminary form as journal articles; I thank the respective editors for permission to adapt these essays: "*Psycho*'s Allegory of Seeing," *Literature/Film Quarterly* 24 (1996), 47–51; "Feminism, Deconstruction, and the Pursuit of the Tenable in *Vertigo*," *Hitchcock Annual* (1996–97), 3–25; "The Direction of *North by Northwest*," *Cinema Journal* 36 (1997), 43–56; "*The Lodger*'s Allegory of Seeing," *Film and Philosophy* 4 (1997), 11–19; "*Easy Virtue*'s Frames," *Hitchcock Annual* (1998–99), 20–30; "*Torn Curtain*'s Futile Talk," *Cinema Journal* 39 (1999), 54–73; "Ro/pe," *Film Criticism* 24 (1999–2000), 17–40.

Introduction

Histories of the revolution in criticism during the last quarter-century are familiar.[1] In the late 1960s, the New Critical paradigm for literary studies collapsed; intellectual historians of the future may debate whether that event was signaled by the Johns Hopkins Conference of 1967 or by political events in France and America in the following year.[2] Whatever its origin, the shift away from New Criticism—to structuralism poststructuralism, feminism, reader-response criticism, the new historicism, postcolonial studies, cultural studies, queer theory, deconstruction—has become the subject of allegories, including those that envision the break as a "fall" or the present state of criticism "Babel."[3] Because literature departments are the largest in the humanities, change accelerated more rapidly in them, but new critical discourses became more common in other humanities and social science disciplines, too.

This revolution presented reigning empirical models with four challenges: to Cartesianism (the idea that philosophy begins with the division of the world into subject and object), to signification (the idea that a sign has a necessary relation to its referent), to mimesis (the idea that art is a reflection of reality), and to hermeneutics (the idea that a determinable meaning of a text may be inferred from its analysis).[4] In place of these challenged assumptions, the new discourses proposed different starting points: for example, certain feminists argued for intrinsic features of women's writing; psychoanalytic critics advocated reformulated versions of Freud's idea of the unconscious; new historicists and postcolonial critics redefined literature as allegories of hegemonic power; queer theorists exposed the cultural construction of gender. Within deconstruction, the approach closest to mine, various starting points for critical discourse were proposed, including Jacques Derrida's many neologisms (*différance, supplement, trace*), Paul de Man's concept of the machinal nature of language, and J. Hillis Miller's recent theory of black holes. None of these approaches now enlists a following comparable to that of the New Critics, with the result that the humanities has become a discipline in interminable crisis, if not in ruins.[5]

Research in the humanities now proceeds without appeal to critical authority (as Eliot often provided for New Critics), without agreed-upon canons, and without definitions of the object of literary and cultural studies.[6] Instead, humanities scholars acknowledge many objections to any new *starting point*—to cite the figure I just used in my last paragraph—as a foundation concept for work in a discipline that lacks foundations. Today there is no starting point that does not soon commit the critic to ever-more-vulnerable assumptions. Writing of narrative beginnings, J. Hillis Miller observes that each one "cunningly covers a gap, an absence at the origin."[7] As my arbitrary "historical" opening implies, criticism, too, often adopts the temporal structure of narrative, of a before and after. If the first moves of narrative and critical writing may be imagined as gap coverings, then the most ethical function of criticism at the present time may be to acknowledge its own dysfunction.

Criticism's immediate self-invalidation is apparent even in the critic's choice of topics. To write on a category like thrillers or film noir may be to commit oneself to ideas already called into question by the examples chosen to illustrate it. To write on an author or a film director may be to implicitly commit oneself to that figure's canonization within arbitrary institutions that perpetuate their own hegemony and induce unpredictable effects in the real world.[8] To write on "suspense" or on "Alfred Hitchcock" runs both risks. Kafka allegorized the dilemma of an inability to begin in his parable "Before the Law," where the petitioner, after approaching the law, soon finds his goal more distant; likewise, the first steps taken by Beckett's heroes Murphy or Malloy set them on courses of infinite detour. Martin Heidegger acknowledged the incapacity of starting without contradiction in his commentary on Nietzsche's eternal return: it "expresses the way in which the one who poses the guiding question remains enmeshed in the structure of that question."[9] Alfred Hitchcock's *Easy Virtue* depicts a world in which no opening is possible without the adoption of a frame. To follow the implications of Kafka, Beckett, Heidegger, and Hitchcock places the writer in the position of uncertainty described by Werner Heisenberg, in which attempts to measure the world falsify it.[10] All critical discourses must pass over this threshold of self-invalidation before beginning, but this quick, inevitable movement leaves unanswered questions that will later challenge the argument. Or—in a related figure that reveals the topic and thesis of this book— any beginning leaves unanswered *questions that will hang suspended*.

My title anticipates a definition of suspense developed in the three parts of this book, which I will summarized in a moment. But first a discussion of interdisciplinary approaches to film is in order, because they also shape my study. As the artistic medium that exploits not only traditional theatrical components but also camera technique, film has for years been the art form most hospitable to interdisciplinary inquiry. And because film criticism is written and taught in those same large departments roiled by changes in literary criticism, film scholars now routinely invoke contemporary theory, and their work is categorizable by approach. While for the first three-quarters of the century film theory was dominated by the insights of realist practitioners like Eisenstein and Bazin, the field now includes Marxists, suture-theorists, reader-response critics, feminists, new historicists, Lacanians, and queer theorists, as well as critics influenced by cognitive psychology. The infusion of these new perspectives means that engagement with theories of criticism is now essential. In my first chapter, these and other approaches to suspense are taken up in detail.

Art history has experienced an upheaval parallel to those that occurred in literary and film studies. In the 1970s, the introduction of continental theory into the study of art was facilitated by the journals *New Literary History*, *Critical Inquiry*, and *Representations*. In 1982 *Art Journal* discussed "the crisis in the discipline" brought about by theory. The English translation of Jacques Derrida's *The Truth in Painting* appeared in 1987; in the next year, Norman Bryson edited a collection of essays on "the new art history from France." The work of Svetlana Alpers, W.J.T. Mitchell, and Michael Fried, particularly, has put into question previously received notions of pictorial representation. Robert S. Nelson surveys the debate in art history in his introduction to *Critical Terms for Art History*, a volume consciously modeled on a parallel volume in literary criticism. Nelson's collection reveals how such first principles as "representation," "sign," "meaning" or even "art history" are now so vigorously contested that it is possible to regard critical discussions of them as "short stories."[11] Nelson's dismaying conclusion may portend the same dilemma for art historians as for literary critics in finding consensus or even starting points. In what follows, I provide an overview of the three parts of my book's attempt to define suspense.

A FIGURATIVE, NOT HERMENEUTIC, APPROACH

Suspense is popularly held to be an emotion resembling anxiety induced in a reader or viewer through the experience of a narrative work of art (one that unfolds a story in time) concerning what will happen next, particularly to admired protagonists. Not surprisingly, given the preceding survey of critical diversity, scholars have not been able to agree. Chapter 1 presents a comprehensive overview of the literature, mostly associated with the Cartesian and hermeneutic traditions. One major obstacle for these theorists is the phenomenon known as "recidivist" suspense—or suspense that persists even after multiple readings or viewings of a narrative; in such situations, suspense is deemed to exist independently of "what will happen next." For example, even after several viewings audiences of *Psycho* may experience suspense as Marion Crane prepares for her shower. Recidivist suspense is intuitively apparent to theatregoers who at numerous performances have watched Othello prepare to kill

Desdemona or to readers who follow Marlow's search for Kurtz. Thus to denote the meaning of "suspense," something everyone thinks is real, we do not yet have the right signs.

A second difficulty is that suspense can exist even in the absence of an admired protagonist. Perhaps the long Socratic/Kantian heritage linking knowledge with morality explains these theorists' ideological investment in suspense. In any case, modernism teaches that suspense also arises in connection with the fate of villains. Hitchcock and Truffaut thought that film audiences would hope, with Norman Bates, that Marion Crane's Ford sank all the way to the bottom of the swamp; theatrical audiences exhibit anxiety about the fate of Brecht's unlikeable Mother Courage; readers of *The Stranger* are similarly concerned for the criminal Mersault. A third difficulty is that suspense may continue even after the work has concluded. Everyone acknowledges this in the case of plot discrepancies—the question of Lady Macbeth's children or the way Judy disappeared from the McKittrick Hotel in *Vertigo*; however, a more fundamental uncertainty persists in the case of ambiguous characters. Is Henry V the ideal king? Can we be certain the title character of *The Lodger* is not, at the same time, the Avenger? These examples suggest an intertextual dimension of suspense that makes it inseparable from the act of interpretation. Put another way, the older Cartesian and hermeneutic approaches to suspense may establish a spurious boundary between plot and interpretation, whereas Hitchcock's films suggest that prior interpretative decisions may even *define* plot. *Easy Virtue*, for example, teaches that viewers may not *see* events without first adopting an interpretive frame. In any case, these exceptions to the popular definition of suspense suggest it may be too narrow. Of course, those who defend it have responses to these objections, which are examined in Chapter 1. Still, the existence of counterexamples to the popular understanding of suspense shows why studies drawing on other critical traditions continue to appear.

One tradition is Aristotle's discussion of "catharsis"—a "purgation" or "cleansing" of pity and fear at the end of the tragedy. Is *catharsis* like the supposed closure of suspense? Aristotle's famous formula has always been debated; recent scholars have questioned whether catharsis takes place in the viewer, as most have assumed, or in the action of the play. Whatever its outcome, this new discussion raises two questions for the study of suspense: where it occurs and when it ends. Again, suspense turns out to be not as simple as it first appears. Have popular ideas about suspense been derived from hasty analogies between audiences and literary *characters*? Is it possible that suspense never ends? Chapter 1 raises these questions without answering them, noting only that they bedevil definitions of suspense advanced in the Cartesian and hermeneutic traditions.

Hitchcock's statements about suspense, examined in Chapter 2, suggest an alternative approach: the figurative. In interviews and short essays, Hitchcock struggled to conceptualize the phenomenon that he as well as critics found to define his work, but scholars have been disappointed: some of Hitchcock's remarks are at odds with others; some are contradicted by his practice. The first part of Chapter 2 discusses these deadends, while the second considers Hitchcock's more vivid narratives and analogies for suspense. For instance, he writes about suspense in his cameos (his walk-on roles in his own films) and in his MacGuffins (or plot pretexts). These indirect definitions raise questions about *representation*—about the identity of characters, the meaning of their quests, and the ideas they (or the film as a whole) seem to espouse. Cameos and MacGuffins are figures that do not pretend to provide an abstract definition or referent for suspense; instead they exemplify it. So, in adopting my own figurative approach to suspense, I've followed Hitchcock's lead.

An implication is that suspense may be coextensive with narrative. In remarks amplifying deconstruction's objection to the metaphysical assumptions that inhabit texts, Derrida claimed that suspense was fundamental to literature:

Literature's *being-suspended* neutralizes the "assumption" which it carries; it has this capacity, even if the consciousness of the writer, interpreter or reader (and everyone plays all these roles in some way) can never render this capacity completely effective and present . . . because this capacity is double, equivocal, contradictory, *hanging on* and *hanging between, dependent* and *independent*, an "assumption" both assumed and suspended. [italics in the original][12]

The suspended quality Derrida finds in literature is also a characteristic of film. Though such suspense may initially take the form of undecidability, as of a propositional statement and its opposite, it never rests there but continues, in Derrida's trope, to *hang*. Chapter 2 shows how Hitchcock's figures for suspense imply this larger state of contingency. They authorize my working hypothesis that suspense is best understood not discursively but figuratively.[13] And so it is to the hanging figure that Part II turns.

ETYMOLOGY AND ICONOGRAPHY

For critics in the Cartesian and hermeneutic traditions, a deconstructive and figurative approach to suspense may seem dangerously unstable; however, the weakness of existing theories and Hitchcock's preference for the figural may encourage its pursuit. The major theoretical advantage of deconstruction, outlined in detail in Chapter 1, is that it makes fewer assumptions than other approaches: one need only believe in the existence of a mark. In any case, the first task of my figurative approach is to investigate an overlooked topic that should be of interest in all approaches—the etymology of the word "suspense."[14]

The English word "suspense" is a compound derived from the Latin *sub* and the transitive verb *pendo*, the source of the derivative, intransitive *pendeo*, which means to be suspended or hang. The first sense of the transitive verb means "to place in the scales or weigh," an activity involving both judgment and representation, one that is directly related to its second meaning, "to allot or pay out." For the Romans, to "pend" something would be to weigh it in a scales—a quantity of grain, pieces of gold—in anticipation of disbursing it as payment to someone else. Hence before "suspense" acquired any affective sense of anxiety, its root denoted the necessity for accurate measurement and representation of something of value, before being circulated in the world of exchange; perhaps a faint picture of the scales themselves or of their ideal state of equilibrium may be evoked in the later intransitive form of the verb. In any case, the prospect of beginning with fair representation underlies not only commercial activity but also ethical and philosophical inquiry: before extending money as payment, we must determine—or have full confidence—that it is authentic and the proper amount; likewise, before we speak words like "love" or "God" or "suspense," we must *weigh them carefully*, before allotting them to others in our discourse. But at the same time, this necessity admits there must be doubt: if there were no variety in quantities, weighing would be redundant. Further, if true representation is necessary prior to "use," then we must also be sure that the *scales* are accurate: for instance, any control weights, on the other side of the scale, must themselves be measured and weighed against some *other* standard, which may necessitate a prior weighing, with the prospect here of infinite regress. It is no wonder that beginnings are impossible!

To the extent that a process of weighing prior to disbursal is like thinking prior to saying, thinking, too, may be discovered to be foundationless. (That the analogy is not simply fanciful may be borne out by the fact that *pendo* is also related to the Latin *pondus*, the root for the English verb "ponder"; thus, to think may be already to be in suspense.) The inquiry into the etymology of "suspense" has already manifested this dilemma: seeking some foundation for discourse in etymology, we discover an abyss. Hitchcock's suspense opens up similar prospects of foundationlessness that must be artificially covered over before discourse can start; in my extension of de Man's thesis, acceptance of such a preliminary fiction is a prerequisite even for *seeing* Hitchcock's films, much less talking about them.

The Latin word *pendeo* acquired many meanings: to hang; to be strung up for punishment or in suicide; to have one's name hung up or posted; to be weighed; to hang *upon* something (as on a person's neck or words); to droop; to be perilously perched before an impending fall; to be supported in the air or hover; to float on water; to be left incomplete; to be undetermined or uncertain; to be perplexed; to be hinged or based on; to rely on. The majority of these meanings have to do with spatial position and only a few with affect. Physical positions like these are often depicted in Hitchcock's films. It may be that this director, who cared more for setting and location than for affect, contrived his films to render *visual* suspense through the maximum number and variety of hanging figures.

The thread common to *pendeo*'s many senses is an incapacity to exist autonomously, an idea with implications for the depiction of the self. Changing the Cartesian paradigm, in which the self is an independent *res inextensus* safely housed inside a *res extensus*, Hitchcock depicts the self as an illusion generated by the operation of signs. *Psycho*'s empty interiors and selves are a good example. The self's interminable state of contingency may be related to the prospect for infinite regress opened up by *pendo*'s dilemma of weighing: if no external standard for a weight exists, can one exist for a self, for the person who does the weighing? *Pendo*'s etymology hints that suspense is an undecidability that may *never* be resolvable and, by inference, that closure of the sort envisioned by Cartesian and hermeneutic critics may be a myth. Part II proposes that suspense implies infinite undecidability and that this sense is discernible in visual representations of hanging figures.

Before proceeding with this claim, I must explain my use of the word "figure." Beginning with my title and continuing until the last chapter, this word conveys—at the same time, without distinguishing between them—both of its two main senses: first, as a visual shape or form; second, as a deviation from normal usage. It will be readily asked how a visual image could also partake of the second meaning, which by tradition has to do with *verbal* usage. A preliminary reply is that contemporary theorists have increasingly acknowledged the presence and operation of figures in visual art. Roland Barthes believed images in advertising, photography, and film could be construed as figures.[15] Michael Fried interpreted the paintings of Thomas Eakins as allegories of what it means to "figure."[16] Writing of the term "figuration," the art historian Richard Shiff points to the contemporary conflation of its visual and verbal senses:

But what does it mean to be figured? *This concept is* of the utmost interest to art history because it oscillates between the visual and the textual and between matter and sign. It facilitates diverse kinds of understanding by playing one type of knowledge against another. A figure can be a drawing or any depiction (visual art), but it can also be a metaphor or any description (literary art). Does this imply that a drawing *is* a metaphor and a metaphor a drawing? Or are such assertions, articulated in words, no more than metaphorical themselves? To contain or control the "figure" is no simple matter. Figuration spreads.[17]

Shiff's belief that the oscillation between visual and verbal senses of the word figure may facilitate "diverse kinds of knowledge" agrees with the premise of this book; in fact, establishing the figurative value of the visual is one of its goals. Different proportions of each sense coexist each time the word "figure" appears. Each contributes to the understanding of suspense. In the afterword, I offer a more extensive discussion of the word, in hopes that these larger theoretical questions can then be addressed in the light of this study.

My assumption that visual representations of hanging figures may contribute to knowledge of suspense is in keeping with this book's interdisciplinary approach; in recent years, the study of visual art by scholars from other disciplines has become frequent. Impetus for this trend came initially from the Frankfurt School and seminal essays like Walter Benjamin's "The Work of Art in the Age

of Mechanical Reproduction."[18] Works like Derrida's *The Truth of Painting* and
Miller's *Illustration* show how painting may be examined in deconstructive analysis.[19] A spectrum of even broader interdisciplinary studies—uniting poststruc-
turalist thought with architecture, photography, and television, among others—
is collected in Peter Brunette and David Wills's *Deconstruction and the Visual
Arts*.[20] My analysis of hanging figures in Chapter 3 shares this recent interdisciplinary interest; I test the idea that suspense as undecidability inheres in still
art. If so, still art may have, after all, an ineradicable temporal dimension. A
corollary is that classical accounts of nontemporal arts—and especially the in-
vidious rankings of genres (like Lessing's of poetry over painting)—may require
revision.[21] Another corollary—for those who believe visual representations resemble the real world—is that reality itself may be composed only of referentless figures. I suppose this to be an "ultimate" implication of my study, which
I defer to the afterword.

While my survey of hanging figures in Chapter 3 is brief, it shows that fascination with this image has characterized Western and non-Western cultures
from their origins; that hanging figures sometimes have important religious or
ritualistic functions; that the authentic identity of the hanging figure is put in
doubt; that the attitude of human hanging figures to their supposed suffering is
enigmatic, raising questions about decidability; that they are also readable—in
the vocabulary of contemporary film criticism—as "reflexive," that is, as commentaries on themselves and the condition of suspense they exhibit. For these
reasons, the iconography of the hanging figure seems an appropriate bridge
between the etymology of the word "suspense" and film. For example, because
most hanging figures examined in Chapter 3 are literally *off the ground*, they
are particularly apt explorations of groundlessness or of the abyss of judgment
already hinted at in the Latin verb *pendo*. Both the Egyptian depiction of children hanging from the towers of Canaan and Michelangelo's *Santo Spirito Crucifix* may convey the contradiction that foundationless religious faith
nevertheless requires material embodiment; Titian's depiction of the flaying of
Marsyas complicates the representation of groundless faith by examining its
pagan analogues; Rembrandt's slaughtered ox captures the way "the sacrificial"
must presuppose a frame. These figures depict paradoxical, framed conditions
of groundlessness—the very contradiction opened up by the etymology of suspense.

Extending the study of hanging figures from still art to film, Chapter 4 develops close readings of specific images from four Hitchcock films: *Murder!*
(1930), *Number Seventeen* (1932), *Saboteur* (1942), and *Rear Window* (1954).
Students of Hitchcock will recognize the importance of these scenes. The
trapeze-hanging of the homosexual mulatto Handel Fane in *Murder!* is the prel-
ude to his artistic, climactic, off-camera suicide by hanging. The "strung up"
double-hanging figures of *Number Seventeen* literally embody the issue of the
"construction of the couple" central to film. The Statue of Liberty setting for
the hanging villain in *Saboteur* exemplifies the frequent connection in Hitch-

cock's films between suspense and political ideology. Jeff's hanging from his sill in *Rear Window* focuses attention on the recurring image of the threshold— here between the inner and outer realms that constitute the film's unresolved study of knowing. These scenes insinuate into their own stories a suggestion of undecidability comparable to those conveyed in the paintings of Titian, Winslow Homer, or Toulouse-Lautrec. The diverse domains of undecidability are also remarkable: viewers are led to question whether there are meaningful differences between homosexuality and heterosexuality, between law-breakers and law-enforcers, between patriots and traitors, or between inner and outer worlds. At the level of morality, Hitchcock's hanging figures effect a Nietzschean trans-valuation of values, a signature element of his films. Any decision between moral and political opposites is put in suspense. In its discussion of these images, Chapter 4 offers support from Hitchcock's films for the hypothesis discovered in Chapter 2 and tested in Chapter 3—that in the *figure* of suspense we can learn clues to its operation.

SUSPENSE IN HITCHCOCK AND IN CRITICISM

Part III studies suspense in eleven of Hitchcock's films. Each chapter is in-troduced by a frame-enlargement of a hanging figure whose relevance to the film's suspense is discussed in an italicized caption. Some of these scenes are just as central to their films as those discussed in Chapter 4. For example, Hitchcock and Truffaut agreed that the image of the anonymous protagonist of *The Lodger*, hanging handcuffed from a wrought-iron fence, alluded to the cru-cifixion. *Vertigo*'s introductory shot of Scottie Ferguson dangling from the gutter crystallizes that film's ongoing antithesis of tenability and nothingness. In *North by Northwest*, Thornhill's hoisting up of Eve Kendall, across the face of Mount Rushmore, is one of many moments of political defacement. Other examples of the hanging figure will at first seem marginal but, on reflection, of recognizable importance to the film's suspense. The judge's swinging monocle in *Easy Virtue* is a seemingly trivial detail; nevertheless, the dissolve that likens it to a clock's pendulum and the role it plays in focusing the judge's "vision" allegorizes the "adoption of a perspective" as inevitably prejudicial judgment. *Spellbound*'s figure of John Ballantine's young brother, accidentally impaled on a fence, is so fleeting as to defy legible video-capture; nevertheless, as the "true" origin of the protagonist's amnesia, this hanging figure raises questions about the film's happy ending.

Other examples of the hanging figure are closer to the etymological periphery of "suspense." For example, Alicia in *Notorious* hangs on Devlin as they walk down the staircase to their safety. And while *Rope*'s David Kentley stands on the floor, his position reflects and makes problematic the etymological sense of *pendeo* as "to be strung up." These images illustrate the elasticity of the hanging figure; indeed, elasticity is itself one of its senses. Of course, Part II had already established that a spatially hanging *human* figure was not essential to the category: if suspense is readable in pendants or Jeff Koons's basketballs, it is also present in Marion Crane's sinking Ford or the birds hovering in Bodega Bay. In this way, Part III reinforces my conclusion that images of hanging figures— human or abstract—are not privileged signs *necessary* to the understanding of suspense. On the contrary, a hanging figure is only a sign, like any other sign, without any necessary connection to the suspense that seems to accompany it. Another way of putting this is to say that suspense may be inherent not only in literature, as Derrida argued, but in the visual images or art and life. At the outset, then, readers are advised of the eventual decoupling of my heuristic hanging figure from its supposedly signified referent, suspense.

In its emphasis on the infinite postponement of meaning, my understanding of suspense may at first seem to recall Derrida's early neologism *différance*; each idea, however, has a distinct scope. *"Différance"* in Derrida's essay constitutes language, whereas suspense in this book is only an accompaniment to both language and the visual. There is a major theoretical difference, too. Despite Derrida's disclaimers, concepts like *différance* (or the trace, the supplement, the call, or chora[22]) may be regarded as metaphysical terms: that is, they serve as foundation concepts, starting points, or new first principles for philosophy, in much the same way as Kant's categories, Hegel's spirit, Husserl's *epochē*, or Heidegger's *physis*. As Rodolphe Gasché points out, Derrida's first allegiance is to the Western philosophical tradition and not to literature or art.[23] There is little doubt that he sees his work as a continuation of the Enlightenment project of ground-clearing that may eventually lead to philosophy's proper resituation of itself on first principles or *archē*.[24] Derrida's adherence to this noble tradition is all the more evident when his approach to deconstruction is contrasted with de Man's: for the latter, language was figurative and ironic before being referential, and so it was to the rhetorical (not the constative) functions of language that de Man turned his attention. (Of course, de Man was hardly immune to the allure of metaphysics, since in his late works he speculated on the existence of language as an autonomously functioning system.[25]) In this respect, my definition of suspense is indebted more to de Man than to Derrida: in fact, I adopt de Man's view of reading as a useful analogy for the experience of viewing films. As my eventual decoupling of the hanging figure and suspense implies, these two terms are only coincidental, parallel figures, not figures *for* each other. My exploration of their co-presence is simply another heuristic—a MacGuffin—that allows discussion of suspense and Hitchcock's films from a new angle.[26]

That critical discussion has already embodied suspense is evident first from its obsessional character: the same images are constantly revisited, with no consensus or end in sight. We shall never reach agreement on the function of the rotating helix in *Vertigo* or the eye/drain dissolve in *Psycho*; each new reading is inaugural. Competing approaches quickly become self-canceling, particularly with regard to closure. For example, it is often a custom of hermeneutic criticism to evaluate the societal norm established at the end of a film, especially as reflected in the creation of the couple, in the light of the template critics bring to bear on that norm: for such critics, the achievement, subversion, or modification of that norm provides a readable end to suspense.[27] But Hitchcock's endings frustrate this expectation. Consider the last scenes of *Rear Window*. Virginia Wright Wexman thinks the ending idealizes—in the fate of the couples in the apartments across from Jeff—numerous examples of a companionate relationship that Jeff and Lisa are themselves unable to realize.[28] On the other hand, Robin Wood thinks the "very neatness of all this tying up of loose ends emphasizes its superficiality."[29] While the existence of opposed conclusions is no surprise, the remarkable frequency of such stalemate attests to Hitchcock's transvaluation of moral values: the same characters are read as examples of authenticity or fraudulence. *Rear Window*'s ending is only an obvious instance in which such conclusions do not end suspense: Paula Marantz Cohen thinks it "escapes narrative closure,"[30] and Thomas Leitch goes farther, generalizing from it—rightly in my view—that in "most of Hitchcock's films" the ending "does not resolve the problems the film has posed."[31] This book extends the insights of Cohen and Leitch by treating the criticism of Hitchcock, too, as perpetuating suspense.

Criticism has generated its own figures for irresolution. Andrew Britton's devastating critique of psychoanalysis in *Spellbound* helped me see psychiatric reading (and reading in general) as just another instance of that film's traumatic MacGuffin, the construction of arbitrary black shapes on white. My chapter on *Rope* develops a metaphor (narrative as inherently interrupted transfer) suggested by Thomas Hemmeter's excellent account of that film's dramatization of foundationless language. Susan White's learned study of *Vertigo* prompted my exploration of the trope of tenability. Robert Corber's analysis of the ambiguous motivations of Sam and Marion in *Psycho* converted these characters into new figures for the film's undecidability. Discussions of the MacGuffin by Thomas Elsaesser and Tom Cohen enabled me to read that parable as an allegory of reading and viewing. At the same time, citing prior interpretations also discloses the way misrepresentation becomes a condition of critical discourse, too: citations reframe the original works they were derived from. Wexman's view of *Rear Window*'s ending is part of her larger project to modify new historicism in the light of Habermas; Robin Wood's opposite view is part of his larger exposure of dehumanization in Hitchcock; Robert Corber wanted to call attention to the dangerous "postwar settlement" in America, not to undecidability; and so on. As relays that reframe the work they adapt, new works of criticism, too, struggle against misrepresentation.

The metaphor of an intertextual relay, as old as Plato, was given this expropriative sense by Derrida in his account of the postal network in *The Post-Card*; being enmeshed in such a grid is a recurrent feature of Hitchcock's world.[32] From the newspaper reports of crime and scandal that introduce *The Lodger* and *Easy Virtue*, through the summons to analysis in *Spellbound* or the relayed jury verdict of *Notorious*, to the scenes of dictation and cablegram-delivery that open

North by Northwest and *Torn Curtain*, Hitchcock's world begins in relayed messages coincident with or anterior to our knowledge of the main characters. Afterward this world becomes saturated with messages cut off from origins, words that misrepresent author and subject matter, and signs of all sorts that circulate independently of the human subjects they give the illusion of authenticating. Derrida's theme in *The Post-Card* is that "the letter never arrives at its destination"; this is his maxim for the self-division or spacing of language that makes its *non*-referentiality a condition of legibility. Hitchcock's hanging figures become visible amid relays of such suspended discourse The lodger hangs caught between the (false?) accusations of the mob and the (true?) discourses of the mass media. The judge in *Easy Virtue* pauses before delivering a verdict misrepresenting Larita, whose empty identity is signaled at the end of the film when she punningly tells photographers, "Shoot, there's nothing left to kill." In *Spellbound*, John's recollection of a hanging figure is evoked by a psychoanalytic relay constructed by Constance, who passes along the distorted words of *her* analyst, Brulov, who passes along the distorted words of Freud. John's remembered hanging figure is supposed to establish identity but instead defers it. In *Rope*, David Kentley becomes the missing conversation piece, the absent referent, first between Phillip and Brandon, then among their company. The dangling cargo in *Torn Curtain* is only a late example of that film's series of images of transferred exteriors misrepresenting interior contents; this one takes place at a relay point. Like the characters in Hitchcock's films, criticism passes these relays along as it creates new figures; to the extent we inhabit a world like Hitchcock's, we inevitably misrepresent.

Most viewers would not care to see themselves in the Swiftian images of audiences and readers Hitchcock provides. In his first film, *The Lodger*, Hitchcock depicts us as a vigilante mob intent on enforcing unjust interpretations we passionately believe and as the Buntings—a hypocritical, credulous couple awestruck by visual display. In *Easy Virtue* we are like prejudiced, voyeuristic jurors; in *The Ring* we are like howling fans at boxing matches. By *North by Northwest*, we are like the CIA. Through his cameos Hitchcock always impugned himself, too, by acknowledging his role in the relay; perhaps this helps convey a spirit in his work one critic called Jansenist.[33] Savage indictments of the gullibility and dangerous self-deception of senders and receivers of film signs continued throughout his career. Some might argue that the commercial success of his films depended on their being *mis*read in this respect. On the other hand, analysis of Hitchcock's endings shows that from the beginning of his career he devised the means to achieve immediate popular appeal despite a condemnation of reading that becomes evident in retrospect.

Hitchcock calls this world a "glamorously dangerous charade."[34] The world is a charade because, as already indicated, individual claims to identity are spurious. The world is glamorous because its signs often allure viewers. The world is dangerous because the necessity for assuming that its signs refer to something, as a premise of reading, always leads to unforeseeable results. (For example, my interpretation of Wexman, Wood, and others could hardly have been fore-seen by them.) As a "glamorously dangerous charade," Hitchcock's depicted world echoes the two-stage process the viewer experiences when watching his films. This process is a visual parallel to the one Paul de Man discerned in reading:

The paradigm for all texts consists of a figure (or a system of figures) and its decon-struction. But since this model cannot be closed off by a final reading, it engenders, in its turn, a supplementary figural super-position which narrates the unreadability of the prior narration. As distinguished from primary deconstructive narratives centered on fig-ures and ultimately always on metaphor, we can call such narratives to the second (or the third) degree *allegories*.[35]

For de Man, reading consists first of the encounter with a deconstructed figure that is inherently suspenseful (it "cannot be closed off by a final reading"); subsequently this encounter, which is deemed to be arbitrary (we learn "the unreadability of the prior narration"), becomes the *subject* of new narrations, which de Man calls allegories of reading. In my extension of de Man's two-stage process, viewing may be seen as beginning in an initial encounter with a visual spectacle taken to be real, followed by the deconstruction of that visual image as arbitrary. We read the visual world similarly to the way we read texts: first we mistakenly believe what we perceive has meaning, and then we reject that illusion; but in doing so we construct what de Man calls a new *allegory* or—in my terminology—the hanging figures of criticism. This process generates interpretation of all varieties; it helps explain why my own approach remains avowedly and merely figurative, retaining the sign without the referent.

HANGING FIGURES IN THE MUSEUM

On February 24, 2001, I drove some of my students to Montreal to see "Hitch-cock and Art: Fatal Coincidences"; to my knowledge this was the first major exhibition devoted to the work of a film director. Drawn by signs that had beckoned me to offer the seminar and my students to take it, we undertook a postmodern pilgrimage, from a relay point full of mostly verbal signs to another made up of mostly visual signs. In embarking on it we automatically became part of a narrative generated by journalists and museum officials, one that im-plicated us, too, in a process of canon formation. The pilgrimage required new border crossings, currency exchanges, entry fees and the acquisition of new signs—especially the purchase of the lavish catalogue, *Hitchcock and Art: Fatal Coincidences*.[36] If Hitchcock's Nietzschean transvaluation of values was to be believed, then any emancipatory effects of books and art had to be balanced—had to be weighed or suspended before being meted out—against the exhibi-tion's potential political effects. The glamorous signs that beckoned and can-onized also multiplied the wealth and reputation of what the Frankfurt School called the *Kulturindustrie*—first, Hitchcock's Hollywood studios, with their protected copyrights, and now the Montreal Museum of Fine Arts and its corporate partner. The never-predictable dangers of alluring signs is the continuing lesson of the MacGuffin: if you search for "the thirty-nine steps," the wife of a crofter who helps you may be beaten; if you search for the Nazis' secret, an innocent woman's life may be jeopardized; if you search for "Ambrose Chapel," pandemonium may come to Albert Hall. Acquiring new signs like the beautiful exhibit catalogue will have effects in the grid of circulating signs that I must ignore in order to get on with life. The value of what we do when we attend an exhibit or read or write a book can always be transvalued; the religious implications of "pilgrimage" as applied to my trip to the Montreal Museum of Fine Arts must be resisted.

"Looking for Hitchcock in a museum" forced me to recall the number of times museums in Hitchcock's films had been depicted as places of nonrecognition. As *Blackmail*'s criminal Tracy hangs from a rope in the British Museum, in front of a huge Egyptian statue, he never notices the dead quality of art's aspiration to immortality. As *Vertigo*'s Scottie observes Judy's supposed obsession with the portrait of Carlotta Valdes in the Palace of the Legion of Honor, he is unaware he is being manipulated. As *Torn Curtain*'s Armstrong and Sarah rush through the East Berlin *Staatsmuseum*, they are incapable of appreciating values that communists may share with capitalists. Museums are hardly singled out as places of misrecognition. A partial list of public places that prevent the transmission of true knowledge through visual spectacle must include such other delusive relay points as the music halls of *The Lodger* or *The 39 Steps*; the amusement parks of *The Ring* or *Strangers on a Train*; the courtrooms of *Easy Virtue* and *The Paradine Case*; the theatres of *Murder!* and *Stage Fright*; the aquarium and movie theatre of *Sabotage*; the observation decks in *Saboteur* and *North by Northwest*; the gambling casino of *To Catch a Thief*; the Casablanca bazaar in *The Man Who Knew Too Much* (1956). In these settings, Hitchcock's films question whether true knowledge can be derived from interpretations of the visual. In all films this doubt is extended to the real world by analogy; in certain films like *Rear Window* and *The Birds*, this extension is an explicit part of the plot. So the intellectual premise of the Montreal exhibition—that authentic knowledge of Hitchcock was to be derived from the juxtaposition of his films' signs with other visual signs—may have been subverted ahead of time by the objects exhibited.

The organizers of this exhibition assembled works of nineteenth-and twentieth-century visual art in successive rooms, each illustrating different and asymmetrical rubrics: the dying woman; Poe; the music-hall milieu; Catholicism; the kiss; abstract shapes; etc. A special room was devoted to Dalí's collaboration on *Spellbound*. Each room also included frame enlargements and recursive video clips from Hitchcock's films, all soliciting from the museumgoer obvious hermeneutic inferences—*influence? theme? archetype?* The exhibitors' use of the word "coincidences" was a well-chosen correlative to the thesis I had tried to establish on whatever residue was left from the thoughts of de Man and others: that signs, like hanging figures, and suspense simply coexist, without any natural or causal relation. For the exhibitors, the word preserved institutional neutrality with regard to the public's anticipated inferences.

A quotation from Jean-Luc Godard appeared at the entry to the exhibition—signs on a threshold promising referents within:

Perhaps there are ten thousand people who haven't forgotten Cézanne's apple, but there must be a billion spectators who will remember the lighter of the stranger on the train, and the reason why Alfred Hitchcock became the only *poete maudit* to meet with success was that he was the greatest creator of forms of the twentieth century, and it's forms that tell us finally what lies at the bottom of things.[37]

Godard's sweeping generalization and *hommage* need not detain us, but of great importance for this book is his conviction that Hitchcock's greatness lies in the evocation of objects—like the cigarette-lighter in *Strangers on a Train*—that are also "forms" or what I call "figures." (The relation between "form" and "figure" is touched on in my afterword.) Construed in this way, Godard's threshold quote is also the opening premise of this book. With regard to Godard's conclusion (that these figures finally tell us "what lies at the bottom of things"), I maintain that at the bottom of things lie new figures.

Godard's emphasis on the variety of object-signs in Hitchcock's films is another point of agreement between the exhibit and my book. As noted earlier, the hanging figure is only one example, but I could as easily have chosen vehicles, doors, clothes, or any number of other objects that seem to signify. Part of Hitchcock's genius is the creation of so many objects that withhold or withdraw significance in interminable suspense, a thought that the exhibit corroborated. After reading Godard's epigraph, I passed through the first door, where the exhibitors had displayed in a darkened room more than twenty props, on loan mostly from the studios, on black velvet under glass cases; in the language of the catalogue, "Objects signifying the films' identities give the exhibition a metonymical dimension: a rope (*Rope*), a cigarette lighter (*Strangers on a Train*), the mummified head of Norman Bates's mother (*Psycho*), a glass of milk (*Suspicion*), a bottle of Pommard wine filled with uranium (*Notorious*), Carlotta Valdes's jewelled pendant (*Vertigo*), and so on."[38] That the authors of the catalogue considered these objects metonymies reinforced my conviction that the real world, as well as painted objects and language, could be read as figuration. (The authors claimed to know—but withheld their knowledge of—what "the films' identities" *were*.) From unseen speakers came Bernard Herrmann's theme of longing from *Vertigo*, adapted from Wagner, and the overall effect of the room—*mise-en-scène* is not hyperbole—was to elevate these Hollywood trinkets to the stature of precious jewels.

I thought of the frames that would register these objects to perception. A new historicist critic like Corber or Wexman might have linked this opulent/tawdry display to the reifying effects of capitalism. A feminist critic might have resented the organizers' solicitation to scopophilia. A Lacanian critic might have meditated on the room's revelation of fetishism. I looked down on each case, hanging over them, looking though the glass. It was surely not lost on the exhibitors that gazing at an untouchable object trapped behind glass, as if in a jewelry shop, is itself an apt metaphor for the cinematic viewing process. Some would say filmed objects are "really" only photons—a speculation I take up in the afterword—but few of us ever see film that way, not even the most vigilant critics. (On the other hand, Hitchcock may have seen film this way; witness his remark to Truffaut, "There's no such thing as a face, because until the light hits it, it's nonexistent."[39]) The great majority of us must mistake signs for referents before later becoming aware of our error. These flickering pulses of light—what the French call *clignotements*—become beckoning signs the moment they appear on the screen in front of us, unobtainable; we effortlessly appropriate them into some referential narrative and, beyond that, into books of criticism.

The objects I gazed at under the glass at first seemed figures for what takes place in reading film. But after I realized my mistake, I could no longer say what these objects meant, and so they appeared to me then, as they now do in memory, only as hanging figures.

ONE

Theories of Suspense

1

Current Theories of Suspense

Only in the past thirty years has the subject of suspense attracted the serious interest of scholars; one survey of research cites only two articles prior to 1969 and no book-length treatments.[1] Prior neglect may reflect the fact that suspense falls across the disciplinary boundaries of psychology, psychoanalysis, literary and film criticism, and philosophy. In the late sixties, scholars in these disciplines began to develop models of literary and cinematic suspense, but their interest coincided with the revolution in critical theory outlined in the introduction. As a result, efforts to understand suspense have not been exempt from theoretical controversy. For example, Cartesian and hermeneutic approaches assume the presence of a cognitive or emotive subject representable in language; studies of cinematic and literary closure make the hermeneutic assumption that the meaning of a work's themes are readable in its endings; psychoanalytic approaches assume the presence of an unconscious that is representable in language. These approaches assume it is possible to say when suspense begins and ends. After a review of the literature, this chapter sketches in the advantages of my figurative and deconstructive approach.

CARTESIAN AND HERMENEUTIC THEORIES

Cognitive and Behavioral Psychology

In 1996, sixteen American and European studies were collected and published as *Suspense: Conceptualizations, Theoretical Analyses, and Empirical Explorations*; nearly all contributors adopted a paradigm of cognitive or behavioral psychology according to which the text is stimulus and suspense is the response.[2] Within this conceptualization, five important issues surface: the role of affect; the relation between suspense and plot; the problem of "recidivist" suspense; the definition of when suspense ends; the problem of the moral approbation of the hero.

The place of affect in psychological definitions of suspense is problematic. For example, Minet de Wied defines suspense as an "anticipatory stress reaction," distinguishable in intensity from cognitive uncertainty and

prompted by an initiating event in the discourse structure [novel or film], and terminated by the actual presentation of the harmful outcome event. The strength or intensity of suspense is found to depend on character valence of the endangered characters, degree of outcome uncertainty, and duration of harm anticipation.[3]

For de Wied, "strength or intensity" denotes the affective essence of suspense; for other psychologists the representation of emotion is sometimes taken for granted, sometimes ignored, or subject to conflicting interpretations. For example, David Bordwell concedes that his approach "does not have much to say about affect" beyond the fact that "emotion is bound up with expectation and its interrupted or delayed fulfillment."[4] Like Bordwell, the cognitivists Ohler and Nieding subordinate affect, the very essence of the concept they are attempting to define:

Emotional processes evoked by the viewing of audiovisual texts are seen as subordinate to the cognitive processing of the film. Before the viewer can experience the emotional impact of a film, the text must be mentally represented—at least in rudimentary form. Motivational processes are seen as the energy-related components of cognitive processing mechanisms.[5]

Ohler and Nieding assume that suspense requires cognitive representation; however, they also imply that affect, subordinate but seemingly essential, is not separately representable. But if this is the case, then a circularity in the cognitive approaches to suspense may be unavoidable: on the one hand, affect or "intensity" is essential to distinguish suspense from cognitive uncertainty, but on the other hand, it cannot be separately articulated.

Some psychologists try to avoid such circularity in studies that measure indications of "intensity" empirically, through physiological categories (heartrate, systolic and diastolic blood pressure, etc.), through observations of expressive behavior, and through self-reports.[6] The long-term goal of such research is to learn whether the observable indicators of suspense are specific (i.e., attributable *only* to suspense) and independent of persons and situations (i.e., co-varying with changes in suspense in differing contexts), in order to determine ultimate reliability. Mattenklott's review of the current state of research found weaknesses in the first two measures and recommended beginning on the basis of self-reports, as the most nuanced representations.[7] But even assuming that empirical research could someday establish a reliable correlation between physiological or behavioral indicators and textual stimuli, the question of the true meaning or *referent* of the signs of suspense would still remain unanswered. Does a set of indicators *mean* an anticipatory stress reaction in the organism consistent with the Darwinian paradigm for this model?[8] Or instead, as we shall see in psychoanalytic studies of suspense, might the set of indicators signify an *unconscious anxiety*? In other words, even if the affective component of suspense correlated with a set of physiological signs, their meaning would still depend on the interpretive frame brought to bear on these signs. Such a dilemma highlights the relevance of Hitchcock's dramatization of the inevitability of frames in *Easy Virtue*.

A second problem with psychological definitions of suspense is their restriction of the suspense-stimulus to the plot. This limitation is reflected in de Wied's use of the phrase "outcome event" for the end of suspense. Noel Carroll also reflects this predisposition when he cites "bombs attached to fizzling fuses or ticking timepieces" as examples of suspense.[9] David Bordwell defines suspense as a hypothesis about what will happen in the future; he cites Jeff, in Hitchcock's *Rear Window*, as an analogue for the cinematic spectator who experiences suspense as he guesses what has happened in Thorwald's apartment.[10] In these instances, the outcome that supposedly ends suspense is assumed to be a plot-event—an explosion or the solution to the mystery. Behavioral and cognitive psychologists, perhaps influenced by Aristotelian categories of mimesis, tend to understand suspense as initiated and terminated, as de Wied says, in the *events* of the discourse structure; their work pays less attention to suspense that accompanies the political and philosophical questions raised by literary or cinematic texts—for example, the urgency of D. H. Lawrence's attack on industrialization or of Gillo Pontecorvo's call to resist imperialism in *The Battle of Algiers*. If suspense ends with a diegetic event, then it must be absent not only from subsequent viewings, performances, or critical responses but also from ideological debates provoked by the diegesis. But these later viewings and debates *seem* suspenseful, too. In this way, restriction of suspense to plot events uncovers the more fundamental problem of recidivist suspense.

This phenomenon raises issues of genuine theoretical importance for cognitive and behavioral psychology, since its very existence challenges the discipline's theoretical foundations—that cognition triggers arousal, that all emotion is mediated by consciousness and that there can be no unconscious emotion.[11] If this foundation is true, how could affect exist in the absence of cognitive stimulus *unless it had nothing to do with consciousness*? William F. Brewer concedes that the issue of rereading "provides serious constraints on theories of suspense."[12] Noel Carroll sees the fact of recidivism as a challenge to the very idea of the rationality of the viewer.[13] Richard J. Gerrig concludes that the "resilience" of suspense necessitates a modification of the way we think about the "inherent properties of cognitive architecture."[14] In response to this threat to their discipline's premises, psychologists have proposed and tested numerous hypotheses. Gerrig suggested that rereaders consciously ignore an otherwise structural "expectation of uniqueness" in the psyche; however, it is hard to distinguish such a condition from unconscious affect.[15] Brewer surveyed several explanations but found most were inadequate to account for the observed phenomenon that some affect, albeit reduced, accompanies rereading.[16] Both Brewer and Carroll thought that some "concern about outcome," independent of cognitive knowledge of outcome, might account for recidivism. But these ideas, like Gerrig's, have raised new questions.[17]

The theoretical vulnerability of psychology also surfaces in discussions of the "resolution" or "termination" of suspense. That both words are used to indicate closure betrays an uncertainty regarding irrevocability: "termination" implies a definitive end, whereas "resolution" implies a temporary arrest. Some researchers further distinguish between "satisfying" and "dissatisfying" resolutions.[18] Are endings terminations of suspense? Psychologist Dolf Zillmann concedes that physiological indicators of suspense may persist even after the termination of its stimulus,[19] and in this he concurs with reader-response critics who argue that the boundaries of aesthetic experience never match those of a specific text.[20]

Two examples from Hitchcock may illustrate the difficulty. According to the original ending of *Vertigo*, Scottie and Midge listen on a car radio to a report of the arrest of Gavin Elster; it may be that this original ending was intended to comply with the moribund Production Code stipulation that villains should be punished. In any case, the suppressed ending can't be erased from the minds of viewers who are aware of it. While not a part of what psychologists would recognize as "stimulus," this fragment from "beyond" the film creates new uncertainty—the meaning of Midge's final relationship with Scottie. No doubt this extra-diegetic suspense could be "resolved" as the renewal of their college romance, but now this interpretation challenges readings of the released film that saw the death of Judy/Madeleine as betokening the impossibility of human love. In effect, the unreleased footage sets up undecidability between two interpretations of the film. A second example is the revised ending of *The Birds*. Hitchcock had originally planned a sequence in which the Brenners drive away from Bodega Bay, only to approach Golden Gate Bridge and see it covered with birds. This suppressed ending, once known, initiates new suspense because viewers cannot know whether the more ominous threat makes the Brenners' attempted escape futile. These intertextual examples reveal a bias toward textual autonomy in cognitive research that has been challenged by other approaches.[21]

Finally, Cartesian definitions of suspense are weakened by the requirement for moral approbation of an endangered hero. While differing in emphasis, Carroll, Zillmann, and Vorderer claim that suspense is possible only when the viewer morally approves of the hero. For Carroll, approval is a cognitive decision; for Zillmann and Vorderer, approval and affect are intertwined. (Zillmann concludes that "liked characters are always moral and good and disliked characters are always immoral and evil."[22]) To widen the opportunity for viewer endorsement of protagonists, Carroll liberalizes the conditions for approval. First, he claims that films permit identification with morally dubious characters who are rendered temporarily sympathetic by some redeeming character-trait— for example, the ingenuity of the heroes of caper films. Second, he argues that the moral standards by which viewers judge characters are established by the film. Hence it is possible to identify with a moral value embodied by a hero while later, on reflection, disapproving of it. For example, an anti-imperialist might for the duration of the film root for the colonialists in *Zulu*. Carroll's broadening of the cognitive position may seek to pre-empt objections from many viewers, especially audiences of Hitchcock's films, who claim concern for the fate of Hitchcock's villains. Robin Wood's eloquent recollection of his adolescent concern for the fate of Brandon and Phillip, the cold-blooded killers in *Rope*, is one example; Deborah Knight and George McKnight cite several others.[23]

Carroll's position on the temporary acceptance of a film's morality is opposed by the reception-centered theorists Ohler and Nieding, who see in this idea nothing more than "an ongoing scene-specific adoption of protagonist-specific perspectives."[24] Zillmann expressed his disagreement even more distinctly:

Carroll (1984, 1990) emphasized the role of moral considerations in the creation of suspense. He argued, essentially, that respondents hope for morally correct outcomes and fear evil ones. To the extent that morally correct outcomes translate to benefaction of protagonists and evil outcomes to their calamity, this accords with our dispositional conceptualization. However, Carroll granted fiction sole responsibility for the moral judgment of events in drama . . . Here our conceptualization differs. We recognize that the moral judgment of respondents is highly personal and varies considerably (Kohlberg, 1964), and that respondents bring their own, unique moral considerations to fiction— considerations capable of overwhelming the morality built into narratives.[25]

The dispute between Zillmann and Carroll reveals a sharp divergence within Cartesian approaches. Text-centered theorists like Carroll may argue that moral approbation may be determined by the textual stimulus on the hermeneutic assumption that it represents the author or director, whereas reception-centered theorists like Zillmann consider moral approbation part of the viewer's bias or personal belief-system. For the latter, it would be impossible for the stimulus-text to create a moral world that the viewer's preconceptions world not "overwhelm"; the differences between these approaches are not easy to reconcile.[26] For text-centered critics, an implication of reception-centered approaches may be moral relativism: without some governing representation of morality, narratives may become detached from any truth and degenerate into utter irrationality that makes moral judgment impossible. Text-centered approaches preserve the possibility of a Kantian hermeneutics of objective understanding, whereas the reception-centered approaches seem to accept the prospect of radical subjectivism or anarchy in interpretation.

In summary, the unresolved problems of psychological approaches to suspense include the necessity for affect but an incapacity to represent it, especially in cases of recidivism; the tendency to equate the outcome of reading with the understanding of the diegetic events; the assumption of the referential property of the text; the definition of the termination of suspense; and the moral approbation of the hero. Some of these problems flow from psychologists' Cartesian assumption that a text is a Cartesian "object"/stimulus and suspense is cognitive/affective response; others flow from traditional assumptions of hermeneutics.

Iser's Indeterminacy Theory and Reader-Response Criticism

Some of these shortcomings are avoided in the indeterminacy theory of the reader-response critic, Wolfgang Iser. Like the cognitivists, Iser sees reading as a process of hypothesis-formation; in his language, he thinks readers must make inferences regarding the "schematized views" of reality taken by characters and even authors in literary texts, and "between the 'schematized views' there is a no-man's land of indeterminacy, which results precisely from the determinacy of each individual view" (11). For Iser, this means that most literary texts are full of "gaps" that readers must imaginatively fill. They are obvious during the publication of serial novels, like those of Dickens, but similar techniques for the withholding of information and prolongation of suspense are present to some degree in every literary work:

The serialized novel uses a cutting technique. It interrupts the action usually where a certain tension has been built up that demands to be resolved, or where one is anxious to learn the outcome of the events one has just read about . . . One could draw up a whole list of such cutting techniques, which for the most part are more sophisticated than the primitive, though highly effective method of suspense.[27]

The metaphor of "cutting" is suggestive for the study of film because of its implication that suspense may inhere in even its smallest constituent units. For Iser, it exemplifies the ongoing process of gap-filling that can never end in any final closure. His theory of indeterminate gaps has been criticized by cognitivists for overemphasizing "imprecision" in the text, but at the same time, this criticism reveals the formalism of the cognitivists' position that suspense begins and ends with the story.[28] Of course, Iser's view is vulnerable to some of the same criticisms made against Cartesian-based psychologists: for example, like them, he assumes readers are rational and autonomous. Still, his work is less committed to the assumption of the referential property of the text or to the cotermination of suspense and narrative.

Studies of Cinematic Closure

Film critics have examined closure primarily from the point of view of cinematic convention. Thus Bordwell studied the "unmotivated happy ending" in

American films of the forties and concluded that in such films as *You Only Live Once, Woman in the Window, The Wrong Man,* and *Suspicion,* happy endings that reversed the normal expectations of the diegesis forced viewers "to recognize the conventions that rule classical cinema."[29] Following a semiotic model, Richard Neupert proposed a fourfold classification of films based on the degree of closure in both the diegesis and the narration. Neupert's categories distinguish films that are open in both text and discourse—those of Robbe-Grillet or Godard—from those closed in one respect or both.[30] Following Bordwell, Neupert understands suspense as a process of cognitive hypothesis-building in which cinematic conventions, especially those derived from genre, prompt viewer expectation as to theme; Neupert's extends Bordwell's analysis by tracing the process of prompt, expectation and closure at the narrational level, too. Neither theorist questions the existence of closure. Both understand the concept hermeneutically, assuming that the only means of determining thematic content is through the binary of the expected closure's presence or absence.

Studies of Literary Closure

Literary critics have studied closure through philosophical approaches to diegetic endings that sometimes doubt the existence of cognition and resolution. Two contributions of this sort are Frank Kermode's *The Sense of an Ending* and D. A. Miller's *Narrative and Its Discontents.*[31] The former's ostensibly Cartesian approach masks the way his thesis transcends the cognitivists' conflation of suspense and plot; the latter, as its title allusion suggests, is substantially indebted to Freud and directly addresses key issues of representation—as noted above, a crux for Cartesian thinkers—and introduces the category of the "narratable," to which we will have occasion to return.

Kermode's thesis in *The Sense of the Ending* is that human beings live in a condition of suspense he calls the "middest," a condition borne of our inability to know true beginnings and endings. Because we dwell in what Wallace Stevens calls "poverty" or meaningless temporal succession (time conceived as *chronos,* which we cannot bear), we interpret it as portentous crisis (time conceived as *kairos*). The gospel writers, forced to change their idea of the *eschaton* from imminent to immanent, were among the most eloquent creators of such temporal concord, and for Kermode, great literature, especially tragedy and poetry, continues to respond to the human need for concordance between past, present, and future: in a way analogous to that of the principle of complementarity in physics, such literature temporarily reconciles the contradictions of time by providing fictions of closure—what Kermode means by the *sense* of an ending, as opposed to a "true" ending. Modern literature, responding to shocks brought about by the scientific understanding of time, struggles to provide the secular version of the concord previously effected by the New Testament; in the work of Shakespeare, Wordsworth, Stevens, and others, Kermode discovers the heroic but continually flawed effort to achieve what Stevens called the "supreme fiction."

Kermode's argument differs from that of previously discussed studies in its implication that there can be no hope for true closure or termination of the literary and existential suspense of clock time: modern systems of thought, like fascism, which promise apocalypse, are fraudulent and immoral—the result of the degeneration of conscious fiction into political myth. In tragedy (like *Macbeth* and *King Lear*) and in poetry (like the work of Stevens or Larkin), the human struggle to reconcile time can at least be dramatized and articulated. Kermode pictures the reader's situation as "a common project, truth in poverty, and a common need, solidarity of plight in diversity of state" (164). Through these and other characterizations, Kermode defends his Arnoldian thesis that literature in the modern world has assumed the illuminative and consolatory functions of religion.[32] Kermode's idea that the intractable dilemma of time can at least be dramatized, even if it can't be resolved, opens up a new way of understanding diegetic suspense—as the allegory of a permanent human incapacity.

Like Kermode, D. A. Miller understands narrative closure as the symptom of an intractability, but in his case the incommensurate terms are not simply human time and the *eschaton* but, more abjectly, the conditions of narrative representation. Like Freud's civilization, Miller's narrative is sustained at the cost of a lie. Novelistic closure is an arbitrary if necessary imposition of meaning on narrative materials that threaten at every moment to expose its fraudulence. Miller's examples come from Jane Austen, George Eliot (Mary Ann Evans), and Stendahl (Marie Henri Beyle). Each writer deals with the necessity for such transparently false closure in different ways: Austen makes a direct ideological intervention; Eliot disavows the supposed finality of closure by alternately entertaining mutually contradictory interpretations of her novel's conflicts; Stendahl reverses traditional binaries like "bound" and "free" closures as a means of keeping his novel in a state of suspense or "dispersion" (257).[33] In each case, the dilemma is that narratives are shown to be incapable of making true dispositions of their own ideational content; in such a situation, there can never be a "true" closure (of the sort envisioned, say, by Bordwell or Neupert). The pressure that this gradually revealed incapacity exerts on narrative strategies is Miller's theme: each of the three studied remedies is drastic; indeed, Stendahl's recourse—the final substitution of conversation for narrative—acknowledges the impossibility of any attempt to "anchor" the novel's meaning. From this perspective, Miller's Stendahl becomes a narrative precursor to the Freud who, by the end of the twentieth century, will be understood through Lacan and Derrida.

The advantage of the contributions of Kermode and Miller stems from the reduced number of assumptions, from their refusal to assume that suspense is a subjective response to a stimulus. Instead, Kermode finds suspense implicit in time; Miller, in narrative. It is as if suspense could be understood without appeal to either the Cartesian subject or object. Neither writer supposes that suspense requires moral approbation of the protagonist or that it ends when the story does. Each finds suspense to be a kind of primordial condition whose miseries may be allegorized in texts that are nevertheless incapable of accurately reflecting, describing, or summarizing it. Such is the meager result of Kermode's and Miller's intellectual austerity. Definitions of suspense more modest than those of the psychologists are also a feature of psychoanalytic studies.

Psychoanalytic Studies: Freud

Freud wrote no works on literary or cinematic affect. The concept closest to suspense in the Freudian lexicon is anxiety, to which he devoted a chapter in *A General Introduction to Psychoanalysis*. There Freud distinguished the psychoanalytic concept of anxiety from the Darwinian explanation that anxiety reflected the instinct for self-preservation in the face of danger to the organism. On the contrary, for Freud anxiety and its extreme form, phobia, were symptoms of Oedipal repression and undischarged libido: repressed longing for the mother may be displaced onto otherwise insignificant objects: "the phobia may be compared to an entrenchment against an external danger which now represents the dreaded libido."[34] It is of interest that Freud considered anxiety to be inevitable and permanent; in fact, he believed anxiety could be understood as "the universally current coinage" exchangeable for all affect:

... when we have a hysterical anxiety-state before us, its unconscious correlate may be an impulse of a similar character—anxiety, shame, embarrassment, or just as easily, a positive libidinal excitation or a hostile aggressive one, such as rage or anger. Anxiety is therefore the universally current coinage for which *any* affective impulse is or can be exchanged, if the ideational content attached to it is subjected to repression.[35]

Freud's idea that anxiety is the *lingua franca* for affect goes far toward showing why the study of suspense, its near-synonym, is so important: if anxiety is the common denominator of all affect, and if some anxiety-like affect is a criterion of suspense (as psychologists claim but find difficulty in representing), then what we learn of narrative suspense may help us understand that common denominator. The question of whether the etiology of anxiety could be replicated through identification with characters in narratives was one that Freud never addressed. In his famous analyses of the work of Shakespeare and Dostoevsky, Freud held that Oedipal anxiety could be diagetically represented; by analogy, it might be elicited.[36] At the same time, Freudian anxiety is clearly distinguishable from suspense as defined in Cartesian studies, which allow only *conscious* anticipatory stress reactions.

Psychoanalytically inflected film criticism examines unconscious affect in numerous ways; one survey outlined six distinct approaches to the subject.[37] Three recent trends are of interest in understanding suspense: first, Lacanian studies—especially "suture" theory and the writings of Christian Metz and Slavoj Žižek—

that theorize suspense in terms of the viewer's unsuccessful struggle to escape
the delusion of selfhood generated in the process Lacan calls the mirror-stage;
second, feminist-Lacanian studies that take up the subject of the gendered construction and positioning of subjectivity by film;[38] third, Lacanian studies influenced by queer theory. The chief advantage of Lacanian approaches over those
of empiricist theorists lies in their refusal to assume the existence of a Cartesian
subject prior to language; their chief disadvantage lies in their reliance upon the
metaphysical concept of the unconscious.

Psychoanalytic Studies: Lacan and Suture Theory

There have been several valuable introductions to Lacanian film criticism and
suture theory.[39] Briefly, Lacanians believe that the cinematic experience is
closely analogous to the fundamental formation of the self during what Lacan
calls "the mirror-stage." In that constitutive process, which need not take place
before a physical mirror, the self is established in a moment of illusion and
thereafter considers itself unified and whole when in fact it remains irrevocably
fragmented, broken, and driven by the unconscious—the Freudian concept Lacan renames "the Other." Identifying with characters on a screen who are in
reality fictions created by a mechanical apparatus that must be "forgotten," viewers gain spurious confidence in their own subjective autonomy through this
duplication of the moment of their own psychic origin. "Suture" theorists claim
that film reinforces this false confidence by "suturing" or ideologically positioning a self—most notoriously, as passive, male, consumerist—where none exists.
Cinematic experience is thus an overdetermined and peculiarly revelatory instance of our more general alienation in what Lacan calls the Symbolic order—
that is, the day-to-day miasma of lies, sublimations, and misrecognitions that
constitutes human existence. The question of whether or not any "cure" for this
alienation is available to analyst and analysand is taken up in Lacan's clinical
writings.[40] Lacanian film criticism has been understandably attacked by empir-
icists like Carroll.[41] Still, before proceeding to the critique of the theory, it will
be helpful to consider its findings regarding suspense.

Lacan claimed the unconscious or Other could be understood as "the gaze":
"In our relation to things, insofar as this relation is constituted by the way of
vision, and ordered in the figures of representation, something slips, passes, is
transmitted, from stage to stage, and is always to some degree eluded in it—
that is what we call the gaze."[42] The idea that the unconscious is like a gaze
animates the work of several Lacanian film critics and lays the groundwork for
their analysis of suspense. For example, Pascal Bonitzer argues that Hitchcockian suspense is produced by the audience's ever-present knowledge that individual characters in the film narrative, especially lovers, are never depicted as
autonomous but instead as continually open and vulnerable to the intervention
of some third entity: "There is thus always a third party in a couple, a gaze
welding it together."[43] Bonitzer and other Lacanian critics frequently associate

this gaze with the camera; as a result, films may be regarded as narratives of the Lacanian instantiation of the self. The characters' delusion of autonomy is figured in their obliviousness to the camera's gaze, which nevertheless determines them, just as the viewer's delusion of autonomy is manifested in his or her "forgetting" of the projector that is the pre-requisite for understanding the film.[44] All of this is consistent with a view of the self as produced and determined by some unconscious agency from which the ego in daily life is permanently cut off. Bonitzer argues that within such narratives, suspense may be understood as a durational "stretching," a "viscosity of time [which] is related to eroticism, and it concerns the eroticized time in the prolonged, necessarily disturbing undecidability of an event . . . the erotic prolongation of the trajectory of a coin thrown up into the air, before it falls on one side (tails: yes) or the other (heads: no)."[45] Bonitzer's examples are the cigar-lighting scene in *Blackmail* and the murder of Marion Crane in *Psycho*; in both cases, the effect of slowed time is created through editing and is sustained by the gaze. (Bonitzer's belief that suspense is pleasurable responds to another of the many paradoxes of this field, one that Cartesian theorists have also addressed, with mixed results.[46]) From a psychoanalytic perspective, pleasure in the prolongation of undecidability can be accounted for by the viewer's temporary, unconscious identification with prohibited behavior in the story.

Žižek shares Bonitzer's confidence that the critic can articulate the "absolute Otherness" that dwells "beyond the wall of language" and the pleasures of identification. He cites the example of Hitchcock's arousal in the viewer of a " 'sadistic' desire to see the hero crush the bad guy" (for instance, in *Torn Curtain*) only to have that desire exposed (for example, by the hideous murder of Gromek) as manipulated by the director in his role as the emissary of the unconscious. Žižek also cites the "God's view" shot of Bodega Bay in *The Birds* and the conclusion of *Psycho*, when the dissolve from Norman's face to his mother's skull reveals the "the subject not yet caught in the web of language."[47] At such rare moments, Žižek claims, viewers are forced to break their suspense-identifications and to reflect on their pleasure and anxiety by adopting the perspective of the unconscious and by seeing themselves as determined by the Other.

Žižek's assumption that such ultimate moments are possible has implications for the idea of closure. As Lacanians see it, ordinary closure provides viewers with false reassurances of the unity of self achieved through the mirror stage: Žižek cites film noir, in which a voice-over narration often completes a self whose fragmentary past was narrated in flashback. But Hitchcock's films mock such conventionally reassuring closure. While Hitchcock "pretends to comply fully with the rules of closure," the "standard effect of closure remains unfulfilled," his endings "undermine the very notion of personal identity." Suspense ends in such fleeting intuitions of self-construction. Of course, Žižek's assumption that it is possible to articulate such a space "beyond the gaze" and oracularly unveil the unconscious is metaphysical and has been vigorously contested for this reason.[48]

Garry Leonard summarizes the relation between suspense and closure in Lacanian theory: "Suspense activates the potentially soothing process of *suture*, but only in order to generate a situation where the suturing effect might be ripped open . . . a suspense film or story will, in a subtle but unsettling manner, suggest the possibility of the sutured reality splitting open again."[49] Leonard analyzes Hitchcock's *Vertigo* and *Psycho* to show how their conclusions imply the collapse of protagonists' and readers' identities that had been painstakingly put together during the course of the narrations. Like Bonitzer and Žižek, Leonard equates the alienating gaze of the Other which accomplishes this dissolution with signs of the intervention of the director himself.

Psychoanalytic Studies: Feminist/Lacanian Studies

In Lacanianism and suture theory, some feminists found vocabularies for analyzing the reification of women in classical Hollywood films and the oppressive subject-positioning of women as spectators. Assisted by Laura Mulvey's essay, "Visual Pleasure and Narrative Cinema," feminist critics sought to expose patriarchal assumptions in Hollywood and in film criticism as well as to explore the possibilities for alternative, emancipatory cinematic narratives. These efforts were accompanied by the risks entailed in an arm's-length adaptation of patriarchal theory.[50] Kaja Silverman's work is representative of the struggles of such critics to use Lacanian/suture theory to recuperate for feminism against-the-grain readings of classical Hollywood films. These reconceive women not as victims of the gaze of the Other but as its agents, freed from dominant models whereby women are constituted in the moment of lack precipitated by male castration. For example, Silverman's analysis of *The Best Years of Our Lives* focuses on the way that film's women refuse to define themselves with regard to the scene of amputation/castration/impotence brought about by the traumas of history; instead, at the wedding at the end of the film, the women succeed in isolating themselves from society's dominant fiction and instead make their own gaze at last prevail. Through such a reading, Silverman argues that the Lacanian options of deluded subjectivity or recognition of the gaze's determination are not the only alternative resolutions of cinematic suspense. Feminist/Lacanians like Silverman advance a heretical adaptation of Lacan, though they do so at a price: like Žižek's criticism, Silverman's can't escape the metaphysical and hermeneutic assumption that also haunts cognitive and Cartesian studies—that in the "right" reading of the film's ending lies the resolution of its suspense.

Queer Theory

Queer theorists extend the feminist revision of Lacan's idea of the unconscious-as-gaze. As Silverman's work suggests, the political orientation of feminist/Lacanian studies shifted them toward a cultural understanding of suspense that sought to liberate the viewer from dominant patriarchal discourses like Freud's. Queer theory moved even further in this direction, as may be seen in Robert Samuels's *Hitchcock's Bi-Textuality*. Samuels adapts Žižek's approach to Hitchcock but emphasizes the bisexual and multidimensional character of the unconscious; he sees Hitchcock's films as narrating the irruption into everyday life of those unconscious elements—for example, the feminine and homoerotic instincts—that most threaten the maintenance of the dominant patriarchal, heterosexual, and ideological order. Samuels believes the preservation of that order is a consequence of cinematic representation in general and Hitchcock's personal anxieties, in particular;[51] nevertheless, like Žižek and Silverman, he argues that critics can on occasion glimpse the repressed unconscious in Hitchcock's closures: an example is the confrontation between Jeffries and Thorwald at the end of *Rear Window*: "For just a brief moment, Jeffries was face-to-face with the true object that causes his desire. His response to this was to block his and his object's vision, just as Hitchcock has blocked the representation of the scene of homosexuality." This closure of Jeff's anxiety is brought about by "the encounter with the gaze of the Other from the position of true desire." In such passages Samuels, like other psychoanalytic critics, assumes that suspense ends and the unconscious becomes readable.[52]

A psychoanalytic study of Hitchcock that reflects many of the same concerns as Samuels's book is Robert J. Corber's *In the Name of National Security*.[53] Corber modifies the Lacanian paradigm in two important ways. First, he situates the films in the political context of the "post-war settlement," the nascent cold war, in which the Oedipal process valorized by the films reinforced a cultural ideology that stigmatized any variations from it, especially homosexuality. Second, Corber argues for restoration of the original Freudian sense of "identification," which emphasizes its function as a defense against repressed homoerotic instincts. In both ways Corber modifies the concept of subject-positioning developed by "suture theory": instead of seeing the male subject as fixed by the film into a stable heterosexual position, Corber sees the process of identification as only partly successful:

As the primary mode of address of classical Hollywood cinema, identification restages the male spectator's feminine attitude toward the father during the pre-Oedipal phase and thereby encourages the formation of a polymorphous, rather than a fixed, heterosexual identity.

In commentaries on *Strangers on a Train* and on the pair *North by Northwest* and *Psycho*, for example, Corber studies the way their themes of "normative Oedipalization" become compromised by acknowledgements of homoerotic or other putatively "deviant" object-choices. Thus the coded-homosexual Bruno "is more charismatic than the all-American Guy, and his potentially destabilizing presence can only be contained by his violent expulsion from the diegesis." In

North by Northwest, Roger Thornhill's "erratic" and "irresponsible" multiplication of identities is at long last fixed, but in *Psycho*, viewer identification with Norman reveals the pleasures in remaining outside the law. In these examples, Corber argues that the viewer's identification with Hollywood's ego-ideals is never complete; on the contrary, suspense consists of the indulgence of such repressed instincts up to the very moment when the ending closes them off in a final imposition of Oedipal "victory," whose psychic costs in films like *Strangers on a Train* and *North by Northwest* are fully revealed in *Psycho*.[54]

Like Lacanian feminism, queer theory sees suspense as the anxiety induced by a dominant discourse that cannot avoid, at the same time, revealing the arbitrariness of the ideological system through which it attempts to mold characters and viewers into an Oedipal structure. Samuels and Corber believe the arbitrariness of the system is readable and that in the films' closures—in Jeff's attraction to Thorwald, or in the face of Norman's mother, for example—a true representation of the repressed unconscious is discernible. Both critics resolve the ambiguity of the endings in such a way as to expose ideological struggle. For Samuels, the struggle reflects Hitchcock's personal conflicts; for Corber, the larger political scene of postwar America. Neither critic doubts that Hitchcock's films faithfully represent inner or outer conflicts. Thus psychoanalytic studies of Hitchcock move away from Freudian determinism and toward assumptions of mimesis and ego-autonomy that also characterize Cartesian approaches to suspense.

Studies of Catharsis

The difficulties of current theories of suspense parallel those encountered in discussions of the Aristotelian idea of catharsis. Suspense and catharsis bear certain similarities: both have been considered important dimensions of the experience of literature; both envision the stimulation of a not wholly pleasurable affect that is dissipated. Certain writers have claimed that suspense has a "cathartic" or "purgative" or "cleansing" effect on viewers, so in this respect the concepts are close. Originally formulated by Aristotle in *The Poetics* and limited to tragedy, the concept of catharsis was extended to epic and other genres by Italian critics in the late Renaissance; contemporary theorists have proposed its existence in comedy.[55] The classical scholar G. F. Else summarizes its breadth:

The great virtue, but also the great vice, of 'catharsis' in modern interpretations has been its incurable vagueness. Every variety of moral, aesthetic, and therapeutic effect that is or could be experienced from tragedy has been subsumed under the venerable word at one time or another.[56]

Among classicists there are three main approaches to catharsis. The first defines it as an exclusively emotional cleansing in the viewer that occurs as the result of the elicitation of pity and fear by the performance; the second, as a purification of the acts of events of the play, which only secondarily produces affect; the third, as a thematic clarification that works first on the intellect, then on the emotions.[57] It is interesting that this debate echoes the dispute among text-centered and reception-centered psychologists: if catharsis and suspense are subjective, how can they be defined? If textual signs elicit emotion, which ones are they? These dead ends suggest the way Cartesian and hermeneutic definitions of suspense—whether they are psychological, psychoanalytic, or literary—founder because they begin with subjects and objects and assume the referentiality of language.

TOWARD A FIGURATIVE APPROACH: SOME PHILOSOPHICAL ANALOGUES FOR SUSPENSE

To begin with fewer assumptions, I examine below certain philosophical *analogies* for suspense without regard for their place in the author's philosophical system or for their signified referent. To do so is to consider them not as concepts but as figures: as we've seen, the verbal sense of the word "figure" is the use of a word that "deviates from its normal or expected usage." None of the concepts listed below was conceived as literary or cinematic suspense; nevertheless, they may serve as prompts to thinking about suspense in fresh ways. The prominence of suspense-like conditions in philosophy, especially in the twentieth century, suggest it may be approachable from larger, less restrictive perspectives than those of psychology, psychoanalysis, and literary criticism. Chapter 2 shows that Hitchcock preferred figures to such conceptual theorizing. In what follows, then, several analogies to suspense from Western philosophy are offered—not as abstractions to be "applied" in future chapters (for the most part they are not) but as samples of alternative thinking and introductions to the figural approach.

In *Outlines of Pyrrhonism*, Sextus Empiricus (ca. 270 CE) developed what he called the "ephectic" drive of philosophy—the idea that a "suspension of judgement" was the default response to problems for which no philosophical answer could be determined.[58] Sextus's thought, which stimulated Enlightenment skeptics like Hume, was revived by Nietzsche, who saw the ephectic drive as a first stage in the restoration of health to philosophy.[59] In *The Concept of Dread*, the proto-existentialist and Christian theologian Søren Kierkegaard studied the suspense-like condition of dread, finding it first in paganism and sensuousness, but then inquiring as to its object: "If we then ask further what is the object of dread, the answer as usual must be that it is nothing. Dread and nothing regularly correspond to one another. So soon as the actuality of freedom and of the spirit is posited, dread is annulled (*aufgehoben*). But what then is signified more particularly by the nothing of dread? It is fate."[60] For Kierkegaard, nothingness and fate—two non-Cartesian entities—define dread, which is only annulled through the spirit. The corollary is clear that without spirit, and ultimately without God, existence would be definable only as dread. Adapting Sextus's ephectic drive and the secular portion of Kierkegaard's thought for the study of film, we may consider suspense a clue to some unavoidable incapacity or emptiness prior to consciousness whose existence may nevertheless be allegorized in film. Taking the ideas of Sextus and Kierkegaard as figures suggests non-Freudian ways of looking at states of anxiety, conditions that need no grounding in a metaphysical unconscious.

A third analogy is available in the thought of Edmund Husserl, who in *Ideas* developed the concept of the phenomenological *epoché*, which he translated as "abstention," or the ability to bracket or put aside all presuppositions when entering into philosophical investigations; Husserl viewed the *epoché* as an extension and intensification of skepticism but one that also turned doubt onto Descartes's foundational concept, the *cogito*.[61] Adapting Husserl's idea as an figure, we may understand film as effecting such a bracketing prior to any theorizing: understood without regard to a referent, film may allow abstention from hermeneutic and Cartesian perspectives. In *Being and Time*, Husserl's student Heidegger put the *epoché* in practice through an analysis of *Dasein* that did not assume any connection between Being and the Cartesian subject. As part of this analysis, Heidegger discussed *angst*—which many readers, especially in the postwar era, understood as a subjective state—as one distinctive way in which *Dasein* is disclosed. To the consternation of humanists, Heidegger held that *angst* could be understood as authenticating not the self but only the subordination of the self to Being.[62] In such a non-Cartesian light, suspense is more like a primordial condition, one that resembles Kierkegaard's fated dread. What suspense teaches is not anxiety or dread within the subject but the subordination of the human.

Sextus's ephectic drive, Kierkegaard's dread, Husserl's *epoché*, and Heidegger's *angst* are figures or analogies for unending suspense, just as "the hanging figure" itself is.

In *Speech and Phenomenon*, Jacques Derrida extended the Husserlian *epoché* in a new direction, by challenging the priority of speech over writing that Husserl took for granted. Derrida followed Saussure, whose premise of "the arbitrary nature of the sign" called into question presumptions of referentiality. In his essay "Différance" and in *The Post-Card*, Derrida claimed that the linguistic sign could not exist unless it differed from itself; such an original "difference," in turn, meant that any achievement of meaning in language was ultimately deferred.[63] Derrida's hypothesis of the infinite deferral of meaning in language, with its suggestion that suspense may be interminable, is an important corollary of the hanging figure: it permits examination of suspense without the hermeneutic assumptions that affective catharsis or closure occurs or that literary/ cinematic meanings become readable in endings.

In *Philosophical Investigations*, Ludwig Wittgenstein introduced the concept "seeing-as" to help him convey philosophy's frustration in being unable to truly articulate sense-data. Wittgenstein analyzed Jastrow's ambiguous line drawing that could be perceived as either a duck or a rabbit. The moment the shape of the duck was seen in the rabbit Wittgenstein called "dawning" or "aspect-shift"; at that moment, "ordinary" seeing was replaced by "seeing-as" (or what ordinarily is called "recognizing"). But Wittgenstein could devise no protocol for understanding how "seeing" and "seeing-as" in fact differed: there manifestly *was* a difference, but it could not be articulated. Looked at in a different way, his frustration allows the inference that there is no *real* or originary seeing but only "seeing-as." Wittgenstein even extended the problem to the recognition of other people. At first he considers "seeing-as" an amalgamation of seeing and thinking; later he speculates that the newly apprehended meaning of "seeing-as" is "experienced." But in the end, he abandons this distinction, too. Some of Wittgenstein's commentators dismiss the "seeing/seeing-as" quandary as a disgression in *Philosophical Investigations.*[64] Nevertheless, the problem Wittgenstein couldn't solve may be of continuing importance to the figure of suspense in visual art: it foregrounds the necessary *delay* in visual recognition, leaves the nature of recognition in doubt, and treats the entire perceptual manifold as a "figure" that lacks a fixed ground or referent but nevertheless must be read. In the next chapter we shall see how the uncertainty in reading such figures is conveyed through Hitchcock's cameos; in the afterword we will take up the idea that the world as a whole may be only a figure.

For the study of suspense, the most productive figure in Paul de Man's thought is his discussion of irony as a "permanent parabasis"—a moment of pause or interruption in a narrative when the impossibility of representing the self becomes evident; we shall see that a moment of suspense very similar to this is particularly compelling in Hitchcock's film *Rope.* As noted in the introduction, de Man believed that literary and philosophical texts could be read as allegories of this very dilemma.[65] Both de Manian ideas will be useful in understanding the way suspense exceeds textual boundaries.

This brief survey has examined several concepts that, when seen as figures, suggest alternative and interdisciplinary contexts for studying suspense that do not rely on the Cartesian and hermeneutic assumptions that have led prior theorists to contradiction. That the work of these writers for the most part accompanied the twentieth-century evolution of film links the two suspense-engendering endeavors in ways that will be explored in the chapters following.

2

Hitchcock on Suspense

Perplexed, Deborah Knight and George McKnight introduce their recent study of Hitchcock's comments on suspense in this way: "Hitchcock's films do not always conform well with the theories that purport to capture what is basic to suspense. . . . Equally noteworthy, many signature moments in Hitchcock's films do not correspond to his own pronouncements . . . [Our starting point is] this lack of fit between basic theories of suspense and Hitchcock's work."[1] "Lack of fit" seems a generous understatement. Hitchcock makes distinctions that quickly collapse and introduces others belied by his practice; worse, he confounds theorists by expanding the criteria for suspense so much that it might be found anywhere. His most consistent remarks, however, comport well with the broader approach to suspense discussed at the end of the last chapter. For example, in discussing the MacGuffin, Hitchcock develops a Saussurian concept of the arbitrary nature of the sign; in discussing the cameo, he conveys a Wittgensteinian doubt as to what recognition means. As in Heidegger, human identity is itself suspenseful, as if any individual "self" were only a dependent mask, a persona with no person. In some ways, too, Hitchcock's ideas seem close to de Manian deconstruction: he thinks film suspense can expose the "glamorously dangerous charade" of the world, but only while it is a part of another charade. These remarks suggest the limits of conceptualizing suspense; they reflect a preference for indirect accounts, analogies and narratives—like the MacGuffin, the cameo, the seductive woman. The inference—that there is no referential sign for suspense apart from figuration—may be taken as Hitchcock's most important contribution to the study of suspense.

THEORETICAL COMMENTS

Hitchcock often claimed that suspense is best achieved when viewers are maximally informed, an idea he articulates in the "Lecture at Columbia University" (1939), "Let 'Em Play God" (1948), "The Enjoyment of Fear" (1949), and in responses to Truffaut.[2] He distinguishes suspense from both terror and surprise: suspense is like a buzz bomb whose chugging noise advertises its arrival, whereas terror and surprise are like the noiseless V-2. (The similes suggest his attraction to figures.) He concludes that "you have suspense when you let the audience play God" because maximum knowledge increases the opportunity for anticipation.[3] But as Knight and McKnight have pointed out, in films like *Vertigo* and *Psycho* Hitchcock violates this requirement.[4] Other blatant examples include *Spellbound*, where the identity of the villain is not revealed until the final moments; *Stage Fright*, in which from the outset the audience is given *mis*information; and *Torn Curtain*, in which the protagonist's role as a kind of volunteer double agent is unknown until halfway through the film. Withholding knowledge can extend even beyond diegetic endings: at the end of *The Lodger*, viewers continue to wonder whether the title character may not still be the criminal Avenger; at the end of *Suspicion*, it is undecidable whether Johnnie Aysgarth wants to make love to his wife or murder her; by the end of *The Birds*, no reason for the bird attack has been given.[5] Thus, Hitchcock often contradicts his own criterion for suspense.

In another essay Hitchcock argues for the *opposite* of maximum knowledge— for what he calls "subjective" rather than "objective" suspense. He finds objective suspense in "the chase" or the Griffithian montage of "the race to the scaffold" where the viewer sees the alternation of two sides—for example, galloping hooves and condemned man—in an unfolding climax; by contrast, in subjective suspense, the director suppresses details and shows mainly one side.[6]

In the French Revolution, probably someone said to Danton, "Will you please hurry on your horse," but [I] never show him getting on the horse. Let the audience worry whether the horse has even started, you see. This is making the audience play its part.

The old way used to be that the audience was presented with just an objective view of this galloping horse, and they just said they hoped the horse got there in time. I think it should go further than that. Not only "I hope he gets there in time," but "I hope he has started off," you see. That is a more intensive development. (272–73)

Hitchcock's advocacy of maintaining ignorance is belied by the fact that he often follows Griffith's famous formula: in *Strangers on a Train*, shots of Guy's tennis match alternate with Bruno's efforts to plant incriminating evidence; in *The Man Who Knew Too Much*, shots of orchestra musicians alternate with the face of the anxious Jo McKenna, searching for signs of an imminent assassination attempt.

Though Hitchcock cites no examples of subjective suspense from his own films, they are not hard to find. At the end of *Rear Window*, the detective Tom Doyle telephones Jeff and learns of Thorwald's guilt, but when Jeff hangs up the viewer is left to wonder whether Doyle will rescue Jeff. In both versions of *The Man Who Knew Too Much* (1934 and 1956), there is an interval between the kidnapping of the child and the first time the kidnappers make contact with the child's parents; during these intervals, suspense may be said to be subjective, in Hitchcock's terms, since the viewer has no way of knowing whether their threats will be carried out. The intervals of ignorance in both examples are very short: in the first case, only a short scene separates the viewer's knowledge of both sides; in the second case, only a dissolve. In fact, brief moments of subjective suspense or narrative opaqueness seem presupposed by the fact that suspense unfolds in time. Subjective suspense still uses montage, just less of it. In short, Hitchcock's theoretical statements on informing the audience say tautologically that suspense can come from both knowledge and ignorance.[7]

More decisive was his position that any character could elicit suspense. In his interview with Truffaut, Hitchcock made clear that a time bomb ticking in the briefcase under the conference table would be suspenseful even if Hitler sat there: "What it means," Hitchcock added, "is that the apprehension of the bomb is more powerful than the feelings of sympathy or dislike for the characters involved." In later parts of the interview, Hitchcock cites the audience-sympathy for the killer Charlie in *Shadow of a Doubt* and for Norman Bates (Tony Perkins) in *Psycho*: "When Perkins is looking at the car sinking in the pond, even though he's burying a body, when the car stops sinking for a moment, the public is thinking, 'I hope it goes all the way down!' It's a natural instinct."[8] Hitchcock concurred with Truffaut's wry response—in such scenes "the viewer's emotions are not exactly wholesome." Their point challenges the views of Noel Carroll and David Bordwell, who think suspense must be limited to situations in which the morally good is in jeopardy; in fact, this broadened application of suspense seems to insulate it from moral assessment.

Hitchcock further broadened suspense by telling Truffaut it could be understood independently of fear.[9] Of course, psychologists have long held that fear and hope constitute a dyad of future-oriented affect; their definitions of suspense often simply redefine hope as the desire to avert threats.[10] Hitchcock's definition goes further by including not only hope for avoiding threats but also altruistic hope. To illustrate his point, Hitchcock cites the scene in *Easy Virtue* where the telephone operator eavesdrops on the conversation of a man proposing to a woman; the scene depicts the operator's anxious identification with the overheard voices, which culminates in apparent relief and rapture. Inclusion of such altruistic hope makes suspense nearly a universal affect: what emotion would *not* exemplify it? Hitchcock spoke to this subject in his 1939 lecture at Columbia University: "I think that nearly all stories can do with suspense. Even a love story can have it. We used to feel that suspense was saving someone from the scaffold, or something like that, but there is also the suspense of whether the man will get the girl. I really feel that suspense has to do largely with the audience's own desires or wishes."[11] Here Hitchcock implies that the capacity for suspense is inherent in any narrative. (If we substitute "anxiety" for "desires and wishes" in this passage, Hitchcock's broad view of suspense may come to resemble Freud's position that anxiety is the "universal currency" of all affect.) And if suspense, like anxiety, is the *lingua franca* of narrative, it is all the more interesting that in Hitchcock's example, the telephone operator, a surrogate for the film audience, is clearly engaged in a process of *constructing a narrative* from the anonymous sounds she listens to and interprets. To the extent the operator resembles us, Hitchcock implies that suspense-affect may be the same as interpretation.

Hitchcock's theoretical distinctions (the desirability of both knowledge and ignorance) are tautological and in any case belied by his own practice. His broadening of the referent of suspense to include potentially all people, all narratives, and all affect makes its domain virtually universal. It would appear that theorizing makes the concept even more problematic. The frustration of the attempt to conceptualize suspense is captured at the end of an interview response. Hitchcock had been discussing what happens on the set in those role-reversing moments when he performed his cameos and the rest of the cast watched; he wonders about a parallel with interviewers: "I find myself tempted to try the same trick with some of the press people, when they come for a full-dress interview. I have a secret yen to interview them, to pose them for still pictures. I would like to focus a press camera on some photographer and ask him to 'express menace and suspense,' please."[12] The hostility of Hitchcock's gauntlet-throwing in the last sentence recalls his repeated insistence that "in real life people's faces don't reveal what they think or feel"—a recurrent theme of his films.[13] But the deeper insinuation—that to "express menace and suspense" may be futile—is also established.

THE MacGUFFIN

An important figure for suspense is Hitchcock's parable of the MacGuffin. Hitchcock borrowed the neologism from his early colleague in the London Film Society, Angus MacPhail, who used it as early as 1939. In the story, a man traveling on an English train notices a package on the shelf above another man.

"What's that package?" asked the first man.
"Oh, that's a MacGuffin," replied his companion.
"What's a MacGuffin?"
"It's an apparatus for trapping lions in the Scottish highlands."
"But there are no lions in the Scottish highlands."
"Then that's no MacGuffin."[14]

Hitchcock calls the MacGuffin "something that the characters in the film care a lot about, but the audience doesn't worry about it too much"; he cites the examples of the wedding ring in *Rear Window*, the aircraft formula in *The 39 Steps*, the uranium-sand in *Notorious*, or the government secrets in *North by Northwest*.[15] From these examples, critics in the past have interpreted the MacGuffin to mean the "plot pretext"; on the other hand, Hitchcock himself saw the MacGuffin more broadly, as "the key element of any suspense story" and argued for its potential in non-espionage films, too.[16] The MacGuffin is most functional in certain revelatory plots that best generate suspense:

> To my way of thinking, the best suspense drama is that which weaves commonplace people in what appears to be a routine situation, until it is revealed (and fairly early in the game) as a glamorously dangerous charade. The spy stories of pre-war years fit these specifications perfectly. . . . The "MacGuffin" has obviously got to change. It can no longer be the business of breaking a code. And yet these very same elements, disguised to fit the times, must still be there.[17]

It is the MacGuffin that reveals the world is a "glamorously dangerous charade." What were its essential "elements" that could be "disguised to fit the [postwar] times"? The most important is the contrast between the significance of the MacGuffin to the characters and its insignificance to the audience—a contrast which, like the anecdote, calls into question its *meaning*.

In its exposure of the arbitrary, the MacGuffin functions less as a plot pretext than as a principle of reading, one that anticipates deconstruction in its unending dyad of figures used to expose figures. Suspense inheres in that moment—"fairly early in the game"—in which ordinary people come to see existence as a dangerous charade because at that moment, meaning itself, for characters and viewers, is put in suspense. The idea that the MacGuffin functions as a Saussurian sign that discloses the world's lack of ontological foundation has been increasingly favored by recent interpreters. In 1981, Thomas Elsaesser likened the MacGuffin (and Hitchcock's anecdote defining it) to a " 'pure signifier' to which no signified corresponds."[18] In 1994 Tom Cohen analyzed the anecdote and concluded that a MacGuffin "is (also) something other than the very thing that [Hitchcock] *seems* to call it"; for Cohen, the circularity of the story illustrates the idea of the MacGuffin as an only tenuously sustainable "*signifying loop* that is close to implosion."[19] Other studies of Hitchcock films have seen the MacGuffin as a de Manian challenge to hermeneutics.[20] In the light of these new interpretations, it will help to analyze in detail both the anecdote of the MacGuffin and examples of it from Hitchcock's films.

Cohen concludes that Hitchcock's story tells us that we still don't know what a MacGuffin is; his conclusion underscores the term's opacity. In addition, Hitchcock's parable *narrates* this suspense of meaning or deconstructive reading process whereby naming is first established then discarded in a new act of faulty figuration. The parable narrates the naming moment or the scene of denotation, of "What is that?" In the absence of the only alternative, silence, some sign must appear. The reply—that a MacGuffin is "a device for trapping lions in the

Scottish highlands"—shows that it is useless and, since lions were never indigenous to Scotland, always has been useless. It is as if the reply made matters worse. We are also told that the MacGuffin is a "package": thus the entity ostensibly defined by the parable is simultaneously a proper noun and a common noun, a fact that further unsettles the idea of the referent.[21] And if the word "MacGuffin" also means "package," it may be taken figuratively, as either metonymy or synecdoche: if "MacGuffin" is supposed to signify something *in* the package, then to identify the MacGuffin with the package is a metonymy; if "MacGuffin" is supposed to signify *a package with no contents*, then the figure is synecdoche, since in this case the part and whole are synonymous. Of course, in both cases, no "contents" of the package are ever revealed. As a result, the initial reply, "That's a MacGuffin," spoken of a package, is figural and undecidable even before the question of its empirical verification can arise. The meaning of "MacGuffin" was "always, already" undecidable.[22] It is as if a request for a name, once having been uttered, only puts the prospect of its true definition further out of reach. In this way, Hitchcock's parable for the "key element of suspense" recreates an undecidability similar to that which was observed in the discussion of the etymology of the word "suspense," in the introduction: before being "given out" in circulation, anything of value—grain, words or coins—must be weighed, but the very process of weighing revealed the arbitrary determination of values.

That MacGuffins should *not* be restricted to "plot pretext" is clear from Hitchcock's first example, the wedding ring in *Rear Window*. In that film, Lisa becomes convinced of Thorwald's guilt when she spies his wife's wedding ring on a night table. The interpretation she offers to Jeff ("No woman would *voluntarily* part with her wedding ring.") is for her axiomatic. Lisa's reading moment occurs two-thirds of the way through the film and prompts her first direct intervention in the case: in her evening gown she climbs through Thorwald's window, now a willing agent of the plot's peripeteia. Thus the wedding ring is not the pretext for *Rear Window*'s plot, which would more accurately be described as having been set in motion by Jeff's accident or his many prior inferences about the Thorwalds' marriage. But if the wedding ring *is* a MacGuffin but *is not* a plot pretext, what is it?

It is a sign. Like all signs, the wedding ring is not what it is: insofar as a wedding ring is a sign of the unity of two people and their pledge of mutual love, this particular wedding ring represents the opposite—murder. In this way Mrs. Thorwald's wedding ring demonstrates the truth of every sign, that its meaning cannot inhere in itself. In the words of Saussure, all signs are arbitrary; Lisa's interpretation of the ring is an act of reading understood as the bestowal of figural significance upon the arbitrary. As the story continues, we realize a second property of signs: insofar as they imply *promises*, none can ensure its own fulfillment, and no interpretation can be truly performative. Lisa's intervention into Thorwald's apartment—her movement from theoria to praxis—results in an outcome just opposite to the one she had conceived. Confronted by the returning Thorwald, Lisa's position quickly changes, Oedipus-like, from that of discoverer to discovered, from reader to victim, from knower to known. It is almost as if the "pure" knowledge Lisa gained through her interpretation of the ring can be valid only so long as it is withheld and never "applied" or "inserted" into the actual world, where it can only become vulnerable to the exigencies of new interpretations or—what may be the same thing—to the depredations of power. Thus the wedding ring counts as a MacGuffin not because it instigates the action but because it reveals the world as a "glamorously dangerous charade" made up of figures.

Hitchcock's second example, the aircraft formula in *The 39 Steps*, shows that exposure of the charade does not end suspense. Cohen has admirably analyzed two crucial features of this MacGuffin. First, as an ungrammatical string of numbers and letters uttered by Mr. Memory, the formula exemplifies not only the arbitrary character of language but also the spurious learning of the protagonist, Hannay. Second, as the title of the film itself, "the thirty-nine steps" links Hannay's misinterpretation with that of the film viewer, too, who may at first be tempted to read the film hermeneutically, as the construction of a normative couple or as the vindication of Hannay's quest to establish his moral innocence. Cohen's analysis shows that far from providing closure, Mr. Memory's recitation prompts new reading dilemmas.[23] The "glamorously dangerous charade" he exposes is a world given over to war, just as the "revelation" of Hannay's reading is only more suspense. That the climax takes place just offstage at the Palladium seems an ironic answer to those psychological theorists of suspense who compare its resolution to a "curtain fall", the persistence of Hannay's and the viewer's suspense even after the revelation of the MacGuffin of *The 39 Steps* belies such theories of closure.[24]

The uranium-sand in the champagne bottle in *Notorious* also exposes the world as a glamorously dangerous charade: the trappings of high civilization enclose the potential for its total destruction. The grotesque relation between sign (label or container) and referent (contents) may be understood in the contrast between the pop of the champagne cork and a nuclear detonation. Devlin's seizure of the sand, like Lisa's appropriation of the wedding ring, ought to presage some true and emancipatory knowledge. However, the apparent apprehension of meaning leads not to truth or freedom but instead to new figuration, doubt, and suspense. Of course, the uranium-sand (like the wedding ring or aircraft formula) is in itself morally neutral. The question of whether the sand— or nuclear weapons—should be possessed by the Americans or the "ex-Nazis" (here perhaps surrogates for communists) can never be settled by the sand itself—just as the question of the Thorwald's guilt cannot be settled by the ring. The muteness of the MacGuffin in response to the moral urgency of the questions it gives rise to shows its performative incapacity: the contents of the bottle may have dangerous effects in the real world, but these can never be mastered by acquiring it.

The mute MacGuffin of *Notorious* turns attention back to the film's consistent analogies between the Americans and the ex-Nazis. Like Alicia's father, Devlin trades on his knowledge of her affection for him to exploit her for political purposes. Like the ex-Nazis, the American CIA operates outside the rule of law: a motorcycle policeman in Miami defers to Devlin; both Americans and Nazis acquiesce in the elimination of members once their usefulness has been compromised; the love of Alex Sebastian for Alicia is much less compromised (and arguably much more genuine) than Devlin's. Given the moral undecidability of the two sides depicted in *Notorious*, the viewer might well ask, "To which side should the uranium-sand *naturally* belong?" MacGuffins create such unanswerable questions. Of course, the principal cinematic signifiers of the film—its stars, costumes, lighting, soundtrack—are positioned so as to rationalize for its target audience the CIA's lawbreaking on behalf of American national interest. Arrayed like the labels of the wine bottles, the film's glamorously dangerous sign-system is revealed to be arbitrary by the viewer who, like Devlin, momentarily breaks its surface; in retrospect, the world's amoral charade is *both* the Nazis' plot and Devlin's exposure of it. (The analogy between Devlin and the viewer as readers, both of whom seek what's inside by extraordinary means, may also be reducible to the crude linearity of Alex Sebastian's elementary reading moment—he finds a 1940 bottle substituted in a line of 1934 bottles. The perception of difference in signs is a prerequisite for any reading.) Like both characters, viewers of *Notorious* must consider whether their guidance by glamorous signs results in truth or delusion.

Hitchcock talked about the uranium sand on three occasions.[25] In one version, he explains how in 1944 his producer had asked about the nature of the Germans' activity in Rio; when Hitchcock replied, "Uranium-235," the producer continued: "What's that?" Hitchcock said, "That's the stuff they're going to make the atom bomb out of." When the producer said, "What atom bomb? I've never heard of it." Hitchcock replied, "No, it isn't out yet." The echo of the dialogue in the MacGuffin parable is striking: in this story, the innocent or nonexistent device to "trap lions in the Scottish highlands" becomes the stuff of the atomic bomb. The morally abysmal parallel between a movie concept and nuclear war once more calls attention to the incommensurable gap in meaning central to the MacGuffin. In a coda to his reminiscence, Hitchcock explains how "as a result of this mistake," the producer sold the property for only half of its value; Hitchcock's concludes, "He could have made 100 percent had he not made that cardinal error . . . And so those producers lost all kinds of money for the wrong kind of thinking. But they still think that way. They still think that if the film's a spy film that it's all about . . . well, the MacGuffin." For Hitchcock, a film with a MacGuffin is not *about* the MacGuffin; his account of the producer's "mistake" succinctly narrates the inevitability of error in interpretations of the MacGuffin.

We are never told specifically what the producer's motive *was*, so we guess: fear of negative publicity from political controversy? Hitchcock's omission is in keeping with the spirit of the MacGuffin; the indeterminacy shows the way interpretations of the MacGuffin (first the producer's, then Hitchcock's, then ours) further darken the opacity of the original story. Even the supposed vindication of Hitchcock's prescience isn't the unambiguous referent of this MacGuffin, since his interpretation must be challenged, too. The story mocks the producer's greedy reluctance to risk a profit, but it reveals Hitchcock's appropriation of the MacGuffin as being just as self-serving.[26]

Hitchcock cited the MacGuffin in *North by Northwest* as an example of his refusal "to use the kind of thing which most people think is very important." In fact, *North by Northwest* never describes its MacGuffin—microfilm to be spirited out of the country by the ideologically unidentified Vandamm—as anything more than "government secrets."[27] To this degree, the MacGuffin of *North by Northwest* may seem even purer than earlier ones, since nearly all referents (as, "Thorwald's wedding" or "air defense" or "nuclear weapons") have been stripped from it; as a result, the film may allegorize a struggle for the purest MacGuffin or for figuration itself. In his interview with Truffaut, Hitchcock seemed to recognize its simplicity:

Grant, referring to the James Mason character, asks, "What does he do?" The counterintelligence man replies, "Let's just say that he's an importer and exporter." "But what does he sell?" "Oh, just government secrets!" is the answer. Here, you see, the MacGuffin has been boiled down to its purest expression: nothing at all![28]

The minimal content of this MacGuffin is evoked by its illegibility: compared with *The 39 Steps*, where we hear the recitation of the aircraft formula or *Notorious* and *Rear Window* where we see the uranium-sand and wedding ring, the MacGuffin in *North by Northwest* is practically invisible. When the statuette cracks open, a strip of microfilm appears for an instant. To be sure, not *all* semantic value has disappeared, since the secret bears some generic relationship to state power. Such a residual value in this distilled MacGuffin may prompt speculation as to whether, for Hitchcock, the arbitrariness of the sign can ever be theorized outside of politics or what Foucault would call the discourses of power. Such an implication of the MacGuffin suits *The 39 Steps* and *Notorious* very well, too, since the prized valences of the aircraft formula and uranium-sign are set upon them by the state. *Rear Window*'s wedding ring might at first seem explicable without regard to state power; however, the film's romance plot focuses on the legitimation of human relationships in marriage—a prospect readable in the film's juxtaposition of the marriage question with the arrival of the police. The legitimation of sex in state-sanctioned marriage is a speech act like the arrests of criminals by the police; however, the dysfunction of these performatives is conveyed through the film's ambiguous ending, which is silent on the subject of the formation of the couple.

The suspense of *North by Northwest*'s MacGuffin is both political and linguistic. As in *Notorious*, the MacGuffin is conspicuously located in a container—in this case, an Eastern art-object, a small statue. The illegible secrets that now comprise the interior of a container permit a clearer understanding of the MacGuffin-sign as a linguistic structure of interior and exterior. The arbitrary relation of exterior to interior is reinforced by the statuette's "Eastern" provenance—an enigmatic or portentous exterior with perhaps an even less obvious relation to its interior than *Notorious*'s champagne bottle had with its interior—sand whose dark color might at least feign the profile of wine. That this MacGuffin's exterior is Eastern and its interior Western deepens the undecidability of a film that depicts national security at odds with the international ideals of the United Nations: as in *Notorious*, the morally appalling nature of both sides that struggle for the MacGuffin insures that the identity of its "true" owner is indeterminable. By giving the lie to any image of international unity or harmony, *North by Northwest*'s MacGuffin, like the others, exposes the glamorously dangerous charade of the world. Finally, the MacGuffin as microfilm suggests links with both Western technology and the film itself. As a textual technology, microfilm implies the same application of the arbitrary onto the material that is evinced in Roger Thornhill's advertising career or in the vacant modernism of the Seagram's building or Vandamm's mountain retreat; these are only a few of the cultural markers of a worldwide charade. And of course as a manifestation of *film*, the MacGuffin becomes self-referential, transferring recognition of the necessary futility of the pursuit of the MacGuffin from the characters onto the film viewers.

HITCHCOCK'S CAMEOS

In a passage typically Hitchcockian in its blend of humor and seriousness, ambiguous pronoun references, and plethora of puns and figuration, Hitchcock's 1950 essay on suspense linked the MacGuffin with his cameos:

In *Stage Fright* I have been told that my performance is quite juicy. I have been told this with a certain air of tolerance, implying that I have now achieved the maximum limits of directorial ham in the movie sandwich.

It just isn't true. There may have been a "MacGuffin" in my film appearance, but not a ham. My motives have always been more devious, or, if you prefer a more devious word, sinister. I have wormed my way into my own pictures as a spy. A director should see how the other half lives. I manage that by shifting to the front side of the camera and letting my company shoot me, so I can see what it is like to be shot by my company.[29]

Hitchcock's seeming salute to his critics' "air of tolerance" may mask his anger at their accusation that his cameos are self-serving. By construing his cameo as MacGuffin, Hitchcock counters the charge by demonstrating the way all language is self- or, better, persona-creating. This implication is conveyed in the way cameos unsettle the distinction between actor and non-actor.[30]

The tone of the passage is enigmatic: it is hard to say whether his critics' "air of tolerance" and his own rejoinder are to be understood seriously. On the one hand, cameos seem unnecessary and trivial—Hitchcock's last for only a few seconds and never influence the course of the diegesis. On the other hand, cameos also exemplify the indispensable *enunciative* principle in art, any feature that momentarily reveals its constructed or figural nature.[31] Whether it is the sculpture's pedestal or painting's frame, the literary persona or the dramatic *mise en scene*, the enunciative principle, no matter how trivial, can never be eradicated from art. It is understandable, then, that Hitchcock calls his cameo a MacGuffin: both are simultaneously trivial and urgent, both disclose the glamorously dangerous charade of the world—and also its representation in art. Critical discussions of cameos perpetuate this suspense when their significance is put in doubt.[32]

Hitchcock's reference to the cameo in *Stage Fright* places it on an equal footing with the MacGuffin as a vehicle of suspense. There is no generic term from either traditional rhetoric or the rhetoric of cinema for cameos, so for the moment I propose the neologism "reverse parabasis." Simple or unmodified "parabasis" names that moment in theatre when an actor steps out of his or her role and addresses the audience directly, as at the conclusion of *The Tempest*.[33] At first glance, this term might appear useful in analyzing parallel moments in film, especially comedy—as for example when Groucho Marx, W. C. Fields, or Woody Allen turns to address the camera directly. Hitchcock's cameos seem to work in the reverse way, since in his case someone who is not really a character is inserted into the diegesis. But a moment's reflection shows it is obvious that both simple and reverse parabasis conceal similar contradictions: how do we know that a recognizable director who plays a minor part, like any actor who appears to have cast off his character, has not simply—has not *necessarily*— just assumed another role? The question is easy to answer in the cases of Marx, Fields, and Allen, since their shedding of diegetic roles surely reveals no new or genuine self but only a familiar comic persona carefully constructed over years of performance. Perhaps by virtue of its gigantic persona-creating machinery, film makes explicit what was implicit but not much noticed in the parabasis or even curtain calls of drama: that in *any* parabasis, the "true" self unveiled is instantly discovered to have been inauthentic from the start. Film and drama teach how viewers are also suspended in a permanent state of self-construction from which we can never escape to emerge as our "natural" or "normal" or "original" selves. J. Hillis Miller, following Paul de Man, calls this the moment of "permanent parabasis."[34] What Hitchcock calls the "sinister" motive of his cameos may be connected with this unsettling moment and may explain why parabasis is often accompanied by disbelief, laughter or terror.

Put another way, in Hitchcock's cameos we witness an emptying-out of the idea of the Cartesian self, arrived at from a slightly different direction than in normal parabasis. Instead of momentarily seeing a "real" person behind a character's unmasking, viewers of Hitchcock films are first confronted with a figure that was not diegetic in the first place, one that struggles unsuccessfully to achieve momentary diegetic existence, only to be replaced by a seemingly real "Hitchcock," but in an another instant that figure is exposed as a persona, leading to the suspicion that there may never have been a true Hitchcock independent of it. Thus, there is no difference, after all, in the function of normal and reverse parabasis; both induce a state of suspense from the real. Hitchcock's cameos create such pauses when character, Cartesian self, and persona seem for a moment to alternate distinctly but then dissolve into each other, promising but withholding authentic revelation. In this process, they recapitulate the suspense of the MacGuffin, in which the exposure of the "glamorously dangerous charade" of the world can be effected only by new artifice. Neither actor nor audience emerges from behind an immovable looking glass.

That Hitchcock chose *Stage Fright* as the film for theorizing his equation between the cameo and the MacGuffin reinforces the similarities between theatrical and cinematic parabasis, since in this film human life is everywhere depicted as simply an extension of theatrical role playing. From the curtain-raising which accompanies the credits to the "revelation" induced in theatrical space, *Stage Fright* develops the kind of parabasis first seen in *The 39 Steps*: in both films, characters are introduced as indigenous to theatrical rather than natural space. The futility of their efforts to "reestablish" natural identities through disguise and courtship becomes evident. Eve Gill and Ordinary Smith, in *Stage Fright*, function like Richard Hannay and Pamela in *The 39 Steps*, substituting one constructed identity for another in a process that ends only when an imposition of the law arbitrarily halts the potentially unending series of exchanges. Into *Stage Fright*'s world of disguises without selves, Hitchcock inserts his cameo.

His six-second appearance occurs during Eve Gill's effort to protect her friend Jonathan Cooper, whom she wrongly believes to be innocent, and to speak to Charlotte Inwood, whom she wrongly believes to be guilty. As an actress with the Royal Academy of Dramatic Art, Eve has long prided herself on her ability to play any part; as Hitchcock's cameo approaches, she has begun to play two. First she impersonates a newspaper reporter, who interviews and bribes Nellie Goode, Charlotte's maid, the witness to the escape of the murderer. Eve gains Nellie's permission to impersonate her cousin, Doris Tinsdale, in order to get access to Charlotte by claiming that Nellie, sick, sent her as a substitute. Eve fashions a disguise as Doris and, uncertain of its effectiveness, walks down a sidewalk toward the camera, holding a piece of paper in front of her and rehearsing her lines, "I'm Doris Tinsdale; I'm from Nellie." It is at this moment that Hitchcock, walking on Eve's left in the opposite direction, passes Eve, overhears her, and peers over his left shoulder. Is his glance quizzical? Supercilious? Unaware of it, Eve walks on while Hitchcock resumes speed and turns a corner.

What the camera shows us in this cameo is Alfred Hitchcock, the director of *Stage Fright*, pretending to be a nameless passerby in London, turning to look at Jane Wyman, an actress he has hired to play the role of the actress Eve Gill,

Figure 2.1: *Stage Fright* (1950). © Warner Bros. Pictures Corp.

who has earlier impersonated a newspaper reporter as a means of later impersonating Doris Tinsdale. Establishing the true referents of these two identities
with certainty would be as difficult as pronouncing their names simultaneously.
"Whoever he is" overhears someone saying, "I'm Doris Tinsdale, sent from
Nellie." The look that accompanies Hitchcock's glance—like all looks—is un-
interpretable: no knowledge of its import is possible. For example, could the
passerby be someone who knows the real Eve or real Doris and hence knows
that the words spoken are lies? Could the passerby turn because he recognized
the name "Nellie"? Could the passerby be acquainted with someone *else* by the
name of Doris Tinsdale? In this case, the passerby would undergo a moment of
"potential recognition" that would after all be signlessly revised as cognitive
dissonance. Could the passerby be a non-English speaker and his turning and
glance be precipitated by no more than the mere sounds of the words, apart
from their signification? Is it possible to know whether Eve's words were even
heard, since a lustful but deaf passerby might have turned his head because of
Eve's appearance, not her words? These questions are not quibbles: they ask
the same questions about the meaning of the word "recognition" that Wittgenstein asked in *Philosophical Investigations*:

I meet someone whom I have not seen for years; I see him clearly, but fail to know him.
Suddenly I know him, I see the old face in the altered one. I believe that I should do a
different portrait of him now if I could paint. Now, when I know my acquaintance in a

crowd, perhaps after looking in his direction for quite a while—is this a special sort of seeing? Is it a case of both seeing and thinking? Or an amalgam of the two, as I should almost like to say? The question is: *why* does one want to say this?[35]

For Wittgenstein, the fact that the signs of recognition were indistinguishable from the signs of nonrecognition called the concept of recognition itself into question. All seeing may be "seeing-as." In the case of *Stage Fright*, it is easy to see how the indeterminacy of the cameo serves as a synecdoche for the film's many other moments of supposed but unprovable recognition—for example, Eve's lame, late protests to Ordinary Smith ("I wasn't acting!") or to Jonathan ("I feel desperately sorry for you!"), statements that can only be taken on faith, statements made in the charade of life. Any "recognition" derivable from the cameo cannot be distinguished from false-recognition or non-recognition.

The situation is no better "outside" the film. Can we interpret the meaning of Hitchcock's look at Jane Wyman? Does it mean, "She is playing this scene well" or "All actors are cattle"? To Truffaut, Hitchcock later complained:

In her disguise as a lady's maid, [Wyman] should have appeared rather unglamorous; after all, she was supposed to be impersonating an unattractive maid. But every time she saw the rushes and how she looked alongside Marlene Dietrich, she would burst into tears. She couldn't accept the idea of her face being in character, while Dietrich looked so glamorous, so she kept improving her appearance every day and that's how she failed to maintain the character.[36]

Before accepting Hitchcock's complaint at face value, we should ask whether directors' interpretations of their films are more privileged than those of critics. (Certainly, Hitchcock's critics have been astute in detecting the way his replies to Truffaut enhanced his lifelong persona-building project.[37]) His complaint in the quotation raises new questions. For example, his interpretation of Wyman is inseparable from and perhaps even conditioned by his assessment of the character she plays, Eve Gill, the apprentice actress, in her relationship to the more experienced and glamorous femme fatale, Charlotte Inwood, played by Marlene Dietrich. Thus, an off-camera interpretation has become contaminated by the story and can't be freed from it—a compelling example of parabasis. Hitchcock's comments here assume that the correlation between Wyman's face and character are independent of the "real" person and are instead the product of her persona's rivalry with Marlene Dietrich's. Of course, it is impossible to miss the way Hitchcock's comments to Truffaut preserve his *own* persona as the imperious and on occasion misogynistic manipulator of the women he hired. In summary, critical interpretation of Hitchcock's presence in *Stage Fright* is no more productive of truth than is study of the passerby's glance: considered from either vantage point, the six-second performance is a stunning (or in the title's hint, frightening) demonstration of parabasis—the suspense of being permanently trapped in a fraudulent or fictional self.

CAMEOS, MacGUFFINS AND THE SUSPENSE OF STILL ART

As we've seen, Hitchcock's cameo in *Stage Fright* recalls an analogue in one of the films it rewrites, *The 39 Steps*: in that film, Hitchcock was a passerby at a bus stop while in *Stage Fright*, a double-decker bus appears in the background as he walks past Eve/Jane. Hitchcock's cameos are frequently sites of transfer—on sidewalks, streets, railway cars, elevators—in which the director's persona is read in the context of the essence of his medium, movement. In *Blackmail*, he appears reading a book on a train; in *Number Seventeen* he is a walking paparazzi; in *Spellbound*, he emerges from an elevator into a hotel lobby; in *North by Northwest*, he is excluded from a bus he seeks to board; in *The Birds* he walks dogs out of a pet store onto the sidewalk. Each such moment interrogates what was accomplished by the movement of the persona, by its going from here to there. Each moment associates the act of film direction with the most questionable transfer of all, the shift from sign to referent. Each cameo may be studied as a part of Hitchcock's evolving film theory: like the cameo in *Stage Fright*, each offers different contexts for understanding the parabasis of identity.

In the cameo and the MacGuffin, Hitchcock found figures for suspense less vulnerable to the contradiction that marks both his own expository writing and that of scholars of suspense. Suspense accompanies the infinite deferral of the MacGuffin's meaning and the undecidability of identity that the cameo transfers, by association, to all other characters. In these figures, suspense theory becomes indistinguishable from the viewing of films; what suspense *is* becomes inseparable from the viewer's visual and verbal experience. The close scrutiny of one frame of Hitchcock's cameo in *Stage Fright* suggests another hypothesis of this book—that suspense may inhere in still photographs (and by extension other still art) as well as in the traditional "temporal" genres of literary and cinematic narrative; this hypothesis will be tested in the next chapter.

Definitions of suspense falter when they try to abstract from narratives formulaic or universally applicable criteria; by contrast, Hitchcock's MacGuffins and cameos suggest that suspense is *figure without formula, criteria, or referent*, a condition of transience observable even in still art, one that referential discourses, including this chapter, misrepresent. In Part II, visual renderings of hanging figures are examined as metaphors for this condition.

TWO

The Iconography of the Hanging Figure

INTRODUCTION TO PART II

The contradictions in current theories of suspense flow from their Cartesian assumptions about the existence of self and object and from their hermeneutic assumptions that signs have natural meanings. Hitchcock's theoretical observations were just as contradictory, but his *figures* for suspense—the MacGuffin and the cameo—harmonized with the thematic undecidability of his films; close attention to one frame of a cameo suggested the possibility of suspense in nontemporal art, too. The intellectual advantage of a figural approach to suspense is that it assumes less—only signs, which may not have referents. Austerity was also part of the rationale for beginning with the etymology of suspense rather than its supposed referents. As noted in the introduction, "suspense" is derived from the Latin *pendere*, meaning "to cause to hang," which is itself derived from the transitive form *pendo*, "to weigh prior to circulating." The introduction also noted the way this original sense of the word harbored its own undecidability. Now we turn attention to the undecidability of "hanging," as that has been rendered in visual art. Physically suspended figures provide metaphors for states of contingency and deferral of meaning analogous to those already noted in Hitchcock's discussions of MacGuffins and cameos. From the perspective gained in this chapter, suspense may be understood as part of a radical uncertainty already readable in the history of visual art.

By themselves, hanging figures have no meaning; they appear significant only when interpreted in relation with other signs. This Saussurian idea has always been more easily understood in the study of literature, where alphabetic systems

are demonstrably arbitrary, than it has been in visual art, where signs often seem
to convey "natural" meaning. In *Philosophical Investigations*, Wittgenstein
questioned this assumption, arguing that a drawing of a happy facial expression
could never convey any inherent meaning, any more than could an alphabetic
character.[1] It is not just that the meaning of smiles is culturally specific; rather,
there is nothing in the smile itself that should inherently "mean" anything. In
The Truth in Painting, Derrida explained the divorce between visual representation and the truth by developing the theory of the frame: what made painting
possible—the *parergon*, or adoption of a frame—simultaneously required its
own exclusion from the representation.[2] For both writers, visual images are
inescapably textual; they are not exempt from Saussure's insistence on the arbitrary relation between sign and referent. For Derrida, all visual images are
"caught within a network of differences that give them a textual structure."[3]

To take a familiar example, it is clear that the referent of the crucifixion is
by no means inherent in its image: for Christians the meaning of "victory over
death" arises only in the context of a limited range of interpretations of certain
texts; for non-Christians, the image's referent may be physical suffering or even
justifiable punishment. Reinforcing the arbitrary character of this image is this
chapter's conclusion that the expected suffering of hanging figures cannot be
taken for granted: the Christian idea that the crucifixion may be painful *only in
part* is paralleled in several non-Christian examples, too—in the native American sun dance, in Titian's rendering of Marsyas, and in the Hanged Man of the
Tarot cards.

But paradoxical expressions of pain—perhaps as pain/joy—also manifest
Wittgenstein's or Derrida's deeper undecidability about meaning. As we shall
see in the case of pendants, the act of hanging converts a part of the natural
world into art, with the result that the previously assumed signification of both
now becomes open to question. Put another way, when an object becomes a
pendant, it ceases to be fully continuous with nature and becomes a questionable
sign; the material world becomes explicit only when newly regarded as a sign
or figure. This making-explicit occurs only *after* some semantic or cultural value
for the figure (for example, the pendant) has first been apprehended in it. The
built-in disillusionment of the experience of visual art repeats the two-step process Paul de Man observed in the reading of literary texts—in the first place,
readers commit themselves to referents as they grasp the semantic sense of a
visual sign that, in the second place, is revealed to be arbitrary, after all. This
process means that reading hanging figures will involve initial interpretations
that are understood to be mistakes, but only in retrospect. For example, it is
necessary first to mistake the crucifixion as having a semantic content like the
victory over death or the paradox of pain before seeing that those particular
contents are cultural constructions. As indicated in the introduction, this "allegory of seeing" transfers de Man's thesis about reading to the visual arts.

Two influential scholars have argued that hanging figures *do* have decidable
referential meaning—they stopped, as it were, after the first of de Man's two

steps. In *The Golden Bough*, Sir James Frazer surveyed mythological and religious examples of hanging deities, beginning with the figure of Marsyas, a satyr sometimes identified with Silenus, whom Frazer considered a double of Attis, an important vegetation god. (Titian's painting of Marsyas will be discussed later in this chapter.) Marsyas was tied to a pine tree and flayed; his skin was later hung from a cave next to the river that bore his name. Frazer interpreted the hanging, death, resurrection and subsequent worship of deities like Marsyas as magical or apotropaic acts undertaken to ward off sterility and help promote fertility. Marsyas, Attis, and Adonis were types of the scapegoat god whose death was thought necessary to the continuation of seasonal and agricultural cycles. Frazer believed that the crucifixion of Jesus was best understood in the same context—in this case as an avatar of the sacrifice of Haman, the mock king who died at the Babylonian Sacaea festival, which later influenced the Jewish festival of Purim. For Frazer these hanging figures served a unifying social, cultural, and religious function; the figure was not arbitrary but the emblem of a universal truth discoverable by anthropological research.[4]

In *Discipline and Punish*, Michel Foucault considered the hanging figure as the secular "spectacle of the scaffold," the principal means by which the display of power legitimized and sustained the European state through the eighteenth century.[5] Visual representations of that spectacle from the twelfth to the nineteenth century—including horrific depictions of public hangings, burnings, flayings, drownings, breakings on the wheel—have been analyzed by Lionelli Puppi, who follows Foucault and Albert Camus in claiming that the severity of public torture and capital punishment was reinforced by the tradition of Christian martyrdom: states constantly reasserted their legitimacy by making deviant subjects the mirror image of the physical suffering inflicted on saints and before them, on Jesus.[6] For these writers, the iconography of the hanging figure discloses the political character of suspense: those who are hanged attest, willy nilly, to the supposed legitimacy of the executioner's discourse.

The worldly functions that Frazer and Foucault assign to the hanging figure are comprehensible only when its signs are deemed performative—that is, only within the domain of superstitious or magical thought: some Christians, like their pagan counterparts, believe that signs themselves, crosses or amulets, have predictable powers, just as monarchs and dictators have often believed that the mere spectacle of the scaffold is sufficient to control populations. In this chapter, religious and political performative values are first discussed as if they were fixed, in the manner Frazer and Foucault recommend; however, it is inevitable that signs later become readable as only constative and arbitrary. At such moments referential meanings evaporate, and hanging figures could be representative only if the world itself is thought of as a figure.

Two examples will illustrate the process. A long tradition of art criticism has associated Rembrandt's *The Flayed Ox* (see Figure 3.7) with both the crucifixion and older sacrificial traditions; these religious meanings are balanced by the painting's naturalism. But this potential paradox is anticipated in the ox's wooden frame, which draws attention to the arbitrary quality of Rembrandt's art and of perception in general. Hence both religious and naturalistic referents "hold" only so long as the viewer does not attend to the painting as also a "framed" collocation, of arbitrary colors. When viewers identify with the young woman in the background—seeing something ponderous whose display is made possible by a frame—the hanging figure loses its referential capacity, thereby leaving its audience in suspense. Experiencing Homer's *The Life-Line* (see Figure 3.8) also involves these two steps. In the first, the scene's existential allegory of human vulnerability, technological frailty, and repressed sexuality is quickly assimilated, as numerous art critics have attested. But when the title's referent is explored in its many contexts—ropes in use, ropes hanging uselessly, and the artist's "lines"—it becomes clear that the existential allegory is only made possible by painterly artifice whose limitations are also allegorized in the scene. Thus hanging figures in visual art tell us first about the world—its religious and existential terror—but then, by revealing their arbitrary and constructed nature, they put these lessons in suspense. Through this two-step operation they define what it is to *be* a hanging figure.

Chapter 4 shows this process at work in Hitchcock's films. For example, in *Murder!* Handel Fane is understandable as an actor whose sexual and racial ambiguity may give the lie to the assumptions of "natural" white, male, heterosexual, aristocratic privilege embodied in the film's ostensible hero, Sir John. But as he swings on his trapeze, the back-and-forth motion of this elaborately costumed performer—tracked by the camera, in front of a transfixed audience—forms a parallel to the visual experience of Hitchcock's viewers. This reflexivity or *enunciation* of the camera exposes the constructed nature of the scene, just as Rembrandt's frame or Homer's rope did for their paintings. In short, whenever the artwork exhibits its own construction, its signs are seen as, after all, only framed and arbitrary constatives, as hanging figures themselves that denote only emptiness, the inescapability of figuration, and the deferral of meaning.

The iconography of the hanging figure begins with pendants and persists in postmodernism.

3

The Hanging Figure in Non-Cinematic Visual Art

PENDANTS AND POSTMODERNISM

Pendants date from the Paleolithic period. Ivory pendants with scores of beads found in Middle-Paleolithic burial mounds in Russia required forty-five minutes for the shaping of each bead, and such pendants were worn everywhere—across the forehead and temples, across the body, down the arms and legs and around the ankles.[1] As with the preparation of cave paintings, the painstaking process of pendant manufacture attests to a degree of sophistication that may belie meliorist accounts of history. Archeological speculation as to the function of pendants often invokes performative religious or political explanations: pendants with apotropaic properties—especially those portraying gods and within Egyptology—are considered amulets.[2] Some pendants have been interpreted as having astronomical or calendrical functions;[3] others remain enigmatic. For example, the archeologist Holly Pittman concludes her study of a proto-Elamite "shell pendant" (Figure 3.1) with the conclusion that it served "perhaps as a permanent record of a transaction, perhaps deposited as a 'votive object' in a sacred space."[4]

Pendants change natural objects like stone into a suspended form; this conversion defines art in a moment of rupture that afterward calls into question both the object's original and newly proposed meaning. In this way, an object on a pendant may be analogous to an allusion or citation—an excision transferred from one realm to another, with the hanging material (thong, rope, etc.) analogous to quotation marks. Hanging a stone on a rope is like quoting a predecessor poet. T. S. Eliot famously preached and practiced that the citation

Figure 3.1: *Proto-Elamite Shell Pendant* (ca. 3300–2800 B.C.). Courtesy Staatliche Museum zu Berlin and Ägyptisches Museum.

of prior art and the creation of each new work of art changes the canon—Chaucer's Prologue can never be read the same way after the opening of *The Waste Land*. Pendants illustrate the extension of Eliot's dictum to the human manipulation of the natural world. Pendants create signs as sites of transfer; they manifest the iterative property of signs. That is, in order to *be*, signs must be citable, quotable, iterative.[5] Pendants also raise the prospect that the world itself may be figurative: rocks can never be read the same way after having been seen as a pendant maker's quarry. Postmodern art often conveys the same iterative essence of the sign by depicting ever more boldly the exact point or threshold that constitutes art as such a site of transfer. Rosalind Krauss has shown how the marked earth sites of the seventies and eighties—from cavities incised in the landscape to Christo's *Running Fence*—reconceive sculpture as the mark of an ontological absence.[6] In much the same spirit, Damien Hirst's dissected animals or Jeff Koons's suspended basketballs (Figure 3.2) propose that meaning can be understood as the temporary suspension of the natural or artificial object in a moment that disables its utilitarian or semantic functions. These avant-garde experiments often dramatize the liminal moment in which the material world becomes figuration. From this perspective, the prehistoric pendant is only an early instance of art understood as an allusion or quotation that suspends the privilege-claim of the natural world. The fact that pendants were worn in such profusion and redundancy, on so many parts of the body, attests to art's *prox-*

Figure 3.2: Jeff Koons, *Two Ball 50/50 Tank* (1985). Courtesy
Sonnabend Gallery, New York.

imity to the human—as if from the outset it was impossible to imagine life
without art understood as its condition of articulation in signs of suspended
meaning.

The early shell pendant discussed by Pittman reveals two further sides of
suspense. First, its appearance just prior to the introduction of writing suggests
a parallel between graphic representation and hanging figures, a parallel that
obviously comments on the way signs outlive the human. Pittman identified the

pendant as a copy in more durable material, stone, of an early logographic or pictographic tablet originally made of the more perishable medium of clay; hence this pendant shares an aspiration to permanence with the library, archive or the cemetery stone. Like the formal writing systems that soon followed, this trait of the pendant may attest to some spurious human association between immortality and signs. Durable signs presuppose the same mortality and death of the subject that their greater empirical longevity demonstrates to perception. Nevertheless, the desire to imitate "lasting signs" or the hope that life may endure as long as signs (later associated with literature and "literary immortality") may already be present in the proto-Elamite pendant. The fact that such an association is also evident in signs that predate writing may support Derrida's speculation that the presupposition of death in signs and their independence from metaphysical presence may be a condition "older" than history.[7] From this perspective, the pictographic pendant functions as eloquently as any verbal sign.

Second, along with its depiction of natural objects, including the cattle that are carved into its surface, *this pendant also depicts, around the cattle's necks, pendants*. This is an early instance of the "Chinese box" or "Quaker Oats box" effect, implying the possibility of infinite regress; one archeologist has already noted the wit of this pendant's reflexivity.[8] Paul de Man thought that the potential for vertiginous regress was inherent in signs; he called this "dissolving irony," and we shall see its functions in several of Hitchcock's films, including *Rope*.[9] In this detail, the proto-Elamite pendant anticipates the possibility of the infinite recursivity of signs, whether ominous or comic, as that is later manifested in the novels of Laurence Sterne or John Barth.

To summarize, a pendant is a hanging figure made by a "quotation" from nature, one that calls into question both nature and signs; it presupposes death and may reveal some human desire for immortality; despite this, a pendant may acknowledge that it is nevertheless just a constative sign, and that it may be, after all, only a sign of itself. These functions of the pendant are echoed in postmodernism.

NON-WESTERN AND PRE-CHRISTIAN ICONOGRAPHY

In the Sun Dance of the Plains Indians (not illustrated[10]), warriors lacerate their skin and thread it with leather thongs attached to a central pillar. Over the several-day course of the dance, participants pull back against the thongs with such force that they temporarily hang from the post. According to tradition, the voluntary infliction of pain purifies the warrior while infusing him with the spirit of the tribe's god, whose totems (especially buffalo) hang from the post; the arrival of the spirit's power is accompanied by visions and climactic, ecstatic gesticulations. The Sun Dance reverses the order of the pendant: instead of the transformation of a natural object into suspended proximity with the human, the Sun Dance transforms the human. It is as if the human subject becomes the post's pendant; the post "wears" the brave, and dancing transfers the undecid-

Figure 3.3: Egyptian Attack on Ashkelon (from *Altlus zur altaegyptischen Kultur-geschichte* by Walter Wreszinski). The drawing appears courtesy Editions Slatkine, Geneva, Switzerland.

ability of the pendant's stone onto the human being. From this perspective, the Plains Indians can be considered more rigorous than their Paleolithic ancestors, since they include human beings as well as natural objects in the category of undecidability established by the work of art. On the other hand, this ceremony, like all other religious ones, also presupposes a performative view of the rite: drumbeats, chants, and accompanying symbols are thought capable of precipitating an infusion of divine power into the warrior whose endurance of pain solicited it.[11]

Western pre-Christian traditions begin with the Greek and Near-Eastern mythologies Frazer describes; the legends of hanging vegetation gods find parallels in ancient customs of human sacrifice. For example, among the Canaanites the practice of sacrificing and hanging children from the ramparts of besieged cities is attested to in Egyptian art (Figure 3.3).[12] Some scholars believe that such sacrifice was also practiced—whether inside or outside Yahwistic law is the point of contention—by the pre-Exilic Israelites.[13] While the Jews never worshiped a hanging figure, the function of Temple sacrifices was understood as propitiatory and expiatory: the ritual purged or cleansed celebrants of transgression, a function that may have influenced later Christian veneration of a hanging figure.

SANTO SPIRITO CRUCIFIX (1492–93)

The Western Christian tradition centers on the crucifixion. The gospel writers interpreted Isaiah's description of the servant who has "made himself an offering for reparation" as predicting the arrival and passion of Jesus, whom John referred to as the Lamb of God. Christian depictions of the hanging figure clearly violated Jewish strictures against the representation of God, but the construction of the new image paradoxically jeopardized its own referent. The *Santo Spirito Crucifix* (Figures 3.4 and 3.5), a wooden sculpture attributed to Michelangelo, may be studied as an example of this process. At first glance it maintains a straightforward relationship with its referent, the passion of Christ. The Church's high estimation of Michelangelo's work is evident in its unembarrassed display of the ceiling of the Sistine Chapel; among art historians, few names surpass that of Michelangelo. And because the *Santo Spirito* sculpture is one of only a few renderings of the crucifixion by Michelangelo, it is of particular interest.[14]

But as a subject for artistic representation, the crucifixion is enigmatic, since no undisputed eyewitness to the event also wrote about it. Scholars find it increasingly difficult to sustain the early tradition that the apostle John was also the Evangelist; in any case, to equate them requires the prior interpretation of a trope, the Evangelist's antonomasia or self-identification, written in the third person, as the "Beloved Disciple."[15]

Michelangelo's statue requires other interpretive frames. From a distance it appears entirely nude, without even the traditional crown of thorns, but on close inspection, painted drops of blood and small holes in the forehead provide an *impression* of a now-absent crown of thorns (see Figure 3.5). As a result of this rendering, we see the crucifixion as taking place both *with and without the crown*, a double perspective that may on second thought reflect a striving for accuracy, since the gospel writers differ: three mention the crown, but Luke does not. In this situation, the "reality" of the crucifixion cannot be rendered without some selection that privileges some gospels at the expense of others, so in sculpting a statue viewable in two ways, Michelangelo may have done his best to resolve gospel contradiction.

The treatment of the crown makes that detail parallel to the inscription—both are detachable signs that are *supposed* to identify a specific figure but, from another perspective, may not. The sign over the cross is attested to in four gospels, although the varying accounts in each do affect semantic meaning; indeed, these produce a statue representing parabasis or an *aspiration to identity*

Figure 3.4: Michelangelo Buonarroti (attributed), *Santo Spírito Crucifix* (ca. 1492–93). Courtesy Casa Buonarroti and Chiesa di Santo Spirito, Florence.

under a sign of linguistic differences.[16] Michelangelo chose the most elaborate version of the inscription, John's, in which the sign reads "Jesus of Nazareth, King of the Jews," in Hebrew, Latin, and Greek. John's version of the inscription may have promoted the shift in proselytizing, from Jews to Gentiles, but it also

Figure 3.5: *Santo Spírito Crucifix* (detail).

reminds readers of the etiology of foreign languages in Genesis; in so doing, it reveals the crucifixion—and its function in manifesting the identity of Jesus— as also a site of translation. The three languages, written in different alphabets, indicate that particular answers to the question of Jesus's identity may already be at odds with each other. John's sign places Jesus in the world of Babel, even before the meaning of the names is deciphered.

In numerous writings, Jacques Derrida has argued for the essential untranslatability of any language. In *The Ear of the Other*, he reads Genesis' narration of Yahweh's forcible imposition on the Shemites of a proper name, Babel, as resulting in this unresolvable dilemma: humans are commanded to translate but also made aware that translations cannot succeed, if only because now no single language could ever reproduce the condition of multilingualism from which it had to be artificially abstracted. No language is now privileged, and none can be complete. The meaning of the supposedly proper noun "Babel" is "confusion," a definition evident in what Derrida calls the "wretchedness" of every supposed proper noun—since after Babel, none can be, after all, "proper."[17] In *Aporias* Derrida goes further, finding untranslatability inherent in any language's self-division, so that "Babelization does not therefore wait for the multiplicity of languages."[18] Proper nouns aspire to name uniquely one particular referent, yet untranslatability makes such a dream of definitive and unique naming illusory. Michelangelo's hanging figure recalls John writing a sacred text in Greek that implies that Greek (or any language) can only desacralize the entity it seeks to name and identify definitively. The story of Pilate's composition of the sign adds new irony to this scene of necessary and impossible translation.[19] Michelangelo's crucifix asks us to see the hanging figure—before it becomes theological, before we ask the question of whether it represents Christ or what the word "Christ" means—as first of all a body-in-Babel whose supposedly definitive signs (the crown of thorns, the words on the sign) cannot, after all, tell us truly who he is In this way, the signs of the crucifixion effect parabasis, the aspiration to authentic identity that remains permanently suspended.

(The suspension of the crucifixion's meaning to some future date in the imminent or far-off *parousia* is a crucial feature of the canonical gospels. The extent to which this future orientation may be reinforced by the physical condition of hanging dependency—a proleptic state between life and death—cannot be known. No similar deferral of meaning attached itself to the life of an earlier Messiah, from Qumrun, who was *not* crucified but instead left for dead in the streets.[20])

For viewers habituated to conventional representations of the crucifixion, the absence of the loincloth is Michelangelo's most shocking departure from tradition, one that few artists have repeated. This challenge to convention calls attention to its arbitrariness. According to art historian Gertrud Schiller, the early Church fathers believed Jesus was crucified naked; the tradition of the loincloth may have begun when Gregory of Tours (died ca. 594) objected to a naked crucifixion in the cathedral of Saint-Just in Narbonne and ordered it veiled.[21] On the surface it would appear illogical that the crucifying authorities who in other respects sought to humiliate Jesus (the mock robes, the crown of thorns, the vinegar) would preserve his dignity with a loincloth. The gospel accounts are ambiguous: Jesus's "garments" were restored to him after a mock robe was removed; these were later divided by Roman soldiers prior to the removal of the body from the cross by Joseph of Arimathea. Michelangelo's crucifixion assumes that the word "garments" includes undergarments and hence that Jesus was crucified nude.[22]

Michelangelo's depiction of genitalia unavoidably raises the divisive issue of the place of circumcision in Christianity, part of the larger dispute narrated in Acts between Paul and the Jerusalem church (led by James, the brother of Jesus) over the necessity for Gentile converts' observance of the Law and, beyond that argument, over the unanswerable question of the signs of election. The early Church's adoption of the Pauline position led to an iconographical tradition in which the crucified Jesus had to be represented as bearing a stronger resemblance to Jews than to the burgeoning majority of his Gentile followers. Of course, the circumcision of Jesus was no secret: paintings of the surgery on the infant Jesus appeared during the Renaissance and details of the circumcision were long a part of popular lore.[23] Still, Michelangelo's depiction of genitalia lends credence to the non-Pauline position of James or Matthew—that Jesus's life may be understood as a vindication, not a repudiation, of the Torah. Put another way, the idea of Jesus the Jew expressed—truthfully? mockingly?—in the multilingual inscriptions may also be evident in the body, but this undecidability was always, already implicit in the formative years of the Church. The boldness of Michelangelo's violation of convention puts the circumcision in the same category as the crown of thorns and the inscription atop the cross: no external signs can identify the hanging figure or to tell us truly what it means. At the same time—in the Pandora's box opened by Paul—the dysfunction of signs calls into question *any* means of representing the truth of Christianity. It may be that Michelangelo's *Santo Spirito Crucifix* suggests the way future heresy, Protestantism and even romanticism may germinate in the gospels, Acts, and the writings of Paul.

Michelangelo's statue struggles to achieve fidelity to contradictory texts but ends by eliciting the undecidability of Christianity. Could a painter solve Michelangelo's problem by representing the crucified Jesus at such a great distance that the details of the inscription as well as the crown and loincloth might be obscured? This recourse would still place the body of Jesus under an indecipherable sign, leaving the viewer in the same place—with a figure that must but cannot be read. So the artist's dream of rendering the truth of Christianity issues again in parabasis, in the representation of identity as interminable suspense.

THE FLAYING OF MARSYAS (1570–75)

Titian's *The Flaying of Marsyas* (Figure 3.6) reproduces the climactic moment of Ovid's story of Marsyas, a Phyrgian satyr in the service of Cybele, who is flayed by Apollo as punishment for losing a music contest. The story originates with Athena playing a flute in the company of other goddesses, some of whom laugh when her effort to blow into the instrument distorts her features. When Athena understands the reason for their laughter, she discards the flute in disgust,

Figure 3.6: Titian, *The Flaying of Marsyas* (ca. 1570–75). Courtesy Arcibiskupský zámek a zahrady v Kroměříži. Kroměříž, Czech Republic.

whereupon it is found by Marsyas. (If readers could remember in time, Athena's experience might have warned them of art's power to *dis*figure.) The music Marsyas plays on the flute charms his fellow nymphs and satyrs to such a degree that he proclaims himself a musician superior to Apollo. When the god learns of this boast, he challenges Marsyas to a contest, to be judged by the Muses, with the winner able to dictate the loser's fate. When the Muses cannot decide, Apollo continues to play, this time with his lyre inverted. When he is unable to draw forth any sound from his inverted flute, Marsyas is declared the loser. As his reward, Apollo requires that Marsyas be hung from a tree and flayed alive. Titian's painting represents Apollo in the act of flaying Marsyas. After his death,

Marsyas's blood and tears were supposed to have created the river that bears his name.[24]

As an enormous, complex rendering of a tale that cautions against artistic hubris, Titian's paradoxical painting soon casts suspense over both its classical and Christian contexts. From the Christian perspective, Titian's painting may be regarded as narrating the hubris and dead end of the classical world, the sense in which human aspirations to perfect expression are doomed to end not only in artistic failure but also in excruciating torment: Apollo ensures that the highest art remains inaccessible to humans and demonstrates the futility of trying. The intellectual helplessness of the pagan world may be observed in the ludicrous effort of Marsyas's fellow satyr carrying a bucket to the scene of his friend's flaying. But the apparent indictment of classicism is undermined by the untroubled expression on the face of Marsyas, which one critic calls "beatific."[25] Another speaks of the way the terrible scene is "bathed in a light of honey and an atmosphere of elegiac fulfillment."[26]

These responses prompt a dizzying series of ironies that dramatize an unresolvable dialogue between Christianity and classicism. Surely Marsyas undergoes the most profound torture, but his serenity also exposes the injustice of his tormenter, in a way that suggests—three centuries before Frazer made the connection—the parallel between the fates of Marsyas and Jesus; the emphasis on Marsyas's blood and on the futility of efforts to comfort him may extend the analogy. But since Marsyas is also a *satyr*, with a goat's legs, the sympathetic parallel between Marsyas and Jesus may now run the risk of blasphemy. But this charge could be countered, too, by reading the painting as envisioning the Incarnation as the divine assumption of *completely* animal flesh. Such an explanation now frees the painting to serve for Christians as a *via negativa*—as a demonstration of the pagan world's *need* for some different spectacle of suffering-that-is-not-suffering in the flesh. (After all, this is a painting whose *topic* may be regarded as flesh: the flesh of a satyr that calls into question the distinction between humans and animals; the flesh that can be stripped away with knives; the relative vulnerability of the conspicuously exposed flesh of the god, satyr and four humans; the wholly animal flesh of the dogs.) In furtherance of this pious interpretation, the painting may teach that the need for transcendence of the flesh did not end with the advent of Christianity: at the extreme left is an anachronism, a violinist, who focuses his gaze entirely on Marsyas's flute without seeing his tortured condition, heedless of his predecessor artist's cautionary lesson. In this detail Titian may be read as condemning secularist tendencies in the art of his own day.[27]

But a Christian interpretation of the painting that survived such a field of ironies would still encounter problems. If Marsyas's beatific expression exposes Apollo's unjust condemnation of mortal art and the need for Christ, then Titian, as Marsyas's artistic descendent, implicitly asserts *himself* capable of attaining, after all, the same godlike capacity for artistic expression that was denied to Marsyas. In this reading, Titian would have to exempt himself from both classical hubris and Christian presumption; as truth-knower and truth-teller, he would no longer need the redemption that *The Flaying of Marsyas* implied the necessity for. As the creator of the beatific expression that foretells the need for its supersession by a new order, Titian, like Dante, might be said to aspire to the status of a new gospel writer envisioning figural and providential history, one whose representation of reality must be accepted apodictically. Of course, the contradiction here is obvious: to the extent that any "correct" religious allegory is intelligible, then not only its moral warning but also the painting itself—or any other human art, for that matter—become unnecessary, since human artists have been shown capable of superseding the religion they represent. The dilemma is that Titian's painting conceives of classical art as incapable of anything but foreshadowing Christianity and of Christian art as oxymoronic.

It may be that Titian addressed this problem in the same way Dante did—through a self-representation, a cameo—in the artwork: critics have seen his likeness in the old man wearing a crown who gazes down and away from the bucket-carrying satyr, in the general direction of Marsyas's head or of the dog that laps his blood.[28] Begun when Titian was eighty, *The Flaying of Marsyas* represents the artist as biographers might—as old, wealthy, and recognized; however, his indeterminate gaze makes the allegory of his "view" of his subject matter end in an insoluble enigma, for we cannot know for sure what that subject matter is. Is it the physical world of bodies in which skin can be flayed and dogs drink human blood? the torment of art? the limitations of the classical world? Titian's own *debt* to the classical world? the supersession of that world by Christianity or of Christianity by art? the wish that the undecidability of the Muses' verdict had been left alone? the meaning of Marsyas's facial expression or of any facial expression? the meaning of his own painting? the contradiction in attempting to represent providential history? an acknowledgment, through the cameo, that as a Christian he is fallen and thus *cannot* claim divine knowledge? an admission of the disingenuousness of trying to exempt himself from the charge of presumption through the trick of the cameo?

Just as a pendant disables the referentiality of objects in the natural world, so the beatific face of the hanging figure of Marsyas deconstructs Titian's painting by neutralizing these questions in advance and suspending answers to them. If the hanging figure both authorizes and condemns the painting's critique of classicism and Christianity, its beatific gaze finds no correspondence in the worried look of the elderly artist who like all mortals can only continue to ponder the questions that his painting has rendered unanswerable.

THE FLAYED OX (1655)

In Rembrandt's *The Flayed Ox* (Figure 3.7), the hanging figure is a spread-eagled, disemboweled ox suspended upside-down from a wooden frame. From a doorway in the background, a young woman, probably a maid, looks out toward the carcass and past it, to the viewer. Most critics find this work atypical

Figure 3.7: Rembrandt van Rijn, *The Flayed Ox* (1655). Courtesy Musée du Louvre, Paris.

of Rembrandt's various genres, though its extreme naturalism may link it to Rembrandt's late self-portraits or *The Anatomy Lesson of Dr. Tulp*. Certainly these paintings' intensive focus on carnality makes them disconcerting expressions of the same artist whose Biblical scenes, for most critics, seem to marry realism with profound religiosity or mystery. On the other hand, while *The Flayed Ox* does not depict a crucifixion, critics understand the allusion to be present.[29] The contradiction suggests Rembrandt's painting may convey an undecidability in divine identity similar to Michelangelo's in the *Santo Spirito Crucifix*.

The art critic Avigdor Posèq traced the recurrent images of hanging carcasses in twentieth-century Jewish art through their antecedents in Rembrandt to the pre-Exilic Jewish rites of human sacrifice (noted earlier in this chapter); the relation between those practices and Yahweh's call for the sacrifice of Isaac has been the subject of much debate.[30] According to Posèq, John's appropriation of Isaiah's vision of the suffering servant is paralleled in Paul's comparison between Jesus's role as the Paschal lamb sacrificed in atonement and the earlier purification of the Tabernacle with blood offerings (Heb. 9:10–26). Posèq also examines the iconographic association between the slaughter of the fatted calf, in the parable of the Prodigal Son, and the crucifixion of Jesus.[31] Thus while Rembrandt's painting of a flayed ox lacks any overt Christian context, Posèq's study shows how it assumes a place in this tradition intertextually.

The spectacle of the flayed ox works on the viewer in two stages: first, the viewer considers the body as carcass and life as purely animal existence without any soul or hope for Christian salvation; next, through the ox's allusiveness, the viewer perceives two drastic, Dostoevskian alternatives: *either* we are animals who die like this flayed ox, *or* we can see "behind" or "within" the flayed ox a second referent, the crucifixion, which holds forth the prospect of some nullification of this spectacle of meaningless death. Because of its intertextuality, the ox presents both alternatives objectively, without any indication of the artist's preference. So far, Rembrandt's *The Flayed Ox* may be considered a visual paradox, a *concordia discors* of the sort New Critics praised. But like *The Flaying of Marsyas*, the painting never achieves aesthetic stability of this kind; it never rests in intellectual equipoise. Instead, its meaning is indefinitely "opened up," just as the carcass itself has been "opened up"; in fact, the viewer may be said to be viewing the site of *the opening up of a hanging figure*.[32] What creates this suspense is both the composition of the mass and the figure of the young woman.

It is obvious that the flayed ox monopolizes the space of the canvas. Its enormous bulk marginalizes the woman who peeps out at it. Fully illuminated by some basement window to the viewer's upper right, the ox casts nearly everything else in dark shadow, save for the weak light behind the woman. If we needed a visual allegory of the hegemonic, then Rembrandt's *The Flayed Ox* might serve as a plausible example—of the blatant, almost violent subordination of humanity to this carcass, whether that is allegorized as matter or religion. As a metaphor for materialism—the anatomical discourses of Gabriel Harvey or of Dr. Tulp (in Rembrandt's *The Anatomy Lesson*), for example— the hegemony of the ox expresses the eclipse of the human by science and its view of death as terminus; as a metaphor for Christianity, the hegemony of the ox expresses the awesome supremacy of the divine sacrifice in relation to the insignificance of humanity. In both cases, the magnificent centrality of the discourse seems to be achieved *at the expense of* the ordinary observer who stands diminished and marginalized by it. Christian and naturalistic interpretations of the ox begin to cancel each other, just as they did in Titian's painting.

Religious interpretations are further weakened when Rembrandt's young woman is seen as recalling the women present at the crucifixion "who looked on from afar"; of these, Mary Magdalene is the most fully attested.[33] A possessed woman once healed by Jesus, Mary Magdalene is traditionally considered a repentant sinner and the woman who loved Jesus most ardently. The gaze of Rembrandt's maid could be interpreted as the longing of love, but once considered in this light, the religious significance of the dead ox becomes harder to sustain, as Mary Magdalene's look at the dead body of Jesus would scarcely be read as the continuation of her desire. As a result, the gaze of Rembrandt's maid is more plausibly read as, "This ox is a provision for the future," or, "This ox will feed the family well." Put another way, the ox as crucifixion allusion may imply the possibility of redemption, but it does so by reducing the rest of the world to caricatures of bourgeois appetite. This is the logic of Calvinism at its most painful.

The hanging figure's true identity is again inaccessible: to the extent that we don't know whether humans are only meat or meat with souls, we don't know whether the crucifixion of Jesus was the death of a god or a man. But this uncertainty is not the painting's final suspense; in addition, Rembrandt positions the woman, our surrogate as a viewer of the flesh, in such a way that *her view of the ox, like ours, is dependent on its frame.* Our view of the ox at first seems complete and univocal—even though the process of thinking about its meaning may have led us to doubt. But because the woman's full view of the ox is obstructed by the frame, the painting now suggests that an incapacity to see truly may be inherent in very act of perception, in the necessary adoption of a conceptual stance or "frame." To focus on the hanging figure is to momentarily forget this. The woman in the background may be common humanity as Mary Magdalene, loving even the ravaged body from which the divinity of Christ has departed. Or, the woman in the background may be a bourgeois burgher feeling more secure about the next week's meals. The woman in the background is one or the other, depending on the viewer's adoption of a frame, which is as necessary to reading as it is also blind and exclusive. Of course, these uncertainties are doubled by the painting's reflexivity: the flayed ox hangs in a frame *just as Rembrandt's painting does.* Thus in *The Flayed Ox*, Rembrandt opens up the hanging figure to discover the suspense attendant upon the necessary adoption of the frame in art and life.

THE LIFE-LINE (1884)

In Winslow Homer's *The Life-Line* (Figure 3.8) two figures are suspended in a breeches buoy: a surfman and an unconscious (perhaps dead) woman he is rescuing from a shipwreck, which is barely noticeable at the left.[34] Homer began the painting after seeing this device used in Atlantic City, New Jersey, during the summer of 1883. Following its initial appearance at the Exhibition of the National Academy of Design in New York, *The Life-Line* became his most famous painting.

The precision of the scene's rendering seems greater than photographic, especially given the state of photography in 1884: close scrutiny reveals drops of water hanging from the right side of the hawser (the rope at the top) and other drops falling from the hand of the rescued woman. The effect of such preternatural realism is enhanced by its juxtaposition with the formless gathering waves and exploding surf. The tension between two such diverse perceptual registers may correspond to the pressure dramatized in the narrative, to the downward pull exerted by the gravity and weight of the human on the pulley's ring—in short, to the visual center of the painting. This suspense may also anticipate the conflicting ways the scene is read.

For example, from the painting's first reception viewers were drawn not only to the scene's obvious dangers (and predictable existential allegory) but also to its sexual implications. That such a critical response is not simply the heritage of Freudianism is evident from the scene's composition: contemporary sources confirm that the breeches buoy was "hardly suitable for women and children," for whom a "life-car"—a covered boat pulled by ropes—was preferable.[35] Franklin Kelly observes: "Although safety was doubtless a primary reason for not using the breeches buoy for the rescue of women, the use of a covered boat suggests that matters of decorum were also at work."[36] Of course, Homer's choice of subject matter can be justified in narrative terms: the surf was too rough to permit operation of the life-car; the life-car was unavailable, etc. But the effect is to invite commentary of precisely the sort the painting received even in its day. An anonymous reviewer in 1884 called the woman "a buxom lassie, by no means ill-favored in figure and face."[37] One recent critic argued that *The Life-Line* manifested Homer's unconscious and read it in the tradition of sublimation that includes works by Fuseli, Fragonard and Lacret.[38] Another found parallels for Homer's work in Millet's drawing *The Lovers* and Rodin's sculpture *The Kiss*.[39] Thus reading *The Life-Line* today demands not only close scrutiny of the hanging figures but attention to intertextuality and hermeneutics.

Jules Prown sees in *The Life-Line* both a humanist endorsement of interdependence in an indifferent universe and sexual repression; such a New Critical reading renders a Freudian paradox of manifest and latent content.[40] At the same time, readings of this sort assume that the painting's signs, including its many lines, correspond only to the Freudian/Cartesian category of the self, however inwardly conflicted. Doubt of that assumption may be readable in the painting's

Figure 3.8: Winslow Homer, *The Life-Line* (1884). Courtesy Philadelphia Museum of Art: The George W. Elkins Collection.

most conspicuous detail—the woven scarf or shawl that wholly obscures the surfman's face. According to a contemporary account, Homer's painting originally did show the face but the artist, "finding that it scattered the interest, boldly threw over it the shawl of the fainting woman who lies in his arms."[41] Deliberately blocking the painting's most important detail has many effects. As the reviewer suggests, interest shifts from the man to the woman and the pulley. The woman's unperturbed face suggests that she is not conscious. That she must have been conscious when boarding the breeches buoy is established by her grip on the rope; the fact that she maintains the grip suggests that she is now either unconscious or dead—the maintenance of the grip being made possible by *rigor mortis*. The deflection of attention from rescuer to rescued, therefore, ends in an emphasis on liminal states—of conscious/unconscious or life/death. As is the case of the many hanging figures readable in the tradition of the crucifixion, what art renders is not life but undecidability. The pulley apparatus is made up of twelve circles, easily detectable when the painting is viewed at full size: two vertical rings depending from the pulley, two horizontal wheels inside the pulley-housing, and eight circular holes on the housing's exterior. These twelve small circles echo the large circle of the buoy itself, making thirteen circles; these vacant circles may be regarded as abstractions of the surfman's missing face. Following the reviewer's suggestion, then, the woman's scarf may rewrite the painting as the record of a *defacement* or displacement in reading—an act of occlusion that substitutes new signs for the once-privileged, now empty, sign of the human. From this perspective the painting is less a narrative of the human predicament or sexual repression than it is an allegory of two kinds of blindness—physiological (in the woman's case) and figurative (in the surfman's and reader's)—that together pose a challenge to the representational capacity of art.

The scarf's erasure of the face is a trope for the unretrievability—the *unrescuability*—of the human subject. Prown makes the interesting suggestion that the scarf is "tied to the rope to signal [to those on shore] the location of the breeches buoy";[42] this seems likely. Even though the general location of the breeches buoy would be known to those on shore pulling on the rope, a sudden surge of high waves might make the dark-clothed passengers on the buoy temporarily invisible, so in this case the (bright red) scarf could offer a second clue to their whereabouts. To say that this scarf is tied to the rope requires scrutiny that has evidently satisfied Prown; other viewers might allow that however attached, the scarf seems very much in jeopardy of being instantly blown away. It is this detail that seems most intriguing for an understanding of the painting's representation of identity: the human face has been replaced by an artificial and arbitrary sign that at any moment may be perceived as superfluous, unnecessary, or wholly unrelated to life. It is at best a flag, a color, a woven entanglement of textiles. Its only purpose is to momentarily capture attention before being ignominiously discarded. In these properties, the red scarf serves as a figure for the suspense of human identity, for visual art in general and for this painting in particular.

The idea of reading the painting as an allegory of art is reinforced when the viewer's position is taken into account. Put in an impossible place by the artist, the viewer must look directly at two signs of the denial of the human—the woman's liminal condition and the man's occluded face. Viewers must think of themselves as perched on a second life-line, a metaphoric breeches buoy some dozen feet from these hanging bodies; and if like most viewers we have no experience with breeches buoys our condition must resemble that of the woman more than that of the surfman. By this interpretation, we can read ourselves as being in an insensible swoon or death-in-life. As for the surfman, he may well be readable as a figure for the blind artist—Homer's pun on his name—the guide who attempts to bring people to a different, better place but whose efforts are also ludicrous. In any case, figuring the artist as blind guide forces us to ask what it is we see and whether our position is any more secure or perspicacious than that of the woman we are made parallel to or the unseeing artist who has brought us this far—who has brought us only as far as art *can* bring its audience.

Of course, what we may most perspicaciously see is only colored paint on canvas arranged in lines, planes, and shapes. Consistent with Paul de Man's thesis, such a collapse of the painting's representational system can occur only after we have first understood the painting naturalistically in hermeneutic terms, as a scene of maritime danger. In this secondary, deconstructive reading, the painting becomes like the red scarf, an arbitrary signifier. At the same time, this reading is also enabled by the painting's title *The Life-Line*, which ostensibly names the device represented in the painting. But "life-line" is also an inclusive term that could apply to flotation devices on ropes, to the hawser for a life-car, or even to a single rope; in this painting we take the phrase as a synecdoche that refers to either the hawser or the pull-line, as the technology that first makes the rescue possible. But there is another line in the painting, too: off to the left, we see a rope dangling from the now-dysfunctional rigging of the wreck. This line was once rigid and crucial to the life of its vessel but now of course is not; similarly, the unused length of the pull-line dangling behind the buoy is not now a life-line. These ropes now have a delicate curved quality they may not have possessed while in use. Disabling their utilitarian function has made them aesthetic objects, like pendants or Jeff Koons's basketballs. These details suggest that the property of being a life-line is not inherent in the object (the rope) but instead is a semiological function, apparent only when put in use. As a result, it is possible to see the painting's title as having only temporary "applicability" to its supposed referent. Put another way, the possibility that any life-line may become a meaningless, beautiful curve may be inherent not just in the perilous narrative predicament but also in painted lines.

Hence the title also refers to lines of paint, especially to those etched or blurred boundaries between sea and land, sea and sky, life and death that constitute the Homer's two perceptual registers. The painting intertwines these lines. Maybe it subverts their distinctions. Just as the bodies of the hanging figures are intertwined, and the ropes supporting the breeches buoy are made up of intertwined strands, and the hem of the woman's dress is made up of sewn-together strips of cloth, and her scarf is made up of intertwined skeins of yarn—so the painting is itself an intertwining of lines, great and small, that temporarily guide thought up to a certain point and then desist. As well as betokening some mechanical means of rescue, *The Life-Line* also implies the contingent, suspenseful, futile lifeline of art.

LE PENDU (1892)

In addition to his work as a painter in the early nineties, Henri Toulouse-Lautrec designed posters for the Montmartre cabarets he frequented and for Parisian periodicals, including *Le Matin*, *La Revue blanche*, and *La Depeche de Toulouse*. Toulouse-Lautrec never regarded posters as a genre inferior to painting; on the contrary, as Julia Frey observes, he saw posters as an integral part of his work: "Increasingly, the poster was his preferred art form. '*L'affiche y a qu'ca!*' (The poster, that's all there is!), he is said to have declared . . . One of [his] most consistent behaviour patterns since childhood had always been to *s'afficher*, to show off . . . This word, which means to attract public notice or notoriety, comes directly from the word *affiche*, or poster."[43] Frey believes Toulouse-Lautrec's posters accomplished several serious purposes: psychologically, they fulfilled exhibitionistic urges that carried out the artist's defiance of his physical disabilities; intellectually, the posters attested to Toulouse-Lautrec's modernist understanding of the growing power of publicity (including negative publicity), self-advertisement, and the implication of art in commerce.[44] Students of the avant-garde often connect the overthrow of canonical genre distinctions with the exaggerated and parodic visual displays characteristic of *fin de siecle* France and England; for Toulouse-Lautrec, high and popular art merged in an art that made his deformed figure, his persona and his nearly illegible signature famous in Paris.[45]

Le Pendu was an early poster designed as one part of an advertisement for the journal *La Depeche de Toulouse* (Toulouse Dispatches), which on April 27, 1892 began serializing a historical novel titled *Les Drames de Toulouse* (Toulouse Dramas) by A. Siegel; one of its three parts was a retelling of the notorious Calas affair of 1761. On October 13 of that year, Marc-Antoine Calas, the son of the textile merchant Jean Calas, was found dead. The body was first discovered by Marc-Antoine's younger brother Pierre, who held a candle as he led a young dinner guest, Gaubert Lavaisse, from the family's second-floor living quarters to the front door, by way of the family's first-floor shop. Following an investigation, Jean Calas was accused of having murdered his son to prevent him from converting to Catholicism; he was condemned, publicly broken on the wheel, strangled, and burned to death. Voltaire later became interested in the case and through a vigorous press campaign brought about a judicial review. In 1765, a fifty-judge panel reversed Calas's conviction and paid the family an indemnity, developments that led Voltaire to write his famous essay, "Traite sur

Figure 3.9: Henri Toulouse-Lautrec, *Le Pendu* (1892). Courtesy the Collection of Irene and Howard Stein, High Museum of Art, Atlanta, Georgia.

la tolerance." Nevertheless, neither the cause of Marc-Antoine's death nor the guilt or innocence of Calas was ever definitively proven, and the episode remained a flashpoint for French political and religious polemics.[46]

Toulouse-Lautrec's rendering of this scene (Figure 3.9) is noteworthy on several counts. In its depiction of the discovery of the hanging body of Marc-

Antoine, the poster is already an interpretation, already a side-taking in the controversy, since according to the family's first account given to the police, the body was discovered lying on the floor. It was only thirty-six hours later that the family members changed their story and said the body was discovered hanging in a doorway by a rope. When pressed by police, Pierre and Jean Calas as well as the dinner guest Lavaisse explained that their initial story was designed to shield the family from the disgrace of a suicide, but the police were suspicious.[47] Since the only witnesses to the scene gave contradictory testimony, *any* representation of Marc-Antoine's body must *already* reflect a prior decision as to the guilt or innocence of Calas and hence the validity of the original verdict. In Michelangelo's crucifixion we saw that the selections of details like the crown or the sign already privilege one or another Gospel account; in Rembrandt's ox we saw the necessity for a frame. Likewise, the representation of Marc-Antoine's death implies that an undecidable reality can be represented only with the prior adoption of some interpretive frame—in this case one with political and religious consequences. Toulouse-Lautrec's composition of the hanging figure suggests his alignment with Voltaire against the Catholic authorities in an affair in which it was notoriously impossible not to take sides.

The artist's choice of a commission that played blatantly on his aristocratic name—it was part of the newspaper title and novel title—also has the effect of making his poster supersede the verbal art it advertised: neither the "acts of" Toulouse nor the "dispatches of" Toulouse can match the bold immediacy of this "*affiche* of" Toulouse [-Lautrec]. Supplanting both the historical reality and its verbal representation, the poster implies the superior longevity of the artist's name, or of any name for that matter, over the referent it ostensibly signifies. The slogan "*L'affiche, y a qu'eu!*" ("The poster—that's all there is!")—becomes an aesthetic and philosophical manifesto: the self-promotion and self-commodification of the artist in the world of ephemera—enhanced by new technologies of mass media in the *fin de siecle*—attest to the triumph of the figural over the referential.

Conspicuous among the poster's formal elements is the viewpoint from below, a characteristic perspective adopted by the five-foot artist that became not only a reflexive device but also a commentary on the sordid or louche figures he drew: the Calas family, eighteenth-century bourgeoisie, fare no better than the fat, lascivious club-hoppers he caught in the footlights of the Moulin Rouge. Also prominent in *Le Pendu* is the liquid, laid-on quality of the candle light that calls just as much attention to nature of illumination as it does to its object. In its allusion to Voltaire, the painting may serve as a commentary on the Enlightenment project as a whole: here in the darkness of an undecidable suicide/murder is the place we are brought to by our light. The light of reason or art extravagantly illuminates the surfaces of the world, its figure, while leaving its reality dark, with questions of causality, meaning and truth held in suspense, like the hanging figure.[48]

THE HANGED MAN OF THE TAROT CARDS (1392–present[49])

The poetry of Yeats and Eliot introduced the otherwise scandalous Tarot cards into Anglo-American intellectual life: both poets' early conflations of the cards' divinatory properties with the myths of Frazer or with Jungian archetypes were exemplary modernist moves that challenged readers to find some basis for distinguishing mainstream philosophical and religious discourses from their underground, esoteric, or fugitive counterparts.[50] Like such poetry, the quasi-scholarly histories of the Tarot, which speculate on the cards' Egyptian, Oriental, and Central European origins, may be read as deconstructions of the genealogical assumptions of Western religion, philology, archeology, and intellectual history. For example, in Tarot scholarship—as in the kabbalah, to which it is linked— readers are advised that any written record may just as often misrepresent as preserve the "authentic" oral tradition; true comprehension, if it ever occurs, requires that an initiate ultimately transcend written interpretation.[51] Thus even before beginning to interpret a single card, readers must understand that written guides not only miss truths (like those that emerge from divinations) but also may deliberately perpetuate *dis*information, in order to deflect naive initiates from the cards' unpronounceable esoteric truth. The Kafkaesque idea that written guides mislead makes scholarship as to the meaning of the Tarot and the Kabbalah exercises in intellectual despair.

Nowhere is that futility more evident than in discussions of the meaning of specific cards. The Hanged Man or "Le Pendu" (Figure 3.10) is the twelfth card of the Tarot category called the Major Arcana (or "Trumps Major"), but its significance—like that of any of the cards—is entirely a matter of its context. Basil Ivan Rakoczi summarizes the first principle of divination: "First, the simple meaning given in ordinary divination, *read with reference, not only to whether the card falls upside down or right way up, but to what relation it bears to other cards spread about it and to the card chosen to represent the questor*" [i.e., person seeking the divination] (italics in the original).[52] Assumptions like these link the Tarot cards with linguistic systems in general, in which the basic constituent units—alaphones and phonemes, in oral systems—are meaningless in themselves and make sense only in combination with other insignificant linguistic units. When commentators discuss the supposed inherent meaning of the Hanged Man, hermeneutics quickly becomes equivocation. The English writer Arthur Edward Waite claims "the figure, as a whole, suggests life in suspension" but concludes after all that "the significance is veiled."[53] The French commentator Papus [M. Gerard Encausse] at first says the signification of the Hanged Man is "Trials, Sacrifice" but goes on to assert that any attempt to understand the card is finally dependent on its placement.[54] Rakoczi summarizes seven likely meanings but then adds another six that are possible when the card is reversed.[55] As we've seen, the key feature of reversibility is often marked in the iconography of the hanging figure—as in the Sun Dance ritual of voluntary hanging. Of course, the figure in the deck of cards *is* "Le Pendu," the hanging

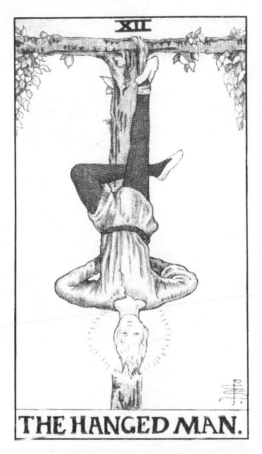

Figure 3.10: *The Hanged Man*. The Hanged Man from The Universal Waite Tarot deck reproduced by permission of U.S. Games Systems, Inc., Stamford, CT, 06902. Copyright © 1990 by U.S. Games Systems, Inc., Stamford, CT. Further reproduction prohibited.

man, yet at the same time, interpreters of the card invite us to consider his identity equally well disclosed in the opposite position, when he appears to stand, not hang, as if the hanging man *both is and is not a hanging man*. The self-cancellation of identity may be only a more striking instance of the parabasis or undecidability observable in the sun dancer, Jesus, Marsyas, the flayed ox, or *Le Pendu*; it may account for the figure's disturbing facial expression, one that echoes the beatific look on the face of Marsyas. The hanging man's smile not only calls into question the suffering of sacrificial versions of this figure; it questions identity itself as it illustrates the way the meaning of a figure never inheres in it. Instead, the Tarot's hanging man, like Homer's surfman, is suspended between identity and nothingness.

RELATED FIGURES

As noted in the introduction, the etymology of suspense includes not only the expected sense of hanging free but also numerous related conditions of partial support or buoyancy where the object is seen as no longer autonomous but immobile, on display or vulnerable. To convey the breadth of the tradition, this survey of iconography concludes with discussions of three examples. Rubens's *Prometheus Bound*, like Titian's *Marsyas*, adopts pagan mythology to render an undecidability between Christianity and classicism. For Christian audiences, partly supported figures may recall the deposition of Jesus, in which the body as a whole no longer hangs but is carried—by Joseph of Arimetheia or the virgin Mary—while the lifeless arm suggests the agony of the crucifixion just completed. Secular art often echoes such positions: for example, in Homer's *The Life-Line*, the rescued woman's arm conveys a deposition-like quality. Jacques-Louis David's painting of Marat, which has been compared with both a crucifixion and deposition, extends suspense to the realm of politics. Already noted in connection with pendants, Jeff Koons's *Two Ball 50/50 Tank* exemplifies the suspense of floating as it conveys a self-canceling cultural critique.

Prometheus Bound (1611–18)

According to some modern authorities, Prometheus actually did "hang" from his rock, though in his *Prometheus Bound* (Figure 3.11), Rubens depicts him as lying supine.[56] He is chained to a cliff at the extreme border between Europe and Asia, usually the Caucasus Mountains, where an eagle comes every day to eat his ever-replenished liver. The nature of Prometheus's transgression is well known: by stealing fire from the Olympians, he brought to mortals the arts of civilization, including numbers and language. Zeus's retaliation against Prometheus is at first understood to be interminable, but an ultimate reconciliation forms the plot of a trilogy by Aeschylus, of which only the first play is extant, and of Shelley's *Prometheus Unbound*.[57]

Zeus's punishment is depicted as iterative: the transgressor's liver is eaten and replenished daily, with the result that justice is always repeated and never concluded. The torture also seems overdetermined—it consists of chains, the bird's bite, and the talon in the forehead—as if the expression of justice required multiple violations of the body. Repeated and multiple punishments indicate inherent flaws in justice, since the divine verdict, which ought to be a self-executing performative, in fact requires both agency (the eagle) and iteration (no single punishment is adequate). Rubens depicts divine justice in human terms—in the world of Derrida's postal, where a permanent gap, disjuncture or space intervenes between the sending of the message and its meaning, between

Figure 3.11: Peter Paul Rubens, *Prometheus Bound* (1611–18). Courtesy The W.P. Wilstach Collection, Philadelphia Museum of Art.

sign and referent; this gap exists *because* of the iterative property of signs. Put another way, the painting implies that God's *im*perfection, even *in*justice, is inherent in the utterance of a verdict. This defect in the application of a divine decree to human affairs is reinforced by the gargantuan proportions of the canvas, as if the futility of artistic attempts to represent justice should be foreseeable in the painting's recourse to mere size and repetition.

Zeus's punishment reveals the vulnerability of the body to laceration; this piercing of the flesh may recall the Indian Sun Dance and, through the tradition of Christian parallels between Prometheus and Jesus, the stigmata. These analogies began with Tertullian, who referred to the Christian God as "verus Prometheus" and compared the Titan's punishment to a "Caucasian crucifixion"; after him Fulgentius saw Prometheus as a symbol of divine providence. Augustine and Lactantius were struck by the parallels between Genesis and the legend that Prometheus created human beings out of clay. Tertullian directly linked the lacerations of Prometheus with the stigmata and blasphemy when he argued as part of his polemic against Marcion that "the true Prometheus, almighty God, is being slashed by [Marcion's] blasphemies."[58] But if this allusive tradition makes Prometheus analogous to Jesus, then Rubens's chained, reclining figure becomes not only a subject of divine judgment, a suffering sinner, *but also the means of release from that judgment.* This interpretation removes the need for divine salvation and may substitute for Jesus the victims of divine punishment, who become their own saviors. Considered in this light, Rubens's Prometheus anticipates romanticism: in much the same way Blake's rewriting of Milton's Satan makes explicit an undecidability at the core of providence in *Paradise Lost,* so Rubens's Prometheus blends classical and Christian iconography to the point of undecidability. If his Prometheus suggests the torment of the damned, he also anticipates Shelley's *Prometheus Unbound.* Looked at in one way, the hanging figure is a type of eternal damnation; looked at in another, it predicts a human means of redeeming humanity from such a sentence.

This undecidability is also evident in the lacerations. Tertullian said that blasphemies like those of the heretic Marcion re-inflicted the stigmata on the crucified Jesus; this concept has a long history in medieval strictures against oaths, including a memorable allusion in Chaucer's *The Pardoner's Tale* (lines 470–76). To the early Church, Marcion was both blasphemer and heretic, whose doctrines are said to have "slashed" Christ. Thus for Tertullian, heresies were performatives: they had immediate and predictable results, no matter what the context. Rubens's painting may suggest this reasoning, whereby a heretic's misrepresentation is to Jesus as Zeus's verdict, through the eagle, is to Prometheus—words that continually re-pierce an already immobilized, suspended body.

For orthodox observers, these renewed lacerations presage the violence of Jesus at the Last Judgment, and suspense refers to the fate that awaits the unwary tormenter or viewer. Through its network of allusions to the crucifixion, Rubens's Prometheus warns all who judge to expect additional retaliation for heresy or—what may be indistinguishable—for misinterpretation: "Interpret if you dare" may be the painting's subtext, robbing the viewer of the capacity for judgment if exercising it might re-inflict wounds and increase future torment! For Christianity, the institutional definition of misinterpretation results temporally in the Inquisition or excommunication and eschatologically in the Last Judgment. Foucault's idea that the scene of punishment attested to the legitimacy of the executioner is ironically borne out, since ultimately all temporal persecutors, heretics, or interpreters will be overthrown.

Beyond this orthodox implication, Rubens's Prometheus implies its opposite—

that the hanging figure may after all subvert God—even within human history. In this interpretation, the parallel between Prometheus and Jesus is blasphemous. If Prometheus is a figure for the damned but is also analogous to Jesus, then the damned may one day end their captivity and suffering, just as Prometheus did in Aeschylus and Shelley, without the intervention of a deity. Looked at from this perspective, Rubens's Prometheus is itself a gigantic, blasphemous, Promethean act. Of course, if the same hanging figure can be viewed in such antithetical ways—as both a warning against and incitement to rebellion—then it becomes impossible to distinguish religious figures from blasphemy. If both the orthodoxy of Tertullian and the apostasy of Marcion and Shelley are latent in the Promethean hanging figure that recalls the crucifixion, then the question of whether the hanged man signifies salvation or damnation, reverence or blasphemy, can never be decided but only suspended.

The Death of Marat (1793)

Modern critics of David's Marat (Figure 3.12), like eighteenth-century audiences, think the painting recalls the crucified Jesus; one even finds an allusion to Rembrandt's flayed ox.[59] Of the painting's many titles, the most familiar, *Marat à son dernier soupir*, indicates the way Marat is rendered at a liminal moment, between life and death; it encourages us to see the painting's subject as this moment of undecidability characteristic of so many hanging figures. David extends the hanging figure's condition of undecidability to the world of politics, which the French Revolution had envisioned as the greatest achievement of the Enlightenment. The importance of David's deconstruction of politics to future artists can be gauged by its frequent revisitings, especially in the work of Munch and Picasso.[60]

As a physician, a lonely man of integrity, a *citoyen* and the *ami du peuple*, Marat was known for his Kantian aphorism of setting principle above people; likewise, David's parallel role as the sublime aesthetician/propagandist of a Neo-Classicism that easily accommodated and officially endorsed the Rights of Man has been established in several studies.[61] David's painting, the most famous of numerous contemporaneous works depicting Marat as martyr, ostensibly exalts the Jacobite leader; however, in his sordid death at the hands of Charlotte Corday, David also announces the stillbirth of politics as the working-out of the Enlightenment. The painting's allusion to the crucifixion makes its relation to the supposed object of the homage problematic, and in the light of the iconography of the hanging figure, it is not surprising that this slumped body has been read as subverting both human identity and political principle.[62]

There is at the outset the problem of what to call this painting. Five titles, none privileged, have from time to time been attributed to the canvas; *Marat à son dernier soupir* has become the default choice.[63] But this situation of arrested nomination may also be understood as the *subject* of the painting, which is focused at least as much on the interruption of verbal representation as it is on

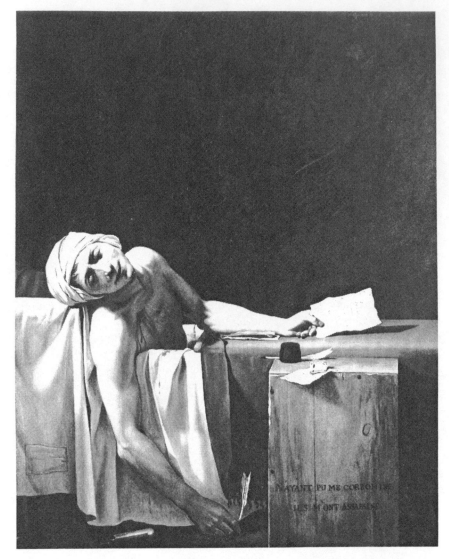

Figure 3.12: Jacques-Louis David, *The Death of Marat* (1793). Courtesy Musées royaux des Beaux-Artes de Belgique, Brussels.

the assassination. The details of Marat's dying are subordinated to those depicting him in the act of writing: Charlotte Corday's small knife and the stylized blood, as opposed to the *two* quills, the *two* notes, and the inkstand. It is as if the scene were composed to show the murder as secondary and the halting of discourse as primary, as if death is understood as a collateral effect of discourse, as what Paul de Man called "a displaced name for a linguistic predicament."[64]

Moreover, this redistributed emphasis takes up only *half* of the canvas, the other half of which consists of a black wall: human mortality may be said to be one fourth of the painter's concern, verbal discourse one fourth, and nothingness the remaining half.

Marat's tub is a scene of relay, one of those nodal points of sending and receiving studied by Derrida in *La carte postale*. The letter Marat holds is Corday's duplicitous plea to be allowed into his presence; Marat's naive belief in the truth of its referents causes his death. The letter Marat was in the midst of composing—an order to convey money to the deserving widow of a republican soldier—remains atop the writing table, its trajectory toward its destination halted, suspended.[65] Thus, before the painting's political content can even be known, the scene shows us "the death of the author"—the extinguished subject who is supposed to be the sender and recipient of letters but is cut off from them *and cut down by them*. This sense of language's permanent suspense over the subordinate human is reinforced when the political details of the letters are understood. Helen Weston has shown how the fragment of the letter Marat holds inscribes the difference between the *ancien régime* (the aristocratic "Marie Anne Charlotte Corday") and the republic (the address to *"citoyen* Marat"); she finds in this difference evidence of David's sympathy for Marat.[66] Yet this difference also exemplifies the way the Revolution's political agenda may be reconceived as rhetorical, as only *reducible to* or *inscribed in* the perlocutionary or performative dimension of language. Just as Marat's Jacobinism may temporarily triumph through his verbal representations and broadsides, so may Charlotte Corday's Girondiste terrorism triumph through *her* manipulation of language. And of course it is language as *manipulated*—as something moved with deliberation by a now useless hand— that David's *Marat* forcefully reveals.

As a scene of writing, David's painting discovers in Marat the contradiction of the Enlightenment—that politically "neutral" principles or Kantian regulative justice cannot escape dependence on the same arbitrary representations of the state they would reform. The journalist and man of principle Marat, who dispenses justice to the deserving, must do so through the same arbitrary system of signification that causes his death. There is an interchangeability between Marat's justice to the widow and Corday's justice to Marat: Jacobite and Girondiste "deliver" justice through arbitrary signs. In Foucault's famous thesis, the spectacle of the scaffold merely evolves, under the liberal bourgeois state, from the guillotine to the panopticon to the orthopaedic discourses of psychoanalysis and surveillance.[67] Put another way, the principles of the revolution, reflected in the letter Marat writes to the widow, are ideals or promises, performative statements whose truth is suspended to the future: their juxtaposition here with Marat's slumped body dramatizes the ultimate failure of the performative to be self-executing. The effects in the real world of the principles of the revolution, like the effects of any political principles, can never be predicted.

Accompanying David's deconstruction of politics is a parallel deconstruction of art, of authorship, and of the artist as creator; this is accomplished in the conspicuous dedication, in the lower right-hand corner, "A Marat, David," which seems imprinted on the writing table beside Marat's bath. Mantion and Lomas both note the painting's metonymic chain that associates Charlotte Corday's knife with the quills and with David's brush.[68] Each implement is the vehicle of a signature—an incision or inscription that implies only an absent self: Charlotte Corday, Marat, and David himself. Weston sees David's dedication as a means of immortalizing the artist and sharing in Marat's glory; Lomas sees it as David's act of self-sacrifice; Mantion sees Marat assuming the intertextual role of Plato in commemorating the death of Socrates—the subject of one of David's earlier paintings. In all cases, the dedication calls attention to the presence/absence of the creator within the painting as an analogy to the presence/absence of the murderess Charlotte Corday. Through this parallel, the artist's supposed homage becomes an acknowledgment of complicity in the destruction of its object. The painting implies that art cannot represent or espouse principles because the signs that are supposed to convey them are exposed as dysfunctional as soon as they are read. All art can do is dramatize the scene of that exposure.

Read in the context of its dead recipient, the dedication "A Marat, David" calls into question the name "Marat," which here could mean only "the memory of Marat," as in an elegy; that is to say, the sign "Marat," like all signs and particularly like all "proper names," outlives and thereby vitiates again its putative referent; in this respect, the dedication, too—like Marat's unsent letter—evokes the Derridean notion that a sign never arrives at its destination. And if these signs were always, already cut off from their referents, then the scene narrates not only the death of the principles of the French Revolution or any revolution, but also the deaths of authors, artistic creators, and interpreters, too—extinctions effected in the act of representation.[69]

Two Ball 50/50 Tank (1985)

Floating objects also suggest the condition of suspense. Often hanging between two elements (earth and air, water and air), floating objects express both stasis and dependency. In offering themselves up for display or contemplation, floating objects sometimes imply "more below the surface" but disappoint this expectation when the hidden or profound "more" is in fact only more of the same: thus do signs promise referents that turn out to be signs. This potentially vast category could in theory include most nautical representation, from Noah's ark, Odysseus's raft and the *Pequod* to James Cameron's *Titanic*, as well as such human figures as Millais's *The Death of Ophelia*. In his "Equilibrium Series," conceptual artist Jeff Koons may be regarded as both continuing and satirizing this tradition with his aquarium tanks containing Spaulding basketballs. In some of the tanks, the balls floated; in others, the artist alternated layers of normal and "heavy" water to variously position the balls *on* the surface or even *below* the surface. (In *Two Ball 50/50 Tank*, Figure 3.2, the balls float an equal distance above and below the surface.) Thus the balls' different positions encompass a spectrum of representations of suspense. The tanks made up one part of the "Equilibrium Series" installation; other objects included framed posters advertising Nike basketball shoes and various flotation devices—a rubber raft, a snorkel vest, an aqualung—which had been cast in bronze.[70] As we shall see, hermeneutic interpretation of these objects suggests a moral and political critique of contemporary society that on reflection, however, remains suspended. In this two-stage process of reading them, Koons's equilibrium tanks recapitulate the deconstruction of the hanging figure experienced everywhere, beginning with the Paleolithic pendant.

Koons's installation appropriates the icons of American leisure society to demystify culture: the tanks isolate for contemplation the centrality of sports in what Guy DeBord called the society of spectatorship—sports as creator of sites and viewers; sports as promoter of the cultural ideology of capitalism, whereby endemic racism can be supposedly "overcome" by the free market's "ticket out of the ghetto" of professional sports; basketball as conjuring visual images of floating, both of the ball itself and of players whose leaps seem to defy gravity— images strengthened by the link between the Nike posters and the absent/present Michael Jordan as superstar spokesperson for Nike's "Air Jordan" shoes. Such a critique is reinforced by the bronzed flotation devices. In ossifying these once-pliable human "life-savers" and rendering them specular and unusable, Koons's sculpture suggests both the futility of the culture's mania to defeat death and the fetishization of objects that hold forth the promise of doing so. There is a link, here, with Homer's *The Life-Line*. The bronze flotation devices function aesthetically in the same way as the variously immersed basketballs: once deprived of their utilitarian function, these cultural objects are freed to inspire moral and political critique. Koons's art stimulates this process through its respect for what the artist calls "the integrity of the object"—he isolates brand-new Spaulding basketballs for contemplation—though here the word "integrity" also denotes "undecidability."[71]

Just as David's Marat finally questions the achievement of Enlightenment justice even in the apparent celebration of its martyr, so Koons's basketballs turn their moral and political critique back upon the viewer. If the capitalist commodification of sports in the specular arena is suggested by the way the balls galvanize viewers' gazes, so too is the operation of the museum itself. If these isolated balls engender a moral and political critique of society, they are at the same time both *empty* and *arbitrary* forms bearing an uncomfortable correspondence to the viewers who make the critiques. Koons said the balls reminded him of "a brain cell or a foetus or some biological form"; he imagined the proximate balls forming some pattern of communication with each other or even constituting "an artificial intelligence, a womblike situation."[72] Whatever the value of these and other associations inspired by the balls, it is clear that if signs like the balls can be understood as referring to the political world, they can and perhaps *must* refer to the onlooking subject, too. If we see in the balls the obsessions and delusions of capitalism, we must also see ourselves, empty and in various degrees of moral and epistemological submergence. Perhaps the nearly unstoppable urge to interpret the object has always concealed the hope that by doing so the interpreter can smuggle in unnoticed the category of the subject, the human as definer of the figure of suspense; this may have been the hidden agenda of interpretation all along.

THE FRAME

All representation, and especially visual representation, presupposes some frame, margin, border, boundary, or perimeter. For the purposes of this chapter, the most obvious are picture frames, pedestals, or the chains from which pendants hang; in cinematic representation, the constitutive unit of discourse is of course *acknowledged* to be a frame. Derrida's concept of the "parergon" has led art critics to explore what it is that frames of all sorts leave out or repress as the price of making any particular representation possible.[73] For example, Jean-Claude Lebensztejn adopts a Derridean approach to the frame in the history of European painting, from Renaissance gilt-edge monumentality through twentieth-century experiments that exposed the arbitrary nature of the frame, to a contemporary return to the rectangle.[74] European painting has often interrogated the naive idea of the frame as window, through the effects of *trompe l'oeil* and, more crucially, the introduction of interior frame; this phenomenon supports this study's claim that beginning with Paleolithic pendants, hanging figures have undermined whatever ideas they ostensibly represent. Reviewing a few of these interior frames will show how hanging figures may be read as figures for figuration itself.

On the one hand, frames seem trivial backdrops. Jesus's cross, Prometheus's rocky crag, and the trees from which Marsyas and the Hanged Man dangle are given cursory artistic treatment; they seem negligible in comparison to the figure. More important, they seem arbitrary: *any* cross, rock face, or tree would do. On the other hand, this seeming subordination is a mirage, because the hanging figures are *attached*, to cross, tree, or cliff, and thus in the paintings are shown to be dependent on expressionless matter. The paradox of pain and transcendence that would give their lives meaning can never be dissociated from the miserable mute earth to which they are tied. The humiliating condition of achieving maximal expression while being dependent on the dumb, undifferentiated material world makes these figures an apt type of every sign, which becomes capable of expression only insofar as it abstracts itself from matter. Paul de Man called this condition "the prosaic materiality of the letter." Without for a moment conceding that language could *represent* presence, de Man argued that its operation presupposed materiality.[75] Put another way: every expressive hanging figure must be "grounded," but that to which it is grounded is completely arbitrary. Derrida and de Man, whose work uncovered it, both sought to evade this bitter dilemma of deconstruction, through appeals to the metaphysical. The hanging figure grants a kind of provisional access to the unavoidably suspenseful nature of signs: if meaning must be grounded, but only on the arbitrary, language and suspense will be inseparable.

The humiliating condemnation of meaning's attachment to the arbitrary is articulated in varying degrees in the frames that accompany the many hanging figures in this chapter. The ugly wooden frame of Rembrandt's flayed ox permits its display at the cost of forever after impinging on any attempt to see it "unframed." The painting might be considered a visual analogue of Heisenberg's uncertainty principle: to see the ox truly, to see it "whole and in the round," the carcass must be framed, but the act of framing ensures the ox will never be seen wholly and in the round. The ox must be attached to a frame just as Rembrandt's painting must be circumscribed within a frame; both efforts to bring the truth of the object's presence nearer only reveal, as in the figure of the servant in the doorway, both the viewer's distance and obstructed sight.

An interior frame in Homer's *The Life-Line* is the hawser, which forms a second border across the top of the painting. The connection of the hanging figures to this frame provides the visual focus; it is as if idea of attachment itself were the painting's point. The painting insists on the precariousness of humanity's dependence of the arbitrary, whether that should be glossed hermeneutically (as the technology of rescue, the psychology of identity, the concept of salvation) or deconstructively (as the faulty life-lines of representation itself).

In Toulouse-Lautrec's poster, Marc-Antoine Calas is discovered hanging from a thick wooden stick, which in the trial accounts was said to be the spindle around which the yard goods in his father's shop were wrapped. In the family's second account, Marc-Antoine had evidently wedged the stick between the tops of two partly open double doors. Thus there are two lines that form interior frames of his body—the spindle and the door jambs. Like Rembrandt's ox-frame, these emphasize the inherent selectivity of representation. In Toulouse-Lautrec's vision, it is impossible to tell whether the doors open toward or away from the viewer; this ambiguity invites the viewer into the frame, as a double to Pierre, the bearer of the candle (of, hermeneutically, light, knowledge, Enlightenment). Toulouse-Lautrec's composition puts viewers, like the painted figures, in a liminal position, on the threshold of knowledge that permanently escapes them, just as the truth of the Calas affair was permanently lost in its representation; in this way the architectural frame doubles the artistic frame's false window on the truth.

David's Marat is framed by his bathtub and writing board; these interior frames betray the futility of the grounding afforded both to life and to its written representation. The Enlightenment ideal that writing can be politically meliorative (or even its modern version, that writing can be personally therapeutic) is shown to be as futile as Marat's attempt to heal himself in his tub. The frame that would heal in fact creates new vulnerability. The triumph of the degenerative inheres in the scene's reductive equation between pen and sword: if writing is seen as always, already extinguishing the subject, the tools are analogous. In this case, the attachment of the figure to its frame is envisioned as immersion, as the impossibility of the act of writing's ever liberating itself from the arbitrary constructions that made its operation possible.

Prompted by the etymology of the word "suspense," this chapter has examined visual representations of hanging figures to help determine its meaning. After a first reading, the religious, psychological, philosophical, and political meanings of these figures give way to undecidable states—whether the examples come from Western or non-Western, classical or Christian, ancient or contemporary civilizations. Because this yielding of the semantic to the rhetorical seems to happen everywhere, and so frequently, the chapter hypothesizes that hanging figures and their frames may best be understood as figures for figuration itself. If so, these images may teach us about themselves—that is, about the process of figuration—or about the world, to the extent the world itself may be thought of as an undecidable figure. Both prospects will be kept in mind as we turn to the hanging figures in Hitchcock's films.

4

The Hanging Figure in Hitchcock's Films

The iconography of the hanging figure discloses a condition of suspense more fundamental than audience anxiety at the fate of an admired surrogate: a world where the meaning of events is forever mistaken and human identity unknowable. In contrast to the conclusions of Frazer and Foucault, hanging figures express no religious or political truth, only undecidability; they question any religious, political, or artistic solutions to human problems. Where hanging figures are abstracted from narratives, their stories never achieve significance from diegetic endings; on the contrary, hanging is a synecdoche for an infinite deferral of meaning all along the narrative line and beyond its boundaries, if any exist. In the images of Jesus, Marsyas, the flayed ox, Prometheus, and Marat, Western art discovered this interminable suspense in its principal intellectual traditions—classicism, Christianity, and the Enlightenment. In the images of the proto-Elamite pendant, Canaanite sacrifice, the sun dance, and the Hanging Man of the Tarot Cards, non-Western art expressed it, too. In austerely exposing their own incapacities, these images prompt wider speculation on figures in general and on the world itself as a place of figuration.

Speculation about "the world as figure" is reserved for the afterword. In this chapter, hanging figures from Hitchcock's narratives are studied as part of the tradition of suspense as undecidability and deferral outlined in chapter 3; my hope is that these images may afford similar access to the broadest meaning of suspense. The following parallels anticipate that similarity:

As in Homer's *The Life-Line*, Hitchcock's films depict human relations as futile in the light of unknowable identity. *Murder!*'s enigmatic villain Handel Fane, for example, exposes the groundlessness of identity in "normal" society.

But as we shall see, the film's endemic "feigning" is not simply a matter of masks concealing true selves; instead, *Murder!* narrates identity as one of many supposed referents absent from a world of empty theatrical posturing. In the end, Fane becomes a figure for the necessity of figuration.

As in David's *Marat*, Hitchcock's hanging figures undermine Enlightenment rationality and its transmission through letters. *Number Seventeen* narrates the way all the detective prowess of its hero, Barton, ends in a massive train wreck. In the frame isolated for study, he is unaware that his hanging (and that of the woman he is tied to) has been brought about by his misplaced confidence that his telegram would arrive at its destination. What's more, this hanging couple only *seems* to be a couple: any supposed mutuality is enforced and artificial, like the many scenes of handcuffed lovers. The scene anticipates any number of false couples in Hitchcock's work and gives the lie to efforts to find in the final "construction of the couple" any moral or ethical norm.

As in Koons's *50/50 Tank*, Hitchcock's films present cultural critiques that show viewers to be just as inauthentic as the "glamorously dangerous charade" they are invited to judge. In the wartime film *Saboteur*, Hitchcock daringly compares American patriotism and Nazism, while also indicting the film and its audience as collusive in the empty visual spectacles that sustain both ideologies.

Just as the Hanged Man of the Tarot Cards can be read as a figure for the undecidability of reading, so *Rear Window*'s Jeff exemplifies irrational interpretation. He is ousted from his interpretive chair when he can't reply to a challenge as to why he is interpreting. His hanging from the windowsill is a visual reminder of the "groundlessness" of the process that brought him to this point.

In their instantiation of such themes, Hitchcock's hanging figures continue the tradition of suspense in visual art and also disabuse moviegoers of their independence from it.

MURDER!

The circus performer Handel Fane, a murderer who realizes his capture is imminent, swings on his trapeze, his shadow caught in the spotlight (Figure 4.1); then he fashions a noose from a rope, fastens it around his neck and jumps. Viewers then see only a swinging rope under tension—a visual metonymy for both suspense and the invisible corpse, a figure without a visual referent.[1] The hanging corpse is nonexistent, wholly the reader's construction. This unrevealed hanging erases the faint anticipation of a *second* unrevealed hanging—the imminent execution of Diana Baring, falsely accused of the murder Fane committed. These present and absent ropes, with their present and absent referents, are figures for the parabasis of identity in *Murder!*, a story depicting a charade of shifting masks or signs that do not conceal any underlying self.

Critics have interpreted the numerous theatrical metaphors in *Murder!* as implying a Hitchcockian distinction between false role and true identity.[2] They

Figure 4.1: *Murder!* (1930). Canal + Images UK, Ltd.

associate the latter variously with Sir John, Handel Fane, Hitchcock, or both.[3] For these critics, the characters' adopted roles are considered deviations from some normative perspective that the director endorses. However, in *Murder!'*s displaced representation of the hanging figure, an arbitrary sign, a rope, supplants the human subject; this is only one indication that Cartesian and hermeneutic faith in the autonomy of the self may be mistaken. The subordination of the human to the arbitrary has also been illustrated from the start of the film, when random shapes and sounds precede the introduction of the human. Genesis-like, *Murder!* opens with oppositions between light and dark, sound and silence: the silent night is interrupted by sounds of an unidentifiable knocking, a dog barking, and a decontextualized scream. To the extent a Flaubertian homology established here may equate the human voice with animal sounds, the accompanying shots of flying bats, scampering cats, and silhouettes also equate the human with chaotic visual movement. This is the condition Marc Vernet refers to as the *clignotements* of the black-and-white film—its blinking, flashing, and flickering constitution, which are prior to any subsequent visual interpretation.[4] Film narrative emerges from such random light, making the construal of human identity—much less any moral or romantic intentionality—the work of fiction. False teeth enable Ted to articulate, and Doucie's corset is responsible for her silhouette—in these images we see human beings as false constructs even *before* their names are known. This preamble ensures that when we later meet characters "playing roles"—on or offstage at the theatre, in a boarding-house, in a courtroom, jury room or circus—these roles will be superimposed not on real selves but on fictional constructs.

This is parabasis, the suspense of authentic identity, roles in place of selves—just as we saw in Hitchcock's cameos. Sir John is always already an actor/aristocrat, while Diana Baring is always already an actress/working-class girl who wants to become a star. After Sir John plays roles as concerned juror, detective, and playwright or Diana plays roles as harried witness, suffering prisoner, and redeemed victim, they reassume not authentic selves but their opening parts. While their assumed personae temporarily make their previous existences seem natural by contrast, the "characters" are never separable from fictional roles. Discussing the supposed authenticity of Sir John's quest to disclose the truth, Slavoj Žižek gets close to this sense of universal charade when he claims that the film's ultimate achievement is "to unmask man's act itself as the supreme form of performance."[5] Permanent parabasis is disclosed in the ubiquity of the film's theatre analogy, especially in its final shot, when the seemingly natural kiss of Sir John and Diana is gradually revealed to be a stage kiss. Sir John's motive for detection, which presumably parallels the viewers,' is to determine "the inner life of the Baring case," but this project turns out to be another fiction, a play by that title he writes and stages. "Baring" in the sense of revealing truth never occurs; instead, putative revelations occur only through new fiction, as in Handel Fane's rehearsal of Sir John's draft, a "confession" of murder that reveals, as we shall see, new unrevealed secrets. The characters in *Murder!* are quickly shifting disguises-of-nothing. Even as the police interrogate the Coventry Stage Group, trying to fix their identities and knowledge, Handel Fane becomes a woman, then a policeman, and Ion Stewart reverses the order. The film depicts a spontaneous metamorphosis of human roles that never gives viewers confidence in some authentic inner identity. The idea that the removal of a disguise reveals not truth but further enigma is narrated in Handel Fane's climactic entry into the circus ring, wearing his feathered and bejeweled "wings." Following his ascent to the trapeze platform, he removes his cape and stares straight into the camera, but nothing emerges from this false baring.

Instead, the death of Fane—the homonym of *feign* has often been noted—suggests the impossibility of the unfeigned life or of existence unmarked by a sign. To be a half-caste or mulatto, as Fane is, is to be branded with a sign from birth. Like Faulkner's Joe Christmas, another hanging mulatto, Handel Fane is doomed in his impossible pursuit of identity. Children of mixed racial ancestry are thus a special case of suffering the universal inescapability of the sign visibly and in the body; for others (especially those harboring illusions of Cartesian autonomy), this condition may be easier to blithely ignore.

The subordination of human identity to the sign is also dramatized in Sir John's plan to force Fane to incriminate himself, Claudius-style, when auditioning for Sir John's version of Hamlet's "Mousetrap," the partly written *Inner Life of the Baring Case*. From this strategem, Sir John and the viewer may infer new acknowledgments of Fane's guilt, but the actor is careful to avoid confessing while reading Sir John's script and to preserve the opportunity for his own narration later. The crucial moment in the audition comes when Fane is asked to read lines that end the page with "don't know that he's a half-," whereupon the next page turns up blank. Fane's response ("What a pity the scene isn't finished . . . I was getting quite worked up") clearly indicates the strength of his *acting*, his instantaneous ability to shift from one role to another. At the same time, the blank that follows the prefix "half" shows how identity is a blank or cipher to be filled in by an arbitrary sign—identity on the model of textual construction. Doubtless Sir John would want Fane to fill in the blank with "caste," but Fane's sang-froid—his feigning—suggests that even "half-caste" misrepresents who he is.

The stability of Fane's identity as "half-caste" was further shaken in 1972, when Hitchcock asserted that Fane was "a half-caste homosexual"; this remark supported the speculation of a few earlier critics. (Later critics, oddly, ignored it.[6]) Of course, directors' interpretations of their films are no more privileged than those of their critics; this reopening of the meaning of "half-caste" merely extends suspense in new directions. According to the written message Fane leaves for Sir John, his motive for killing Edna Druce was to prevent her from divulging "his secret" to "the woman he dared to love." But of course, if Fane was a homosexual, why and how did he "dare to love" Diana? Rothman speculates that Fane might see Edna as a threat to a possible marriage of convenience with Diana; however, Rothman himself rejects that explanation, and nothing in the film supports it. The controversy has now become wholly undecidable, since we can never know *the content of the secret Edna was going to divulge*. Was it Fane's mixed racial ancestry? His homosexuality? Both? Neither? At the heart of *Murder!* is a sign—"Fane's secret"—that may or may not have a referent; we are blocked from knowing. This is but another way of formulating the MacGuffin, Hitchcock's parable for interminable suspense.

As MacGuffin or referentless sign, Fane challenges readings of the film that enlist him as a representative of some authentic state of being in contrast to the charade-world all around him. Following Eve Kosofsky Sedgwick, Tania Modleski sees in Fane a "feminizing potential" that Sir John must vanquish in himself.[7] Alenka Zupančič goes further, seeing in Fane's suicide an example of Kant's definition of "pure autonomy."[8] Each believes Fane speaks for the director from a position of truth. But the unmaskings in *Murder!* come about not through Fane but through a reading process that is independent of him and other characters. It begins with Sir John's shift from juror to critic of the jury's deliberations, exchanging the supposedly performative function of verdicts for open-ended, referent-questioning, suspenseful reading. The process continues in the shavingscene, where the "signified verdict" is challenged. Fane's death never provides the world with a critical perspective more authentic than Sir John's melodramatic and egocentric work of detection; in the concluding scene from *The Inner Life of the Baring Case*, art and life continue to be as indistinguishably merged as they are in Fane's swinging from a rope. Far from being an authentic alternative to this world, Fane may be said to be its root, its radicle, or its embryonic stemcell: the homonym of Fane, "feign," is one of the etymological sources of the word "figure." In the character of Fane we may read a figure of figuration itself, the capacity to assume any role in the absence of any authentic human identity.

Murder!'s endless charade can be understood only in retrospect, only after its figures have been taken for signified referents, and when it is, readers may recall the film's beginning in random knockings and bat flights—arbitrary sounds and black-and-white flickerings on a screen from which the world of figures was constructed.

NUMBER SEVENTEEN

The hanging figure in *Number Seventeen* is for the first time plural—Rose Ackroyd dangles with the detective Barton from the ceiling, where they have been suspended by the criminals Barton had hoped to apprehend (Figure 4.2). As a joint hanging, the scene anticipates other perilously suspended couples— in *The 39 Steps, Shadow of a Doubt, To Catch a Thief, Vertigo, North by Northwest*, and *Torn Curtain*.[9] Barton and Rose are not a romantic couple, though their hanging together may raise that expectation. *Number Seventeen* challenges the idea that Hitchcock's films endorse norms of romantic union. Any idea of the normative couple assumes that each partner has an articulable identity, but *Number Seventeen* puts that idea in question. The film's enunciative details make the characters' identities appear not just questionable but unknowable.

The inauthenticity of this hanging couple is evident in their self-deception. Barton, the film's representative of rationality and legal authority, is the author of the telegram that initiates the plot. (The film's opening scene—in which he must chase his windblown hat—hints that his rationality and control may be illusory.) As he hangs suspended with Rose Ackroyd, Barton never admits his responsibility for their plight. Attempting to catch the criminal Doyle, Barton wired Rose's father, asking him to keep an eye on Number 17, the house they are now suspended in. His plan was to arrive at the house and arrest both Sheldrake, a jewel thief about to escape to France, and Doyle, who he hopes will be drawn to the house in search of Sheldrake. However, the telegram from Barton to Mr. Ackroyd was never delivered: Rose received it and was in the process of searching for her father when she fell through the roof of Number 17. Barton had not been aware that Ackroyd observed Number 17, entered it and fought with Sheldrake, only to be left for dead. He is unaware that his telegram was in the first place redundant and in the second place dangerous to Rose. Barton's authoring thus situates him within the Derridean world of the postal, in which senders of messages imagine themselves to be in control of their letters' destination and meaning, only to learn belatedly (if at

Figure 4.2: *Number Seventeen* (1932). Canal + Images UK, Ltd.

all) the delusion of such Cartesian thinking; in Barton's case, such learning never comes.

Barton's misplaced confidence in the rationality of detection also endangers Ben, the homeless Cockney sailor, whom Barton had discovered on the scene and forced to stay, without disclosing his identity. Throughout the film, Barton's prolonged withholding of his identity makes it impossible for viewers to distinguish his coercive behavior from that of the criminals—until the very end, when new problems arise. (Viewers who "instinctively" take Barton's side must question their own predisposition to accept as moral the handsome leading man.) To Ben, Barton assumes a kind of class-based prerogative of control, against which the poor sailor protests in vain. Barton's deaf ear to Ben's understandable requests to "call a copper" strikes him—as it may first-time viewers—as criminally arrogant. From the perspective of police work, Barton's solo operation—his "self"-reliance—becomes increasingly dangerous.

Soon even his implicit motive of zealous law enforcement rings hollow: when the criminals begin their rush to the train, Ben once again asks Barton to call the police, and Barton replies, "And have [Nora] arrested? Not if I can help it." Barton could have exonerated Nora even if she was arrested; his impulsive decision to continue the chase—even by bus, when he is kicked off the train—can only reflect a desire for Nora that has become all-consuming. His reckless chase of jewel thieves—who do not possess the stolen jewels—soon results in the train's stoker being shot dead, in a bus driver and his passengers put at risk, and in the wreckage of a train and ferry. As a law enforcement official whose pursuit of outlaws rationalizes the death of innocent people and the massive destruction of property, Barton anticipates a long line of supposedly sympathetic upholders of the law in Hitchcock's films, "authorities" whose blithe amorality calls both their cause, their self-knowledge and identity into question: Devlin in *Notorious*, Rupert in *Rope*, the Professor in *North by Northwest*, Armstrong in *Torn Curtain*. Like these supposedly Enlightenment figures, Barton never understands that his irrational motives remain closed to him and that his actions are as morally reprehensible as those of his opponents. So this scene of hanging is one in which Barton, at least, does not know who he is.

As for Rose Ackroyd, her apparent innocence also masks an undecidability, since it cannot be known whether she and her father arrived at Number 17 to help catch Sheldrake, as Barton assumes, or to commandeer the diamonds for themselves. What little we know of Ackroyd's motivation is revealed when he begins to untie Rose and Barton:

Ackroyd: I've been watching this house for some time.

Barton: For the police?

Ackroyd: Something like that.

Ackroyd carries a gun and handcuffs, just as Doyle does. If Ackroyd worked for the police, it is unclear why Barton was ignorant of his prior surveillance and needed to enlist it. Rose's wink at her father may simply betoken recognition or—just as plausibly—the complicity of father and daughter in an interrupted conspiracy of their own. We can't tell if either should be judged as ethical or unethical. To conclude that either half of this hanging couple has a determinable identity is to construct a fiction from undecidability.

The hanging couple's position seems to mime vertical sexual intercourse, and the presence of handcuffs lends a suggestion of erotic pleasure in restraint; in this Hitchcock's hanging couple conveys an enigma not unlike that of Marsyas or the Hanging Man of the Tarot. Such pleasure/pain is more than paradoxical: it calls into question perhaps the most universally accepted signs, the signs of pleasure. The cognitive dissonance is reinforced by the dialogue. As she dangles, Rose claims with apparent pleasure to have fainted; then after looking down at the floor, she actually faints. Her double take links the painful sensation of fainting from vertigo with orgasm understood as utter abandonment or loss of control. When the signs of pleasure and pain are exchangeable, as here, critical assessment of emotion—not to speak of the normative couple—is better suspended, especially since an apparently feigned emotion is followed by an apparently real one. To the extent that the hanging couple of *Number Seventeen* depicts emotion as indeterminable or indistinguishable from acting, articulation of their identity is put in suspense.

This suspense is consistent with the way human identity is represented elsewhere in *Number Seventeen*. Identity is frequently associated with aliases or arbitrary, illegible calling cards. To gain access to the house, Doyle represents himself as Brant's nephew; both claim to be midnight house-hunters. Inexplicably, Nora represents herself as deaf and dumb sufficiently well to deceive everyone. When she finally speaks, Barton immediately interprets her act as "a fake" and the "trick of a crook," while on the other hand her return to untie him *might* be interpreted as honest *if* she had any way of knowing Barton's true identity; the film holds forth no prospect of truth beneath these masks or roles. Nora's own breathless explanation to Barton of her motives for staying with the crooks ("It's the best thing I can do; besides, it's safer for you") is unfathomable. Until the very end, she like Rose has no reason for considering Barton to be anything but another crook, and the viewer has no reason to consider either woman innocent. The assumption of roles is rife: Barton claims to be Fordyce; Ben calls himself Lloyd George; Ackroyd successfully poses as Sheldrake to Doyle; at one point, Sheldrake believes Doyle is Barton. When Barton first discovers Ben and accuses him of murdering the man on the landing, Ben sarcastically mocks the accusations by emptying his pockets and producing a piece of string that he says was used to "stab" the corpse and a piece of sausage that was used to knock him over the head. Barton rebukes him ("It's best to play it straight when you're innocent") in such a way as to imply that even innocence may be read as an act. In this proliferation of adopted roles, the plot of *Number Seventeen* represents life as the convergence of masks in a surreal space where nonrecognition is the norm and strangers—like viewers—mistake characters and their motives. Of course, the film's climactic recognition scene aspires to transform this state of indeterminacy; however, it shares a *deus ex machina* quality with other Hitchcock films, such as *The Lodger, Murder!, Spellbound, Stage Fright, Psycho,* and *Frenzy*. In these films, the final revelations of guilt and innocence are brought about so swiftly, incongruously and self-mockingly as to subvert the authenticity of character revelation. For example, at the end of *Number Seventeen*, the criminal Doyle momentarily pretends to be Barton, but this misidentification actually takes on plausibility in the light of the moral undecidability that marks Barton's character for so much of the film. Who *is* Barton? In his masks covering undecidability, is Barton anything other than everyone?

In an irony that makes the expression of character identity inseparable from narrative, Barton says: "You're Doyle. The necklace would draw Sheldrake and Sheldrake would draw you, Henry Doyle. The comic part of it is, I'm Barton." Here Barton "resolves" the suspense of his identity by appealing to a genre of fiction. But the film itself has blurred the line between comedy and melodrama: that is to say, the film is continuously ironic, in de Man's sense. In its first half, the action is rendered expressionistically, almost surreally: dark shadows and canted camera angles recall Hitchcock's style in *The Lodger*, inflected by his exposure in Germany to the work of Murnau. Barton remains wholly unresponsive to Ben's humor. The melodrama of the chase sequence is punctured by highly reflexive details, especially the use of models. While the ending aspires to restore order, the stoker's death is unassimilated into the conclusion. In the context of these mixed genres, Barton's declaration ("The comic part of it is, I'm Barton") implies that his own identity is another such a derivative mixture. Barton's fictional self-revelation has the effect of undermining the attributions of other character identities, too. If they are finally "truly named" by someone whose identity is itself fictional, then everyone's identity is up for grabs. The film's recognition that identity is derived from narrative was prefigured in the scene of hanging:

Rose: It's like the pictures, isn't it?
Barton: Too much for my liking.

Barton's claim that his situation resembles films "too much" acknowledges his fictive identity: if we did not do so before, henceforth we will see "Barton" also as an actor playing a part. Like the parabasis of Hitchcock's cameos, this reflexive remark allegorizes the way the articulation of identity in language prevents the reassumption of any natural or true self we thought we once possessed. In film, reflexivity vitiates characters just as in life, names vitiate identity.

The film likens its characters' fraudulence to the audience through other reflexive details, too, especially the telegram Barton sent to Ackroyd, which asks him to "Watch number 17." This admonition makes Ackroyd parallel to every viewer of Hitchcock's films. As we've seen, Ackroyd's identity—like everyone else's—is undecidable. His "watching" of house number 17 has resulted in his unforeseeable, inextricable entanglement in a chaos of misrepresentation. A similar predicament ensnares the viewers who "watch *Number Seventeen*." In the first of de Man's two steps we must construe light and shadow—Vernet's *clignotements*—as figures, as autonomous selves or even as a potential couple; but in the second step, through the inevitable reflexivity of reading or viewing, we must renounce these prior interpretations as illusions.

This deconstruction of presence happens automatically or "uncontrollably" in reading or viewing films: it is as if we must read words or view figures before we understand they are false. The ending of *Number Seventeen* may allegorize that process. Barton's rational quest seeks to reveal the identity of the malefactors (while preserving his own subjectivity as autonomous and safely hidden). His self-vindicating project presupposes that signs have referents, just as he believes his telegram must arrive at its destination. Once these assumptions are doubted, his rational order predicated on reading begins to quickly, uncontrollably collapse. The montage in which shots of Doyle's out-of-control train alternate with shots of Barton's commandered bus parodies the Griffithian "race to the scaffold"—a tradition that had already become a cliché. In Hitchcock's parody, the alternating sides are created not from real trains or buses but from models; this new reflexive detail undermines the reading process just as Barton's reference to films did. As we read *Number Seventeen*, we interpret not a model of reality but a model of a model. The potential for infinite regress and dissolving irony is even more vertiginous when the frequent analogy between films and trains is entertained: both made up of joined units that "carry" characters from one boxy frame to another on a kind of track. In any case, *Number Seventeen*'s chase subverts Barton's supposed rationality by showing his reliance on coercion (the gun he holds to the bus driver) and by identifying it with an out-of-control train, an engineerless or headless vehicle—an image prefigured in the film's first scene when Barton chases his windblown hat. As an analogy with communication, this spectacle of vehicles hurtling toward a massive wreck analogizes the out-of-control chase with Barton's authoring and his ratiocination. Once rationality has begun to exercise itself on the world of signs through a process of reading that questions the necessary referent of a sign, the result may be an accelerated encounter with chaos that can only be arbitrarily halted. The hanging figures of *Number Seventeen* may remind viewers of the tenuousness of our stay against such free fall and the imminence of the out-of-control.

SABOTEUR

The hanging figure in *Saboteur* appears in the film's climax as the saboteur Fry hangs with both hands from the base of the Statue of Liberty's hand; Barry Kane, an aircraft worker wrongly accused of having been a saboteur, holds onto Fry's sleeve while they wait for the police to bring a rope (Figure 4.3). Under the tension, the stitching on Fry's jacket gradually pops open and as Fry falls to his death, his sleeve comes off in Kane's hand. Hitchcock's wartime audience

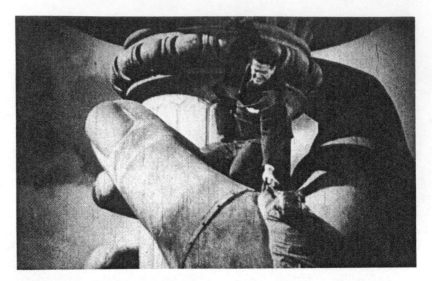

Figure 4.3: *Saboteur* (1942). Copyright © 2002 by Universal Studios. Courtesy of Universal Studios Publishing Rights, a Division of Universal Studios Licensing, Inc. All rights reserved.

saw this hanging figure as a villain, a Nazi sympathizer who sabotaged American security, facing his opposite—the wrongly accused hero who speaks out on behalf of love and America. Because this American hero risks his life to save the villain who betrayed and tried to kill him, *Saboteur*'s final tableau may suggest moral absolutes: American selflessness and Christian charity pitted against totalitarianism.

But the film shows these absolutes can't be distinguished from their opposites. Knowing that police and FBI agents are inside the Statue of Liberty, Barry Kane nevertheless takes the law into his own hands by picking up Fry's gun and stalking him on the Statue's torch; after Fry raises his hands—revealing his humanity in the posture of the Statue of Liberty—Kane feigns an assault that makes Fry fall backward over the railing. The effectiveness of Kane's one-hand grip on Fry's sleeve may be open to question: it is a gesture perhaps in the tradition of Hitchcockian drollery. In any case, Kane's supposedly selfless rescue attempt may now appear futile or ironic: Christian charity may be easier to extend when the chances of its actually being effective are slight. Finally, the reflexive elements of this climactic moment—the conspicuous use of models, the sudden cessation of non-diegetic sound, the close-up on the popping stitches, Fry's stylized fall—ensure that its allegory of moral absolutes will be inseparable from questions about its *representation*, and these have accumulated throughout the film.

The arbitrariness of that representation is emphasized by Hitchcock's depiction of the world of the postal—the world of signs cut off from referents and destinations. As in *Number Seventeen*, the plot gets underway with the misde-livery of a message—in this case, Kane picks up and returns Fry's letter. At the cafeteria, Kane calls out "Fry!" and the man turns—a scene repeated in the Statue of Liberty, when Patricia calls out the name. In these naming or identi-ficatory moments, language appears to be performative: the swivel of a head seems automatically elicited by a word. But the arbitrariness of names quickly becomes evident. The truck driver who gives Kane a lift refers to a friend who died in an accident as having been "fried"; the use of the name "Kane" for someone thought to have maliciously killed a brother-figure raises familiar bib-lical associations; at Miller's cabin, Kane easily adopts the alias "Mason"; the Siamese twins challenge the validity of names from the perspective of the sup-posed referent. This subversion of proper names and language's referential func-tion is demonstrated again by the sabotage of the ceremonial christening of the USS *Alaska*, when it becomes apparent that the performative or naming moment may just as easily destroy as designate its referent.

The popping of Fry's jacket seams suggests the way tension and suspense make manifest the concealed construction of artifice. By analogy, viewers may wonder about the fabricated nature of the seemingly solid Statue of Liberty—it was built on a sound-stage—and the values to which it supposedly refers. The statue's artifice is emphasized when Patricia reminds Fry that it was a gift from France and by her recitation of the famous words attributed to the statue ("Give me . . ."). Moreover, the statue's interior, in which uniformed and plainclothes police hunt down someone suspected of disloyalty to the state, contradicts its exterior, which promises the rule of law (including the presumption of inno-cence) and acceptance of immigrants. The statue's idealistic exterior promise is literally hollow unless enforced by the interior *realpolitik* of brute power; in fact, Hitchcock's close-ups on his model make the statue's exterior visage appear both slightly androgynous and menacing. The outsized statue that rises from the waves parallels the gigantic battleship USS *Alaska*, sabotaged on its side before launch. Both images suggest a stillbirth or contradiction inherent in the vain-glorious, military defense of freedom.

The dawning interchangeability of the hanging and rescuing figures suggests other qualifications of the supposed clash of absolutes. While serving as the champion of democracy and law, Barry Kane briefly takes a little girl hostage and steals a horse: the ensuing chase across the western landscape positions Barry as the American cowboy. The genre is also recalled in the ghost town (Soda City), as well as the truck driver's linked, canvas-covered vehicles and the carnival's series of trucks, both of which resemble wagon trains. As a genre, the western depicts America as the place where neither black hat nor white hat respects the law. When the police arrest Kane, they brush aside his insistence that they produce a warrant and take for granted that the length of his sentence will depend on the quality of the lawyer he hires. Americans' contempt for their own legal system is also evident when the truck driver helps Kane escape by misdirecting the police.[10] Patricia's initial respect for the law might arguably be cited as a counter-example, but she, too, becomes an accessory to Kane's flight despite new indications of his capacity for violence.[11] Contrasting such morally compromised figures is the blind pianist Philip Martin, a seeming epitome of the American ethic of openness to strangers and the presumption of innocence. Whether his benevolence is made possible by his freedom from awe-inspiring visual displays of power is impossible to say; nevertheless, his status as a genuine alternative to the compromised world is qualified by his inaccessibility, vulnerability, and ephemerality.[12] For their part, the saboteurs are depicted as deeply committed to family values: Freeman admires Tobin's love for his granddaughter and describes his own joy when cutting his son's hair or taking him to the Philharmonic. These contrasts have the effect of transvaluing the valuations of the western genre and its conventional, disingenuous patriotism; in doing so Hitchcock neutralizes any simple opposition of absolutes.

The flawed rationality of democracy is also allegorized in the scene when the circus performers vote on Kane's fate. Bones, democracy's spokesman, records the vote on the basis of his intuition of how some will vote; Esmeralda's tie-breaking vote, cast on the basis of her assessment of Patricia's appearance, puts the troupe in a position of rebellion against the established law. This is the familiar paradox of Rousseauistic or Jeffersonian democracy: if governments derive their legitimacy from the social contract, existing laws carry no authority in themselves. The circus performers merely put into political practice the same disparagement of the law exhibited by the truck driver. Democracy votes to defy law. We may look at the scene in at least these two ways: as outcasts helping outcasts or as grotesque performers deluded about their rationality.

America's capitalist ideology is made to seem indistinguishable from Nazism. In his dialogue with Kane, Tobin defends totalitarian regimes by saying he seeks a more "profitable" form of government and that he "wants power as much as you want your power." This bald appeal to power and profit is only a more explicit version of the corporate ethos of America as seen in the opening factory sequence—a place driven by precisely those principles. Before his journey east, Freeman stops to look admiringly at the Hoover Dam and to speculate with Kane on its power; in fact, the dam as a spectacle of power is later made the object of the saboteurs' telescopic sight. This visual fascination with power recurs in the USS *Alaska*, the Statue of Liberty, and the movie theatre, where viewers sit enthralled with the spectacle of film noir. This reflexive detail links Hollywood and Hitchcock's own role in the *Kulturindustrie* with the profitability of gargantuan size and visual intimidation. Capitalism's need to reproduce what Guy DeBord called the society of the spectacle is also registered in the many huge billboards Kane passes; these advertise a nation where everything is for sale.[13] The saboteurs mimic commercial enterprises like the Newsreel Company and hatch their plans in corporate office buildings; they refer to their organization as "the firm." At the pinnacle of American high society, the duchess's ball, the task of differentiating American from totalitarian sides has become impossible: all are shown to be captivated by the mesmerizing effect of an auction of jewelry; in this they simply repeat the deluded, degraded condition of film audiences who pay to be dazzled by the cinematic baubles of capitalism. But this was true from the very beginning of the film, when we were caught by the spectacle of a body apparently on fire. Mistaking film's black-and-white flicker—its *clignotements*—for a human being suffering in a political conflict was only one of the initial figure-creating errors necessary to comprehend a narrative whose apparent political values, on reflection, were just as deceiving.

REAR WINDOW

Having been pushed out his window by his nemesis, Thorwald, Jeff dangles from the sill (Figure 4.4). His hanging is liminal and figurative if only because the history of Hitchcock criticism has so frequently construed his window allegorically. *Rear Window* has always been read as a parable: Jeff *represents* something—the alienated urban dweller, the sexual voyeur, the patriarchal male, the film viewer, the film director, the McCarthyite subject, or some amalgam of these—even before he is understood as a disabled photographer, much less as an assemblage of shapes and colors on a screen. Jeff's window is variously understood as his eye, his opening on the world, his perspective, his camera. These ballooning identifications show the triumph of film criticism understood as hermeneutics, as the attribution of meaning to signs. In Jeff's hanging scene, the hermeneutic impulse generates speculation: here Jeff begins to pay for his arrogant isolation from humanity; here Jeff changes from gazer to gazed-at; here Jeff experiences the limitations of aesthetics; here Jeff learns the necessity for mutual dependence or human community. As in *Saboteur*, the scene of hanging precedes a rescue and so produces an expectation of resolution that the final scene nevertheless frustrates. Because the hanging figure of *Rear Window* dangles from a site separating inner and outer realms, the Cartesian model of life, it is easier to see that what the film puts in suspense may be just this paradigm.

My effort to define *Rear Window*'s suspense requires that I first mistake the flickering screen as Jeff and then identify him as a Cartesian interpreter. Until he is pushed onto his sill, Jeff's main activity consists of reading signs. Being on the sill seems to change all that—for the first time, he is turned away from his field of vision and analysis; for the first time he makes no interpretations. While he hangs, Jeff is suspended between reading and non-reading. What has brought him to this liminal position? Jeff dangles because Thorwald, the main object of his reading, has confronted him and demanded to know, "What is it that you want from me?" Jeff does not answer. (Of course, Thorwald is a criminal who now realizes that he's been under Jeff's surveillance and that incriminating evidence in the form of the wedding ring may be on its way to the authorities, so the plot context can't explain Jeff's inability to speak.) It requires only a small effort of the imagination to understand Thorwald's demand as an unanswerable demand asked of any reader *by whatever it is that is being inter-*

Figure 4.4: *Rear Window* (1954). Copyright © 2002 by Universal
Studios. Courtesy of Universal Studios Publishing Rights, a Division
of Universal Studios Licensing, Inc. All rights reserved.

preted—a film, a pendant, a hanging figure. Critics may imagine the question
as being addressed by Hitchcock to any reader—in the case of this book, to me.
     Understood in this way, the question is first a challenge to our supposed
intellectual curiosity—to acknowledge its lack of neutrality, to admit that the
act of reading is an unjustifiable appropriation in which the reader keeps safe
and surreptitiously *gains*. Jeff is silent. It would be laughable for him, *l'homme
moyen sensuel*, to reply to Thorwald that the obsessional reading of his apartment window sprang solely from an objective, Kantian effort to uphold public
morality. Like all of the hanging figures surveyed in this chapter, Jeff is not

above reproach. He makes his living photographing scenes of suffering; he has no objections to voyeurism; he is cruel to Lisa; he exhibits no compunctions about violating the civil liberties of others. When the pronouns of Thorwald's question are emphasized ("What is it that *you* want from *me*?"), it becomes even clearer that one reason for Jeff's silence may be a recognition that like Thorwald, he is a case study in amorality, too, maybe just less acted-out. In this way Thorwald's question first exposes the moral pretentiousness of the interpreter.

But a more fundamental reason for Jeff's silence is evident if Thorwald's question is paraphrased simply as "Why?" with regard to the totality of Jeff's quest to understand. Jeff's interpretation of Thorwald's behavior begins as a seemingly involuntary thought, on the morning after he witnesses Thorwald's argument with his wife. Lisa dismisses Jeff's theory of murder and dismemberment as having no basis in the signs he has read. His reading hypothesis is what existentialists call an *acte gratuit*, an entirely random event that simply happens in the midst of numerous other interpretations of the world. There is no rational way of understanding the grounds for his hypothesis, just as there is no necessary support for any of Jeff's other theories—about the sunbathers, the newlyweds, Miss Lonelyhearts, the sculptress, the pianist, or the married couple. In all of these instances, the unfounded nature of interpretation is emphasized by the airy distance between interpreter and interpreted. It is as if a story of the fate of a reader of signs could be understood more deeply, more clinically and with fewer distractions if studied in a kind of close-up or controlled experiment where the two entities, reader and signs, were clearly defined and separated, across a courtyard, and where one particular narrative of interpretation was chosen for detailed inspection from the midst of numerous others. From this perspective, the Thorwald case might be understood as what Gestalt psychologists call a *figure* which is suddenly singled out for interpretation against a *ground* of potentially infinite number of other readable signs. From the perspective of Wittgenstein, Jeff's interpretive moment is the shift from *seeing* to *seeing-as*—or "aspect-dawning."[14]

The accidental genesis of Jeff's reading is the reason he cannot reply to Thorwald's question, "Why?" Prior to Jeff's mad or inspired hypothesis about the disappearance of Thorwald's wife, his vision and reading might be considered a kind of *skimming*, a wandering survey of signs to whose referent he and the film viewer remained mostly indifferent. (A corollary is that film viewers or any other readers are unable to say why one interpretation, rather than countless others, grips them at any particular moment.) After the inexplicable moment of hypothesis formation ("How would you cut up a human body?"), referents are now assigned to signs that lacked them beforehand. In such a moment, unavoidable in retrospect, the construction of narrative begins. The de Manian paradox is that reading must *necessarily* misrepresent its arbitrary origin. Consistent with his role as reader, Jeff sits in his room, just as Descartes' *ego* sat inside its machine, an allusion reinforced by his position in his wheelchair. As in Beckett's *Endgame*, we have a visual figure of man as the thinking machine. In these works the reading mind is "seated," and within a confined enclosure there seems to be no alternative to interpretation. It happens involuntarily. Jeff's hanging from his windowsill may be likened to the making-visible of reason, when Thorwald's violent assault seems literally to "unseat" it, as if the mind or reading capacity might momentarily appear *almost* outside its confined exterior.

Thorwald's invasion of Jeff's reading site and his interrogation of reading's purpose can be understood in this allegory. Jeff cannot explain the grounds of his reading; his privileged position surveying all objects is a fiction that can be exposed only by teaching him the arbitrary nature of his own site and role as reader. Shoving Jeff from his reading site discloses to the viewer of *Rear Window*, at least, the arrogant appropriation inherent in Jeff's "point of view." As Jeff hangs from the sill, we can see both the necessity of reading (his "interior") and reading's arbitrary construction (Jeff's window that frames the world). Hanging on to such a perspective on reading is not easy—we all need to return to the idea that reading discloses meaning, and so to this end we need to go back safely inside, too, and readopt our rational but foundationless perspectives on the world. The hope is that doing so after reading *Rear Window* will at least allow us to see our own continuing enclosure in the Cartesian, framing space of hermeneutics as our probably unrenounceable error.

Jeff is unable to answer Thorwald's deepest and most open-ended question because to do so would be tantamount to explaining why reading occurs. In a similar way, I cannot answer the question, "What is it that you want from Hitchcock?" What was it I gained from the signs at my window, the signs on the screen, as opposed to what I may have derived from immersion in any number of other potential narratives? Any response to such questions misrepresents the arbitrary. Instead, Jeff replies only when Thorwald rephrases his question, to ask about a particular sign—the wedding ring, this film's Mac-Guffin. As we've seen in chapter 2, the MacGuffin functions as the pure sign, the material correlative of the inarticulable or undecidable; Thorwald's rage to get it back betrays the illusion of both his and Jeff's hermeneutics—that the meaning of the sign is inherent in it. This illusion has been dramatized in the many casual interpretations of other stories. For example, reading the signs of Miss Torso generated Jeff's and Lisa's conflicting interpretations, which are not resolvable even by the return of the serviceman, her apparent lover; the newlyweds' eventual quarreling gives the lie to all interpretations of love, including that between the pianist and Miss Lonelyhearts or Jeff and Lisa. In these interpretations we can see reading continually exposed as undertaken on the basis of unjustifiable assumptions.

The ending of *Rear Window* returns the viewer to an even more ironic scene of reading as the belated exposure of illusion. While a few critics suppose that Jeff and Lisa resolve the film's suspense by achieving the normative status of the Hollywood couple, most other commentators point to new evidence of friction in the supposedly happy couple. These competing interpretations raise new prospects of hermeneutic undecidability; in any case, it is unclear why critics might believe their interpretations of the closing shot of Jeff and Lisa would be in any way more valid than Lisa and Jeff's interpretation of the couples across the way.[15] But whatever the couple's moral or intellectual coming together, it is easy to see that Jeff's second fracture ensures that when he awakens he will be all the more confined to his reading position; for the time being, his function as an object of Lisa's visual field reveals the never-ending interpretive process. Lisa's reading while practicing deception seems to link these activities. Resuming the position and act of reading, respectively, Jeff and Lisa now fully reinhabit the world of ordinary, Cartesian, mystified suspense, of the infinite deferral of meaning. The contrasting scene of Jeff dangling from the sill may have seemed to visualize some ecstatic alternative to reading—some ability to jump outside "perspective" and figuration—but in the end the hanging figure of *Rear Window* only exaggerates and caricatures a condition of human suspense that cannot, after all, be escaped.

Hanging figures in Hitchcock convey the broadest range of suspense—as it inheres in character identity, political and cultural critiques, and the act of interpretation itself. These images doubtless elicit anxiety from moviegoers, but when that emotion subsides, the residual and ineradicable suspense may be examined in the light of less terminable dilemmas. If hanging figures provide one way—though not a privileged way—of understanding such suspenseful dilemmas, they may serve as useful points of entry for other Hitchcock films.

THREE

Suspense in Hitchcock

5

The Lodger: Deferred Identity in the Crucified Figure

Nobody knows the name of Hitchcock's first hanging figure—by default he is called "the lodger."[1] *He is accused of being a serial killer who also lacks a true name, someone nicknamed "the Avenger" by the press. Arrested and handcuffed but escaped from custody, he is chased vigilante style by a crowd convinced he is the killer. Cornered when his handcuffs catch on the wrought-iron fence he tries to scale (Figure 5.1), the lodger is beaten by the crowd and rescued only when word comes from reporters that the real Avenger, after all, has been apprehended. The injured lodger is then taken down from the fence, and after he recovers from his injuries, it is learned that he is a man of great wealth.*

Hitchcock called *The Lodger* "the first true 'Hitchcock movie.' "[2] It begins in a scene of murder, the death of the subject; it ends in unresolved identity and postponement of meaning.

In keeping with iconographic tradition, Hitchcock's first hanging figure literalizes suspense by making identity undecidable. Suspicions are raised that the lodger may be the serial killer sought by the police, and these are supposedly put to rest by the surprise ending. But despite the seeming finality of the conclusion, critics *continue* to doubt, especially since the object of the police quest—the "true referent" of its signs, the Avenger—is never shown. For William Rothman, this uncertainty and the camera's ambiguous role in flashback scenes leave room for the possibility that the lodger "could still be the Avenger."[3] Citing evidence that the Avenger may have had an accomplice and that the lodger should be understood in the tradition of the *doppelganger*, Ken Mogg concurs.[4] This critical acknowledgment of the protagonist's undecidability

Figure 5.1: *The Lodger* (1926). Reproduced courtesy of Carlton International Media Limited.

shows how the film's suspense extends beyond its ending. Moreover, if we can never know whether the protagonist is hero or villain, moral criteria for suspense cannot be invoked. Indeed, any viewer expectations of neat closure seem to be mocked by the laconic, tautological message of its concluding intertitle: "Every story has an ending." As noted in chapter 1, such amoral and beyond-the-story suspense is anomalous for Cartesian and hermeneutic theories; however, in this book's deconstructive and figurative approach, the indeterminacy of the lodger's identity can be understood as only the most blatant of the film's many absent referents. In its identityless state, the hanging figure of *The Lodger* is not only paradigmatic for the rest of Hitchcock's films but consistent with the undecidable meaning of its many predecessors, including Jesus, Marsyas, and Prometheus.

UNDECIDABLE LODGER AND DIRECTOR

At first glance, Hitchcock's comments to Truffaut seemed to deny any ambiguity in the lodger:

Francois Truffaut: I gather that you would have preferred the hero to turn out to be Jack the Ripper?

Alfred Hitchcock: Not necessarily. But in a story of this kind I might have liked him to go off in the night, so that we would never really know for sure. But with the hero played by a big star [Ivor Novello], one can't do that. You have to clearly spell it out in big letters: "He is innocent."

Truffaut: You know, I am rather surprised that you would consider an ending that failed to provide the public with the answer to its question.

Hitchcock: In this case, if your suspense revolves around the question: "Is he or is he not Jack the Ripper?" and you reply, "Yes, he *is* Jack the Ripper," you've merely confirmed a suspicion. To me this is not dramatic. But here we went in the other direction and showed that he wasn't Jack the Ripper at all.[5]

Hitchcock's claim is that studio pressures forced him to ensure Ivor Novello's innocence; however, the work of Rothman and Mogg shows that *Hitchcock had his way after all*, despite the studios. He had found a way to *appear* to respond to external constraints while in fact defying them. A careful reading of the passage shows that he by no means concurs that the lodger's identity *is* settled by the film. Hitchcock says only that "He [Novello, not the lodger] is innocent" and never confirms to Truffaut the moral guilt of the film's principal *character*. When Hitchcock says, "[The lodger] wasn't Jack the Ripper at all," he is accurate, since the film was only *inspired* by the career of Jack the Ripper. The criminal in *The Lodger* is called "the Avenger." To say that the lodger is not Jack the Ripper is not the same as saying that he is not the Avenger. All Hitchcock says is that the integrity of his leading man, Ivor Novello, was not compromised and that the lodger was not Jack the Ripper. Other interpretations of the protagonist's identity, including Rothman's and Mogg's, can be entertained, as can the idea that identity is a fictional construct made necessary in the process of reading arbitrary signs.

The fact that within the acting community Novello's homosexuality was well known lends a reflexive dimension to the issue of the lodger's identity.[6] For those aware of Novello's sexual orientation, the fact that his character wound up in a closing embrace with a woman further undermines its closure: their apparent affection both is and is not the sign of the end of suspense in some image of "the normative."

Within the diegesis, the lodger's undecidable identity may be further understood by Maurice Yacowar's observation that he is a lower-case avenger—since he claims to have come to London searching for the killer, in response to his sister's death and in furtherance of a promise made to his dying mother. Now when the question is asked orally, "Is the avenger the same as the Avenger?" it is easier to see how the determination of identity is inseparable from the artifices of representation, in this case as arbitrary as conventions for capitalization. The question whether this word should be capitalized in film criticism, while seemingly trivial, raises the perennial issue of the status of proper nouns. To capitalize "Avenger" is to imply that there may be a specific one, though the film also suggests that everyone may in some sense be an avenger—a person provoked to irrational action by arbitrary signs. The term "lodger" raises a similar uncertainty: If there is one specific Lodger, as the credits suggest, does this imply that others are *not* lodgers? The Buntings' house has presumably been occupied by any number of lodgers. To define someone who is *not* a lodger, a temporary occupant, raises new questions, for whose dwelling in the world is permanent? A story about serial killings narrates successive dislodgments from the world. The many referents for the film's supposedly proper names, for its hero and villain, may suggest that it narrates, instead, the way supposedly unique identities are established only in the arbitrary constructs of language.[7]

Hitchcock's acknowledgment of the scene's allusion to the crucifixion links Ivor Novello's hanging with the most famous example of the iconographic tradition:

Truffaut: Is it far-fetched to suggest that in the scene where the man in handcuffs is backed up against the railing, you were trying to evoke the figure of Christ?

Hitchcock: When the people try to lift him and his arms are tied together? Naturally, that thought did occur to me.[8]

Before analyzing the allusion's implications outside the film, we may consider its relation to the film's other crucifixion, the one on Mrs. Bunting's night table.[9] One sense of this visual echo is the simple cultural critique that any metaphysical significance of the lodger's hanging may remain inaccessible in a world of signs like "lodger" or "avenger" or "golden curls" that have no undisputed referent. The lodger's reprise of his landlady's crucifix extends the film's critique of Christianity, which is less a matter of satire than of depicting the ubiquitous leveling of signs in the Derridean world of the postal: for example, the beckoning function of the crucifix sign is on the same level as newspaper headlines and the blinking neon of "TONIGHT—GOLDEN CURLS." Immersion in these signs defines the world of the Buntings, Hitchcock's examples of bourgeois striving. The owners of the lodgings value respectable appearances and are horrified at the contemplation of sex-murders; at the same time, they remain blind to their own participation—through Daisy—in a world of fashion and erotic allure that seems only a sublimated version of the dance halls that are, in their turn, sublimations of the erotic incitements of the Avenger's murders. Moreover, the Buntings' interest in lurid media representations of the Avenger marks them as the perfect consumers of the newspapers' commodification of crime. Their wholesale acceptance of bourgeois values appears in the film's conclusion, when they cravenly fawn over the lodger and his pretentious home, unaware that their earlier misjudgment of the lodger reveals their blindness to anything but appearances.

A religious alternative to such a world, one that might permit authentic judgement of it, is simply reified in the bedroom crucifixion where it becomes indistinguishable from other signs; thus, like the crucifix, the lodger's fence-hanging provides no vantage point from which to judge either his or society's moral life. His "resurrection" into the restored world of the haute-bourgeoisie ensures that no alternative value system will threaten the world of the sublimation and delusion he inhabits. His inability to change is paralleled in the Buntings, who anticipate all the well-meaning, blind, sublimated, bourgeois families Hitchcock ever imagined—the McKennas of *The Man Who Knew Too Much*, the Newtons of *Shadow of a Doubt* or Brenners of *The Birds*—families whose moral rectitude depends on the repression and disavowal of any instinct that might threaten to expose the "glamorously dangerous charade" of life. The reintegration of the resurrected hanging man into this world is supposed to be achieved in the closing embrace; but if we cannot know the characters' true identities (or if whatever we do know contradicts the image of closure), then this supposed resolution is vitiated. In its place we are left with the world of signs—the amoral, blinking, indeterminate postal world that is visible behind the embracing lovers in the beckoning sign that began the film: "TONIGHT—GOLDEN CURLS."

In addition to its cultural critique, the hanging figure's allusion to the crucifixion also works the other way, providing additional perspectives on Christianity. If the lodger is like Jesus but may also be both innocent and guilty, then we may imagine Jesus, too, as both passive sufferer and avenger. Although Jesus's passion is usually associated with the unjust punishment of innocence, Hitchcock's parallel between the lodger and Jesus asks us to see on the cross an *avenger*, too. Such a reading comports well with the image of Jesus as a horseman with a sword, a divinity who avenges sin; the parallel reimagines Jesus as *simultaneously* innocent and vengeful, a characteristic that deepens the figure's unknowable and suspended identity, already indicated in the *Santo Spirito Crucifix*. In addition, the lodger's handcuffs, which anticipate scenes of suspense in later Hitchcock films, add an emotional component to the figure's suffering. Hitchcock associated the handcuffs with sexual fetishes and "sexual aberrations through restraint"; in *The Lodger* this association becomes evident when Daisy's unrequited lover Joe "playfully" handcuffs her to the bannister.[10] Applied to the scenes of the lodger's crucifixion, this association suggests that physical suffering can also be pleasurable. In the secular world of *The Lodger*, it is easy to see this motive in Daisy—in her rapt, masochistic infatuation with a menacing dandy whom one critic compared to a predatory vampire.[11] With regard to the crucifixion, Hitchcock's allusion suggests that Jesus's expression may evince joy as well as suffering, thus placing the figure even more clearly within the iconographic tradition that includes the undecidable expressions of joy/pain of Marsyas or the Hanged Man of the Tarot Cards.

The undecidability of identity here is compounded because this is also the scene of Hitchcock's cameo—he is present as a member of the avenging crowd observing the spectacle that he created. The problem of "recognizing the identity of the lodger" is now made parallel to that of "recognizing Hitchcock." In chapter 2, Hitchcock's cameos were discussed as cinematic versions of what Paul de Man called "parabasis"—that is, moments when the apparent recognition of true identity dissolved, on reflection, into the "recognition" of mere persona. (These moments resembled the way "seeing-as," in Wittgenstein's thought, could not be distinguished, after all, from mere "seeing.") So when an unidentified man in the crowd is recognized as "Hitchcock" gazing down at his created protagonist, the viewer at first thinks authentic identity has been established; then, on reflection, this sense of authenticity dissolves as questions about just who "Hitchcock" is, apart from his persona, cannot be answered. A similar process is at work with all cinematic viewing: when we "recognize" Ivor Novello "behind" the lodger, we immediately question what it is we have learned.

Hitchcock's cameo allegorizes the way illusions of personal identity vitiate film criticism, too, because it shows the director/persona "making observations on" his character/actor; the scene becomes a miniature version of Hitchcock the interview-respondent or, by analogy, of any work of film criticism. To the extent that hermeneutic film criticism seeks to establish "the director's view" of his characters, plot, and so forth, this scene already dramatizes it as being silent and unrevelatory. The scene shows what is true for every film: the director has arrived on the scene before his viewers have finished watching the film, so there is implicit in the viewing experience the promise of significance. But when we, too, arrive at the director's position, when we seem to meet him and even to identify with him, we find not truth but only the spectacle of a spectator, only the image of our own silent construction of visual figures.

OPENING FOG

Thus *The Lodger* allegorizes seeing in the two senses of vision and understanding; it dramatizes the way visual clues lead to misunderstanding. In reading the story of a man wrongly suspected of guilt, viewers learn that the many signs that supposedly constitute human identity are both necessary and—only in retrospect—illusory. We must make the mistake of reading before later learning our error. In retrospect the dysfunction of visual referentiality might have been apparent from the beginning—from the film's title, subtitle, credits, and opening. Analyzing these introductory elements will show the film's anticipation of the way its ending fails to close off suspense.

A clue to the continued undecidability of identity is available in the title word "lodger." If the word means "temporary occupant," then it stands for nothing specific: everyone is really a "lodger," even the supposed referent of the film's title, the aristocratic owner of a mansion so imposing that it daunts the Buntings and perhaps even film audiences into momentarily considering him something other than or superior to a "mere" lodger. The sense that at first a word has a fixed meaning that is subsequently dissipated recurs in the nickname "Avenger," the meaning of which becomes the goal of its characters and critics. As noted above, the film depicts many avengers, but it may also apply to critics: this is one implication of the mob scene. Like the mob, we viewers want to "hunt down" our quarry of meaning; we *must* fix identities and characters as part of that process. (It would be salutary to think that Hitchcock's silent viewing— watching us, the mob of identifiers—is a warning to us that some kind of be- mused detachment from the frenzy of interpretive apprehension is preferable; on the other hand, even to attribute such a "Buddhistic" view to the director is to suspend a false construction over a blank face. And besides, Hitchcock's cameo teaches that gaining such a position of detachment is possible only by first joining the mob, as we must first read) But if the identity of the "lodger" will always escape interpretation, so will the larger quarry of the film's theme or idea. Thus the title of the first true Hitchcock movie functions like a MacGuffin thirteen years before the term was coined: "the lodger" seems to designate a specific, apprehensible referent that on close scrutiny disappears.

The title's instability is repeated in the subtitle, "A Story of London Fog," which equates human-identity-as-temporary-occupancy with both a fiction ("a story") and the film's recurrent image of the inapprehensible. T. S. Eliot's mem- orable use of the image, evocative of a cityscape of serial deaths, appeared only three years earlier:

Unreal City,
Under the brown fog of a winter dawn,
A crowd flowed over London Bridge, so many,
I had not thought death had undone so many.

A metaphor for the borderline between nothing and something, light and dark, sense and nonsense, fog blurs the binaries that comprise the world's condition of intelligibility. Such binaries (and others, like guilt/innocence or love/hate, hermeneutics/deconstruction) seem themselves like "lodgers"—temporary oc- cupants or referents of thought, perhaps metaphors for thought as a boundaryless place where no "figure" can be genuinely at home.

Fog and its interior analogues, smoke and steam, appear frequently in *The Lodger*. Fog defines the scenes of the murders and the first appearance of the lodger, in effect adding a blur at the outset to any attributions of identity. London's fog also encircles the gas lamps under which the lovers seek to know each other, and it penetrates into the smoky interiors of pubs. Inside the Buntings' residence, smoke curls from Mr. Bunting's pipe or from the lodger's cigarette, and steam rises from Daisy's bath. The fogs of both exterior and interior assist in the subversion of that distinction, usually so crucial for the interpretation of identity.

Another image that erases it is the "wrapped face." Hitchcock often exploited this metaphor: its memorable manifestations include the blackface disguising the killer in *Young and Innocent*; Handell Fane's makeup in *Murder!*; Doctor Peterson's glasses in *Spellbound*; Louis Bernard's facial makeup in *The Man Who Knew Too Much* (1956); the cosmeticized face(s) of Judy/Madeleine in *Vertigo*; Norman Bates's wig and disguise in *Psycho*. Disguised faces cast doubt on "real" faces throughout Hitchcock's films by instantiating *Macbeth*'s theme:

> There's no art to know the mind's construction
> In the face.

In *The Lodger* the face of the "true" Avenger, if such a person exists, is so fully "wrapped" it is never seen. Witnesses claim the murderer's face is wrapped in a scarf, but as soon as it is mentioned, this sign is imitated or iterated by an anonymous man in the crowd. (The crowd in "the first true Hitchcock movie" is the first of many that may be likened reflexively to the film audience and critics; in its gathering around the site of a murder, the death of the subject, curious to affix causality and identity, the crowd embodies the attitude of hermeneutic readers.) The imitation of the sign suggests the way attributes of identity other than names are also iterable or citable and not inherently meaningful; it also suggests the way *all* faces, not just the Avenger's, may be wrapped and unplumbable. Unwrapping them reveals not truth behind illusion but only new illusion. Thus the first scene of the first true Hitchcock movie announces the death of the subject, the alienability of signs, the unrecuperability of human identity, and (despite these) the human obsession to know.

The idea that only new illusion lurks under the wrapped face is reinforced by the early parallel drawn between the face and the circulation of news in the mass media. News is expressed first in the faces of the crowd of onlookers, then transferred to the faces of the newspaper reporters and radio announcers, whose faces dissolve into each other: journalism itself is equated with some "generic," impassive, expressionless face. Interestingly, Hitchcock drew a sketch for Truffaut that showed his early plan to make the back of a newspaper delivery van resemble a human face.[12] The misrepresentations of the media are likened to the unknowable face. A correlation between faces and blank signs is evident, too, in the heavy facial makeup of both Ivor Novello and his leading lady, June

Tripp: under the lodger's scarf lies an actor in makeup; under Daisy's dresses is a "mannequin." (This identification of her role, in the credits, conveys the senses of both living model and inert dummy.) There is no authentic identity beneath the layers of signs—marks of nonexistent character—that comprise either this film's hanging figure or the woman he loves. The distinction between male and female blurs—as close-ups of the lodger's ghostly or dandified white face with prominent lipstick and eyeshadow alternate with Daisy's more conventionally constructed visage. It is as if the fog as distinction-blurring device penetrates even to gender, as if the iterability of name, scarf, makeup, wig, and clothes confounds in advance any attempt to ground gender in anything other than sign.[13] The modest questioning of the referent of gender in *The Lodger* may anticipate the full-scale interrogation we saw in the last chapter's analysis of Handel Fane in *Murder!*.

Questioning is apparent in the film's scenes of modeling, too. In the first, Daisy wears a coat with a white exterior and black interior, as if flaunting for both her modeling and film audiences the composition of film; she is followed by another model, who puts a wig with black curls on Daisy's "golden curls," once again exemplifying the arbitrary construction of identity. In a third scene, the lodger's gaze at Daisy is doubled by that of an anonymous woman who stares admiringly at him as he sits resplendent in a silk smoking jacket. This scene of doubled gazing, of a longing directed at signs of eros, glamor and wealth, evokes Hitchcock's "glamorously dangerous charade"—the world conceived of as visual signs that promise meaning beneath or behind or beyond them, lures that seduce the lodger, too, when he buys the dress Daisy wears and has it delivered to her. Mr. Bunting's elaborate unwrapping and rewrapping of the parcel that contains the dress (the lure, the visual sign) is a miniature allegory of film criticism—the manipulation of exterior signs as if they concealed interior significance. Modeling and film are visual promises that exterior signs conceal something of value, perhaps some interior identity, when in fact they conceal only mannequins. Criticism, then, is the interminable unfolding and re-folding of layers of wrapping that disclose additional wrappings.

Even the credits visualize the eclipse of human identity: a silhouetted human figure is framed by the shape of a black "V" that closes and reopens. This image anticipates the importance of the frame, already discussed in Chapter 3, as integral to all hanging figures. In *The Lodger*, this "V" or implied triangle shape is repeated in the Avenger's signature and in the maps drawn by the lodger and by the detectives which suggest their rationality, extrapolation, and the drawing of inferences. Just as identity is eclipsed by the triangular "V," so is the confidence in Enlightenment rationality shown by these characters: the "solution" to the crime "pointed to" by these maps arrives not through ratiocination but through the spontaneous intervention of the press, a *deus ex machina* ending that challenges the process by which Joe, the lodger, the police, and the viewer try to infer the identity of the culprit. Their efforts lead to the apprehension of the wrong person, or better, to undecidability—just as Barton's, in *Number*

Seventeen, led to a train wreck. The delusions of hermeneutics that are everywhere satirized in Hitchcock's films appear first in *The Lodger*.

If the Avenger's triangular "V" implies the death of the subject that accompanies language conceived as arbitrary (and here, alphabetical) shapes, this relation was already established in the visual eclipse of the human by the credits'
closing and opening "V" frame. The credits' frame is a figure, finally, for a
camera's aperture—suggesting that film's efforts to represent human identity
will only further disclose it to be framed, to be a display of faces without
interiors or signs without referents, a temporary illusion of meaning, a
"lodger."[14]

READING FILM

The film's undermining of interior identity and Enlightenment reason suggest
that reading, as the construction of arbitrary shapes, will always fail. The film's
famous opening of a de-contextualized scream presents nearly a pure example
of sign purged of referent. Like all silent film, this shot requires the viewer to
supply a voice to arbitrary shapes of black and white: it is nearly impossible to
read the face as mere photons, as *clignotements* or arrangements of flickering
light and shadow. At the same time, nothing in the opening shot logically requires a meaning beyond itself. For example, lest we assume that such a face
"naturally" implies the existence of an offscreen victimizer, the film soon provides an instance of another scream, induced by the man in the crowd's scarf
prank. And lest we believe a screaming face "naturally" means internal terror,
we are later shown chorus girls imitating victims' cries and Daisy indignantly
protesting Joe's "pretend" handcuffing. Reading the screaming face requires the
attribution not only of voice but also of some interior identity. But the whole
point of the plot of *The Lodger* is that its seemingly inevitable identification of
one man's culpability is a false assumption. Taken together with the V-frame
of the credits, the decontextualized screaming face warns the viewer that such
seemingly necessary misreading might have been known from the outset, perhaps even from the very conditions of photography. The decontextualized
screaming face is a kind of cinematic correlative of the childish faces Wittgenstein drew to suggest the arbitrary, potentially infinite interpretability of lines.[15]

A second famous shot—the glass ceiling—demonstrates the imperviousness
of figures to any reading of their interiors. The Buntings and Joe—curious about
the lodger pacing above them—look toward the ceiling, and, in an elaborately
contrived example of subjective camera, the film audience looks up, as the
characters do, to see through a glass ceiling the bottom of the lodger's shoes as
he paces. In the story this shot probably is a manifestation of group imagination—the Buntings' curiosity about what the mysterious lodger is doing or who
he really is. But the shot is also a witty cinematic trope for illusory transparency:
it suggests that even if characters and audiences could penetrate behind or
through the barriers of signs that seem to separate them from the truth, they

would be met only with new opacity. The glass ceiling literalizes the illusion of clarity. Unwrap the scarf and you still have the enigma of the expressionless face; see through the ceiling, and you have but another walking figure—knowledge you might have known at the outset. The scenes of seeing or reading in *The Lodger* recoil against readers, viewers, imaginers: seeing or reading leads not to some necessary truth of the interior, but only to new exteriors—or better, to the knowledge that the whole idea of an interior was an assumption cast upon an arbitrary figure in the fog.

How should we evaluate the film's ending? We've seen that endings are mocked by the intertitle, "All stories have an end." We've seen that the identity of the Avenger remains undecidable and that the validity of the closing embrace as a sign of resolution is open to question. The credulous, servile Buntings may be surrogates for the audience in being introduced to and intimidated by new spectacle; the fact that they accord a moral status to visual opulence suggests misinterpretation may be interminable. Viewers of *The Lodger* may be made uncomfortable with the way the ending seems contemptuous of those who constructed the narrative out of arbitrary shapes in the first place. Reflecting on their error, chagrined viewers may leave the theatre with the reading imperative as their only shred of justification—that any film viewing, any understanding of diegesis, presupposes that a cinematic sign must temporarily refer to *something*. It is not at all clear that Hitchcock concurred; in a famous remark to Truffaut he said, "There's no such thing as a face, because until light hits it, it is nonexistent."[16] For their part, most viewers find it almost impossible to see a decontextualized screaming face as merely a play of black and white, just as they prefer seeing Whistler's famous painting as his mother and not as an arrangement in gray, as its title indicates. The human propensity for such unavoidable misinterpretation was the continuous instruction of surrealist film, which taught that we cannot refrain from the attribution of significance to the arbitrary.[17] This tradition implies that film viewers, too, might consider themselves "avengers" in a rush to seize upon and hold onto whatever referents we can, perhaps as a defense against the states of doubt induced by art.

But of course, even such an anti-hermeneutic interpretation of *The Lodger* is still only one more "lodger" of the mind—a temporary occupant of the vacancy glimpsed in the film's final moments.

LOVE AS MISREADING

Daisy loves whatever undecidable entity it is she holds in her arms. How should the reader understand that love?

As in many of Hitchcock's films, love relations are depicted in *The Lodger* as triangular. That is, love between individuals is frequently mediated by some "third term," usually but not always identifiable with a jealous rival. René Girard, who founded a theory of the novel on the existence of triangulated love, thought that the third term could also include an imaginative or fictive entity—a character or a complete work of art—that influences the achievement of the lovers' union; thus Don Quixote's love for Dulcineia is mediated by the romances he has read.[18] The evaluation of fictional love relations by a template like triangulation is frequent in hermeneutic readings that assume gender relations to be the signified referents of narrative; by contrast, deconstructive criticism would make no assumptions beyond the *sign* of such relations, which in the case of *The Lodger* is the triangle.

We've already seen that the triangle as geometric shape has been visible throughout the film, in the credits' "V," the Avenger's logo, the lodger's and policemen's maps. Triangles also appear on the title cards and on the wall behind the hospital bed in which the lodger recovers from his "severe nervous strain." Triangles describe the film's two families—the mother-father-daughter Bunting family and the lodger-mother-sister family—whose shapes are changed by the diegesis. Of course, the triangle describes the relation among the lodger and Daisy and Joe, which seems to represent love according to Girard's mediatory paradigm of the aspiration to unity consequent on the discovery of "true identity," when the third term might be ejected and the triangle flattened, two points becoming a straight line, a closing embrace.

The closing embrace of Daisy and the lodger takes place in front of a window through which the viewer can see blinking lights that form the words, "TO-NIGHT—GOLDEN CURLS." As they kiss, the lovers ignore these words, but viewers may recall them from the opening, reflected in the waters of the Thames, following the screaming face and preceding the discovery of the Avenger's victim. So the blinking lights link beginning and end, closing a circle. The first sign introduced the diegesis (the story's crime and victim) and initiated the long process of reading that, in retrospect, proved so frustrating; the first sign seemed to matter vitally while the last sign is a "mere" sign, which just blinks away, ignored.

If the closing embrace ratifies an idea about love, love may be understood in the end as an obliviousness to signs, which show the constructed or figural nature of desire; in the case of the lodger and Daisy, their obliviousness is to the lighted signs that blink against darkness, *clignotements*, for in the end it is only such signs, drained of content, that the film has shown itself to be. Love is an acquiescence in misreading, in a misinterpretation not yet exposed, in closure instead of suspense.

6

Easy Virtue: Framing Nothing

A monocle hangs from a string held between the fingers of the presiding judge; he swings it back and forth as he listens to the cross-examination of Larita Filton by the prosecutor, rendered by alternating shots of their profiles. Soon the swinging monocle dissolves into the swinging pendulum of a courtroom clock; then after another dissolve we see the monocle again. The hanging figure evokes the tedium of the courtroom, but more as well.

When the judge first looked out over the courtroom, in the film's opening scene, the attorneys and spectators appeared as a blur; putting on his monocle made them visible. But while the monocle improved the judge's ocular vision, it by no means guaranteed that he "saw" the proceedings clearly: the film associates his dubious judgment in favor of Larita's drunken husband with patriarchy, the obtuseness of legal tradition, and the British class system. Thus his monocle is a frame that is necessary for vision but nevertheless leaves it distorted. But it is only one of many such frames in the film.

The swinging movement of the hanging monocle is associated through film editing with both the legal proceedings (the back-and-forth cross-examination in alternating profile) and with time (the swinging pendulum of the courtroom clock). In this way the hanging figure suggests both the futility of courtroom's pretense of rationality and the potential for interminably unresolved suspense, whatever the courtroom's verdict.

Given this film's narrative of a woman's never-ending victimization—by a drunken husband, a lecherous artist, a weak second husband and his manipulative mother, a crowd of invasive male paparazzi—it seems odd that *Easy Virtue* has attracted so little notice from Hitchcock's feminist critics; on reflec-

Figure 6.1: *Easy Virtue* (1927). Reproduced courtesy of Carlton International Media Limited.

tion, however, its unequivocal revelation of a woman's oppression may be problematic for critics, like Tania Modleski, who advocate reading Hitchcock's films "against the grain" in order to discover in them a subversion of patriarchy.[1] By contrast, the obvious feminist argument in *Easy Virtue* seems so entirely "with the grain" as to momentarily unsettle the received construction of Hitchcock the covert or overt misogynist.[2] Of course, reading Hitchcock's films as feminist either against *or* with the grain is already to engage in the grail quest that constrains hermeneutic critics, feminists, and others, to advocate some view of gender identity as the resolution of Hitchcockian suspense.

This chapter proposes a way of understanding this critical need for closure as a correlative of the story's victimization of women. It will be seen that *Easy Virtue* narrates gender oppression as the imposition of the frames or structures of male hegemony onto its protagonist, Larita, but it does so only because it allegorizes *all* reading, and even all seeing, as an analogous imposition of frames, onto arbitrary signs. The judge's hanging monocle is one of many such frames, but the most compelling are the shots of Larita framed in the courthouse dooryard, at the beginning and end of the film, confronting the paparazzi. The two types show two ways of imposing frames: both within the story (the diegetic frames showing patriarchy and other social ills) and *of* the story (the cameramen as our surrogates in adopting a point of view on Larita). Each becomes an example of the inevitably marginalizing frame that seeks to end suspense by privileging inside over outside; in this allegory, the film equates reading, seeing, and misinterpretation. And if error is seen as necessary to comprehension, as when the judge puts on his monocle, then critical pursuit of the film's gender theme may be merely the adoption, the helpless assumption, of just another distorting frame. In this light, Hitchcockian suspense may be regarded as waiting for a world without frames.

NECESSARY FRAMES

That *Easy Virtue* allegorizes framed seeing may be evident from its credits, which appear over the image of a camera, and from key scenes involving photography. For example, the paparazzi aggressively take Larita's picture after her first trial. Later, at the Whittakers' estate, when Larita suspects her past may come to light, she desperately tries to smash a camera—a gesture that illustrates the futility of thinking of the world without frames. And after her second trial paparazzi harass her again. Thus *Easy Virtue* is doubly framed—its plot is encircled with the activity of framing—or triply framed, if the credits are seen as a first frame around this double frame.

With regard to Hitchcock's *oeuvre*, this subject has sometimes been discussed in hermeneutic criticism in terms of "reflexivity," that is, of moral commentary on photography, film-making, the film audience, voyeurism, or the gaze.[3] In this spirit, Maurice Yacowar emphasized the idea of the camera as violator of identity—as a catalyst of Larita's downfall through its unexpungible record of her earlier "shame"; he sees the film's indictment of this violation as part of its broader attack on England's press, judiciary and class systems.[4] There is no doubt that such a cultural critique exists in *Easy Virtue*, just as *The Lodger* satirized the police and the mass media. But at the same time, reflexivity also calls into question the validity of visual representation itself. Framed by the cameras of its credits and ending, *Easy Virtue* also explores the frame as part of its critiques not only of the social system and the individual identities that seem to comprise it, but also of representation itself.

Chapter 3 discussed framing as a metaphor for the necessity for selection and point of view in representation: Rembrandt's *Flayed Ox* cannot be seen fully because of its frame. *Easy Virtue* begins with a highlighted newspaper column that reports legal proceedings: the camera technique duplicates the eye's act of focusing. The circular, lighted portion of the newspaper selects the subject of divorce (British usage is "candidates for division") first from the rest of the news and then from other courtroom topics—probate and admiralty. Through this technique, framing is associated with reading, which is made possible by what is framed, hence by what is excluded, marginalized, or not seen. The framing of the newspaper article is followed by two scenes of interpretation, linked by flashback, which extend this principle to the courtroom and the artist's studio: both are sites where framing is depicted as necessary and taken for granted but also as a futile attempt to end suspense by deciding the undecidable.

In the courtroom, society's privileged site of decidability, the trial is depicted as a transparent fiction, an elaborately costumed stage play performed before a credulous audience. The idea that legal proceedings misrepresent the human subject is suggested by the adversarial, alternating shots of Larita and her husband's attorney in sharp profile. The easy equation of these one-sided representations with moral absolutes like innocence and guilt collapses when Larita's story unfolds in flashback and when the prosecuting lawyer later becomes her confidante. Continuing *The Lodger*'s doubt as to the readability of faces, the courtroom scenes in *Easy Virtue* depict faces framed by wigs, suggesting the way their supposedly expressive countenances are masks and the "subjects" they reveal are actors. The myopic judge, posturing lawyer, and self-conscious jurors are dramatis personae, characters who will jointly construct the verdict of misconduct against Larita.

The dependence of the jury's verdict on a representation of character very much resembles the interpretive process of hermeneutic film criticism. In *Easy Virtue* that connection is made by the gossipy woman juror who passes written notes to a fellow juror during the testimony. While most film critics would not identify themselves with this juror, her role as inquisitive interpreter of a visual spectacle makes the association plausible. Her first note is a question ("Was the maid always present when Mrs. Filton disrobed?") that betrays a voyeuristic interest in the proceedings; her second note is a comment ("The artist and the woman he pitied alone together. Pity is akin to love") that is obtuse in the light of the open declaration of love Claude makes to Larita and irrelevant as a judgement of *Larita*'s (as opposed to Claude's) character. Since neither of these responses supports the final verdict of misconduct against Larita, film criticism may be allegorized here as both necessary—since some verdict must be reached—and mistaken.

The jury's unfounded verdict is made possible, in its turn, by marginalizing instances of the more egregious behavior of both Aubrey Filton and Claude Robson and thus is "framed"—arrived at only at the expense of what is excluded. For example, it is the artist, Robson, who shoots the drunken and jealous Filton, who in fact *did* have grounds for jealousy in Robson's behavior, if not in his wife's. Her behavior is depicted only as mute ambiguous gestures that while unresponsive to Robson's pleas, were not unequivocally dismissive of them, either. Just as it became impossible in *The Lodger* to determine a character's culpability from the "wrapped" or always ambiguous face, so in *Easy Virtue* it is impossible to tell Larita's inner identity from her silent flashback. Indeed, it must be recalled that the entire flashback represents Larita's recollection, which the film viewer like the jurors must accept uncorroborated: the prosecutor's dumbfounding emphasis on the wine decanter only points up the obvious fact that mute objects (like mute faces) can never resolve discrepancies in "he said/she said" testimony. In short, the truth of Larita's past remains a black hole, unknowable except through framed representations. As if to underscore its dependence on frames, the verdict is decided upon and announced in a courtroom presented as a series of enclosures: the accused inside a witness stand, jury inside a box, judge behind bench, observers in orchestra and balcony sections. The courtroom's interior ogives—echoed later in the artist's studio—further define the space of judgment as a series of artificial frames. When Larita leaves the courtroom only to be met in the doorway by a barrage of flash cameras, viewers see that the representations of photography only duplicate prior framings which have been allegorized as first conditions of reading and interpretation. Photography captures not truth but the inevitability of arbitrary frames that seek to end the suspense of undecidability.

The film's juxtaposition of the law's outrageous fictions with artistic representation may be unsettling for the traditional humanistic confidence that art's relation to reality is somehow more authentic than the law's; however, Claude Robson's painting of Larita is just as much a "frame" of identity as is the jurors' verdict, the judge's sentence, the reporter's photograph—or (we may now begin to surmise) the film itself and critical discussion of it. None of these representations tells the truth; none can avoid a frame. Within the painter's literal, rectangular frame is an idealized or sublimated figure, a reduction and abstraction of the plot's triangular frame of desire in which Larita occupies the apex. (As we shall see, triangulation is *Easy Virtue*'s consistent representation of desire and in this it follows the pattern established in *The Lodger*.) The frames of art are evident, too, in the white statue, niched by an ogive and observable behind Larita as she sits for her portrait; the statue as an ossified double of Larita may foreshadow her final acknowledgment ("Shoot . . . there's nothing left to kill") of the death of the subject. In any case, the studio's numerous frames suggest the way artistic interpretations of character, including those of film, may be just as fictional as legal verdicts.

Painting, photography, and film—like the law—are helpless to render the world unframed. In *Easy Virtue*, this debility vitiates Enlightenment reason just as the futility of detection did in *The Lodger*. In a world of inescapable frames, it may be impossible *not* to repeatedly allegorize this failure. By no means restricted to newspaper, courtroom, and studio, frames in *Easy Virtue* become the world's attempt to decide the undecidable and thus to escape suspense.

FALSE ESCAPE

Escape (in the form of hiding her "scarred heart") is what Larita longs for in the south of France, yet she first appears in a hotel lobby framed in white columns; like everyone else, she must enter her name within the ruled lines of the guest register. Here human identity, equated with arbitrary signs within a frame, is again figured as parabasis—identifying oneself in misrepresentation. (That Larita substitutes the surname "Gray" for Filton makes the arbitrary nature of her framed identity even more apparent, since that name reflexively summons up the mixture of black and white that constitutes her cinematic representation; in this gesture she echoes the scenes of modeling in *The Lodger* where Daisy appears in black-and-white apparel. Hitchcock misses few opportunities to evoke the *clignotements* or flickerings constitutive of film's construction of character.) Larita's life in France indicates that identity as the byproduct of framing is not much affected by changes in venue. The room in which Larita finally kisses John Whittaker contains an alcove with a statue—as if she had not left the courtroom or artist's studio. The artifice of the wigs that framed jurists' faces is in France replaced by Larita's eye-concealing or broad-brimmed hats and by the tall silk hats worn by John and his driver. In these ways, the site of Larita's striving to recreate herself only makes more apparent the impossibility of transcending the artificial frames that construct selfhood: she has always already been part of the "glamorously dangerous charade."

Any supposed contrast between the old and new Larita is erased by her presence at the second *court*, another formally framed and delimited space of ritualized conflict. The French tennis court—in history a famous nexus of sport and arbitrary law—is introduced by an impossible to ignore framing shot, by means of which we view the players and bouncing ball first through a racquet. It is as if humans are subordinated to some network or mesh or fate larger than themselves. (There is nothing novel about this theme; it appears first in Aeschylus's *Agamemnon*.) The seesaw motion of the tennis game recalls the courtroom's images of the judge's swinging monocle and the alternating arguments of defense and prosecution; the parallel with tennis first likens the judge and attorneys to the tennis audience then compares all of these to the viewers of both the trial and the film, interpreters of the back-and-forth of human discourse framing suspense.

Larita's exchange of one framed place for another provides no escape from the necessarily framed interpretation of her identity or the continued triangulation of desire. John's pursuit of her begins with the interrupted tennis match and is strengthened by his jealousy of the attentions paid to her by the unseen "Duc de Vallenville." Interestingly, this third term in the triangle presents itself as a mere sign—a calling card with a signature; this framed assertion of identity is a visual echo of Larita's signature in the hotel guest book. It is as if the embodied human triangle of London is replaced in France by the schematically purer arrangement of man-woman-referentless sign. In any case, the depiction of John and Larita as always shadowed by various third terms comes up again in their carriage ride, when the presence of driver, horse, and fellow travelers functions to expose the illusion of private selfhood or romantic union.

Chapter 5 explored the way triangular gender relations in *The Lodger* showed the subordination of human desire to the sign; in *Easy Virtue*, the sign is figured as a frame. The most dramatic example is the famous scene in which a telephone operator eavesdrops on John's proposal to Larita. This scene, praised as a virtuoso example of the way silent film "speaks" purely through visual images, dramatizes the way love is constructed in and through a frame, a pre-existing network—here, a matrix akin to Derrida's notion of the postal—while at the same time the lovers mistakenly believe themselves to be the privileged origin and destination of the discourse.[5] (In fact, an intercepted love message had appeared earlier in the film, when Aubrey Filton discovered Claude's letter to Larita; as a result, this scene's dramatization of the illusion of unframed, private discourse in love is already a redundancy.) The fact that the telephone operator's interception of the proposal interrupts her reading of a romance has the effect of equating the discourses of real and fictional characters. In the light of Larita's troubled future with John, the fact that the operator thinks the phone conversation ends suspense is just another way of dramatizing an audience's illusion of closure.

The operator's vicarious identification with the lovers resembles that of a rapt reader or viewer of film. Indeed, when she shifts the site of her empathic reading, exchanging one framed discourse for another, the operator becomes the audience's surrogate. Her eavesdropping on the "back and forth" movement of the conversation aligns her with earlier spectators, in the English courtroom and at the French tennis court. Her "turning" also mirrors the film viewer's move from the suspense of the undecidable everyday world (which may itself be figural) into the more enthralling movie theatre, in the exchange of one glamorously dangerous charade for another. It is noteworthy that the operator literally turns, from left profile to full face, though this turn only leaves her again conspicuously framed, this time by Hitchcock's camera. Like the telephone operator, film audiences may imagine love and freedom on the condition of momentarily forgetting the frames that have made these dreams possible.

ENDING IN NOTHING

The switchboard scene is the center of a symmetrical film framed by courtrooms, triangulated love, and pictorial representations of Larita: the return to England is marked by a famous metonymic dissolve which replaces a French poodle on a trunk at a waystation with an English bulldog. The celebrated economy of narrative exposition here also condenses the film's allegory of the futility of Larita's, or anyone's, struggle to escape frames, since the film's geographical circularity is another one. The lovers' carriage ride across flat wastelands ends in the Whittakers' moated estate, rendered as a series of oppressive interior frames: the doorway, bedposts, and mirror of Larita's room; the interior ogives that recall the courtroom, artist's studio, and French hotel; the wooden carvings of saints looming over the dining room table; the double landings and balustrades that frame Mrs. Whittaker's first entrance and Larita's final defiance. Thus, the austere rigidity of the judicial frames is duplicated in the domestic world, which gradually "judges" Larita in a manner just as arbitrary as the court's. The dining table repeats the jury room, as the social repeats the earlier legal and aesthetic verdicts.

It is instructive that the catalyst for the Whittakers' condemnation of Larita is a pictorial representation—the magazine photograph that cites Claude Robson's painting. Once again, the implication is that the gross distortion of "framing" human identity is also inescapable, like fate: it will come back because it is never absent. When her ex-husband's attorney shows her the magazine, Larita realizes that the truth cannot be concealed; her subsequent camera-smashing makes it seem as futile to wish human identity unframed, unread, or uninterpreted as it is to attack the mechanical instrument of the framing. If framing is like reading or seeing, it is inherent in existence.

In this context, Larita's alterations of her party dress and defiance of Mrs. Whittaker may signal an acquiescence in the inevitability of false constructions of human identity: since she cannot escape misrepresentation, Larita may as well play the "fallen" role assigned by her critics. Her final words to the courthouse photographers ("Shoot . . . there's nothing left to kill") establish an analogy between camera and weapon—one that Hitchcock would explore more explicitly in *Foreign Correspondent* and *Rear Window*. In *Easy Virtue*, the implication is that since photography is only another in a series of misrepresentations of a subject already shown to be constructed from the inescapable frames of prejudice, social convention, and art, it can do no further damage, certainly no more qualitative damage, than any other. Or, better: the necessity for framing dramatized in Larita's story brings to "nothing" our traditional, tenacious, human illusions of autonomous subjectivity, love, and meaning; once we understand that there is "nothing," in this sense, to shoot, the film ends.

Of course, Larita's defiance of the reporters does not deter them from "shooting." The implication for film criticism may be that hermeneutic interpretation— conceived as the attempt to establish the film's (or the director's, or even the viewer's) perspective on Larita's suffering—cannot be stopped, despite the film's thorough exposure of its futility: reading or seeing the film, interpreting its flickerings as characters, was the condition of arriving at its disillusioning end. *Easy Virtue* implies that film criticism, too, is a fated or necessary error, the result of which will be one more frame of "nothing."

7

The Ring: The Circularity of Reading

Silhouetted, seated children hang suspended from a turning carnival ride. In this silent film, we must supply their laughter or screams, just as we must imagine an individual identity behind or within their dark figures. The originating site of a story about the circularity of human love and ambition, the carnival and its rides showcase humans as inhabitants of a charade world where the signs of love and hate are indistinguishable and where human faces cannot be believed. At the same time, the children are nothing more than figures, cinematic "characters" whose existence is dependent upon a turning apparatus of another sort—a camera or a projector; as anonymous precursors to the named characters who follow, these silhouetted children may be figures for figuration, like Handel Fane in Murder! *Finally, viewers of* The Ring *may identify with the children, too, as customers kept in suspense, who have paid for seats in a place where—they've been promised—they will be manipulated or turned to look at the charade of life from a different perspective. How and whether that suspense is ended is the challenge of* The Ring.

OF RINGS

Like *The Lodger* and *Easy Virtue*, *The Ring* continues Hitchcock's interest in visual frames that depict reading as mistaking and desire as a byproduct of the arbitrary signs that make reading possible. The triangular frame that created the spurious identities of the lodger and Larita continues in *The Ring*; it alternates with another frame, the circle, to convey an even more jaundiced sense of the emptiness of reading and love. Hitchcock's narrative establishes that a ring, a

Figure 7.1: *The Ring* (1927). Canal + Images UK, Ltd.

promise, a wedding, or any other sign of love is worthless. Neither the snake bracelet given to Nelly by Jack's rival Corby nor the wedding ring given to Nelly by Jack correlates with any "authentic affect" she may be said to harbor—especially as that may be considered readable in another frequent sign, the smile. Instead, the film's two plotlines—Will Jack finally defeat Corby in the ring? Does Nelly truly love Corby or Jack?—are held in suspense even beyond the supposedly climactic bout. After we understand the outcome—Jack defeats Corby, Nelly loves Jack—the *meaning* of these "resolutions" remains just as deferred as the lodger's or Larita's true identity. Nelly's embrace of Jack and the referee's decision should be summative and performative signs that announce unambiguous new meaning; instead, both signs only engender new signs.

Critics have noticed that the film's title refers both to the pugilistic site where Jack hopes to establish his identity and to the wedding ring he gives to Nelly.[1] However, the title is equally applicable to many other images: the carnival rides (the flying chairs, the merry-go-round); the wheel of tickets that spins as spectators rush to buy admission to the fight; the very idea of a "round" of boxing; the snake bracelet that encircles Nelly's arm; the concentric ripples of the pond caused when the bracelet falls off; the button that for a moment substitutes for the wedding ring; Jack's punching bag; the spinning jazz records; and the film itself, a circular narrative that begins and ends reflexively, in visual spectacles performed before audiences. These multiple referents sorely test the ostensive function of signs—as if the meaning of the word "the" were being mocked. If "the" ring has potentially universal referents it may also have none: the circularity of human endeavor—especially of love and reading—seems more grimly pronounced in *The Ring* than in *The Lodger* or *Easy Virtue*. For example, the credits of *The Ring* appear over a long shot of a boxing match in which the crowd surrounding the boxers occupies far more of the frame than do the tiny, nearly invisible boxers; the composition suggests that the film's interest lies as much in the experience of viewing boxing or in reading *The Ring* as in boxing itself. At bottom, the film audience may itself be "the ring," a crowd assembled around a visual spectacle which it is under a mandate to view and read. In the film's conclusion, Nelly also becomes our surrogate, the interpreter of the bout's significance. At first seemingly divided in her loyalties, Nelly finally commits herself in a climax that mocks the audience's resolution of suspense in an ending: choosing Jack over Corby has always, already been shown to be an empty preference for interchangeable entities. Like so many rival lovers who seem at first to form serious contrasts—the lodger and Joe, Filton and Whittaker, Devlin and Alex, Midge and Judy, Thornhill and Vandamm, Armstrong and Karl Manfred—Jack and Corby may in the end be only ciphers, interchangeable figures, or schematic points on a triangle. *The Ring* is an excellent film in which to observe that any victory of one lover over the another and any winnings can never end the suspense of characters who remain undecidable.

The viewer's unchanging suspense is discernible in the way the film allegorizes its audience. Just as the film viewer is likened to the fawning, self-congratulatory Buntings at the end of *The Lodger* or to the photographers who frame nothing at the end of *Easy Virtue*, so in *The Ring* we may read our own delusions of rational decision-making in the critical moment when the continuously fickle Nelly finally chooses to root for nearly defeated Jack; our rationality is further impugned by the suggestion that Jack revives *because* of her choice. Everywhere in *The Ring* the conventions of meaning making are established then mocked, leaving the audience with only the taste of ashes as its reward for reading. In what follows, we shall see how *The Ring*'s narrative of the futility of desire and accomplishment broadens the idea of reading's circularity, to include all phases of life and its interpretation, leaving the audience to ponder whether the film's title may also evoke the familiar circle of hermeneutics.[2]

SEMICIRCLE I

A vertiginous multiplication of circles, of frantic and enforced gaiety, accompanies the scenes of carnival pleasure depicted even before Jack's story begins, as if the universe might be conceived as only an indiscriminate heap of circular narratives from which the viewer might choose any single one—any rider of a swing, for instance—and meet with a fate the same as Jack's.[3] The abyssal or Dionysian effect here repeats the opening of *Easy Virtue*, in which the highlighting of the Filtons' divorce proceedings randomly selects it from countless other narratives in progress; this opening looks forward to *Rear Window*'s, where Jeff's selection of Thorwald's story is one arbitrary choice from a potential of many ongoing narratives that might differ from it only in degree. In *Psycho* this assumption is implied by the way the camera chooses to enter one of many hotel windows. These beginnings suggest that the story about to be narrated is but a synecdoche for a universe of similar stories; the idea that the random selections may yield analogous results may be Hitchcock's cinematic variant of Nietzsche's eternal recurrence of the same.

The Ring also opens with the image a round drum being beaten, in which is forecast the film's thinking about the undecidable nature of percussion or battery: a sign fusing both pleasure (music, rhythm, the merry-go-round) and aggression (boxing). A similar correlation between circles and undecidability appears in the carnival test of strength in which a mallet is used to pound a seesaw to "ring" a circular bell. Of what possible significance is the bell? What is the meaning of any sport or game? A numerical scale registering mallet blows is as pointless as the referee's counting to determine the significance of the outcome of a boxing match: all that results is an interchangeability, a tautological equation of numbers and identities. From this perspective, sports may have the unintended effect of disclosing how the *in*significance of character inheres in its easy conversion into numbers.

The cultural critique of Western competition is laid out at the outset, just as in satires of the mass media in *The Lodger* or the judiciary in *Easy Virtue*. For example, the round bell that begins and ends the boxing rounds is an arbitrary marker, like the bell at the end of the seesaw. The fact that these circular sources of meaningless percussive sound occur in a silent film encourages viewers to consider the separability of visual and aural signs, as in Munch's *The Scream* or the decontextualized scream that begins *The Lodger*, or in *The Ring*, in the images of carnivalgoers' grotesque mouths twisted, it may be, in shouts of delight or of horror. These disjunctions between sight and sound prompt consideration of the arbitrary nature of society's "normal" rewards for success and of conventional distinctions between pleasure and aggression, music and noise or sound and silence.

The nauseating possibility of the loss of such distinctions is deepened by the scenes of children at a carnival sideshow throwing balls at a target which, when hit, releases a black man into a dunking-pool. The innocence of their supposed shouts of joy is undermined by their seemingly greater pleasure when, clearly outside the rules of the game, they hurl eggs at the man, who cowers away from them before being hit in the eye. This sequence suggests that the boundary between pleasure and aggression is just as fictional and unstable as the line between what is game and what isn't. A policeman standing behind the boys smiles and laughs at their outside-the-rules violence, so even a representative of the law sanctions this collapse of distinction. (Lest we conclude the law is *reliably* blind—in a world where nothing is reliable—a second policeman shoos the boys away.) In a detail that recurs often in the film, the bared teeth of the audience's smiles occupy the center of the frame: the same sign may convey, undecidably, "innocent" laughter or sublimated sadism. The extent of any racial motivation for the pleasure of aggression is elided here, as in Jack's later qualifying fight with a contender whom the titles identify as a "nigger," but that is just the point: just as Jack's professional motives in advancing through the ranks cannot be separated from his jealousy of Bob, so the children's "harmless" fun cannot be separated from racism. To compound this undecidability, the opposite of racial prejudice—full tolerance—is also exhibited: one of Jack's trainers, an unnamed black man, appears as a welcome friend and guest in Jack's house and is treated with equality by Jack and his white handlers—surely an atypical screen presence, given the conventional stereotypes of twenties filmmaking. The effect is to leave the issue of racial aggression in suspense.

These early deconstructions of sign and referent are soon developed in the main diegesis of Jack, Nelly, and Corby, suggesting the way the supposed meaning of boxing and wedding rings—competition, achievement, love—are only new signs in the "glamorously dangerous charade" of life, signs that may represent pleasure as well as aggression.[4] For example, Jack smiles when Corby seems undecided as to whether to accept the carnival challenge; however, we can't know whether either man's gesture is feigned. Our suspense here repeats the undecidability of the policeman's laughter at the "mischievous" children. As the narration continues, the smiles of Jack and Corby may indicate hostility more often than affection, and the smiles of Nelly are never a reliable guide to any interior affect. In the same way *The Lodger* implies that a wrapped face conceals no true interior and *Easy Virtue* conceives of the self as nothing, *The Ring* dramatizes a theme apparent in all of Hitchcock's films—the impossibility of knowing affect from a face.

Also as in *The Lodger* or *Easy Virtue*, human identity cannot be divorced from an artificial triangulation that pre-exists and frames it. There is no true identity to the lodger apart from his rivalry with Joe for Daisy; there is no true identity to Larita apart from the several triangles by which she is socially constructed. In *The Ring* we come to understand Jack only in the light of his rivalry with Corby for Nelly. The existence of any pre-linguistic or pre-triangulated Jack is nullified when he is introduced by a man carrying a placard; the arbitrary nature of his identity is suggested by the *inversion* of the sign bearing his name. The idea that frames create identity is rendered visually by the aperture in the tent through which Nelly and Corby first view each other, prior to the bout with Jack. Here the woman as prize or signified spoils of competition seems to exist both inside and outside the narration. Within the tent, boxing is mere battery or percussion—a repetitive striking that results in one person, equatable with signs on posters, substituting for another in a ring. From this perspective, the implications of "the ring" and "the round" are mutually reinforcing: life is a succession of strikings or blows, within an arbitrary space, whose goal is the acquisition of something that seems "beyond the ring" of such pointless striving; however, in this quest, each new contest (or "round") is as circular an endeavor as the one that preceded it. With a technique often praised for its economy of exposition, the film records the "progress" of fights when attendants hold up cards announcing its rounds; this technique—like the montage of fighters' names on posters later in the film—has the effect of equating human identity with dumb struggle, numbers and signs.

Signs like Corby's gift of the snake bracelet or the cards in the fortune-telling scene also evoke the triangular or circular framing of identity. After Jack's defeat, Nelly covers up the bracelet—the sign of triangulation or perhaps for the audience a sign of signs. It is never possible to determine which man she loves; the undecidability of her affection paints romantic love as the illusory reward of aggressive rivalry transferred from one side of the ropes to the other. Nelly's hiding the bracelet is the equivalent of Jack's and Corby's unreadable smiles: it is not that affection is being dissimulated but that affection, like everything else, is an unknowable figure, like a bracelet, a ring, or a smile. The idea of identity as arbitrary sign is also depicted in the scene where the gypsy tells Nelly her fortune. She spreads the cards in a circle—a gesture that defines the reading moment as the selection of an arbitrary sign from a continuous and interchangeable series. Choosing a card from the deck is like choosing one divorce case from the many listed in the newspaper in *Easy Virtue* or choosing one narrative from the many stories available at the carnival.

Because the gypsy's prediction of a "tall, rich man" in Nelly's life could apply to either Jack or Corby, the assumption of natural referents for signs is undermined. Nelly's mute rapture cannot disclose the object of her desire: does she love Jack or Corby? Jack's identification with the king of diamonds ("That's me. I'm going to make real money now") dramatizes his illusions of identity and his blindness to the merely numerical distinction of one card (competitor, human) from another. The scene ends with the gypsy turning up the king of hearts: the undermining of Jack's place now makes the triangulation of Nelly, Jack, and Corby complete. Throughout this scene, the equation between identities and cards makes their cipher-like, interchangeable quality apparent.

The arbitrariness of Jack's engagement to Nelly—its dysfunction as a performative—is emphasized in Nelly's reverie on the day Jack fights to qualify as Corby's sparring partner. Distracted as she works at her ticket booth, she imagines Jack being counted out, and her facial expression becomes undecidable: it may indicate anxiety on Jack's behalf but it also may reflect anger at herself for speculating on the prospect that his loss might not, after all, be unwelcome in the light of Corby's attentions to her. Altruism, self-interest, guilt and wish-fulfilment, mixed with indeterminate erotic longings—these "affects" become indistinguishable. The certainty that Jack's victory must automatically mean marriage is further unsettled by the emphasis on the contingent quality of Nelly's receipt of his message: although the wire conveying the news finally arrives, the lazy messenger, who would rather watch the merry-go-round than deliver it—dramatizes the arbitrary link between promise and fulfillment, between the sending and receipt of messages. His wayward delivery in turn makes clear that nothing in Jack's victory *necessitates* his marriage to Nelly. In a larger sense, it makes clear to the viewer that no sign can mandate marriage. The king of diamonds and king of hearts are in some sense interchangeable. A snake bracelet may constitute a promise just as much as an engagement does. The film's second half demonstrates that marriage is no more inherent in signs or in an official engagement than love is inherent in marriage.

SEMICIRCLE 2

The film's deconstruction of the performative function of rings and any other signs continues in the wedding ceremony, which Hitchcock renders comically, as the presumption to human dignity of the carnivalesque. Just as wedding attire cannot transform the tall man, midget, or Siamese twins, neither the ring nor the words of the service can establish Jack's relationship with Nelly. The ceremony is as little performative as the gypsy's prognostications. The metaphysical discourses of the church suggest the way that speech acts are civilization's dissimulation of—and its attempt to halt—the suspense of the infinite unfolding of the carnivalesque world of the postal. When the Siamese twins cannot decide upon a pew, the film's satire of the concept of "union" in marriage is rendered in the mode of the grotesque. The wedding ring's status as just another arbitrary sign is made plain when Jack's manager momentarily confuses it with a button. The fact that we never hear Nelly's response to the minister's questions further destabilizes the supposed performative of marriage. As Derrida notes in "Signature/Event/Context," the performative property of signs is conceivable only in the impossible case that their contexts are completely iterable: the unrepeatable vagaries of any single marriage service are obvious from this highly idiosyncratic event.[5] All weddings are sui generis. The future-oriented promises of the wedding ceremony are likened to the fortune teller's claim to a privileged ability to read: both are humorously subverted when she is conked on the head by a horseshoe. The horseshoe, a mere sign like a ring or the words of the marriage service, "means" only muteness, only percussion. It is as incapable of ensuring significance as the principal characters' smiles, which are also exchanged at the banquet, where protestations of friendship between Jack and Corby cannot be distinguished from threats of revenge.

The undecidability of human affect here is deepened when Jack and Corby spar in front of Nelly and other women. Here an analogy between the ring that encircles sparring boxers and the marriage ring shows the undecidability of whatever "interior" is mutually joined or framed. Indeed, sparring is an apt description of the supposedly normal relations among the three main characters: aggression and suspicion that are not yet wholly manifested. As a contender, Jack's progress to a shot at the title is rendered in a series of dissolves revealing new prizefight posters, on which his name gradually ascends. In this way we witness the way a career fraught with conflict, jealousy, and violence can be equated with a change in the position of signs. The upward movement of Jack's name on the signs is accompanied by images of the changing seasons—blowing leaves, falling snow, spring flowers. It is as if time—or the toil of life, the struggle to achieve—is envisioned as the ascent of one name above another up a scale whose terminus is a tautology: the identity of the first is the victor over the second. The meaning of Jack's life is defined by the signs of his "place"; it is as if the physiological battery that bespatters the ring floor with blood is necessary to the movement of the signs to which it is reducible.

The long party sequence at Jack's apartment unites the film's depictions of aggression and desire in the flappers, whose dancing gesticulations also resemble sparring: exhausted, the dancers flop into chairs, to be revived by waiters who wave napkins over their faces. The hallucinatory effects that conclude the party sequence contribute to the overall effect of the unfixed, indeterminable, vertiginous nature of artificially induced desire: the shots of the spinning record join the empty, circular hedonism of the dance with the image of the ring, while the elongated, undulating piano keys make music itself seem fluid. The scene evokes Nietzsche's principle of the Dionysian—the dissolution of form, individuation, and discrimination under the influence of the inchoate, the erotic, the intoxicating, the musical. Indeed, it ends in a breakdown between the real and the imaginary: Jack looks on the Dionysian scene in a mirror that he sees through a door frame and hallway. His facial expression may at first appear to be longing. Is he tempted by the promise of oblivion, of some escape from the world's charade of signs like triangles or rings? The sequence ends in Jack's vision of Nelly and Corby kissing, a scene whose diegetic status can't be determined. Like the "real" sequences, it is inseparable from frames. Here, existence as framed, sign-induced sparring becomes indistinguishable from a complete ontological breakdown, suggesting the final uncertainty, that the world itself may be only dream or figure.

Donald Spoto was one of the first to question the film's supposedly happy ending.[6] The hollow lifelessness of the victory that finally makes Jack eligible to fight Corby is rendered visually in the flat champagne: once more, neither triumph nor its sign necessarily results in the "signified prize," Nelly. That Jack's violence can shift toward Nelly—he now stalks her and grabs at her dress— reveals anew the equation between of love and aggression, which culminates in the juxtaposed scenes of Jack confronting Corby in the nightclub and in the championship match. In the first, Jack's animosity is given expression on the dance floor; in the second, Jack's defeat of Corby is accomplished only after Nelly's presence in the audience seems first to jeopardize, then to enhance his chances. In each case it is triangulation that determines behavior and outcome; as a result, the closing embrace in *The Ring* seems as delusional as *The Lodger*'s: in both cases, the lovers' union is represented as ignorance of the arbitrary nature of the signs that have governed their fate.

In *The Ring*, the lovers' embrace is quickly followed by the discovery of the snake bracelet Nelly had cast aside, in a supposedly decisive gesture demonstrating her newfound, unequivocal love for Jack. But when Corby throws it away, we may see in his iteration the undermining of Nelly's act: neither wearing nor discarding the sign can be significant. The snake bracelet was always, already insignificant, its only meaning some illusion extended to or constructed upon it. To discard the metal bracelet may indicate some hope of escaping the ring or tyranny of signs, but Nelly's kisses and smiles at the victorious Jack are, like Corby's shrug, simply new invitations to interpretations, new rings. It is impossible to be signless, and film itself is no exception to this fate. It is as if *The Ring* leads viewers to the threshold of an understanding of both the misery and inescapability of life conceived as a ring of signs, as figure, but then must renounce even this decidable theme because it, too, is a figure. The film's acknowledgment of its participation in the dilemma it narrates is signaled in many reflexive images.

In a recent essay, Tom Gunning argued that the earliest films should be understood as a "cinema of attractions," that is, as a pure visual spectacle whose aesthetic is analogous to that of the fairground.[7] The reflexivity of *The Ring* begins in its opening, in the fairground scene, in which the restive audience outside the boxing tent is encouraged to come inside and witness a visual spectacle. This scene works on several levels: it replicates the experience of film viewers, caught up in the illusions of commercial artifice, and of film critics, too, who are invited to pass beyond the screen of exterior appearances and into the more privileged space of the referents of the barkers' words. Film criticism is a hermeneutic exercise in which a search for the inner identity of characters and the referents of its figures is both inevitable and futile. The reflexive parallel between film and carnival was not original with Hitchcock: Wiene's *The Cabinet of Doctor Caligari* (1920) famously explored the circus sideshow as a metaphor for film. In that Expressionist classic, the mad doctor's display of his murderous somnambulist takes place inside a tent. Initially skeptical spectators are persuaded to enter by Caligari's promise but later appalled at what they see. (One member of the audience regrets his entry when the somnambulist predicts his death at the end of the day.) It always seems as if the relentless message of mortality conveyed by reading might have been known in advance, but no: *Dum lego, spiro.*[8] In *The Lodger* Hitchcock had imagined the music hall as a site whose beckoning accelerated the encounter with death. In *Easy Virtue* he had envisioned photographic representation as a kind of shooting. *The Ring* depicts film viewers and critics as ushered into a scene of reading that exposes signs as lures that reveal mute battery. He returned to this metaphor in *The 39 Steps* and *Strangers on a Train*, where the lure of the extraordinary spectacle of music hall or carnival prompts viewers to pay entrance fees, only to discover that signs betokening a site of pleasure convey news of death. But while art's redundant message of inevitable mortality might seem predictable, it never deters reading or viewing.

The Ring allegorizes this redundancy in the interpretation of art. One of its title's many senses may imply the "ring" or redundancy of criticism—the hermeneutic circle. For example, the scene of the audience lured into the tent is preceded by a long sequence in which carnival rides and sideshows are depicted.

The merry-go-round and flying chairs employ circular motion to thrill those who have paid for this pleasure. Of course, film itself is generated from circular reels whose turning supposedly provokes pleasure. But we've seen that *The Ring*'s circularity—of truths that ought to have been known ahead of time—concerns the emptiness of the victories of ambition and romantic union; the ending of the film closes a circle that defines an interior emptiness that might have been apparent in the boxing match. As a dumbshow of inarticulation, aggression, and mortality, the ultimate revelation of boxing and love might have been known from the start. So film criticism, on an Enlightenment quest for the truth behind the appearances of its subject matter, finds in the end only what it always should have known.

8

Spellbound: The Suspense of Black Marks on White

To be spellbound is to be in suspense.

At the center of Spellbound *is the trauma that shows the origins of John Ballantine's phobic symptoms. He recalls a terrible childhood experience—his slide down the side of steps that pushed his brother into fatally impaling himself on black wrought-iron fencing. Now John seems to understand why he has been haunted by "parallel black lines"—indentations made by a fork, train tracks, ski tracks. (As a sign whose referent is put in doubt, the parallel lines are this film's MacGuffin.) He recalls the traumatic scene after skiing to a precipice with Dr. Constance Peterson, who is trying to restore his memory of what really happened to Dr. Anthony Edwardes, the man he believes he killed. In a "Eureka!" moment, John concludes that he had unconsciously linked the skiing death of Edwardes with the impalement of his brother and that both were accidental. His new insight may explain his delusion that he killed Edwardes, the psychiatric authority whom he had impersonated as director of Green Manors sanatorium. In other words, the dark lines of John's ski tracks have brought him to a precipice of thought where he confronts figuration or metaphor: one scene is also another.*

This revelatory hanging figure lasts no longer than a second on the screen. The speed of the boy's impalement makes it seem an ellipsis generated in the viewer's mind by John's inexorable slide down the railing toward the pointed fence. Thus the film's seeming resolution of its MacGuffin is a blank or absence that must be filled in or marked, as if the origin of trauma coincided with the origin of signs in figures. The trajectory of the image of "parallel black lines on white" in Spellbound *thus moves from the diegetic source of meaning,*

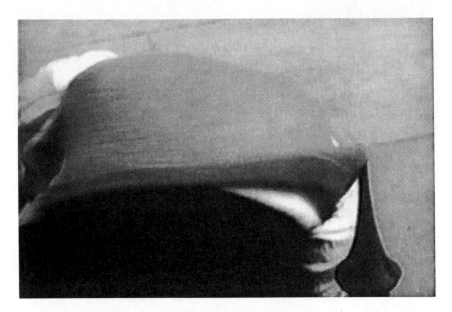

Figure 8.1: *Spellbound* (1945). Courtesy of Buena Vista Television.

through its integration into psychoanalytic theory, to the film audience's act of ellipsis and finally to the film critic's scene of writing. These black marks on white, in imagination or text, are either generated by a hanging figure or are hanging figures themselves, marks whose meaning is suspended.

The suspense of meaning becomes clear when even after John's "Eureka!" moment, new undecidability ensues. His flashback cannot, after all, prove that his brother's death was accidental, since there is never a way viewers can read motive from this boy's or anyone's face; we can only take John at his word that his feelings for his brother were wholly benign as he started to slide. The parallel between the deaths of John's brother and Edwardes now raises the issue of whether Edwardes's fall was accompanied by any aggressive wish on John's part. That these doubts are more than simply a logical possibility is made clear in the scene when John approaches Brulov with a straight razor. Brulov certainly interprets his action as aggressive, and while Constance dismisses the idea, John himself is not so sure, and viewers are left with undecidability. These doubts unsettle confidence in human recollection and intention, but that outcome should hardly be surprising in a Freudian environment that presupposes Oedipal aggression and the rivalry of brothers. Doubts are raised about not only John's understanding of himself, but also Brulov's, Constance's, and Murchison's. And of course if all characters may be deluded, what of the viewer who identifies with them? If we cannot read decidable meaning in visual signs, in outward behavior, or in black marks on white, then MacGuffins like John's flashback will always be hanging figures that promise but withhold meaning. In

Spellbound, *this disillusioning recoil to every act of reading is underscored when it becomes obvious that Ballantine's self-discovery cannot wholly absolve him of guilt after all, when the police inform him that Edwardes was found with a bullet in his back. No "Eureka moment" is allowed to last unquestioned in Hitchcock. The coda of* Spellbound—*in which the figure of the killer emerges only by chance, from Murchison's slip of the tongue—merely affirms what its plot has all along made clear: neither logic nor psychoanalysis can establish the truth of hanging figures, of the arbitrary black-and-white signs of film or writing.*

TWO OPENINGS

Those signs begin in the credits, or first beginning, which appear over black images of dry leaves blowing about bare saplings, against a white background, a juxtaposition that suggests an enervating desuetude or decay of signs even before the film's second beginning can unfold. The instability of signs will later be more boldly asserted in the credits of films like *Psycho* and *The Birds*; in the credits of *Spellbound* these hints look forward to the film's depiction of love, whose beginning is marked by the dry leaves in Constance's hair, and to its MacGuffin, contrasted lines of black on white. (If *Spellbound*'s credits resemble its MacGuffin in this way, then in retrospect the referents of the signs "Gregory Peck" and "Ingrid Bergman" may be just as undecidable as those of "John Ballantine" or "Constance Peterson," implying that the world itself, not just the film, may be only figuration.) *Spellbound*'s second opening follows its credits two epigraphs. The fact that there are two openings and that the second is itself double raises the issue of doubleness in this film about double lines and double identities: when John is most frustrated with Constance's attempts to cure him, he (twice) angrily denounces her "doubletalk." *Spellbound* narrates the double, figural discourses of love and psychoanalysis.

The doubleness of the second beginning consists of two parts: (1) an epigraph that consists of elliptical quote from *Julius Caesar*—"The fault is not in our stars . . . but in ourselves.—Shakespeare"; (2) this anonymous scrolled title:

Our story deals with psychoanalysis, the method by which modern science treats the emotional problems of the sane. The analyst seeks only to induce the patient to talk about his hidden problems to open the locked doors of his mind. Once the complexes that have been disturbing the patient are uncovered and interpreted the illness and confusion disappear . . . and the devils of unreason are driven from the human soul.

Andrew Britton points out that the quotation from Shakespeare has nothing to do with psychological disorders.[1] The speaker, masked by the ellipsis, is the villain Cassius. (The absence of the character's name conflates author and character in a mistake common to hermenetuic readings that try to identify a sought-after "view of the author" with the view of a character; in the case of *Spellbound*,

such critical positions usually equate "Hitchcock's view" with "Constance's.")
The "fault" Cassius alludes to is the fact that he and Brutus are unfairly "un-
derlings," subordinate to Caesar. In thus equating mental illness with inferior
rank or status, the first epigraph works to question psychoanalytic investigation:
for what cause of suffering, after all, do psychiatrists search, and for what reasons? To what extent is mental health the same as social position? To what
standard of normality should patients adjust? Interestingly, a professional hier-
archy among psychiatrists is clearly set forth in the film's first minutes; it is
later critiqued by Constance, Brulov, and Murchison.[2] Murchison's willingness
to kill to maintain his position, while remaining a symbol of psychological
normalcy, goes far to undermine definitions of neurosis espoused by the psychiatric establishment. Michel Foucault's argument that psychoanalytic discourses are complicit with regimes of power is suggested by this emphasis on
professional status. It is also brought home to the viewer by the psychiatric
reliance on coercive force when the talking cure fails—witness Peterson's pre-
scription of drugs for Garmes and Brulov's use of a bromide for Ballantine. The
contradictions of psychoanalysis as therapy are part of the film's cultural critique
from the outset, and any supposed Shakespearean endorsement in the epigraph
recoils against itself.

As to the scrolled "tribute" to psychoanalysis, the figure of "opening the
locked doors" of the mind—where this phrase is not paradoxical—reduces the
work of analysis to an easy gesture.[3] Britton has perceptively shown how this
introductory statement's blatant mixture of empirical and mystical vocabulary
also subverts psychoanalysis by establishing psychoanalysis "as a kind of secular
religion."[4] Its universal acceptance is challenged openly by the patients Carmichael and Garmes and by frequent allusions to professional heterodoxy, but
the major contradiction of psychiatry comprises the film's plot, in which Peterson must violate the rule against counter-transference in order to achieve a cure.
The analyst who falls in love with a patient dramatizes the conflict between the
double discourses of Spellbound, love and psychoanalysis, that critics have uneasily sought to reconcile.[5] In any case, the idea that a film might discredit, not
illustrate, its epigraphs is not a new one for Hitchcock; he plays with the contradiction in The Manxman and in The Man Who Knew Too Much (1956).[6] The
epigraphs and their suspended referentiality are only the first of many hanging
figures.

DOORS

In Spellbound, "Eureka!" moments of seeming discovery are no different from
ordinary acts of recognition and naming: all eventually give way to disillusionment. The process begins with Peterson's greeting of the man she believes to
be Dr. Edwardes. Her falling in love with an imposter becomes the film's major
allegory of the "spellbound" effects of misrecognition, a delusion just as dangerous as Ballantine's amnesia and role-playing. Peterson's moment of forma-

tive misreading occurs as she approaches the door to "Edwardes's" room clutching "his" book: in this way, Hitchcock depicts love as a delusion like hermeneutics—the search for the extra-textual "author" or authority who stands behind the text as a guarantor of its validity. Constance's spellbound love for fraudulent psychiatric authority invalidates in advance each of the film's double discourses. An ironic perspective on this delusion is provided by Miklos Rozsa's swelling violins and in the exaggerated "language of the eyes" that accompanies the characters' transfixed gazes; it is fully established when the lovers' kiss is juxtaposed with shots of opening doors that recall the ambiguity of the epigraphs' "tributes" to psychoanalysis. The embrace of Peterson and "Edwardes" depicts love as made possible by a misidentification that now opens a potentially endless series of ("locked"?) doors, but any new truths that emerge from behind these doors must be bracketed by the error that began to open them. The doors also subvert psychoanalysis. The epigraph had imagined doors as concealing the "hidden problems of the mind," but what is the intrinsic value of psychoanalysis if doors open without it? Viewers may also wonder *whose* mind is being "opened"? On first viewing, the relation between Peterson and "Edwardes" (student and mentor, reader and writer) predicts their love would lead to *her* mind being opened by her grateful absorption of the knowledge of the authority she so admires—an illusion that quickly becomes obvious. Repeat viewers may wonder whether these newly opened doors also include such "truths" as John's "Eureka!" claim of innocence in the deaths of his brother and Edwardes. Finally, the serial door openings also suggest the ultimately interminable nature of psychoanalysis conceived on the model of the search for a psychic referent for signs. Whether opened by love or psychoanalysis, these doors promise only suspense.

IMPOSTERS

In beginning *Spellbound* with a woman who falls in love with an amnesiac imposter, Hitchcock continues to explore the parabasis of identity he had introduced in his early films, where the very introduction of characters initiates doubts as to their identity: the muffled lodger emerging from the fog remains enigmatic even to contemporary film criticism; the contested definition of Larita in court culminates in her realization that she is "nothing"; *The Ring*'s introduction of Jack's name on an inverted placard indicates his arbitrary, "reversible" identity. In *Spellbound* misrecognition is dramatized in the pervasiveness of acting, the glamorously dangerous charade that blocks all attempts to know who or what is being recognized. While it may appear that Ballantine discovers a true identity and Constance always possesses one, the contrast is misleading. Her protean identity is reflected in her quick adoption of a succession of roles— at the Empire Hotel, as a repentant schoolteacher eager to make amends to her husband; at Penn Station, as a wife justifying her husband's fainting; at Brulov's house, as a newlywed. These disguises retroactively expose her profession as a psychoanalyst to be only another such dispensable role; thus, when she attempts to reassert it—in treating John despite her love for him—the result is the ludicrous scene at the Empire Hotel when she passionately kisses John, saying, "Love has nothing to do with this." As for John, his unconscious impersonation is replaced by an equation between his identity and the arbitrary letters, JB, found on his cigarette case. He then becomes John Brown and John Ballantine, though like Constance his supposedly authentic identity is made possible by new impersonations: at Penn Station, he acts as a husband suffering from fainting spells; at Grand Central Station, as "a man passionately kissing a woman" as a train is about to depart. Of course, both of these roles very closely approximate what viewers are supposed to believe is Ballantine's true identity: although he is not Constance's husband, he does suffer from spells; although they are not lovers, they act as lovers.[7] These episodes of iteration, of acting what one is, blur the line between acting and identity; they put acting and identity into the category of doubletalk that John condemns but the viewer soon finds to be unavoidable. When is Constance *really* a psychiatrist and when is she acting as a psychiatrist? When is the couple *really* in love and when are they acting in love? Who is the analyst and who the analysand? (At Brulov's house, Constance insists that the patient take the bed and the analyst the couch, but as matters transpire these roles are reversed, too.) In short, how can viewers distinguish the "real" Constance Peterson or John Ballantine and their enacted roles?

The impossibility of distinguishing real from forged identities is not limited to the principal characters. Brulov acts from the outset, when he pretends to accept Constance's explanation that she and John are newlyweds; he acts again when he diverts John with idle conversation while preparing his bromide-laced glass of milk. And in an acknowledgment that acting may be fundamental to the talking cure, Alex encourages John to talk by saying that he will play the part of his "father image." Each of these deceptions by the film's most valorized psychiatrist raises retroactive questions about Constance. Suppose that between disguises she becomes again an "authentic psychiatrist"—how would such a non-acting character act?

This unending charade is exposed in many scenes of false recognition—moments when apparently genuine communication is shown to be false after all. The initial introduction of "Edwardes" to Constance and the staff of Green Manors is a glaring instance, but not even the first. Constance's analysis of Mary Carmichael results only in their both admitting that lying in analysis is expected; her conversation with Garmes never betrays her alarm at his worsening condition. Later, her response to her curious colleagues on returning from her walk with "Edwardes" defiantly conceals her experiences. Constance's dialogue with the Empire Hotel detective seems typical of the false interchange between characters with invented personas. The interchanges of the staff psychiatrists with Ballantine and Murchison are charades. Even when John's "authentic" character appears to be revealed, his immediate arrest on suspicion of murder requestions that authenticity. When we finally see him again with Constance at the end of the film, at the same gate where they earlier acted the part of lovers, there is little reason to believe we are now in the presence of a man and a woman with identities truer than those disclosed in the earlier charade in front of the gatekeeper. As for Murchison, his elaborated confession–cum–dream interpretation in the presence of Constance shows that the process of the revelation of true identity is literally self-destroying. In *Torn Curtain* Hitchcock depicts a world given over to phony dialogue; whenever in *Spellbound* characters seem engaged in some truthful meeting of the minds, these spellbound moments are subsequently exposed as illusory "Eureka!" moments—false, temporary stays of interminable suspense.

SPELLBOUND READING

As parabasis, character is "always, already" constructed—that is, lacking any "ground" or "norm" of behavior against which to measure subsequent deviations or roles. In his illuminating study of *The Phantom of the Cinema*, Lloyd Michaels argues that in the work of directors like Ingmar Bergman or Errol Morris, character in film is frequently depicted as a series of shifting surfaces concealing no core of inner selfhood; in the films of Hitchcock, Michaels's thesis finds additional substantiation.[8] But while Hitchcock's protagonists are indeed ciphers of identity, his films also narrate the *viewer's* "spellbound" and mistaken act of reading. In previous chapters we've seen that the idea of viewing entailing necessary error is inherent in the films' reflexive dimensions: in obtuse or deluded surrogate viewers, like the Buntings in *The Lodger*, the jurors in *Easy Virtue*, or the ringside crowds in *The Ring*; in repeated reminders of the necessity to frame visual experience; and in the likening of character to the flickering—the *clignotements*—of film itself. Like the characters we construct as real, we viewers have little alternative but to affix identity onto visual phenomena and name what we see. Like Constance introduced to her new supervisor, we name—as, for example, "Dr. Edwardes"—and assume that the attribution is real. But after false identities are discarded, each new act of designation constitutes another framing, another misreading of figures that continue to hang.

The successive quality of misinterpretation is demonstrated in the dream interpretation sequences.

Andrew Britton has shown that the analysts' interpretation of the dream is based on a pre-Freudian rather than psychoanalytic model: understood as corresponding point for point with historical events rather than with condensed or displaced instincts, the dream is interpreted as a code or rebus—for example, the "great pair of wings" chasing John becomes a clue to "San Gabriel Valley." Britton shows that the dream may also be read as an expression of Ballantine's Oedipal anxieties, and both analysts miss this sense. Britton's suggestion proposes a *truer* reading for the one it criticizes; on the other hand, Hitchcock's sequence may also challenge *any* interpretation of the visual, even Britton's.[9] For example, John's dream begins with his famous recollection of the "gambling house" without walls, "just a bunch of curtains with eyes painted on them" and a man "walking along with a long pair of scissors cutting all the drapes in half." None of the analysts interprets the *cutting* of the painted eyes, though Murchison later identifies them as those of the guards at Green Manors. Many critics of *Spellbound*, noting Dalí's participation, connect this scene with the eyeball-slicing opening of *Un Chien Andalou* (1928), and because this intertextual link would also be open to intellectually astute psychiatrists of 1945, its omission from the dream interpretation may further distance the viewers from Brulov and Peterson.

Their indifference to the image of *sliced eyes on curtains* (equaling *screens?*) may suggest to the viewer a connection between the intertextual referents (Dalí's film) and the diegetic (Green Manors and a gambling house). In this analogy, a film like Dalí's or Hitchcock's may be imagined as a site like a sanatorium whose promise of therapy or answers is unreliable—a matter of chance, like the operating assumption of a gambling house. The patients are like both gamblers and the film audience who will not, after all, receive true guidance from the "directors" in whose establishments they have been temporarily placed.

These figures also provide the reason for the permanent disillusionment of art and therapy. On the one hand, the painted eyes, which Murchison likens to the guards, may also suggest the film audience, *with its eyes on screens*. In this allegory, a film audience—taken in by the film's ostensible endorsement of psychoanalysis—will at first be identified with Harry, the muscular enforcer of psychiatric interpretation. Once the weakness of that interpretation is exposed, the cutting of those guard-eyes would register a kind of protest against it: if adopting the perspective of the film's beginning makes the viewer part of the psychiatric police, then in retrospect such a position should be resisted. On the other hand, whenever the painted eyes are cut, new eyes on drapes are immediately revealed behind them, suggesting the way *any* rejected perspective (including the psychoanalytic) is replaced by some new and erroneous perspective that must also in its turn be cut, and so on interminably. The eyes of Cartesian, hermeneutic perspectivalism hang on the curtains, as figures; when they are discovered to be illusions they are cut, but only to be replaced by new hanging figures in a process that will never end.

In the interpretation of John's dream, the identity of the man with scissors has remained unremarked. An analogy between the film director and the *man who cuts* is especially plausible in the light of the sequence's allusion to Dali and *Un Chien Andalou*. (In chapter 13 the analogy between Norman Bates and Alfred Hitchcock as *rapid cutters* is discussed.) In this allegory, the director's exercise of artistic selectivity—the editing that constitutes film—always, already pre-empts any possibility of seeing the narrative subject matter whole and in the round, truthfully. Film editing is like the frame of Rembrandt's *Flayed Ox*, something repressed in the process of making figures visible that also makes their display artificial. The challenge of purging cinematic representation of such framing may have been part of the impetus behind the making of *Rope*. But the inevitable contradictions of an "uncut film" simply show again that the process of exposing cutting out defective construction through newly edited construction is interminable, like the door-openings of thought or other hanging figures.

Hitchcock's camera work in the dream sequence invites the audience to reflect on the necessary errors of interpretation. For example, after the masked proprietor drops the misshapen "wheel" from the "roof" of the building, the camera tracks toward it, focusing finally on its empty center. In her final confrontation with Murchison, Constance construes this "wheel" as the revolver he dropped in the snow after killing Edwardes. But like her silence regarding the painted eyeballs, Constance's "Eureka!" moment of naming misrepresents what the viewer sees; for example, she omits the experience of being guided by the camera toward the absent center of a distorted circle. This movement establishes parallels between the wheel and the eye as *nearly* circular entities with *approximate* centers that are, on closer examination, only holes, apertures, or the seeming results of cuts. In *Vertigo*, Hitchcock depicted another such juxtaposition when he likened the pupil of a woman's eye to an unending abyss; in *Psycho* he fashioned a dissolve from a bathtub drain to Marion Crane's dead eye. In *Spellbound*, the analogy between the irregular wheel's absent center and hanging figures, the painted eyeballs on drapes sliced by scissors, questions the reliability of what the eye takes in. The link between eyes and revolvers emerges again in the final scene, when Murchison points the barrel of his pistol at the camera and, by extension, at the viewer's eye. Hitchcock's characters are immune from the destabilizing potential of these analogies, which point to something deathly or centerless in the act of seeing or interpretation, but for Hitchcock's viewers, these metaphors may contextualize all interpretation, including their own, as new incarnations of the hanging figure—of the unending creation of new figures out of old.

In *Spellbound*'s coda, viewers may expect to see reconstituted, normative figures, the authentic John and Constance, replacing the old amnesiac or love-blinded role-players, if the construction of the couple is to do its work of satisfying the imperatives of the classical Hollywood romance genre. But in keeping with Hitchcock's practice ever since *The Lodger*, the constructed couple is imagined attractively enough to satisfy audiences or producers who may never seriously question visual phenomena; at the same time, consistently with his practice in *The Lodger* and *The Ring*, the constructed couple is also depicted as challenging the happy ending demanded by the mass public. Constance and John smile at each other and kiss in front of the gateman, whose parody of achieved identity is conveyed by the tautological signs of who he is, affixed atop his hat. Then the lovers pass from the camera's range. The gateman is the same character who had earlier watched in astonishment as John and Constance, on the run from the law, "enacted" a kiss in front of him. His astonishment in the former case was clear enough: why would apparent passion animate two lovers at a gate who then, *together*, boarded a train? At the end of the film, the reason for his astonishment may be the same, though there is no way a viewer could know that; on the other hand, the gateman's moment may anticipate the spellbound astonishment of viewers who cannot visually discern any difference between— viewers who are suspended between—couples with authentically realized or enacted identities.

9

Notorious: Thresholds in the Glamorously Dangerous Charade

Poisoned and semi-conscious, Alicia Huberman hangs onto the CIA agent Dev-lin, who is in the process of rescuing her from the Nazis. As he holds her up, they descend the ornate stairway of the Sebastian mansion, where she has served as an undercover agent. They are joined by Madame Sebastian and her son Alex; their attempt to prevent the rescue is foiled by Devlin's knowledge that the revelation of Alicia's mission would spell the death of Alex at the hands of his fellow Nazis, who watch the stairway from below. Alicia, the hanging figure, is wholly dependent on the enigmatic man she clings to for support: a taciturn professional spy who at times seemed attracted to her but nevertheless recruited her to become an American Mata Hari, to "land" Alex Sebastian for the CIA by winning his affections and marrying him. After she succeeded in her mission, Devlin secretly sought transfer to another position and ignored her for five days. This man now has her life in his hands; moments before, he reassured her of his genuine love, and she seemed to believe him. Since from Alicia's point of view, the alternative to belief in Devlin is death at the hands of the Nazis, the quality of the vows of love they just exchanged—the essence of any constructed couple that ratifies normalcy for Hollywood—is at least open to question. Like the man and woman who hang in Number Seventeen, *this may be only an apparent couple.*

As the means of transition between two doors—the door to Alicia's bedroom and the front door of the Sebastian mansion—the stairway highlights the tem-porary and relative nature of the many enclosed or fixed interiors through which the characters have passed in this film. Like Spellbound, Notorious *is made up of doors that open on nothing; like Toulouse-Lautrec's* Le Pendu, *it focuses on*

Figure 9.1: Notorious (1946). Courtesy of Buena Vista Television.

thresholds. Earlier in the film this curving staircase-threshold had been the site of an elaborate tracking shot that emphasized its function as a cinematic place. As an image of continuity accomplished through numerous rectilinear steps or discrete frames, staircases may serve as metaphors for film: to stand on the stairway is to duplicate cinematic representation. So as the film's four principal characters walk down the staircase together, bound within different registers of suspense, they also reveal the cinematic and constructed nature of their identities.

But Alicia's suspense pales besides Alex's, whose descent down the stairs is reluctant to the point of paralysis. Aware of his liminal state, between life and death, he lies to his friends below—he says Alicia is being taken to the hospital—but they immediately see through him. Alex naively loved; for this error he was betrayed by Alicia and is now consigned to death. In this moment when he might have begun to understand the glamorously dangerous charade of life, his only recourse is new fabrication, new construction of what is happening to him. Alex's transparent lie is uttered in panic when he sees the world's and his own fraudulence; it is only one of the last of the film's many metaphors for art as a sign without referent.

CRITICAL CERTAINTY AS TRUE-FALSE KISS

Critical debate over *Notorious* questions the extent to which the film merely condemns or also transcends the patriarchal political and social order that victimizes Alicia.[1] For Tania Modleski, Devlin's egregious reification and near-murder of Alicia makes sense only when read "against the grain," to show some possibility of a woman's ultimate triumph even in submission; for Robert Corber, *Notorious* harshly exposes the regulation of gender roles during the "postwar settlement." On the other hand, Robin Wood sees Devlin's rescue of Alicia as a personal rebellion against the political order he has all along only restively served. These readings adopt genetic and organicist assumptions about the work of art—that in the Coleridgean issue or fruit of the plot lies the culmination of its development; hence the outcome of their debate hinges on interpretations of the ending.[2] Following this book's figural and deconstructive approach, according to which the work of art is not an organic whole but a hanging figure, this chapter looks at the film's parable of gender and political oppression as a matter of suspense that can be resolved only artificially, only by a species of critical arrests or police actions—acts that *Notorious* itself condemns but cannot prevent in its viewers. Instead, the truths of *Notorious* remain as undecidable as the "enacted" kiss of Devlin and Alicia in the doorway to the wine cellar—the kiss that masks their seizure of the MacGuffin, their appropriation of the signified goal of their quests. The juxtaposition of this true-false kiss with the urgent-insignificant MacGuffin lends the undecidability of the latter to the former; the viewer's reading of Devlin and Alicia's love becomes as risky as their purloinings of key and uranium. If the film depicts love like the MacGuffin as a matter of infinitely deferred suspense, then critical efforts to freeze or define it may seem arbitrary interventions, like those of the American CIA or the Brazilian Nazis.

Interpretations of the ending of *Notorious* presuppose agreement as to what that is or when it begins: such definitions quickly become controversial. If the ending begins with Devlin's decision to return to Alex Sebastian's mansion to check on Alicia, its unmotivated, afterthought character is apparent. Casually eating fruit on a sort of daybed, Devlin's CIA superior Prescott is unconcerned with Alicia's fate. As he speculates that she may be "on quite a bender," Prescott may well assume that Alicia's passion for Alex either is or has become genuine, and Devlin has no reason to suspect otherwise. Neither man comprehends Alicia. Thus, Devlin's decision to return may be prompted as much by jealousy as love; the quandary shows how hard it is to know the difference. Moreover, Devlin has waited five days before deciding. This long delay makes it more likely that his park bench sarcasm represented what he really thought of Alicia. But on the other hand, what *does* sarcasm represent? Does any emotion exist if unexpressed? Just when during the unrepresented five-day interval did Devlin's affect, whatever it was, become genuine love? What kind of narrative would have

ensued if Devlin had waited for a sixth day? Devlin later claims that he concealed his inner feelings of love, but this view reinterprets earlier scenes—their
charade-like park bench meeting and their true-false kiss in the wine cellar. Like
the kisses that conclude *Murder!* or *Spellbound*, the wine cellar kiss fuses both
characters in undecidability: can either character's half of their embrace be said
to be genuine if its motive is to reveal Devlin's passion *to Alex*? Searching for
earlier scenes of authenticity doesn't help, either. Critical efforts to decide the
film's position on gender roles on the basis of its ending are hopeless because
the film *has* no ending that is not continuous with the couple's first meeting at
Alicia's party, when she flirts drunkenly with the silhouetted, rigid, sarcastic
Devlin. Whatever unnameable affect is given expression in the final rescue scene
must have originated in Alicia's (feigned?) high-spirits-as-defiance-of-public-
opinion and Devlin's (feigned?) supercilious, begrudging attention. Both are
self-deceived. In Miami Devlin pours drinks for Alicia; in Rio she is poisoned
by Alex. Thus Devlin's relationship with Alicia begins and ends in scenes in
which he leads her from houses where he has facilitated her poisoning; he
rescues her from intoxications they have mutually brought about. In this way,
the beginning and ending of the film resemble the kiss in its middle: their lives
are "glamorously dangerous charades."

Of course, attributing *some* signified referent like love or politics behind the
charade is a necessary first step in comprehension of the story; viewers are
conditioned to project interior motive behind the closed exterior of the cinematic
sign. In this respect, the viewer's activity parallels that of the characters, who
are driven to learn each other's motives, just as they strive to find the interior
contents of the wine bottles. At first glance a world without interior human
motivation is as incomprehensible as one in which political parties fight for
nothing of value. But that is the essence of the charade. The MacGuffin shows
us, in retrospect, the emptiness of both psychological motivation and political
obsession. If the American CIA and the Nazis are willing to sacrifice morality
in the interests of interior contents to which the viewer may remain indifferent,
then political motivation becomes absurd as well as dangerous. As we shall see,
the reading-disillusionment built in to the process of viewing *Notorious* and its
doorway kiss is also allegorized in other scenes involving doors—scenes of
approaching them, listening through them, and opening and closing them. These
dramatize reading as the apparent disclosure of an interior that only continues
suspense.

THRESHOLDS

The film's first door leads to the Miami courtroom in which John Huberman
is being sentenced; there, the viewer learns the futility of access to interiors
when urgently sought information is depicted as existing behind an "impossible"
door. The closed courtroom door is hinged on the left, so as to open away from
the courtroom on the right. But after a cut, we see a reporter trying to overhear

the proceedings while holding open the door, which now inexplicably opens *into* the courtroom *on the left*. Without warning, the reporter begins to *close* the door, but then, just as inexplicably, after a cut, the door now *opens* on the courtroom, where the judge sentences Huberman. These impossible door movements are reflexive devices made possible by editing; they reinforce the film's insinuation that access to interior significance is a fiction. This built-in disillusionment of reading accompanies the ritualistic judicial scene where Huberman's attempt to honestly express interior emotion is suspended by his lawyers, who advise him to defer and repackage his message. In any case, the content of these "interior disclosures" is quickly forgotten as the reporters pursue Alicia's *reaction* to the news: the constructed truth of the interior acquires referential capacity only when it is passed around in the relay of the mass media. (That the media include film is suggested by the *Notorious*'s opening shot, a photographer's flash camera.) In this way *Notorious* restates the cultural critique of *The Lodger*, that it is not crime or punishment and not interior motivation but their representation in signs that is the object of the world's pursuit.

In chapter 3 we saw that Toulouse-Lautrec's use of the threshold in *Le Pendu* conveyed intellectual suspense; in *Notorious*, doors and thresholds suggest undecidable interiors. When Devlin stands in Alicia's Miami doorway "chivalrously" offering a scarf to protect her exposed midriff on a windy night, his gesture again epitomizes his enigmatic behavior—first at her party and later in the wine cellar. Is his interest in her romantic or professional? Is his manner sophisticated or condescending? Is he sexually aroused or puritanically repelled by the sight of her skin? Can he decide? These imponderables generated on Alicia's doorstep, the threshold of the film's construction of the couple, direct attention to her unreadable interior, too. Is her defiance of public opinion a matter of principle or the exaggerated parody of such a principle? Is her association with wealthy Nazi sympathizers a matter of shared values or social acquaintance? Are these alternatives truly distinguishable? As we've seen, the suspense of flirtation-aggression between characters of undecidable identity was a prominent feature of *The Lodger* and *The Ring*; it addition to *Notorious*, it reappears in *The 39 Steps, Suspicion, North by Northwest*, and *The Birds*.

That this undecidable couple functions as surrogate readers becomes evident when they stand on a threshold listening to the surveillance-record that purports to represent truly Alicia's inner life; like us, they seek to interpret its meaning. The idea that in understanding Alicia's emotional life Devlin places most confidence in the technology of political oppression illustrates self-deception, and also Hitchcock's larger theme that emotion has no reality apart from its presence in the circulating, Derridean "postal" of representation. As for Alicia, her sudden respect for surveillance, coming so soon after scenes of her rage against Devlin's role as a plainclothes "copper," injects suspense into her own motivation. If Devlin believes the voice on the record for professional reasons, Alicia may for personal reasons. Crossing the threshold of desire on the windy night has put each character in the same position as the reporter straining to overhear the voice of Alicia's father in the courtroom, deluded into thinking that interiors are meaningful. Finally, each resembles the film audience in attributing an interior significance to the mechanical reproduction of a voice: their position as listeners on one side of the recording mirrors that of the audience on the other, both sides in the midst of suspended interpretation.

Another threshold, when Devlin joins Alicia for a dinner in Rio, allegorizes the undecidability of their identities. The balcony connected to her apartment is the famous site of the couple's code-evading kisses interrupted by Prescott's telephone call—a moment of reflexivity on the threshold that repeats the sense of cinematically constructed emotion in the courtroom scene.[3] Extending the imagery of *The Ring*, the lovers' dialogue now triangulated by the telephone creates an apt image of love in the postal world; it also repeats the scene of their interpretation of the mechanically reproduced voice on the surveillance recording. Devlin's "forgetting" of the champagne in the offices of the CIA deepens the undecidability of his motivation: his seemingly unconscious lapse— as on other occasions, there is no way to decide if he is feigning—may betoken selfless respect for Alicia (by allowing her to make a professional decision un- swayed by alcohol or romance) or determination to end his own (pretense of?) romance in the interests of professional duty. After pleading to no avail that he disclose his interior feelings, Alicia agrees to Prescott's plan to become a "Mata Hari to Alex Sebastian." She pours herself a drink, and Devlin lights a cigarette. They meet on the threshold to the balcony and, before the scene fades out, have this laconic exchange:

Alicia: We shouldn't have had this [chicken] out here; it's all cold. What are you looking for?

Devlin: I had a bottle of champagne . . . must've left it somewhere.

This doorway-interchange encapsulates the undecidability of both characters and the charade world they inhabit. Standing at a liminal place that joins or divides interiors and exteriors, Alicia and Devlin *seem* to converse, to open to the other, but in fact remain closed. The film's architecturally ambiguous dividing lines and openings onto nothing are figures for the parabasis of identity.

At the Sebastian mansion, the machinations of the Nazis are figured *behind closed doors*, for example, in the library where Emil Kupke's fate is sealed. Standing outside its doors, fearfully intuiting the imminent group verdict against him, Emil is last seen framed in the doorway where he stands with Eric Mathis, his colleague who becomes his executioner. Like Devlin telling Alicia about his lost champagne, Eric turns to Alex and says, "Thank your mother for the dinner . . . the dessert was superb!" The scene extends the lovers' charade to the Nazis. Under the veneer of civilization, they enforce the death penalty for anyone who hints at or points to the interior signified secret of the wine bottle. Indeed, the closed library resembles the wine bottles: under the trappings of high civilization it is filled with the living agents or catalysts of holocaust. Emil's inadvertent "leak" of the secret is recapitulated in his enforced exit from the library. His position in the doorway just prior to his execution associates him with the hanging figure's liminal condition between life and death.

The doors that most recall *Spellbound*'s metaphor for knowledge are the ones Alicia opens after her return from her honeymoon; these seem figures for her assignment to discover Alex's secret and for her claim to full partnership with him in marriage. Her claim is granted when Alex transfers control of the house-keys from his mother to her; this transpires in a scene that depicts both a threshold (where Alicia stands listening) and a closed door (to Mrs. Sebastian's bedroom). Here Alicia plays the same role of the eavesdropper standing on a threshold that Devlin did when playing back her recorded conversation. That she fully accepts Devlin's problematic ethics is evident in her concealing the surveillance. These parallel scenes also put Alex in Alicia's earlier role as victim and Alicia in Devlin's role as Machiavel. When she steals the key to the wine cellar, she repeats the amorality of Devlin's secret recording. If Alicia is to be understood as Devlin's victim, as Modleski, Wood and other critics argue, she must also be seen as adopting his ethic against Alex. In effect, Devlin has seduced her into abandoning her earlier Kantian insistence on the primacy of disinterested principle over family ties—displayed in the rejection of her father's invitation to treason, if we are to believe the record—in favor of the CIA's *realpolitik*. Alicia's position at the bedroom threshold may suggest her equivocal status as both victim and oppressor or simply the difficulty of sustaining that distinction.

The potential interchangeability of moral opposites is one of the possible constructions of the film's most elaborate threshold, the grand stairway in the Sebastian mansion. The importance of this recurrent architectonic feature in Hitchcock's films has been emphasized by Yacowar and Bonitzer: the former sees stairways as functioning as the "crisscross" image does in *Strangers on a Train*, to imply parallels between ostensible heroes and villains; the latter notes the way the famous tracking shot around the staircase in *Notorious* exemplifies the film's preoccupation with visual movements from far to near that imitate desire.[4] Their ideas give warrant for understanding the staircase reflexively, as was suggested in this chapter's caption. In the elaborate shot that ends in Alicia passing the key to Devlin, viewers are invited to imagine the camera itself gliding next to the film's most highly articulated threshold—as if to show the cinematic or directorial capacity to both create and temporarily stand apart from the signs of its own undecidability. In this long tracking movement, the camera may be said to evoke a reflexive kind of suspense of its own—perhaps an illusory dream of release from the path of undecidability that it seems always condemned to follow. Of course, the camera's fluidity and seeming freedom from figuration is an illusion that always ends—as it ends here, in the key that purports to unlock the secret of the MacGuffin. The tracking shot hovers over the stairway-threshold but culminates in the key that firmly returns the viewer to the world of visual metaphor; indeed, as a scene of *transfer*, the delivery of the key deftly dramatizes the very essence of metaphor.

INTERIOR CHARADES

As in Toulouse-Lautrec's *Le Pendu*, the doors and thresholds of *Notorious* are figures for unreadable interiors and figuration itself; as a result, their apparent disclosures of political, gender, or moral authority prove to be illusory. For example, the metaphoric promise of keys in *Notorious* began with Madame Sebastian's yielding her housekeys and influence over Alex; a phallic dimension to the keys is added when Alicia hides her theft during her embrace with Alex. Madame Sebastian's original possession of the keys may position her as the castrating or Bad Mother; Alex's transfer of the keys to Alicia implies a kind of voluntary submission to his wife's supplanting his mother as castratix.[5] The successful transfer of the key from Alicia to Devlin continues the circulation of the sign that figures Alex's emasculation and his wife's emotional infidelity; Devlin's later insertion of the key into the lock completes this symbolic circuit. In this way, the parable of political and sexual authority is continually reabsorbed into the Derridean postal world of figuration. That the conspicuous name of the manufacturer of the key and lock is "Unica" permits another reimagining of the key as verbal sign—specifically, as the Spanish feminine form of "unique." The gender inflection suggests the word's identification with Alicia, self-transferred, as it were, from Alex to Devlin. At the same time, there is latent suspense in both the definition and capitalization of the word "Unica." Like proper nouns it holds forth the impossible promise of an exclusive or privileged referentiality; however, viewers recall that if Alicia is Alex's priceless prize, she is also a common noun, the "notorious" woman or object of Prescott's gossip and even Devlin's sarcasm. Similarly, if "Unica" modifies "Devlin," viewers see that although his discovery of the uranium-sand may appear to be some uniquely meaningful act, it results only in the appropriation of more signs—the arbitrary labels on the bottles concealing mute matter that must in its turn be gathered up, put in an envelope, and interpreted in an endless chain of reading-suspense.

Devlin's spurious "Eureka!" moment promotes more suspense because of its immediate juxtaposition with Alex's discovery of the kiss; the ensuing confrontation features two doors—one an exterior (to the garden) and one an interior (to the wine cellar). Inside the inner sanctum are wine bottles with inner secrets, so spatially the scene evokes the Chinese box effect of containers within containers, discovered interiors that become only new exteriors, in infinite regress or de Manian "dissolving irony."[6] Alicia opens the garden door for Devlin, who uses the "Unica" key to open the lock to the wine cellar. (Alicia's ability to remain in the wine cellar for as long as Devlin does, without arousing suspicions, may raise the question of whether his presence was in fact necessary; these doubts may underscore his self-deception or the political delusions that Mac-

Guffins find at the heart of politics.) Hitchcock's emphasis on the insignificance of all MacGuffins—taken together with the enacted nature of the kiss—calls the significance of both Devlin's and Alex's discoveries into question: the significance of what is read, what is found behind doors, what is on the interior, is a construction whose meaning is always suspended. Alex confronts the couple with a reflexive remark ("I'm sorry to intrude on this tender scene"). The unreadability of the spectacle is conveyed in the word "scene," which reminds us of cinematic artifice, and also the word "tender," which might be plausible to the viewer if Devlin's interior motive is read as sexual, but ironic if read as professional: Alex's apparent sarcasm may mask his own feeling, whatever that is, for Alicia. As critics have pointed out, Alex's emotional vulnerability is frequently glossed over by the film's ideological oppositions; it is worth establishing that—politics aside—Alicia willingly does to Alex what she fears Devlin is doing to her.[7] Criticism has displayed much more sympathy with Alicia's tears at the racetrack than with Alex's confession to his mother, though it is difficult to see how the results of emotional manipulation are morally different, apart from gender stereotypes or preconceptions about American and Nazi ethics. In any case, to the extent that the true-false kiss in the wine cellar still leaves characters and viewers uncertain of characters' interiors, and to the extent that the uranium sand opens an endless series of new political interpretations, the meaning of kiss and sand, on which both plots have converged, is now more than ever suspended.

Alex's discovery of the "Unica" key, newly restored to his ring, anticipates his discovery of the misplaced wine bottle: Devlin and Alicia's coverups are parallel acts of reinserting units in a previously established sequence. These signs seem to point to much more significant meanings but instead suspend that referential function by calling attention to themselves; it is their position *as signs among other signs* that makes them readable—here, by Alex. The recirculation of signs resumes when Alex returns them to his mother's room, a movement that leads to a new sequence of hidden interiors—the poison in successive coffee cups. Here Hitchcock implies a gnostic theme—that the result of the discovery of the uranium may not be political hegemony after all but instead the disguised deaths of those who pointed the way to it. If the Nazi Emil Kupke is its first victim, the American who repudiated Nazism, Alicia Huberman, is slated to be its second. Those who point to the referent of the sign are part of a glamorously dangerous charade in which they are assassinated or poisoned rather than empowered. None of the powerful characters perceives this irony; the extent to which Kupke and Alicia discern it is imponderable. That Alicia's poisoning by the Nazis may be a moral consequence of Devlin's recruitment of her into his charade world is made evident when her distorted perception of Alex and his mother recalls her earlier hungover perception of Devlin urging her to drink orange juice. The parallel scenes suggest a Hitchcockian, Nietzschean equivalence of opposites—health and sickness. To enter Devlin's world is to appear healthier while in fact becoming poisoned. From this perspective, his climactic rescue of her resembles his earlier enforced administration of orange juice: in each case he coerces her to join him in an existence society considers normative but which the film dramatizes as a place where reading and referential pointing are lethal. The blithe assumption of the health of that world by Prescott and Devlin makes them as deluded as the Sebastians.

CLOSING THE DOORS

Hermeneutic critics of *Notorious* have taken a wide spectrum of positions on the film's final construction of the couple. Donald Spoto saw Devlin's rescue of Alicia as resulting in the "perfecting of their relationship."[8] Robin Wood thought Devlin awakened the "natural" essence of Ingrid Bergman, so her union with Devlin presages the possibility for a love that can defy the masculinist social order.[9] Skepticism over the status of the ending began with Tania Modleski's argument that *Notorious* narrates the egregious domesticization of a woman's sexuality; nevertheless, she read the ending as demonstrating not only Devlin's recognition of the dehumanizing effects of his own sadism but also a woman's power beneath apparent masochism.[10] Robert Corber concurs with Modleski's account of the domestication of Alicia's sexuality but finds nothing redeeming in the final construction of the couple; instead both are seen as having acted out fantasies of gender organization authorized by the "postwar settlement."[11] Andrew Britton pointed to the "bleak, ironic dissonance" of Devlin's apparent "conversion," which leads him to assume power over Alex and Alicia at the same time.[12] Richard Abel found the ending ironic, arguing that any endorsement of the constructed couple is accompanied by a tacit, subversive awareness of viewer identification with Alex as the agent that facilitated the construction; hence the apparent pleasure we take in the outcome is perverse.[13] Common to these varying critical positions is the assumption that the meaning of the film is readable in its ending; throughout this chapter the difficulties of that assumption have become evident.

In this context of critical diversity, the closing of the doors in the final scene may be read as a continuation of the film's consistent allegory of the constructed and suspended nature of visual meaning. It is hardly necessary to speculate, as Spoto does, on parallels between Alex's life and Hitchcock's, in order to read the outcast's final lingering and then vanishing from the diegesis as metaphors for the artist's disappearance from his work.[14] After he tells on the staircase the lie no one believes, and having no other escape, Alex concedes defeat. As the story ends, the lowest common denominator of film remains—the suspense of the darkened figure's movement toward empty and misleading light. This is a way of expressing what film is.

As the door to the American car locks him out and the door to his mansion locks him in, Alex completes a circuit in the darkness from one interior, one beckoning light, to another. This was Constance Petersen's circuit as she walked toward the light at the bottom of the director's door in *Spellbound*. It is the viewer's circuit, too. Alex's path visually evokes the circularity of the Enlightenment project that the characters, critics, and the audience, too, have pursued. At the end, interior light delivers death, not knowledge. Viewers who credit film and the glamorously dangerous charade of life embodied in Devlin and Alicia may find either a normative or ironic referent for the film's light. Each case rests on a different construction light and shadow; each tries to arrest the suspense of cinematic signs or *clignotements* in order to abstract these referents. An alternative to such identifications of referents, to such constructions, to such seizures of MacGuffins is for viewers to think of themselves as the dark figure of Alex, moving from a closed door to a light behind a door that is first open, then closed. The door's promise of death as the final referent is inferable but also suspended and never grasped, a hanging figure for moviegoers standing up in their seats who must now retrace their steps, from newly lighted places to the doors of the theatre behind them.

10

Rope: Suspense as the Absent Referent

David Kentley hangs limp between Phillip, who strangles him, and Brandon, who supports him from behind: this is the first interior shot of Rope; *seconds ago, a scream was heard over a shot of the exterior of their penthouse window. So the scream was a sign and the hanging figure its supposed referent. Intervening between the two is a cut, the basic unit of film editing, which creates the illusion that the viewer saw first the exterior, then the interior, of the same penthouse. The window-cut thus separates and joins—cleaves—the sign of the hanging figure to its referent. This cut is reflexive and metaphoric: as the first of ten in a film that is as much about editing as about murder, it characterizes cuts as cinematic thresholds. Thus the cut as the pre-eminent sign of film becomes part of the tradition of the threshold hanging figures already examined in Toulouse-Lautrec's* Le Pendu, *in Jeff's hanging from his window in* Rear Window, *and in the many liminal scenes of* Notorious. *Like those thresholds, cuts create the illusion of referents for signs: the scream* must *have been David Kentley's, we reason fallaciously, because we heard it on one side of the window-cut and saw his hanging figure on the other. In retrospect viewers may grasp their mistaken attribution of meaning. The arbitrary construction of signs—in life as in film viewing—is one of this film's crucial themes.*

Of course, the supposed referent of the scream is only another cinematic sign—the actors Farley Granger and John Dall pantomime the killing of the actor Dick Hogan. Hogan's part in Rope *is like a MacGuffin in being, paradoxically, both crucially significant and utterly trivial: his supposed corpse, hidden in Brandon's "cassone" but never seen, later becomes the unspoken referent of much of the ensuing dialogue. The effect on normal conversation is*

Figure 10.1: Rope (1948). Copyright © 2002 by Universal Studios. Courtesy of Universal Studios Publishing Rights, a Division of Universal Studios Licensing, Inc. All rights reserved.

to always double its meaning: for example, when Janet tells Brandon she is so annoyed she could "strangle" him, the audience for a moment may literalize her figure of speech and think of the person in the box. But such double entendres become triple when we realize that Hogan's mute presence, even in the box, was never required and that not even an actor is in it. It is thus possible to experience Rope *as a conversation which is simultaneously about one of the most consequential human acts—murder or death in general—and also about nothing. Dick Hogan/David Kentley-as-MacGuffin anticipates that pure state of the MacGuffin Hitchcock explained to Truffaut, when the MacGuffin is "nothing at all."[1] Another way of putting this is to say that the murder itself—an undecidable hanging figure—is immediately displaced by constructions of the murder, first by the murderers themselves, later by Rupert Cadell, and always by the audience. The film constantly implies that understanding its hanging figure bears a resemblance to constructions of an absent referent. This is the effect of a film that narrates* both *an ordinary story* and *the evidence of its own construction—in the form of the aspiration to being "uncut." In the first narrative, the answer to the question of the moral responsibility for David's murder is left unresolved; in the second narrative, the succession of hidden and unhidden cuts calls attention to the way the long segments of uncut film—and by analogy film itself—are already constructions of figures. The irresolution of both narratives produces the film's suspense.*

INTRODUCTION

Only *Vertigo* has received the same level of critical response as *Rope*, which has become a site contested by Lacanian psychoanalysis, queer theory, and Derridean deconstruction.[2] In all approaches, *Rope* dramatizes the way constructed identities mask what society groundlessly proscribes—homosexuality and the unconscious instincts. At the same time, each approach shares an aesthetic ideology that commodifies *Rope* as the more or less accurate representation of, respectively, the Lacanian symbolic, the cultural construction of gender, and the binarism of structure and free play. Like other aestheticisms, these exempt critical discourse from the film's suspense; they imply that criticism can produce a suspenseless work or can encompass and tie up its object, like a rope. In contrast, *Rope* will be examined here as a film about the two narratives of absent referents outlined in the caption above. *Rope*'s two narratives—the murder story and the editing story—parallel the two-stage reading/viewing process, modeled on Paul de Man's, set forth in the introduction: storytelling exposes first the characters' illusions, but then the failure of its own representation.[3] Nowhere is the second phase of de Man's two-part definition of narrative more evident than in the film's narrative of its own construction, in its title and central metaphor of rope. J. Hillis Miller analyzed this figure as a recurrent trope of and for narrative itself.[4] The "narrative line," which is always arbitrarily begun, entangled, disentangled, and tied up, may be one of the West's most deeply embedded metaphors for representation. Transposed to film, the metaphor is even more compelling in the light of the physical resemblance between rope and film—both are continuous, pliable, coilable, and recursive; hence, *Rope* literalizes the construction of this metaphor in a reflexive way that prose fiction and even drama could not. The second narrative's aspiration to create an "uncut" film is thus crucial for understanding *Rope*'s suspense. In what follows, *Rope* is examined in its main narrative and reflexive dimension—its technical experiment, credits, irony, and interpolated stories. Both seek to convey narrative meaning but end up defeating the aspirations of narrative—including critical narrative—to comprehend or master suspense.

THE TECHNICAL EXPERIMENT

In the first narrative, *Rope*'s allegory of reading is evident in Brandon's confession; in the reflexive narrative, in the failure of the ideal of the "uncut" film. According to that ideal, film recapitulates its own origin and essence—photography—and its Kantian promise of art as a pure conduit of meaning: in an uncut film as in a photograph, nothing has been hidden, censored or expurgated; what is seen is what was shot. Despite controversy over such claims, photography has long kept alive, especially in the popular imagination, the dream of a perfect, objective, or suspense-free art work, of pure knowledge unmediated by the artist. The photograph or the uncut film may seem the aesthetic counterpart of the

wholly truthful statement, utterance, or confession in the moral realm; this resemblance connects the two narratives.[5] By the end of the film, it is evident that
Rope has been the story of an uncut film that is not really uncut and of a
confession whose moral validity is suspect. The fact that *Rope* makes use of ten
hidden and overt cuts may be read, on the one hand, as Hitchcock's earnest
approximation to an ideal and, on the other hand, as the admission of its logical
impossibility and practical failure—a collapse of aesthetic integrity in the attempt to demonstrate it. Similarly, critics have often observed that Brandon's
conception of his own crime as an artifact *requires* its revelation, rather than
concealment. Thus we witness two collapses, Brandon's and Hitchcock's; both
the main story and the uncut film are suspended projects, hanging figures.

A helpful analogy for the contradiction of an uncut narrative may be drawn
from the study of geometry: if the only true line is infinite in length, all lines
in experience are really only line segments or the connection between two
points; hence for practical purposes, all lines are inherently—are always, already—"cut," just as finite lengths of rope must be cut. Likewise, any narrative
with a beginning and end is already cut, already the simulacrum of a continuity
that can never be truly represented in finite signs. Language proceeds by discrete
signs, one after another, like the large "S" and "R" looming out the window of
Brandon's apartment. Music, exemplified by Phillip's piano playing, proceeds
in the same linear way, one note or chord after another; film proceeds by a
succession of one frame after another. Just as it is impossible to reproduce a
true line through any accumulation of line segments, so the hope to achieve
something "uncut" through the "already cut" is futile. Examination of the credits
and interpolated narratives in *Rope* will show, for example, that narratives are
always arbitrarily "cut," truncated or interrupted. The result for film may be the
same as the condition J. Hillis Miller discovers in novels, that none can be
"unequivocally finished, or for that matter unequivocally unfinished."[6] Instead,
of narrating intellectual completion—as for example some truth of Lacanianism,
gender, or the prison house of language—*Rope* allegorizes suspense.

CREDITS

The questioning of film and photography's popular promises of openness,
immediacy, and truth is demonstrated in the opening credits, which begin with
a still photograph that is soon "animated" to become the film's first frame. The
still scene reveals a vacant sidewalk next to a city street—two parallel "ways"
or passages, two sites of transfer or transport. As "ways," these are literally
"media," paths or avenues; as sites of transfer they suggest metaphor, the process
of carrying across something, from one entity to another, like the transfer of the
key in *Notorious*. So even before the story begins, even before the credits, we
can read on the screen/photograph a metaphor of metaphor, a scene of figuration
that precedes the introduction of the human. Much as *North by Northwest* begins
with an abstract grid or structure that only later becomes the reflection of a

populated office building, the opening of *Rope* suggests that the concept of the human may be only the derivative of a prior, ambiguous locus of potential but empty signification.[7]

That this transfer site cannot be dissociated from signs is reinforced by the presence of the postal box in the lower left-hand corner of the frame. Reminiscent of the numerous evocations of circulating messages in Hitchcock's films beginning with *The Lodger*, and anticipatory of the actual post offices of *Torn Curtain* and *The Birds*, the mailbox at the beginning of *Rope*, set upon vacant ways of transfer, helps set in motion the film's Derridean, Marat-like world of endlessly relayed signifiers, knowledge of whose true origin, content, and destination is suspended. As we shall see, much of the action of *Rope* consists of the retelling of stories cut off from their origin. One example will illustrate this. Janet Walker's phone call to Alice Kentley, asking about the whereabouts of David Kentley, is later returned by Alice; when the phone rings in the penthouse bedroom, Mrs. Atwater takes the message. She learns that repeated telephone calls to others still haven't succeeded in locating her son. These circulating references to nonexistence are cut off from their origins and only paraphrased to the others from Mrs. Atwater's unheard conversation in the dark bedroom. This is only one of many small, inconclusive relayed stories within the main "action" of the film, which consists really of more words concerning a missing referent, David Kentley. The postal box, like the street and sidewalk, anticipates both the boxed-in penthouse living room and its interior container, David's coffin or cassone, as the site of circulating of messages whose referent is suspended.[8]

Also depicted in the opening freeze frame are two conspicuous, removable "covers"—the convertible top of an expensive car and a restaurant's doorway canopy. Exteriors masking interiors, these also prefigure the case or cassone which shrouds the film's putative referent. The restaurant canopy masks a doorway—a threshold or transition point—but nevertheless cannot wholly conceal it and so seems to anticipate the film's masked cuts. These covers function like signs, revealing and concealing at once. They are signs of signs, as if the film's opening street scene arrayed visual metonymies of its allegory of narrative. Over this site of transfer, graphic signifiers (the credits) are superimposed, raising new questions of referentiality—of the identity of named actors and their director—questions later compounded by the end credits.[9]

After the superimposition of title and names, the still photograph becomes a motion picture, a street scene, into which human beings and the questions of morality that cannot be dissociated from them are introduced. This silent action soon encapsulates the film's main issue. A policeman accompanies two young boys across the street, but his seeming altruism is soon unsettled. First, he flouts the law: by jaywalking and stopping traffic with his "halt" gesture, for no apparent reason, the policeman shows that ordinary laws need not apply to him. Thus, he takes his place in Hitchcock's tradition of lawbreaking protagonists: the vigilante lodger in *The Lodger*, who is also an avenger; Constance Petersen in *Spellbound*, who knowingly harbors a fugitive; and Devlin in *Notorious*, whose CIA badge allows him to trump the Miami highway patrolman. *Rope*'s vignette of self-justifying transgression shows that Rupert's intellectual defense of the Nietzschean superman is unnecessary, since it merely describes what happens every day. Brandon and Phillip's murder of David is an extreme example of behavior that is routine. The policeman's seemingly benign motive cannot be confirmed or even known.[10] In any case, viewers may uncomfortably realize that the policeman is an authority figure *who has taken two young men in hand*, as Rupert has. Because this little story is truncated by the edge of the frame, we are put in suspense as to the import or destination of this authority's leading of the young; in a like manner, Rupert—like all speakers—is incapable of knowing in advance the practical application of his words.

The credits' street scene narrates interruption: with upraised hand, the policeman halts the flow of traffic; he cuts continuity at an arbitrary place along the way, an action that makes him parallel to a film director. Now if the policeman bore early resemblance to Rupert, as a superman, the new analogy with the director implies a second parallel, between the Rupert the intellectual superman and Hitchcock. Both figures may be envisioned as men who conceive, visualize, and relay messages of criminal amorality but disclaim responsibility for their application.[11]

These implications of the street narrative are intensified by the scene's reflexivity. Thomas Hemmeter describes it as

an artificial image with a pointed reference to a similar shot from the supposedly idyllic Santa Rosa in *Shadow of a Doubt* (1943). Though *Rope* offers only this one image of the "real world" that Brandon's experimental apartment world perverts, this grounding image alludes not to any documentary or representational world but to an earlier film image, itself a parody of the Norman Rockwell image of America. This multiple referentiality of the film's only exterior image suggests that the world outside Brandon's apartment is no more real than the world within.[12]

Hemmeter adds another reason why narrative film cannot function as a pure conduit of meaning: it is part of an intertextual grid. Hemmeter's understanding of the street scene's allusion to *Shadow of a Doubt* creates a new relay, in addition to its recollection of *The Lodger*, *Spellbound* and *Notorious*; these provide new referents for the scene. Thus *Rope*'s opening, onto a presumably solid street, may after all dramatize *false grounding*. It is a view of the ground from a high-angle shot that calls into question the concept of grounding, foundationalism, or any agreed-upon basis for discourse. Is this a film about transgression or about Hitchcock's earlier films? Put another way, the truncated narrative of *Rope*'s street scene suggests that the real world cannot be dissociated from verbal and visual signs, from figuration, and from a Nietzschean perspective, truly a vision from the heights, which suspends their claims to reference.

IRONY

This suspense appears in verbal exchanges that undermine narrative closure and sow doubt as to what meaning, if any, has been transferred between characters; taken together, this dialogue manifests the potentially infinite or "dissolving" irony that, according to de Man, narrative vainly seeks to arrest.[13] Often it can't be known whether characters are serious; these moments continue the undecidability of character already seen in the lodger, Larita, Jack, Constance Petersen, and Devlin. Do any of *Rope*'s characters have a determinable identity? Are Brandon, Phillip, Rupert, David, and Kenneth anything more than interchangeable forms, figures, trochees? Immediately following the murder, Brandon—laughing at his own cleverness—wonders at the death of this "Harvard undergraduate" while the camera dwells on Phillip's face, contorted in agony. The contrast between his amused demeanor and Phillip's fear is sustained throughout the film, making it impossible to know if the crime—an arbitrary murder, committed to exemplify a theory—is conceived as serious or playful. This undecidability appears in a social context that makes it the extension of, not an exception to, the everyday impossibility of judging discourse.

For example, when the doorbell rings for the first time, Brandon turns to Phillip with a very serious air and declares, "Now the fun begins." After Janet arrives and Brandon laughs at one of her offhand comments, she remarks, "Is that funny? I never know when I'm being funny. When I try, I lay the bomb of all time." Introducing the crude tale of Phillip "strangling chicken," Rupert explains that Phillip has "a very funny reason" for not eating it; later, Phillip calls this "an unfunny joke." Because the phrase "strangling chicken" may also allude to masturbation, we cannot know the import of Rupert's cruel or innocent story. Rupert makes a similarly undecidable comment when he tells Mrs. Wilson that he no longer likes the pâté she bought for him. When she questions him, Rupert says, "Just teasing." Mrs. Wilson replies, "You're awful." The characters' facial expressions, like other signs, are incapable of stabilizing this irony. This instability comprises a kind of white noise or background field of irony that, like the opening shot of a policeman's lawbreaking, creates a context for Rupert's "serious" theory of permissible murder. The theory's indeterminacy is apparent in Mr. Kentley's protests ("Surely you're not serious") and in Brandon's deadpan advocacy of the right of the few to murder. As Rupert adduces examples of permissible homicide, Mrs. Atwater's grin and laughter are frozen, a mask of undecidable civility. Viewers seeking closure might expect some resolution of this suspense, but the film's many undecidable moments makes that unlikely.

Irony is pervasive with respect both to the murder and to homosexuality. (These double entendres set the stage for what I examine later as "triple" entendres or reflexive allusions.) Discovering Kenneth's presence at the party, Janet tells Brandon, "I could really strangle you." When she later suspects Brandon of lying, she asks Kenneth, "Why can't he keep his hands off people?" These and other blithe references to hands, death, skeletons, and graves have been discussed as black comedy, but like all irony, they also illustrate the way speakers cannot determine the meaning of their speech.[14] The double entendres concerning homosexuality reveal irony's infinite or dissolving potential, since as D. A. Miller observes, the "truth" of the homosexuality of Brandon and Phillip—however strongly hinted at—remains forever unknowable; indeed, the same must be acknowledged for the possible homosexuality of Rupert, David, or Kenneth. Double entendres concerning homosexuality suggest a world in which there may be no foundation on which to measure irony's extent. Assessing the film's many hints of homosexuality, D. A. Miller concludes that Hitchcock's technique "reinforces the undecidability that keeps suspicion just that, a thing never substantiated, never cleared."[15]

One effect of undecidability is to render unknowable criticism's search for the "true" cause of the murder, insofar as that might be determinable by psychology. The killers' conscious motive—courageously putting into practice Rupert's abstract philosophy—can never be accepted at face value so long as questions regarding their homosexuality remain unanswerable. To what degree might their crime be the result of unacknowledged or unacknowledgable erotic jealousy among the four principals—Rupert, Brandon, Phillip, and David? By leaving the matter undecidable, Hitchcock suspends in advance any critical quest for psychological causality. By developing a narrative in which the facts of the crime are taken for granted from the outset, *Rope* re-creates the experience of Greek tragic plots, based on publicly known myths, and tests the popular view of tragedy's noblest aspiration: that the mind's mastery of the *logos* or cause of irrationality vindicates our capacity to control chaos. If Brandon and Phillip are rational, is the murder of David justifiable? Can we accept Brandon and Phillip's explanation of their own rationality? Can we believe *Rupert*'s explanation of his own moral innocence? Far from vindicating human reason, the solution to the murder of David (like the solution to the murder of Laius or the riddle of the sphinx) becomes a sign pointing to new signs that never rest in a psychological referent but instead circulate in a permanent condition of suspense.

Irony in *Rope* is depicted as inherent in language and independent of human intention; its autonomy affords a way of understanding Brandon's apparently voluntary confession: "We've always said that moral concepts of right and wrong don't apply to superior individuals; that's all we've done. [Phillip] and I have lived what you and I have talked." Normally a confession is thought to be a voluntary act, one that shows language's subordination to human will. But Brandon thinks of his murder as a "work of art" and the dinner party as his artist's "signature" on a "masterpiece."[16] In other words, his experiment *requires* confession, since a signature, like any sign, exists only when read; thus, Brandon's signature ensures his eventual apprehension. As Rupert finally "gets it," Phillip tells Brandon: "This is just what you wanted, isn't it? Having someone else to know how brilliant you are, just like in school!" Phillip's earlier objections to Brandon's increasingly transparent hints to Rupert all along miss the point of the *inevitability* of the confession. Brandon has been neither unwary nor careless; Rupert's "solving" the mystery does small credit to his rationality, because a public acknowledgment was pre-ordained by the necessity for him to read Brandon's signature.

In this challenge to Enlightenment rationality, *Rope* continues the tradition examined in David's *Marat*, as well as in such Hitchcock films as *Number Seventeen*, where the detective Barton's ratiocination leads to a train wreck; *Spellbound*, where the rationality of psychoanalysis masks delusion; and *Notorious*, where Devlin's national-security mindset only by chance averts disaster. The tradition is also evident in Poe's "The Purloined Letter," a text that also informs *Rope*. Each work begins by planting incriminating evidence in a position so prominent as to be undiscoverable by traditional rationality—in Poe's case, by the police inspector; in Hitchcock's, by the "normal" guests or even by Rupert's unaided intellect. It is only when Brandon guides Rupert to suspicion, and only later when that suspicion is intensified by David Kentley's initials on his hatband, that what has been all along obvious becomes recognized by ratiocination.

Rupert is also linked with Oedipus. The bad leg he suffered in the war may recall the hero with injured feet. His obsessive need to determine reason or rationality appears as early as his abrupt response ("Why?") to Kenneth's mild greeting ("It's awfully good to see you again.") He cross examines characters and interprets new information brought into the room. At the moment he discovers the crime, Rupert describes himself as a man of *logos*: "Until this moment the people of this world have always been dark to me, and I've tried to clear my way with logic and superior intellect." This is the familiar language of Oedipus's quest for knowledge— to bring light to darkness and to clear paths. As J. Hillis Miller points out, Oedipus's discovery or *anaxagoris* does not endorse logos or perspecuity: on the contrary, understanding the identity of the criminal leaves in the dark the problem of the gods' intentions in foreordaining the crime. Rupert's moment of insight is similarly unenlightening, because identification of the killer has still not determined the responsibility of the killer's "author"—Rupert himself.

Rupert's contradictory rationality—the Enlightenment man who advocates Nietzscheanism—is mocked not only by the many broad hints that Brandon (replacing him as a mentor) supplies, but also by the fact that Rupert's solution to the crime involves an appeal to the psychological that elides an undecidability. Thomas Hemmeter notes that Rupert's climactic moment of insight asserts the presence of a signified referent—a "something" wrong inside Brandon—as an ultimate anchor of discourse: "The phrase "something deep inside" further undermines Rupert's attempt to use language to escape language, for his previous use of the term *something* suggests quite the opposite of a stable term whose stability might anchor his meanings."[17] As Hemmeter implies, Rupert's "discovery of the truth" requires that he invoke some hermeneutic basis for discourse by which to distinguish himself from Brandon. As the moment of recognition draws near, Phillip cries, "He's got it! He's got it! He knows!" The "getting" here is hermeneutic apprehension of the truth, "based" on the "something" that supposedly distinguishes Rupert from Brandon. But Rupert fails to recognize a moral culpability in himself that corresponds to Rupert's criminal responsibility. In fact, at the end of the film, Brandon has reached a position of moral superiority to Rupert, at least in accepting responsibility for his words and actions. The crime of Phillip and Brandon is only the most egregious example of what *Rope* dramatizes everywhere—that in a world of endless ironic relays without an anchor for interpretation or "something" inside, there is never a final destination, for signs. By contrast, Rupert's insistence on his innocence indicates the way he remains trapped, like Oedipus, in the hermeneutic need to assume some cause, reason, and *logos* as language's natural referent. His condemnation of Brandon's inhumanity seeks to provide a ground or reason that will bring all irony to a rest, but like the psychiatrist's speech that concludes *Psycho*, Rupert's monologue opens new questions. The wailing police sirens and disembodied voices from the street are the only responses to the final tableau; they yield no answer to the viewer's question of "Why?", insofar as that can be asked of Rupert's teachings. The moral and intellectual stalemate reflects the same fundamental silence that Jimmy Stewart's Jeff was forced to exhibit when confronted by Thorwald in *Rear Window*. The disembodied voices coming from below dramatize language cut off from ground. Instead of producing *anaxagoris* or recognition for the viewer, the sirens and voices are only the film's last signs.

INTERPOLATED STORIES

That suspense may coincide with language and narrative is suggested by the film's three short interpolated stories, each of which is also a relay suspended or cut off from origin and destination, illustrative of the idea of narrative as an inherently and arbitrarily cut line: (1) "The Mistletoe Bough";[18] (2) the story of Phillip killing the chicken; (3) the story of Janet's past. Each narrative is interrupted or cut at certain points; each becomes analogous to a story-line, to rope, or to the film itself. The interruptions are sometimes obvious, sometimes masked. And while each narrative sets out to prove or illustrate a point, each instead only indicates new signs of undecidability.

Rupert begins the tale of "The Mistletoe Bough" after Brandon uses the word "cassone"; he wants to show how his former student could "find a new use for a chest. One was always turning up in the bedtime stories he told in prep school." In its hint of past bedroom meetings between housemaster and student who hold each other in high esteem, Rupert's introductory detail—like the film's other ambiguous signs of homosexuality—may reveal more than he intends. The arbitrary nature of narrative beginnings is emphasized as Rupert falters and Henry Kentley takes over the interrupted narration:

Rupert: I don't remember exactly how it started. It was about a lovely young girl . . .

Henry: She was a bride-to-be, and on her wedding day she playfully hid herself in a chest. Unfortunately it had a spring lock. Fifty years later, they found her skeleton.

Janet: I don't think I'll ever get *that* playful.

Of course, Brandon's "original" meaning in telling the story, back at prep school, is unrecoverable, illustrating how narrative meaning is reconfigured as soon as it is retold (and this tale is *twice* retold—first by Rupert, then by Mr. Kentley). Whatever significance Rupert intended to convey by this story is also lost: Rupert may relay this recollection of a prep school intimacy vindictively, to humiliate Brandon, or solicitously, in an effort to remind, seduce or re-seduce Brandon. Just as plausibly, as an account of the failure of heterosexual love, the story may serve as Rupert's rebuke to or private joke with Brandon, whose self-avowed romance with Janet is imponderable. (D. A. Miller correctly points out that there is no way to know whether Brandon's allusion to his own heterosexual experience *is or is not* a mask.[19]) But these interpretations, opposite to begin with, must be realigned when Rupert's retelling is supplanted by Henry Kentley's: narrated now by an older man, perhaps more apparently heterosexual, the story may be read as a lament for a potential marriage doomed by an excessive spirit of "play." Janet Walker understands the story in this sense, but confidence in her resolution never to become "playful" must be weighed in the balance with her own later self-criticisms—for example, of being an "Idiot girl" (as she tells Kenneth), one whose genuine affections seem obscure to the point of un-readability. The self-deceptions of both homosexual and heterosexual love reinforce Hitchcock's savage attack on their folly.

Each interpretation of "The Mistletoe Bough" is destabilized for the viewer of *Rope* by the knowledge of David's body inside the cassone—he is the "princess" dead in the box. He is the MacGuffin or long-sought interior of the film's exterior signs. But like the Chinese box effect of the nested exteriors of *Notorious*, *Rope*'s hypothetical referent generates only new signs. Indeed, it was a word, "cassone," that initiated the telling of "The Mistletoe Bough." These proliferating ironies threaten to overwhelm "The Mistletoe Bough" in interminable ramification. For example, if David is likened to the princess, the association may imply that he partly brought on his own death through a spirit of "play," thereby augmenting the homoerotic subtext in his fatal assignation with Phillip and Brandon. Finally, "The Mistletoe Bough" foreshadows the eventual exposure of the corpse and secret. All of these narrative ironies dramatize the autonomy of language, the way it cannot be prevented from expressing more and other than any sender of a message intended.[20]

The interpretive frames of "The Mistletoe Bough" suggest the way the meaning of any narrative changes with every iteration, somewhat in the manner of Borges's fable of "Pierre Menard" in which the narrative of *Don Quixote* changes even when its Spanish text is rewritten word for word by someone whose native language is (or even may be) French.²¹ If the "original bedtime story" told by Brandon had no privileged meaning apart from its undecidability, perhaps its only function is to allegorize that feature. Of course, such an allegory of reading—in de Man's sense—could itself be recovered only through later retellings (like those of the narrator[s], the director, and the film critic) which further distance signifier and signified, as is illustrated here. The interruption of the narration of "The Mistletoe Bough" mimics this process of cutting or truncating stories from their origins, signs from their intended meaning. In this respect it is instructive that the story is interrupted *even before it can begin*, suggesting a way every "new" narrative may really tell only the same story over and over again, of its exile from the truth.

The second interpolated story is of Phillip strangling chickens. We have already seen that this story's allusion to masturbation suspends its ostensible meaning; it adds new relays to phrases like Brandon's, that the chicken "rose" or Phillip's, that the episode is not "a suitable topic of conversation." If any subtext is intended, something that is impossible to know, then Brandon's glee in telling the story may be reinscribed as the desire to humiliate Phillip. But even without its subtext, the story illustrates the suspension of meaning. Like "The Mistletoe Bough," it attempts to provide a ground or reason—in this case, an explanation of why Phillip doesn't want to eat chicken:

Janet: There must be a reason. Freud says there's a reason for everything, even me.

Rupert: As I remember, you have a very funny reason, doesn't he, Brandon?

Brandon: Yes, it's nothing too much.

Rupert: I think it's quite fascinating.

Brandon: It happened about three years ago in Connecticut . . .

As in the case of "The Mistletoe Bough," Rupert recalls a narrative that is then retold by someone else; here, he laterals the story to Brandon. After a second interruption we learn that Rupert's knowledge of Phillip's chicken-strangling ability came from an experience of one year ago, whereas Brandon narrates a different story, from three years before, when a partially strangled chicken revived. In the dialogue above, the story Brandon tells *is* the reason for Phillip's aversion: both are the antecedents of the word "it." But the referent of this "it" is not established because each character thinks a different story is the referent. Each story accounts for Phillip's aversion differently: in Brandon's story, Phillip's disgust comes from an unsuccessful killing; in Rupert's, Phillip is successful. The attempt to account for the same phenomenon on the basis of narratives with opposite referents may give the lie to the Kantian or Freudian effort to enlist stories in the service of truth.

The climax of Brandon's story narrates the suspense of truncation in another sense—of the cutting-off of life:

Brandon: But on this particular morning [Phillip's] touch was perhaps a trifle too delicate, because one of the subjects for our dinner table suddenly rebelled. Like
Lazarus he rose . . .

Ultimately the story of the chicken-strangling is a story of a strangling that is
not a strangling, a death that is not a death, a subject that is not its subject. It
functions like "The Mistletoe Bough," as a de Manian allegory of reading. In
its allusion to Lazarus, Brandon's story may further illustrate the way the recurrent "subject" of stories—their truncation from origins—is resurrected in
each retelling. This idea makes all interpretation redundant error. Why begin a
story at all if it will only illustrate its own dysfunction? Some sense of this
inevitable failure may be behind Phillip's outburst to Brandon: "There isn't a
word of truth in the whole story! That's a lie! I never strangled a chicken and
you know it." A second interruption now ensues, caused by the heated argument
that follows this outburst, one that "cuts" the story, leaving its details in dispute;
this new truncation emphasizes the same separation between narrative sign and
referent seen in "The Mistletoe Bough." Later, under Rupert's cross-
examination, Phillip concedes the details of the story but continues to deny its
meaning:

Phillip. Well, I just meant that Brandon's story wasn't true. I didn't mean that I hadn't
killed any chicken.
Rupert: That's what you said.
Phillip: Well, I just didn't think it was a suitable topic of conversation while we were
eating.

For the viewer, Phillip's rejoinder may suggest a different reason why Brandon's
story is untrue: that his aversion to eating chicken had less to do with his
strangling chicken than with the strangling death of David. At the same time,
any such interpretation remains only one more guess about an absent referent,
just like the many guesses about the characters' homosexuality. The chicken-
strangling stories leave the viewer in the same indeterminacy as "The Mistletoe
Bough," since both narrate the impossibility of deciding referentiality.

The third story is Janet Walker's embarrassed reminiscence of "the grim Sunday at Harvard," when Kenneth broke up with her. This narrative is told to
Kenneth during the break between the two parts of the chicken-strangling story.
We may guess from Kenneth's refusal to challenge Janet's rueful recollection
("You threw *me* over, chum") one reason for her present embarrassment. Janet
tells the story to explain the truth about this embarrassment and about her present
affections—in other words, what she says purports to be a pure, untainted or
uncut narrative, a confession. This confession also *narrates* a confession. Janet
introduces both with a question about her own veracity:

Janet: You and David used to be such good friends, and you're not now. I'm such
            an idiot girl.

Kenneth: You're not.

Janet: I'm certainly giving a good imitation of one. Why must I try to be so smart
            with everyone except David?

Kenneth: Don't you kid with David?

Janet: I relax with David . . .

The preface to Janet's narration implies that this evening she has been "smart"
and not truthful, since David is absent. An irony of this irony is that Janet was
able to *achieve* her ability to be serious only because of Kenneth's rejection:

Janet: . . . thanks to you.

Kenneth: To me?

Janet: Yes. That . . . that grim Sunday at Harvard, when you called it quits. David
            took me for a walk. My chin was about an inch from the ground. I just couldn't
            be the gay girl. I just relaxed and let everything pour out, the real "real me"
            stuff. Did you hear that little phrase? I hear myself saying things like that! Oh,
            where's David?

If Janet's present confession is true, it may also be false, since it is being told
now to Kenneth, not to the truth-inspiring David, and since she is giving "a
good imitation" of being an idiot girl. Her narrative, too, is and is not itself.
The stutter that initiates her narrative interrupts it and links Janet as storyteller
with Brandon (who also stutters) and Hitchcock (whose narratives repeat each
other). The truth of Janet's confession is further undermined by her phrase, "the
real 'real me' stuff"—words that cancel the possibility of a true representation
of selfhood. What undecidable identity is implied by the quotation marks around
"real me"? How could Kenneth tell the "real 'real me' stuff" from the false?
Here, Janet's insistence on the truth of her confession reveals its fabricated
nature. How could her present confession to Kenneth be more valid than her
past "real, 'real me' stuff"? Even Janet seems to acknowledge these contradictions: her concluding cry ("Oh where's David?") may be heard as a nostalgic
or desperate call for the return of the truth-telling she once believed possible.
If such true communication had ever existed, it has now been eliminated with
the murder of the truth eliciter, David.

The redundancy in Janet's phrase, "the real, real me," exemplifies the repetition common to the stutters, the interpolated stories, and the main narrative.
The deaths in "The Mistletoe Bough" and the chicken-strangling stories are
avatars of the death of David Kentley; the end of Janet's relation with Kenneth
(and before him, Brandon), prefigures the end of her relation with David, too.
The parts and whole of *Rope* repeat themselves, like Janet's phrase and stutter,
Brandon's stutter, or Phillip's perpetual playing of Poulenc's "Mouvement Per-

petuel." These incidental repetitions parallel those of the plot: Mrs. Kentley's repeated calls in search of David and the obsessive return of conversation to the question, "Where's David?" The suspended discourses of *Rope* are different versions of the story told in the credits and in the film; all characterize narrative in general and film narrative in particular as that which both is and is not itself— a narrative line that is uncut and cut, a figure, a "rope."

THE ABSENT REFERENT OF FILM

As narratives within a narrative, the interpolated stories comprise one part of the film's reflexive dimension; like the narrative as a whole, they are told around the cassone, the film's image of absent reference, which also becomes associated with the place of the camera. The cassone illustrates the problem of naming. When Rupert first sees it he asks, "Exactly what is this?" Brandon's reply ("A cassone I got in Italy") converts film's locus of meaning-making into a site of translation, transfer, or interpretation.[22] As in the case of the "Unica" key in *Notorious*, a physical object becomes a verbal sign. (The Afterword considers the material world as only a sign or figure.) The alternation of the "correct" term ("cassone") with "chest" and "case" continues the film's doubt of any necessary relation between signifier and signified; the cassone is a table that is not a table, a fitting image of a misleading basis or foundation. The case that is not a case inspires doubts as to language's reference during the anxious conversations about David Kentley; these are magnified by metonymies that associate the interior meaning of the cassone with food, books, and film. Books take the place of food on the dining room table; late in the evening, Mrs. Wilson and Rupert attempt to put books into the cassone. In the story about Phillip strangling chickens, the food set out to be consumed becomes uncomfortably linked with David's corpse, a conceit with parallels in *Hamlet* ("the funeral-baked meats did coldly furnish forth the marriage tables") and *Sweeney Todd*. Throughout the evening, talk never strays far from the subjects of food, books, film, and killing. These identifications, like the ambiguous cassone, have the cumulative effect of converting life into art: the dead may be imagined as vanished, as conversation pieces or as temporarily consumable, like food, books, or film. At another level these metonymies narrate a process of mortality, whereby the living David Kentley is reimagined as "David Kentley," the sign. What the guests understand as presence, as a living physical object of discourse, is at the same time only the arbitrary name which has supplanted it, just as books supplant their authors and films their directors.[23] In *Rope* Hitchcock dramatizes the way the world may be understood as figure.

From this perspective, the view that art imitates reality is shown to be naive. Janet Walker tells Kenneth she writes a column on "how to keep the body beautiful for an untidy little magazine known as *Allure*." Indifferent to supplanting of bodies by signs allegorized in the cassone's yield of corpse and books, popular writing assumes a direct correspondence between signs and human desire. (Janet's odd identification of her magazine—it is "known as *Allure*"— makes its title seem separable from itself; even as the semantic meaning of *Allure* beckons, her phrase suggests the alienability of sign from referent.) By the same token, Mr. Kentley's antiquarian interest in physical books illustrates his complementary illusion of reducing signs to the material world. Thus, the world's "normal," Cartesian views of writing—as *mimesis* of desire or matter, subject or object—are suspended by the film's narrative relays linking human mortality, food, book and film in discourse surrounding a black box.

The connection with film is established by the gossipy discussion of movies that fills the space between "The Mistletoe Bough" and the chicken-strangling story. This intermediate position suggests the way idle talk, new signs about signs, mask interruptions in narrative; in other words, one way to see this film, or any film, is as a sequence of cut narratives whose beginnings and ends are smoothed over in such talk.[24] Thomas Hemmeter has already drawn attention to the way the words "thing" and "something" in this conversation suggest the emptiness rather than reference of the signifier;[25] the lead-in to the conversation—the mask of the cut—connects this emptiness with mortality and film:

Mr. Kentley: [concluding the story of "The Mistletoe Bough"] . . . fifty years later, they found her skeleton.

Janet: I don't think I'll get *that* playful.

Mrs. Atwater: Talking of skeletons, have you seen that new thing at the Strand?

Janet: Yes, I adored it.

Mrs. Atwater: Did you? Good, though I must say I didn't like the new girl.

The skeleton in the box of "The Mistletoe Bough" becomes the relay-signifier to the next sign, a film, *shown in a place named for rope*.[26] In puns like these, "rope" becomes associated with both the place of the film and the transition masking cuts. It is as if the world is momentarily conceivable as the figure of "rope." The transition here, effected over the cassone or site of transfer, links the dead princess with both David and Janet. Thus while "David Kentley" is the absent subject or floating signifier of the principal and interpolated narratives, other characters soon begin to take on the hypothetical quality of his existence in and through their association with the cassone and its web of its metony-mies.[27] The attenuation of human identity spreads further as the conversation turns to actors: Janet Walker and Mrs. Atwater begin to disappear, to de-ontologize, as their praise of "the new girl" in the film reminds viewers that these dinner guests are themselves, after all, only actors. (The longevity of fic-tionally conferred identity can be glimpsed in the reminders of actors' mortality conveyed in the allusions to movie stars past their prime, Erroll Flynn and Mary Pickford. This effect, possible only in film, gathers increasing impact over time, as the actors and actresses portraying characters age and die. If viewing old films is like watching Lazarus, like hearing the dead talk, then film itself may resemble a skeleton in a box.) An effacement of the human by art accomplished specifically by Hitchcock's films is acknowledged, too, in Mrs. Atwater's recollection of a film with Cary Grant and Ingrid Bergman, which marks her as a possible viewer of *Notorious* (1946). Thus the relay that began in a transitional reference to "skeletons" extends through the characters and actors to film in general and Hitchcock in particular: like whatever film Mrs. Atwater saw at the Strand, *Rope*, too, is a "thing" with no true name, an empty sign about a "skeleton." If this conversation concerns film understood as a skeleton in a box—a speaking about nothing, in the shadow of mortality—then *Rope* depicts the world understood as figure.

The signs of food, book, and film form their own narrative relay, as they circulate around a hidden skeleton without ever arriving at a true destination or referent. The film's attempt to encompass this circular narrative may be figured forth in the image of the stack of books bound by rope, Brandon's way of proffering a gift to Mr. Kentley as he also flaunts his murder weapon. As a figure for Hitchcock's film, Brandon's book-binding rope may suggest art's aspiration to encompass the world of suspended meaning it is condemned to convey—to master it, to summarize it, to tie it up neatly in a narrative. But since it is at the same time the sign of crime that can't be rationally mastered, the rope also portends, as we've seen, the failure of the cinematic ambition to delineate some master narrative that might explain narrative at a distance, without being one. Of course, the same failure haunts critical discourse, too, which like this one patches together truncated and interrupted signs in the vain hope of discovering continuity. What *Rope* teaches is that in order to be tied up, ropes must first be cut. Both aspiration and failure are delivered to a "normal" audience that must initially regard art as commodity—like Mr. Kentley, we pay money for signs—even though subsequent reflection on art invalidates all attempts to commodify it. In this we are doubly disappointed. Like Mr. Kentley, the critic, too, naively and blindly searches for something of value that may be, unbeknownst, already dead; the critic's narrative begins with assumptions of referentiality that only belatedly are shown to be unfounded. This is the unending suspense of criticism. Art is a figure. It is the effort to encompass the world and its failure. It is line and line segment. It is the uncut film that is cut.

11

Vertigo: The Futile Search for Something Tenable

Scottie Ferguson hangs suspended from a gutter and looks down. A policeman trying to help him has just held out his hand to grab Scottie's, lost his footing, and plunged to his death. Scottie watches helplessly, hears the man's falling cry, and glimpses the bottom of an urban canyon. The policeman's death in the abyss is associated with the idea of having nothing to hold onto, but his fall was not the film's first instance of an attempted grasp: in the first frame the criminal *firmly grabs the rung of a ladder that will help him escape. As Scottie hangs, the viewer of* Vertigo *may weigh the transvaluation of values in thoughts of the criminal's successful grasp, of the policeman's grasp of nothing, and of Scottie, the hanging figure, whose grasp is so tenuous he seems fated to fall to his own death. Scottie, our surrogate, hangs suspended between images of chaos (the lawbreaker and the abyss) and the Kantian, rational, regulative law—that nevertheless lacks all support. It seems an impossible position; his reappearance in the next segment, alive and recovering, is never explained.*

These three acts of grasping focus attention on its broader implications— what is tenable in the sense of what can be held or believed. This is Vertigo's *principal subject, embodied primarily in Scottie's love for Madeleine, which he tries to resurrect in his love for Judy. The attainment of desire is also figured as an act of holding: Scottie seems fulfilled when he embraces Judy in Hitchcock's famous 360-degree tracking shot, an embrace of an embrace. But Scottie's story teaches that in trying to "hold" either Madeleine or Judy, he is deceived: atop the bell tower, he learns that what he believed in was fraudulent. Soon his arms, like the policeman's, hold only air; he stares down after Judy's fall as he did after the policeman's. Judy's death suggests Scottie's, too.*

Figure 11.1: *Vertigo* (1958). Courtesy of the Academy of Motion Picture Arts and Sciences. Copyright © 2002 by Universal Studios. Courtesy of Universal Studios Publishing Rights, a Division of Universal Studios Licensing, Inc. All rights reserved.

Scottie's empty arms, like the policeman's, are a metaphor for the human need for something tenable or something to believe in, yet the film as a whole shows us that this need will be thwarted at every turn, and not just in matters of love. The policeman's fall and Judy's dramatize an absence of ground *or foundation that becomes apparent in the exercise of reason itself.* Vertigo's *subversion of acts of interpretations extends to the viewer, too, in its anticipation of critical discourses that might try to "hold it steady," to make it an object of reason. Just as* Rope *challenges the perspicuity of Lacanian criticism, queer theory, deconstruction, and all critical views that seek to tie up or encompass the artwork, so* Vertigo *challenges its many critics to justify what they hold onto.*

CRITICAL SUSPENSE

Feminist critics form one of many schools attracted to this film; controversies over a woman's essential identity are exemplified in their work.[1] Laura Mulvey initially saw the film as an allegory of male spectatorship, then partly disavowed that argument.[2] Susan White and Deborah Linderman explored the film's gender ambiguity in the context of larger epistemological concerns.[3] In these studies, the conflict remained unchanged: the film's interrogation of male constructions of gender occurs alongside a larger subversion of meaning (for White, an "allegory of referentiality"; for Linderman, a "*mise-en-abime*"); but this larger subversion may leave no political space for women. Laura Hinton concluded that "readings of ambiguity and indeterminacy promoted by the film's abyssal structure erode the possibility of feminist critique by inviting then frustrating female agency."[4] Her warning names the problem: because each new hypothesis about a woman's identity derivable from the film is questionable, we wonder what it is we are holding onto. We are indeed "invited and frustrated."[5] Hitchcock's film allegorizes the dilemma not only of feminist approaches but of all others, too, as the pursuit of the tenable—that is, as the pursuit of some referent, ground, or foundation that, after all, vanishes. Such an "invitation and frustration" is observable in the film's arbitrary signifiers and in the undecidablity of its characters, political narrative, and ending, all of which suggest the illusion of tenable points of view on art and life.

WARNINGS AGAINST INTERPRETATION

Like the opening of *Notorious, Vertigo*'s opening dramatizes misleading signs. The credits sequence associates vision or a meaningful point of view with arbitrary signs; Scottie's rooftop chase becomes a synecdoche of the idea of the pursuit of tenability. These redundant proems ought to warn us against allegorizing the film (even, for instance, in terms of gender or the pursuit of tenability); however, they are as powerless to prevent as they are to determine interpretation.

The credits sequence features colored lights in the shape of a woman's divided face; her eye generates the film's title and then its recurrent abstract image, the helix, a shape that resembles an eye. It is as if the subsequent abstract shapes make us momentarily consider the first, the original "eye," truly a referent.

Perception and criticism are born in such nearly irresistible moments of attaching a signified essence to signs, as these two examples attest:

By the linkage, for example, of the signifier "vertigo" to the icon of the eye, the vertigo thematized in the film is designated as a projection of the gaze.[6]

We had been reminded of the figural importance of "cutting," itself a figure for the castration-repression theme, in the first bar image that divides the very first *Vertigo* frame.[7]

All such interpretation of the arbitrary is the result of juxtaposition of signs and is discoverable as such only after reading has occurred. As misleading signifier, this face undermines the traditions both of the "veiled woman" as pursued truth of philosophy, like Isis, and of its opposite, the Medusa that petrifies its seeker.[8] It is conspicuously half-hidden, with this flaunted concealment doubled by cosmetics. The eye becomes perceivable "as figure" against the "ground" of the eye-liner and mascara, lipstick, rouge, and wash of red light. Such a multiply veiled "woman" is nothing but photons promising and concealing something beyond themselves, but a similar deceptive exterior will incite Scottie's doomed search for tenable meaning or criticism's search for essential identity.

Like the rotating helix, the film's title and the names of its makers emerge from this deceiving eye; a resemblance between alphabetic signs and the ideal of visual illusion may be suggested by the simultaneous rotation of the colored helix. Are printed names anything more than swirling shapes? Is there a signified identity to which letters and shapes refer? Is there a signified "essence" of woman? Robin Wood was the first to remark on Judy's finely nuanced character, but her "true" identity is not just complex but undecidable.[9] *Vertigo*'s suspense— its incapacity to establish a tenable meaning for character or story—is anticipated in credits that first set forth the allure of such ungraspable truth then dissolve under swirling lines and colors and the sounds of violins.

The turning helix is also a figure for the title, "vertigo," a word derived from the Latin "vertere" which means "to turn." Thus before it refers to anything in the story—to the French twist in Madeleine's hair, to the staircase in the bell tower, to Scottie's wanderings in San Francisco streets—the colored shape is a figure that refers to the title, to a *word* for turning, a sign of a sign. Applied to the question of identity, this tautological sense of the visual metaphor will raise the question of whether the sign "Madeleine," for example, can refer to any essential individuality or only to other mysterious names or words—to Carlotta, Judy, Eurydice, Galatea, Melusine, Lamia, Proust's madeleine, Mary Magdalene, the Hebrew word *migdal* ("tower") or maybe to "madness" and hence, circularly, back to "vertigo" itself.[10] Hitchcock's rotating helix, like Yeats's interpenetrating gyres, evokes a Heraclitan flux composed of endlessly turning, self-referential signs that precede semantic meaning. In theory, the credits should warn viewers that pursuit of any tenable truth of Madeleine's profile—her hidden identity, her dark side, her role as the unrecuperable place of the mother—may end only in new shadow, in nothingness and tautology. But in practice the pursuit of meaning in film criticism—the hope of catching it, of holding it, of *finding what is tenable*—requires blindness to such warnings.

Hitchcock's second opening *narrates* such a blind pursuit and its "ending" in suspense. As the avatar of Detective Barton, Devlin, Rupert Caddell, Scottie supposedly stands for the law, yet his attempt to implement it is catastrophic. The chase sequence's foreshadowings of the film's larger disasters is reinforced by its detachability from the main story and its dreamlike qualities: the characters, the specific reason for the pursuit, and the rescue of Scottie remain unknown; when the policeman says, "Given me your hand!" to Scottie, his voice is muffled; his plunge is rendered in highly stylized subjective camera. Through these elements, the sequence suggests a scene of "pure pursuit," a vignette that complements the "pure allure" of the credits. Both openings narrate this paradox of reading—that *there must be something tenable* and, at the same time, *nothing is tenable*. The chase sequence's first shot is of the suspect's hand very firmly grasping the rung of a ladder, of literally finding something to hold onto. Holding onto something is a necessary part of the pursuit—here, of the larger quest to catch and hold onto the criminal. But there is some slip or *glissement*, something indicative of belatedness and permanent suspense, that intervenes to make capture impossible and to endanger the pursuer. When the policeman extends his hand, he soon has nothing to hold onto; nothing is tenable, and he plunges to his death. As Scottie hangs from the gutter, it is as if his life depends on holding onto something that is nevertheless very fragile, very vulnerable, ready at any moment to collapse.

Viewers may conclude that any pursuit may end in nothing to hold on to, in air, as it did here for the policeman or at the end for Scottie. Any attempt to fix meaning—whether that is understood in terms of "Hitchcock's point of view" or some interior psychological essence—may likewise end in nothingness, in vulnerability, in dangling in the suspicion that what we now hold onto may be the most fragile illusion. The alternatives are to hang on and look down at nothing, like Scottie, or to turn to our deaths, like the policeman or Judy.

By the end of the second opening, we have been warned twice: first in the credits, where the allure is shown to be arbitrary and empty; then in the chase, where pursuit is shown to result in either death or the subversion of the tenable. Having been warned twice, viewers of Hitchcock's *Vertigo* might well decide to eschew reading, except for the probability that like Scottie or Judy, they may be unable to accept the idea that what they seek may never be tenable. The repeated compulsion to grasp, in the face of all experience of nothingness, may be part of what Nietzsche meant by the eternal recurrence of the same.[11]

As the story proper begins in Midge's apartment, Scottie is trying, without success, to hold onto his cane.

UNTENABLE IDENTITY

Untenable identity is exemplified in Judy. Wood was the first to notice the extraordinary subtlety with which Hitchcock makes it impossible to determine Judy's motivation: we can never be sure, when she acts "Madeleine-pretending-to-fall-in-love," that she is not, simultaneously, "Judy-actually-falling-in-love." The result is a cinematic variant of the more familiar theatrical tradition of roles transforming actors that includes Viola's disguise as Cesario in *Twelfth Night* or Rosalind's as Ganymede in *As You Like It*. Wood's argument that Judy's motives can't fully be known stops short of undecidability, since he, like other critics, also permits himself conclusions about the "real" character behind her masquerade.[12] However, no such "real" character exists. The mistake is clear enough when critics refer to "Madeleine" (as many do, and as I already have) as the object of Scottie's quest; others attempt to circumvent the problem with neologisms like "Judy/Madeleine," but these are no better, since they assume that some relative proportions of the "true" characters of Judy and Madeleine are knowable and blended in this person. But the film's silence with regard to the nature of "Madeleine" also applies to "Judy": we have no more reason to suppose that Judy "represents herself truly"—say, in her memories of her child-hood or in her letter to Scottie—than Scottie has to believe any of the signs that purport to identify the woman.

A similar undecidability is apparent in the case of Midge, a character some-times appealed to in feminist criticism as at least an inspiration for some her-meneutic norm.[13] Like the object of Scottie's pursuit, the uncertainty of her name ("Midge" to Scottie, "Margery" to herself) first puts her identity in doubt. Although she appears to be content with a collegial and motherly relationship with her former fiancée, her face at the drawing board (when Scottie refers to himself as "available Ferguson") may imply—undecidably—either buried love for Scottie or relief at now being free from it. Wood's intuition hints at the larger enigma: "Her look at Scottie when he reminds her that it was she who broke off their three-week-long engagement is one of those moments that reveal the basic strength of the cinema, because it suggests things not really formulat-able in words."[14] But no amount of close scrutiny of this shot will finally yield the "things" Wood intuits: like Hitchcockian faces beginning with the lodger's, Midge's face only appears to be readable. We should have known from the credits that a face is a sign, a figure like a turning helix. Midge herself creates facial undecidability when she paints her portrait of Carlotta. The same painting may be read—and has been read—with opposite meanings: first, as Midge's assertion that she is as worthy of Scottie's gaze as the woman he is pursuing; or second, as a reminder that his obsession, like an adoration of a painting, is idolatrous, egregiously sexist behavior. According to the first interpretation, Midge's painted face refers to herself, to a real person, with real feelings; ac-cording to the second, a "face" may be merely an iterable blank signifier: any face could be painted on the body of Carlotta. Criticism of *Vertigo* has expressed these mutually exclusive interpretations.[15]

That the choice of either interpretation is untenable can be seen in Scottie's reaction. Can his anger also reflect understanding? If Scottie assumes Midge's face represents her interior feelings, then he is guilty of male arrogance; if he reads the face as an arbitrary sign, his continued devotion to Madeleine misreads her point. As a parable of the reading of visual art, Scottie's reaction to Midge's painting discloses undecidability in both the artist's intention and the interpreter's response. It is not that there are two equally tenable interpretations of characters whose motivation is paradoxical; rather, each repeats the failure to understand the arbitrary construction of faces already indicated in the undecidable look of Midge at the drawing board and, before that, in the woman's face in the credits.

As for Scottie, the number of his names and their dependence on the namer makes the question of his identity just as unsettled, at the outset, as Judy's or Midge's. Critics have seen him as both a laudable victim of love and as a satirized representative of patriarchy; however, Wood's questions about Judy's unknowable motivation may also be asked of him. At what point can we say that Scottie's love becomes a conscious or unconscious will to dominate? When his hand lingers on Judy's as he serves her coffee, thinking she is Madeleine? When he says, "No one possesses you"? In this conundrum, Scottie Ferguson repeats the undecidability of Devlin's relation with Alicia. Feminist critics have identified even in seemingly unambiguous expressions of Scottie's love a cover for male dominance. Tania Modleski argues:

When Madeleine jumps into the bay Scottie rescues her and brings her home, later indicating that by saving her he now has a claim over her: "You know, the Chinese say that once you've saved a person's life, you're responsible for it forever." At one point he kisses her feverishly, insisting, "I've got you now"; during another embrace he urgently declares, "No one possesses you"—no one, the implication is, but himself.[16]

Modleski convincingly shows how Scottie's outbursts of love are always just as self-serving as his later, patently sexist makeover of Judy into Madeleine; in fact his chauvinism may be present at his first sight of her, in Ernie's Restaurant: the famous camera work through which Hitchcock captures Scottie's gaze may well imply the kind of possessive vision Mulvey finds definitive of the male viewer. But of course, there is another side to this. Until the necklace scene, the plot also forces us to see Scottie as the *victim* of a cruel delusion and of an alibi for murder sustained by this very woman; therefore, feminist criticism leaves the viewer in the unusual position of seeing the film's protagonist, except at the very end of the film, as simultaneously aggressor against and victim of the same woman.[17]

This means that any hope of rendering Scottie's character decidable rests on an interpretation of the film's ending, but even there he remains unreadable: as he drags Judy up the bell tower, Scottie both embraces and assaults her. Critics have noticed this strange scene's effect of a man who both loves a woman and wants to kill her. Wood's remark that Judy's death "contains elements both of murder and suicide"[18] is typical of the intractable problems of interpreting the ending. One critic sees the nun as "a manifest sign that God is indeed having mercy on Scottie,"[19] and another sees her as Judy's "representation of herself as a spectre."[20] A third sees the nun as reminding the viewer "that the wish for embodiment in the other, the wish to merge and emerge with a knowledge of how that other constitutes ourselves, may be a desire in bad faith."[21] Of course, the credits should have warned these critics against the interpretation of a face. The pursuit of a tenable referent is like the San Francisco police vainly chasing a suspect. Like them, we slip in the pursuit of some readable point of view on the fate of the characters of Scottie and Judy.

The impasse of Scottie's character may be addressed in a new way if the bell tower sequence is taken as an allegory of enlightenment like Plato's parable of the cave: Scottie ascends to a new vantage point; he reaches what he hopes is a tenable point of view about himself, which promises an end to delusion and doubt. However, the acquisition of this new perspective is not emancipating, as it is in Plato, but instantly impoverishing: the "revelation" of the necklace has been, after all, no help in deciding Judy's character. Scottie still must interrogate what he's holding, he must question her word and—like us—read yet another face. So we are brought round to the scene of the credits. New knowledge results not in tenable meaning but in the replacement of one sign by another. This illusion of insight is acted out atop the bell tower, where both characters are blinded to their surroundings and to the presence of the nun stepping out of the shadows. Scottie and Judy perform undecidability, and their fates—death and a life without anything to hold onto—pose alternatives for human beings.

On the other hand, if tenable points of view are illusions, then all perspectives on the film, even about its undecidability, are also illusions. How could this be understood? In the nun and the camera, the film may offer two potential responses to the dilemma, which are of course not answers but simply new points of view on the untenability of points of view. In the oblivious nun may be figured an obsolete theological escape from reading dilemmas. In the camera's movement away from her and from the tower, into empty space—at last hanging in air, in "a position inaccessible to any human being on earth," in the words of William Rothman—may be figured the camera's approximation of pure suspense.[22]

VERTIGO'S PENDANT

The agent of Scottie's false illumination is the necklace of Carlotta, of Madeleine, or of Judy. The necklace is an example of a pendant, that first and most primitive hanging figure from which later images like the Sun Dance, Marsyas, Jesus, Marat, and many others may be derived. As noted in Chapter 3, the pendant seems the essence of the hanging figure, a transformation of nature into art that ever afterward calls the existence of the material world into question. The historic and cross-cultural associations of *Vertigo*'s pendant make it seem a universal figure: its record of the betrayal of Carlotta, Judy, and Scottie suggests the permanence of disappointment. Like *Vertigo*, like any work of art, like language itself, the pendant "invites and frustrates." When Scottie discovers that Judy impersonated Madeleine, he thinks he has discovered authenticity beneath her masks, but his interrogation of her on the bell tower yields nothing. As in the eyeball-slicing dream sequence of *Spellbound*, the destruction of illusion is replaced not by truth but by new illusion. Scottie's insight into Madeleine's fraudulence requires a new blindness—his belief that he now knows who Judy is. That his ultimate disappointment might have been predictable is apparent in Scottie's learning from the pendant: when he puts it around Judy's neck, he recognizes the pendant from the painting. In other words, the pendant as sign refers Scottie not to any real entity in the world but only to previous signs.

UNTENABLE POLITICAL AND CRITICAL NARRATIVES

Although *Vertigo* seems primarily a love story of untenable points of view, its political allegory narrates the public catastrophes of Western civilization, thereby calling into question meliorist theories of history and the "monumental" art that celebrates it. But at the same time, the suspense of even this narrative forestalls critical approaches—associated with recent positions like new historicism, cultural studies, and post-colonialism—that might enlist the film in the service of an argument about history as oppression. If the film's love plot exposed the untenability of fictions of the interior self, its political allegory exposes history as a succession of equally untenable fictions.

Vertigo's political allegory treats the familiar Kantian and Hegelian master narrative of history as the record of increasing freedom, autonomy, and independence, which is set forth when Scottie and Judy read, like tourists, the cross-section of the sequoia tree. There they see history's monumental events on the rings of the tree: the battle of Hastings, the signing of the Magna Carta, the discovery of America, the signing of the Declaration of Independence. (The fact that the events of history are identified through *signings of documents* has the effect of making history synonymous with *recorded* history—that is, history as indissociable from signs.) The Enlightenment history of the West appears in a western national preserve, itself a monumental site, that also suggests its telltale American variant, the doctrine of Manifest Destiny or "ever westward the course of empire." San Francisco is the westernmost point of the advance; in the city and the enforcer of its law, Scottie, may be figured the West's supposed pinnacle of Kantian reason. The historical narrative that began in Hastings and the Declaration is continued—though its benign character may appear less self-evident—in the mission settlements of San Francisco: Juan Bautista, whose mission is the site of the film's climax, founded San Francisco with a military outpost in 1776. Spanish religious and military colonization was fueled by dreams of gold and opulence of the sort displayed in the "Portrait of Carlotta" and the pendant, another of the film's important foci of reading and the gaze. Spanish imperialism was replaced in the nineteenth century by Anglo shipbuilding enterprises, symbolized by Elster, that imply the West's later expansion even farther, beyond the Pacific, making Judy's residence in the Empire Hotel highly appropriate. Through these allusions, the San Francisco of *Vertigo* is depicted as the culminating point of an official *grand recit*: the "triumph" of the European Enlightenment, which in reality masked the rapacity and expropriation narrated in the story of Carlotta Valdes.[23]

Theorists such as Michel Foucault, Stephen Greenblatt, and Gayatri Chakrovorty Spivak have shown how the West's master narrative of emancipation provided the intellectual rationale for centuries of imperialist domination.[24] This underside of the Enlightenment narrative is unconsciously betrayed in Gavin Elster's lament for the twentieth century's loss of the West's "color, excitement, power and freedom." Gesturing toward a picture of nineteenth-century harbors, Elster—here associated with leisure-class capital—complains to Scottie that San Francisco's earlier aura of power and freedom is rapidly disappearing. The point is echoed by Pop Liebl at the Argosy Bookstore, when he says of the abandonment of Carlotta Valdes: "Men could do that in those days. They had the power and freedom." Pop Liebl's story of outrageous sexism, together with his nickname, betrays the way the master narrative of the West is inseparable from patriarchal domination. Of course, Elster's criminal plot gives the lie to his feigned or simply puerile nostalgia for color: the film shows that modern patriarchy—Elster's twentieth-century project of exploiting a woman in order to murder his wife and convert her capital into more leisure—is even more vicious than its nineteenth-century precedent, the "mere" seduction and betrayal of Carlotta Valdes. Through Elster, then, *Vertigo* recounts the attempt of the "westernmost power" to revivify itself. It is a measure of the film's demystification of the Western master narrative that the *Übermensch* Elster is able to manipulate Scottie by playing on his Enlightenment assumption that superstitious mysteries have rational explanations. The fact that Elster succeeds and goes unpunished may be testimony to the film's grim implication that far from being in decline, the forces of imperialist patriarchy masked by and manipulating Enlightenment narratives of freedom have never been more powerful and ruthless.

Feminist studies of *Vertigo* demonstrate how the film's depiction of the obscene triumph of patriarchy is everywhere set against reminders of the wholly cultural construction of gender. The point is evident from the outset, when Scottie complains about his corset to Midge and is surprised to learn that other men may wear them. And the bra Midge is drawing—designed on the principle of the cantilever by a male aircraft engineer—reminds viewers that women's sexuality has long been a male construct (in the recent interests, the film implies, of industrial capitalism). Finally, by reconstructing Judy as Madeleine, Scottie, the detective presumably on the side of justice, is shown to act on the basis of the same patriarchal assumptions that motivated the criminal Elster. The work of Mulvey and Modleski first illuminated this aspect of Hitchcock's cultural criticism.

But Susan White rightly points out that such criticism presupposes "a single, dominating reality" in history; in effect, it mimics the Enlightenment narrative. By way of contrast, she sees in *Vertigo* Paul de Man's very different idea that history, understood as "the telling of the story of the generation of a text," is itself produced by allegory.[25] White's use of de Man here at first seems very apt: the idea that history is nothing other than allegory seems patent in the way Pop Liebl's oral history innocently rehearses as it unconsciously betrays Western master narrative that masks patriarchy and oppression. However, White elides de Man's observation that these allegories tell of the unreadability of history's text and are themselves subject to second (or third) deconstructions, in a potentially endless series. In other words, de Man's argument implies that criticism could deconstruct an allegory like Pop Liebl's—in the manner of Foucault, Greenblatt, Spivak, of feminist critics—only at the cost of committing the same mistake again. And in fact, this inability to avoid new error continues to plague White's analysis and my own.[26]

Suspicions about all theories of history accompany the film's treatment of color: first, in the contradictions in the idea of pursuing "color" in history; second, in the conversion of history into colored, allegorical or "monumental" signs that promise but, in the end, tell no story. The projects of both Elster and Scottie apparently corroborate Elster's lament that the twentieth century lacks the "color" of the nineteenth, their experiences bear out the gray look of San Francisco.[27] Scottie is obviously deluded by the woman in the gray car, wearing a gray suit, black dress, and white coat, who seems to epitomize the era's height of cool fashion. More distinctive color in *Vertigo* is associated with the appearance of the redhead Judy: the green light of the Empire Hotel sign, the purple gown she chooses for dinner, or the shimmering green aura that envelops her as she emerges, remade, from the bathroom. Scottie's desire to bring back the past is figured first as an attraction to color; this reveals how he enacts Elster's lament. On the other hand, the makeover of Judy into Madeleine necessitates the obliteration of these colors. Scottie's simultaneous attraction to and erasure of color gives the lie to Elster's one-way theory of decline. When Scottie finally holds Judy in their embrace amid green light, viewers may understand that the illusion of "finally grasped truth" in the guise of woman is no more tenable in the past or present, with or without color.

The idea that history has some true "color"—for Elster and Liebl, a code for *lese-majeste*; for Scottie, the color of the allure; for feminist critics, the color of patriarchy; for postcolonial critics, the color of political hegemony—is an assumption the film depicts as untenable. It is as if film associates color and interpretation, finding each to be both unavoidable and invalid. The futility of reading the past as a narrative of color/colorlessness (or exploiter/exploited) is reinforced by the scenes showing the interpretation of colored or monumental artifacts and by characters' misreadings of history.

The most conspicuous scene of such reading is the one in which Judy, impersonating Madeleine, gazes at the portrait of Carlotta in the Museum of the Palace of the Legion of Honor. This scene identifies reading, suspense, and the hanging figure, insofar as the pendant is part of the characters' gaze. At first, Judy stares at this assemblage of colors as Scottie, baffled, witnesses; at this moment the painting is, for him, utterly without meaning—no different from any of the paintings that received his indifferent glance before he began his surveillance from a position behind the column. When Judy leaves, Scottie asks the museum guard about the painting. He is told its title (*Portrait of Carlotta*) and given an illustrated catalogue of the collection. This is the reading moment—the bestowal of words on a hitherto meaningless collection of colors. J. Hillis Miller calls such a moment catachresis, that is, and act of "forced or unnatural" bestowal of a name for what cannot be named; in this respect, catachresis is like all denomination, which must helplessly employ arbitrary signs.[28] No name is true. The name "Carlotta Valdes" is not more authentic or meaningful than "Judy" or "Madeleine" or "Scottie/John/Johnny-O/Available Ferguson." But erroneous naming—in the film and about it—is also unavoidable.

Scottie not only "names" the painting, but also interprets Madeleine's reading. Like a film critic, he now interprets the responses of other viewers of visual art: the woman he believes to be Madeleine is suffering from a form of hallucinatory identification with a woman from the past. The mass of color-signifiers on the wall is now, at a stroke, transformed into a signified referent. Scottie now possesses truth; previous viewers (and the woman in front of him) are deluded. The catachresis of the first reading is forgotten in Scottie's certainty at being now in the possession of the tenable truth.

In this interpretive delusion, *Vertigo* shows how supposed insight into the truth of history or art is possible only at the price of blindness. The point is repeated when the necklace scene—with the portrait-reading scene in flashback—turns out not to be illuminative for Scottie: as we've seen, the revelation that "Madeleine" was a delusion is accompanied by blind certainty that the new presence, "Judy," is now knowable. In both instances, Scottie's false insights are elisions of suspense: they anticipate insights by film critics who, in pursuit of the signified idea behind the flickering lights or *clignotements* on a screen, assume a tenable identity for the characters and events of the story. Critics can no sooner say that the experience of *Vertigo* is mere color and sound than Scottie could say the painting of Carlotta was as meaningless as the other paintings in the museum. Like Scottie, we are driven by a fatality to commit the same errors as those we read about.[29]

The camera mimics our repetition of Scottie's errors when it pursues his pursuit through the streets, buildings, and monuments of San Francisco. The viewer's experience of the monumental in *Vertigo* (as, earlier, in *Saboteur* and later, in *North by Northwest*) parallels Scottie's need for something tenable amid historic signs. The Mission Dolores or the Palace of the Legion of Honor are monuments to exalted truths, theological and ethical, that may be imagined but never confirmed, pursuable but untenable. Worse, these dysfunctional monuments sometimes contain, within themselves, additional misleading signs: Sequoia National Park contains the cross-section of the tree; the Palace of the Legion of Honor contains the *Portrait of Carlotta*. In theory, these dysfunctions of art might have been known beforehand, as when we saw in the credits the woman's half-hidden face obscured by red color. In practice, art can only hope to be apotropaic: knowledge of its dysfunctions comes only belatedly, as when Midge understood that her parodic painting could not jar Scottie into his sense or that Mozart could not cure his fugue; as when Scottie stretches out his arms to find nothing tenable; as when film criticism, in reflection, discovers the blindness that generated its insights—as, for example, the concept of tenability. *Vertigo* and its criticism may finally exemplify the kind of repeated, grasping-at-emptiness efforts induced by art or by language that Nietzsche meant by the eternal recurrence of the same. These efforts begin with Scottie's impossible position—hanging onto a gutter so weak that his rescue must be accepted on faith. They end with his arms grasping air. Suspended between the illusion of tenability and the apprehension of nothingness, the catastrophes of *Vertigo* are played out in a kind of Chirocoan cityscape of empty monuments to the pursuit of truth.[30]

12

North by Northwest: Groundless Figuration

Eve grabs the outstretched hand of Thornhill as they ascend Mt. Rushmore in an attempt to escape from Vandamm and his men. The hanging figures are seen against a background of other, monumental figures—representations of highly valorized political faces; in other words, they are visible against a "ground" which is itself made up of figures. (Sometimes even the details of the faces are evident, as when Thornhill and Eve seem to crawl across the nose of Jefferson.) To imply that what we think of as ground may really be only figure is to undermine the whole idea of foundationalism—that personal identity or political ideology "refers" or "rests" or "is based on" something other than figuration. North by Northwest's *allegory of absent grounds extends* Vertigo's *allegory of untenability by consistently exposing the idea of foundationalism as illusory and fraudulent. It depicts a world where signs—names, advertising, telephone and wire messages—are cut off from what they signify and instead circulate freely in the world Derrida characterized as "the postal." Here, all figures hang in suspense, and the idea of rock-solid foundationalism conveyed by Mt. Rushmore or by critical discourses is shown to be illusory.*

THE MASTER NARRATIVES OF CRITICISM

That critics miss *North by Northwest*'s attack on foundationalism is evident from the fact that so many interpretations are based on the same psychological paradigm: a male's movement in the direction of maturation that becomes a prerequisite for marriage.[1] The myth critic Lesley Brill argues that *North by Northwest* follows an archetypal direction of romance, as defined by Northrop

Figure 12.1: *North by Northwest* (1959); © Turner Entertainment Co. An AOL/Time Warner Company. All Rights Reserved.

Frye, in which the hero dies and is reborn in love.[2] The reader-response critic Thomas Leitch sees this direction as the movement away from a debilitating maternal influence, through emancipatory role-playing, toward independence.[3] Richard H. Millington, who like Leitch believes Thornhill's changes may be gauged by his willingness to improvise, sees him as exemplifying an essential American independence from ideology.[4] Reversing these valences but preserving the narrative pattern, Robert J. Corber sees the film's direction as a movement away from gender deviance and irresponsibility, through an internalization of the Oedipal, toward an ironic maturity that exemplifies only the repression of the postwar social order.[5] But as if sensing some slippage in this foundation pattern, these and other critics are also uncomfortable with this master narrative.[6] Thus, George M. Wilson concludes that despite all "self-reform," there is really "too little to a Roger 'Nothing' Thornhill to sustain protracted psychological investigation."[7] Geoffrey Hartman asserts that Thornhill's quest, which "should deliver him from the necessity of testing and role-playing" in fact leads only to "a deferred moment of revelation."[8] In short, the critical consensus that Hitchcock's allegory may be tracked through the direction of the change in Thornhill is both assumed as a foundation but also doubted.

In this chapter, *North by Northwest* is seen as questioning not only the *grand recit* of a hero's maturation but also the meaning of "direction" itself, whether that is understood as character change or as movement toward some representable theme. The film is an allegory that narrates the groundlessness of both character and interpretation, one that fully justifies its climactic scene of figures atop figures. This sense of direction without destination is discussed first in connection with the film's title, which names "mere direction," then in its depiction of the world as "the postal"—a place where the very idea of a changeable human subject arises only as the misinterpretation of arbitrary messages. As in *The Lodger* and *Vertigo*, interior identity is the same as an unreadable face. Hitchcock's ending is understood not in terms of the climax of a *grand recit* of maturation, but in terms of the persistence of groundless interpretation, by both characters and film critics.[9]

THE TITLE

Nobody knows what Hitchcock's title means.

Hitchcock himself said it interested him "primarily because there is no such direction."[10] This Delphic pronouncement and subsequent critical discussion have ensured that its significance will remain in suspense. In a way, suspense *is* arbitrary direction.

Discussion has centered on the possible allusion to Shakespeare's *Hamlet*, II, ii, 360–70, though it is also clear that the phrase "north by northwest" by no means alludes unequivocally to Shakespeare's phrase "north-north-west." But since critical studies accept the allusion, a link has now been established, willy-nilly.[11] Respect for the equivocation suggests how the supposed allusion calls allusiveness itself into question. The title seems to refer to something very specific—a passage in a canonical text—then also retracts or undermines this pointing. (This step forward and back resembles the way criticism both posits then questions Thornhill's maturation.) The title's self-cancellation is echoed in its semantic sense, a seemingly precise direction that nevertheless leaves unstated its end, content, or destination. As a statement of "mere direction," the title thus

implies the possibility of referentiality without content. It suggests parallels between compass points and language or film images: each promises precise denotation, but only within arbitrary systems.

The allusion, if it is one, comes from the scene where Hamlet—made aware
of the players' imminent arrival and after some sparring—finally welcomes Rosencrantz and Guildenstern to Elsinore.

A flourish.

Guildenstern: There are the players.

Hamlet: Gentlemen, you are welcome to Elsinore. Your hands, come then.
                Th'appurtenance of welcome is fashion and ceremony. Let me comply
                with you in this garb, lest my extent to the players, which I tell you must
                show fairly outwards, should more appear like entertainment than yours.
                You are welcome. But my uncle-father and aunt-mother are deceived.

Guildenstern: In what, my dear lord?

Hamlet: I am but mad north-north-west. When the wind is southerly I know a
                hawk from a handsaw.

This passage cancels itself, just as the title did. Hamlet seems to extend a
sincere welcome to Rosencrantz and Guildenstern, but having forced them to
admit they were "sent for," a few lines earlier, he already knows they are capable
of deception. He says he wants to welcome them with "fashion and ceremony"
now so that later, his greeting to the players won't seem more "like entertainment" than this greeting. What can this mean? In each case his welcome will
reflect "fashion and ceremony." Hamlet justifies using deception now so that
later, in comparison with more exaggerated politeness, it will seem more authentic. But comparing the second greeting with the first is to compare figure
with figure, not figure to anything "real." In this small passage, as elsewhere in
Hamlet, we are given a glimpse of the world understood as wholly figuration
or—as Hitchcock called it—as a glamorously dangerous charade.

The title phrase appears in Hamlet's self-diagnosis: "I am but mad north-
north-west. When the wind is southerly I know a hawk from a handsaw." Commentators gloss this as Hamlet's assurance to Guildenstern that he is only
strategically or at certain moments mad; however, the passage raises the imponderable questions, reminiscent of the paradox of the Cretan Liar, of whether
anyone can be believed and of who it is that determines madness—the supposed
"mad self" or some other? The political and forensic implications of this paradox, explored by Foucault,[12] are raised but never resolved in *Hamlet*; instead,
the implication is that a true diagnosis of madness is in suspense. It is as chi-
merical a construct of language as is the distinction between acting and authenticity, between welcome and deception, between uncles and fathers or aunts and
mothers.

In the final sentence, Hamlet appears to support his claim "I am but mad
north-north-west" with the example, "When the wind is southerly I know a hawk

from a handsaw." We might pause here to wonder how an example could illustrate an ambiguous precept, but Hamlet's example does so: it states a distinction illustrative of sanity only to have that distinction collapse. Commentators have noted that the apparent incommensurability of "hawk" and "handsaw" is in fact illusory: both may be tools, and both may be birds.[13] If Hamlet's example was a litmus of sanity, that test canceled itself.

The context of Hamlet's phrase "north-north-west" reveals the possibility that the foundation distinctions of language and literature—between madness and sanity or truth and falsehood—are self-cancelling. That possibility permeates Hitchcock's *North by Northwest*, too, as its affinities with *Hamlet* make clear. Stanley Cavell has listed these affinities, of which the most plausible—Thornhill's efforts to establish his true identity within the context of Oedipal anxiety and malevolent conspiracy—are often assented to in Hitchcock criticism.[14] On the other hand, by seeing Thornhill's victory over Vandamm and his closing embrace with Eve according to the *grand recit* of maturation, such critics must read the film as a cheerful adaptation of Shakespeare—as if Hamlet and Ophelia survived and became engaged, annulling the hero's life questions in love's triumph. But the title's equivocal allusion casts doubt on whether the supposedly happy ending resolves foundation-questions or whether, like the train, these remain in transit, movement, pure direction, suspense.

THE WORLD OF THE POSTAL

The title's implication that language is self-cancellation is borne out in the film's depiction of the world as—in Derrida's phrase—"the postal," that is, as a place where foundationless language is anterior to the subject and creates it in a network of figural relays through which language circulates without ever arriving at any true destination, addressee or referent.[15] Language's anteriority to the human is present from the outset of the film, in its credits, during which we see first an anonymous grid, then words—words placed on the grid, one figure placed atop another. The arrows that emerge from the letters—angled obliquely up from the "h" in "north" and "to the left" in the second "t" of "northwest"—seem to invite viewers to consider letters, too, as "pure pointers," as directions without end, as suspense. Their oblique angles deconstruct the habitual association between compass points and such "true" directions as up or left. Like the title's allusion to *Hamlet*, the credits indicate the arbitrariness of direction in the senses both of spatial position and film *auteur*.

The abstract grid also illustrates spacing or *écarte*, one of the many metaphors Derrida uses for the constitution of language in self-division as a condition of legibility.[16] This grid precedes any "grounded" semantic content (here, Mies van der Rohe's Seagram Building); the human, or the crowds of New York City, is introduced only as a *reflection* on the grid and thereby twice subordinated to its spacing.

The story's beginning in a scene of dictation again dramatizes a world in which language is divided against itself. The *in medias res* (or *verbas*) opening—Thornhill's oral instructions to his secretary Maggie—shows they have "always, already" inhabited the postal, where "As soon as, in a second, the first stroke of a letter divides itself, and must indeed support partition in order to identify itself, there are nothing but postcards . . . our entire library, our entire encyclopedia, our words, our pictures, our figures, our secrets, all an immense house of postcards."[17] At the very moment it illustrates language's self-division, this scene of dictation also reveals the delusion of subjectivity—Thornhill's futile effort to define himself within the postal as the commander or originator of language. The related Madison Avenue delusion—that language can always be manipulated to produce profit—is repeated in Thornhill's chauvinist belief in the powers of his language to effect seduction. Both fallacies flow from the illusion that the subject controls discourse instead of the reverse.

Throughout the film, the depiction of the world as postal or figuration reveals numerous ruptures between sender and recipient—suggestive of Derrida's claims "that a letter can always not arrive at its destination, and that therefore it never arrives."[18] The separation between message and destination is emphasized everywhere: when Thornhill changes his mind, too late, about the message he instructs Maggie to convey to his mother; when the page for Kaplan seems to be answered by Thornhill; when his mother, on the phone, fools the Plaza operator and desk clerk; when the valet and maid identify Thornhill as Kaplan; when Vandamm's men assume they've reached Kaplan on the telephone; when Thornhill intercepts Vandamm's phone message to Eve; when the matchbook with Thornhill's message to Eve is intercepted by Vandamm. In *North by Northwest*, the vulnerability of messages—the sense Derrida conveyed through the metaphor of the postcard—emphasizes the continuing lack of correspondence between sign and referent.

These jeopardized messages find a parallel in the film's extended analogy between transportation and the postal, through which we witness further interruptions, interceptions and detours.[19] An early example is the episode of forced drunken driving, in which Thornhill's presumed destination of death is luckily avoided. This scene also narrates the prospect of a potentially endless chain reaction of interrupted travelers—not just Thornhill, but the motorist colliding with him, the police, and his pursuers. Likewise, the film began with Thornhill and Maggie commandeering someone else's cab (a theft repeated later with Thornhill's mother); later, he steals someone else's pickup truck. All of these scenes illustrate detours or interceptions of vehicles while in transition between origin and destination.

With their "fixed directions" trains may epitomize the naive hermeneutics of absolute certainty in the transfer from origin to destination; however, even *The Twentieth-Century Limited* makes an unscheduled stop to allow detectives to search; the train journey also shows Thornhill that "the real Kaplan," the object of his quest is, first, missing, then murderous, then a fiction. That any planned trajectory can and will be interrupted in the interests of political authority—the law or national security—is part of Hitchcock's cultural critique. The detectives' interruption of the train, like the Professor's later intervention with the Chicago police, illustrates again vulnerability in the movement of a figure to its destination. To the extent that the breakdowns of messages and detours of transportation in *North by Northwest* subvert the concept of "transfer," they also imply a critique of learning—much as we have seen in John Ballantine's false "Eureka!" moment, in *Spellbound*, in the key-passing episode of *Notorious*, in the sites of transfer that introduce *Rope*, or in the revelation of the necklace in *Vertigo*. Movements from place to place ought to result in some gain, in the achievement of objectives, in maturation, insight, or wisdom. Instead, they result in the arrival at another place.

Character names suggest the arbitrary nature of the origins and destinations of meaning. Compounds like Thornhill, Townsend, and Vandamm call attention to the constructed and metaphoric nature of "proper" names; the absurdity of signs of personal identity is conveyed through Thornhill's famous comment on his initialed matchbook: "Rot," he says, "it's my trademark." When Eve asks what the "O" stands for, he replies, "Nothing." The Biblical allusion in "Eve Kendall" suggests enigma while her surname, as Tom Cohen points out, raises the problem of knowing.[20] "The Professor" is an instance of naming—antonomasia—in which the transfer or "true" reference is wholly blocked, as in catachresis. Other details of the dialogue emphasize the way names and protestations of identity are made to appear foolish:

Thornhill: "His name is Emile Klinger . . . Yes, mother, I'm not making it up."

 . . .

Thornhill: "Are you George Kaplan?"

Stranger: "Not the last time I checked."

 . . .

Thornhill: "I'm an advertising man, not a red herring."

That the human subject is not a signified presence but a fiction brought about by language is the whole point of the plot's precipitating event: Thornhill's identity becomes confounded with the fictional Kaplan's. The mistake that calls his identity in doubt is an accident, an *acte gratuit* like Jeff's chance observation of Thorvald when awakened from a fitful sleep. In such moments the subject confronts the constructed nature of identity and the possibility that the world is figuration. That this occurs at another relay point—the hotel page for Kaplan— further underscores the film's depiction of the postal. The incident resembles the opening of Kafka's *The Trial*, in which Joseph K. is mysteriously arrested and given the burden of establishing his identity. The pathetic inadequacy of Joseph K. producing his bicycle license as proof is echoed when Thornhill offers Vandamm his driver's license. In these cases, it is clear that no valid proof of human identity is available in language. Thornhill's attempt to establish his own identity by proving that he is *not* Kaplan cannot result in self-definition, and even after "Kaplan" is exposed as fictional, "Thornhill" remains an empty signifier. Exposing fictions lends a temporary illusion of authenticity to the subject and his name, which on reflection become arbitrary again. The "O" stands for nothing at the beginning and end of Thornhill's adventure.

Thornhill never escapes the postal world of figuration, especially metaphor and catachresis, leaving him unable to establish himself and/or Eve as authentic subjects. Even in the film's so-called happy ending, misnaming cannot be avoided: Thornhill's "Come along, Mrs. Thornhill" is doubtless a prolepsis and in any case blithely posits as true the egregious sexist misnaming of marriage.[21] Eve ends as she began, misnamed, misknown.

TRANSPORTATION AS POSTAL

The analogy between Derrida's postal and the transportation systems in *North by Northwest* indicates the way putative human subjects like Roger Thornhill or Eve Kendall may be viewed as groundless figures. In the famous distinction of New Criticism, they are unjustified "substances" or "tenors" conveyed within exterior "forms" or "vehicles." So enclosed, Thornhill and Kendall at first appear to be "inner," private, authentic subjectivities, but on closer inspection these interiors remain unreadable figures or faces, after all. Roger Thornhill and Eve Kendall take their place in Hitchcock's long tradition of undecidable interiors: in the lodger's wrapped face; in Larita's declaration that she is "nothing"; in the interchangeability of Jack and Corby; in *Spellbound*'s deluded interpreters of the self; in the indeterminable motivations of Devlin and Alicia; in the unreadable affect of *Rope*; and in *Vertigo*'s succession of enigmatic faces—of the credits, of Madeleine and of Judy.

The deconstruction of the exterior/interior distinction in *North by Northwest* begins in the first scene, where Thornhill, on his way to a vehicle, dictates supposedly private letters in the most public of spaces: an office corridor, the sidewalk, the back of a cab. Critics have remarked on Hitchcock's cultural critique, of the "expedient exaggerations" of both advertising and the dehumanized executive who practices it; still, some true alternative to this charade-world is not easy to find in the film.[22] We never see a sympathetic private consciousness, engaged in some authentic, non-exaggerated vocation, a character who might serve as a foil for Thornhill's supposed fraudulence or superficiality. On the contrary, the film depicts Thornhill as only one more talking face in a swarm of mostly anonymous, moving others. The film's opening may as easily be read as denying the existence of any interiority as satirizing its unusual absence in Thornhill.

In the analogy between transportation and the postal, the vehicles that carry characters function as exterior wrappings that should protect and reliably convey a cargo of "significant content," human subjects, but don't. Thornhill's being forced into a chauffeured limousine or stolen Mercedes is comparable, at this level, to the thugs' "mistaking" of his name as Kaplan: the appropriative relation between inner (tenor) and outer (vehicle) is clear as Thornhill is wrestled into these vehicles, a coerced fit of putative meaning into form, a kind of visualization of the trope catachresis.

Like the messages in the film, Thornhill ought to be definable by some inherent essence; instead, the enclosures he inhabits jeopardize any such private interiority. Consider the nesting containers on *The Twentieth-Century*: the train itself; within it the private compartment; and within that, the berth/bathroom. For Thornhill, each provides only the illusion of sanctuary. His hope for anonymity is dashed by Eve's recognition and the train's unscheduled stop; his retreat to Eve's compartment, interrupted by the detectives and porter, makes him withdraw further inward, to upper berth and bathroom. But every inward move brings only new vulnerability—in the berth, Thornhill's protective sunglasses break; in the bathroom, Eve must protect him from exposure. These images of false sanctuary are repeated in the occupation of Townsend's Glen Cove mansion by Vandamm's men, and in Thornhill's frequent illicit entries— of "Kaplan's" hotel room, of a patient's hospital room, and of Vandamm's supposedly secure mountain home. To the extent these penetrations are motivated by some demand for inner truth, they fail and instead expose the myth of the private interior.

The idea that there is no ground or invulnerable interior of the self is visually allegorized in the crop-dusting scene, which presents Thornhill in the absence of any safe place, threatened by a vehicle whose occupant remains unseeable and unknowable. It is tempting to see the scene as the depiction of some primal or originary condition of humanity defined purely as spacing or intersection— as some entity knowable only as the keeper of an unpredictable appointment with death.[23] In such a reading, the invisible pilot is only a less mystified version of the film's people: a vehicle without tenor, a figure with no apprehendable interior or ground. Such a minimalist conception of human identity is, after all, not much different from what we must conclude of the stranger, Thornhill's (and Hitchcock's) double, who is confronted across a deserted highway. (The highway is a transportation link in a grid with no visible origin or destination, a good rendering of a scene of "mere direction.") The stranger's identity is definable as the interval between two vehicles. During this brief existence, he announces contradiction ("That plane's dustin' crops where there ain't no crops") and—like Thornhill—can attest only to what he is *not* called. It is as if the pilot and the stranger are the true synecdoches of human existence who must be—as they soon are—forgotten in the mystified world, where identity, selfhood, love, and national security are the unquestioned assumptions or grounds of human life.

The idea that the emptiness of interiority is elided in a world of contentless relays is apparent in Eve's case, too. Eve is sent by the Professor on a mission of desperate urgency, the content of which remains undisclosed, except insofar as it consists of the pursuit of a sign—a microfilm of the enigmatic. On a mission whose rationale she never questions, Eve at first appears the repository of the most intimate, private, sensitive meaning, protected by her role as double agent and her enveloping exteriors—so many trains, hotel rooms, lodgings; however, the grounds of Eve's subjectivity are just as dubious as Thornhill's. She is a mask without a knowable interior. It is as if her face became the residual, container of the nothingness dissimulated by her layers of protective secrecy; in this respect she is like the cosmeticized face that introduces *Vertigo*. The moments most revelatory of her undecidability include the scenes when she kisses Thornhill just before sending Vandamm the note ("What shall I do with him in the morning?"); when she leaves Thornhill at the Chicago train station, having planned his assassination; when she cries during the art auction; when she leaves Thornhill, in the pine forest, having agreed to the Professor's plan to continue her disguise with Vandamm. In these instances, close-ups on Eve Kendall's face never resolve—they only ask again—the question of her motive: selfless love or selfish duty? Or, in the spirit of the film's deconstruction of interiority, should the adjectives be exchanged? If prosopopoeia may be a constitutive trope of literature, the unreadable face may be its corollary in film.[24]

GROUNDLESS FIGURATION

The dominant master narrative in criticism of *North by Northwest* holds that its ending finds Thornhill matured and its ambiguities resolved in favor of love; however, previous chapters of this book have shown that the creation of the couple never terminates suspense. *North by Northwest*'s apparent climax in romantic love is no exception: it increases rather than quiets the film's accumulating doubts. We have already seen how the film's last words—the prolepsis of Thornhill's invitation to "Mrs. Thornhill"—suggest the future continuation, beyond the film, of inevitable misnaming in the postal. Thornhill and Eve's retreat to an upper berth may also be understood as dramatizing their persistent confidence in a privacy or interiority that the film everywhere challenges. But most unsettling is the way the invitation to the upper berth comports with the scenes that precede and follow it: the famous Mount Rushmore rescue and the scene Hitchcock called his "phallic symbol"—the train entering the tunnel.[25] In this triptych, the scene of ostensible love is bracketed by groundless figuration.

This context has been prepared for throughout the film, when contact with "grounds" works to subvert, not establish, Thornhill's identity, which is appropriately associated with his clothes.[26] Thornhill's had been a life of easy passage through the world untainted by its dirt; but the originary moment in which his name is challenged entails an assault on his impeccably tailored clothes—stained with bourbon by Vandamm's thugs and rumpled at the police station, Thornhill's clothes are just as illusory guarantors of identity as his driver's license. His suit provides only spurious confirmation of his true identity when he lamely compares it to "Kaplan's" smaller jacket: it is as if one figure tries to establish its authenticity on the basis of a comparison with another. In the crop-dusting sequence, Thornhill is driven into the ground and covered with a chemical agent, as if the quest for "grounds" in *North by Northwest* resulted only in the further vulnerability and degradation of the figure of human identity. Eve's later efforts to clean the dust and dirt from his suit may betoken the sense in which love represses any unwelcome hint of the lack of true "grounds," though of course we cannot know—here or anywhere—if her affect is feigned. In any case, the removal of dirt is now a catalyst for the glamorously dangerous charade in which both "lovers" dissemble. When the Professor brings Thornhill new slacks and a shirt in the hospital, clean clothes become associated with bribes and new disguises. By the time Thornhill reaches Mount Rushmore, his clothes, like his name, seem an alienable signifier easily and inevitably dirtied or manipulated: like Eve's unreadable face, both exteriors are arbitrary counters disconnected from identity.

True "grounds" of identity in *North by Northwest* are nonexistent; in their place is an empty abyss. Thornhill and the viewer experience this when—Thornhill's wheels hanging over an embankment—the camera shows firm ground replaced by empty space. This effect is also produced by the high-angle shots that show Vandamm arguing with Thornhill or Thornhill exiting the United Nations. These evocations of acrophobia culminate in the Mount Rushmore sequence, where Thornhill's gropings over a double symbol of solidity—faces in rock which also betoken the foundations of American nationalism—alternate with shots of the empty abyss. Rock and air become elemental constituents, something and nothing; the film's narration of human contact with dust and "grounds" is resolved into this simple binary, through which solidity is only apparent. Geoffrey Hartman noted how the film put in question the idea that "understanding means something firm to stand on."[21] *North by Northwest*'s allegory of missing grounds is an extension of *Vertigo*'s allegory of untenability. Inside the story, the Mount Rushmore sequence undermines name, identity, and national purpose (including the purposes of Eve and the Professor): the dumb presidential faces concealing nothing are magnifications of the masks worn by Thornhill and Eve. He never awakens from his dream of selfhood; she cannot shed her mask or confirm whether her motive has been love or survival. The *grand recit* of redemptive love may also be read as a narrative of two figures turning toward each other their incomprehensible faces.

North by Northwest's questioning of the master narratives of self, country, and love works to undermine the grounds of understanding of film criticism, too, which consists of relentless attempts to attribute an inner referent to the plays of light, the *clignotements*, that seem like figures or faces. The ending forces us to see how we take rock as face, just as we take the play of light through colored celluloid as face. Reading films *requires* such mistakes. In this context of necessary error, the importance of the film's final "phallic symbol" may be something other than a joke. It was Hitchcock who, in a famous remark to Truffaut, "read" the last scene as a "phallic symbol." Like any film viewer, Hitchcock attributes a referent—transfers meaning—to a visual sign. There are several other moments when we seem invited to supply an extra-filmic "signified" to a visual catachresis: early on, when the wheels of Thornhill's car spin over empty air, we may read "cliffhanger." Or as Thornhill listens to the conversation inside Vandamm's house we may read "(E)vesdropping." These witty Hitchockian moments are like the prominent display of Jeff's "cast" during the credits of *Rear Window*. Hitchcock's gloss of "phallic symbol" for train-entering-tunnel may at first illustrate the belated or pathetic quality of criticism. But taken even as definitive—whatever that means—Hitchcock's comment has the effect of equating the act of intercourse with a blank or absent referent which must be filled in, like Roger's initial "O," with interpretation. Interpretation in this case renders the ending more ambiguous, since "intercourse" is an ultimate meaning of the Hollywood couple, the extra-cinematic part of the film that lies beyond the closing embrace. Converting such a transcendental signified into a visual trope transforms it into the contingent, always-intercepted postal: the screen fades out on a scene of coitus (and interpretation) interruptus, suspended.

FIGURES OF STATE POWER

The political world is also groundless.

Political legitimation is impossible when there can be no naturally right message or law, no naturally right sender or recipient of it. The political state of nature is only marked space, like the grid that precedes the credits or the intersection of earth and sky with bullets mailed from an invisible sender to a nameless recipient. Consistent with such a state of nature are Machiavellian adversaries—the Professor and Vandamm, linked only by inference to traditional cold war opponents[28]—each of whom reserves the right to overrule Kantian or regulative law. The Professor's regret at the necessity of having to consign Thornhill to his death or to overrule the Chicago police in no way changes the film's parallels between his own behavior and Vandamm's less mystified depravity. Both men seek the same object—the microfilm/MacGuffin, a sign without content that is enclosed in a "figure." Both men work through intermediaries: the Professor dominates his committee and Eve, his agent. When it comes time to use force to rescue her, he gives an order to fire to a park ranger, an order that shows the homology between the CIA as plainclothes police and a uniformed civilian. From the outset *North by Northwest* has depicted a world in which the civilian world is engaged in a war, as seen in Thornhill's dictation to his secretary about the "war" of capitalism. "Civilian" society's ultimate dependence on force is illustrated by another intermediary, the Professor's chauffeur, who obliges him by knocking out Thornhill when he resists the Professor's plans. This scene makes the Professor parallel with Vandamm, whose stone-faced driver is silent in response to the pleas Thornhill makes from the back seat. The parallels lend force to Thornhill's rebuke to the Professor, when, in the woods, he is told that America's need to win the war justified the machinations of Eve: "Then maybe it's time we started losing a few!" In *North by Northwest*, the CIA is equated with its opponents: civil society is a myth that mystifies the illegitimacy of the Hobbesian or Foucauldian power relations. This depressing political commentary is by now a familiar part of Hitchcock's films: of *The Lodger*, where law enforcers, lawbreakers, and audiences are avengers; of *Notorious*, where Americans and Nazis are morally equivalent; of *Rope*, where Rupert is helpless to distinguish himself morally from his criminal students; in *Vertigo*, where Scottie seems, despite himself, to reenact Elster's ethos of the *Ubermensch*.

The image of brute power wearing the trappings of rationality is promoted by its association with high culture and universities. The name "the Professor" accomplishes this as it denotes an aspiration to signify without reference to content; his title blocks access to any true name. Rhetorically the phrase is catachresis masquerading as antonomasia. Vandamm's seeming erudition and aestheticism are suggested by his presence at the art auction and by the architectural high modernism of his mountainside retreat, but these associations are no more indicative of true identity than his British accent. Vandamm's connection with the university is made in the photograph Thornhill observes, taken in front of a university facade, but this photograph, like the name "Professor," is but another sign cut off from a referent. Even the Professor acknowledges that his "U.S. Intelligence Agency" is "part of the same alphabet soup as the CIA, the FBI, the ONI . . ." The adversaries and their organizations are part of the world conceived as postal; acquiescence in the legitimacy of their referents— reason, nationalism, the CIA, communism—is a delusion shared by characters and film-critics alike, the mark of a hermeneutics impatient with the suspenseful circulation of lying signs and longing to put an end to it.[29]

The only apparent asymmetry between the adversaries is the contrast between the aging, asexual Professor and the apparently bisexual Vandamm; these might suggest that some true "grounds" of identity might be inferrable from the film's depiction of sexuality. However, the significance of Vandamm's libido is, like everything else, dubious. If we believe Eve's claim that her liaison has become purely a matter of patriotic duty, his heterosexual allure is weakened, though Eve's sincerity is open to doubt. Vandamm's homosexual side is weakened by his unresponsiveness to Leonard's competition with Eve for his regard. For queer theorists, Vandamm's bisexual potential might seem to essentialize subjectivity—to position it as an alternative to the illusions of the principals' "normative heterosexuality" or the Professor's asexuality; however, like homosexuality in *Rope*, bisexuality in *North by Northwest* remains only a sign. In *North by Northwest*, sexual orientation is another groundless figure for selfhood.

The outlaw interventions of the Professor and Vandamm recall those of their predecessors, Prescott (or Devlin) and Alex Sebastian in *Notorious*. These are the political equivalents of hermeneutic interpretation of messages in the postal. The suspense of circulating messages is temporarily arrested when they are interpreted as having a content or when they ratify the intervener's belief in cause, referent, or selfhood. Such intervention in the suspenseful circulation of the postal may be a prerequisite for any human communication or political community, but it is nonetheless fictive: Thornhill can no sooner question his identity than the Professor can question national security or Vandamm can question his nefarious scheme or Eve can question her motives. The illusory presences its characters cannot dislodge are as tenacious as the audience's unshakable belief that the flickering lights they see are characters.

FILM CRITICISM AS THE CIA

Figural and deconstructive interpretations of *North by Northwest* are also interventions into the endless postal of groundless signifiers that repeat the errors made by the film's characters and director. The reflexive dimension of the film reinforces this conclusion. Studies of the reflexivity of *North by Northwest* have assumed that some valid point of view on the film is possible, even after frequent demonstrations that the film calls all acts of seeing into question.[30] However, *North by Northwest* teaches viewers that film interpretation is as arbitrary as the CIA, as groundless as Thornhill's search for a true identity, but as inevitable—in Nietzsche's phrase, as "human, all too human"—as belief in the self or in love. Few academic critics see themselves in the Professor. But this chastening analogy is evident when we turn to the film's reflexive side, in which its viewers parallel its characters in the unavoidable, fruitless imposition of meaning on groundless suspended figures.

As Eve bolts on the walk to the runway, Vandamm tells Leonard, "Get that figure back from her!" In this moment it becomes clear that the plot's MacGuffin has always been a figure and its sought-after interior. The figure first appears in the art auction, when its materiality—its literal equation with a price—is established undeniably; at the same time, the film shows that the value of the figure is wholly independent of its price and that the figure itself is inconsequential. The figure begins to signify only when it is assumed that it is a "mere vehicle" for something else, something of supposedly incommensurate value. That something else—a microfilm—is teasingly revealed at the end of the film; so viewers may be led to suspect that film, like any art, culminates in an act of unveiling, of revelation, perhaps of Heideggerian *aletheia*. On the one hand, the microfilm becomes the property of the Professor—no doubt to be put to use for some political or academic purpose; on the other hand, viewers can't read it. According to this allegory, art's undecidability cannot be tolerated in the world; its suspension of meaning is seized by the police, claimed by hermeneutics, pressed into the service of some referent or critical *grand recit*. Hitchcock's withering irony in inviting his audience to compare itself to two sides at war over an unreadable "film" should function like the warnings against interpretation in *Vertigo*, cautioning viewers against such interventions, but by the end of the film such warnings are already belated. A sense of the inevitability of groundless interpretation may have prompted Hitchcock's interest in these obviously artificial, imposed endings, beginning with the *deus ex machina* revelation of the "true" Avenger in *The Lodger* but also evident in Dr. Murchison's slip of the tongue in *Spellbound*, the nun in the bell tower of *Vertigo*, or the psychiatrist's revelation at the end of *Psycho*. In any case, the battle for the unreadable (micro) film in *North by Northwest* suggests how film interpretation is an unavoidable error. As a condition of reading the film, film viewers have scant alternative but to follow the Professor in construing the interior of the figure to be meaningful; the mistake of this conclusion becomes evident, if at all, only after it is committed.

Audience blindness is allegorized in many scenes, where viewers are shown to be ignorant of the meaning of what it is they witness. The crowd in the Plaza elevator laugh sympathetically as Thornhill's mother mistakenly believes she is disabusing her son of his paranoia. The crowd at the United Nations believe they have witnessed Thornhill stabbing Townsend. The crowd at the art auction accept Thornhill's feigned madness. The crowd at the cafeteria accepts Eve's pretend shooting of Thornhill. In these instances, audiences remain mystified by the visual spectacles they've witnessed; as surrogates for film viewers, these people anticipate our misinterpretation.

Of course, it cannot be said that Hitchcock intended this or any other construction of his film; on the contrary, we are led to see that the artwork exists independently of its creator. Through Hitchcock's cameo, the film allegorizes the director as one who "misses the bus," remains on the exterior of the conveyance, himself in suspense, barred from the "vehicle" that ought to be his own before it begins to move. To the extent that the transportation system resembles the postal, the director's message—if one ever existed—remains absent. Whatever is conveyed to the viewer is outside the director's control. The director is as helpless as the viewer in enforcing an interpretation on the interior content of the film, in defining its direction. As the credits should have taught us, the "direction" of *North by Northwest* remains only that—a suspenseful movement or a transfer whose end cannot be said.

13

Psycho: Empty Interiors

Marion Crane's white Ford hangs suspended in a black marsh. The car's windows, top, and trunk are visible; the license plate is half obscured; the lower half of the car lies under the muck. The suspension of the car at precisely this moment interrupts Norman Bates's plans to hide the evidence of his crime. For a minute it seems that he will be exposed, then the car resumes its downward slide.

In its invitation to aesthetic contemplation, the hanging figure's momentary pause may elicit many associations. The car sinking into the mud may suggest the formation of the Freudian unconscious in repression or Plato's related idea of the soul as a chariot driver who steers a white horse and a black horse: the juxtaposition of clear windows with a filthy undercarriage may reinforce the film's insinuations that supposedly rational vision masks depraved human instinct. The half-obscured license plate suggests the way detachable signs of identity may signify only exterior shells enclosing an empty or dead interiors. The trunk lid may remind viewers that inside is Marion's corpse, wrapped in a shower curtain, and the film's MacGuffin—$39,300 in cash, wrapped in a newspaper. Both contents are now rendered parallel in their uselessness. In Psycho *the urgent-insignificant "object" that initiates the plot is here imaginable as a stack of printed signs temporarily removed from circulation in the postal world. Like the submerging license plate, money is as pointless as humans or their news, and all are consigned to oblivion.*

But these multiplying associations of the hanging figure remain uncertain until they can be grounded in the "why" of the film—the psychiatrist's explanation for Norman's motivation. But the Ford as hanging figure sinks into a

Figure 13.1: *Psycho* (1960). Copyright © 2002 by Universal Studios. Courtesy of Universal Studios Publishing Rights, a Division of Universal Studios Licensing, Inc. All rights reserved.

place where all "grounds" may be slippery, slithery, and endowed with the capacity to make the world's most valorized objects disappear. This image frames the psychiatrist's assertion of the grounds for Norman's behavior, be-cause the film's final shot, in which the Ford hangs from a chain pulled by a tow-truck's winch, returns the viewer to the images of groundlessness and the hanging figure. Psycho *depicts a world in which the "why," or rational inter-pretation, is superseded by hanging figures of groundlessness and unending suspense.*

VISION AS MISINTERPRETATION

Psycho's story of the emptiness of interpretation continues the tradition of Jeff's arbitrary theory in *Rear Window* or the accidental challenge to Thornhill's identity in *North by Northwest*; it looks forward to the absence of causality in *The Birds*. *Psycho* shows that seeing is misinterpretation. This theme is traced in the psychiatrist's speech, in the quests of Arbogast and Lila, in the depiction of Sam and Lila as the film's constructed couple, and in the film's reflexive details.

The tradition of seeing as misinterpretation began with *The Lodger*'s explo-ration of visual prejudice that led to the permanent misidentification of the Avenger. In *Easy Virtue* it continued with the idea of necessary visual frames, and in *Spellbound* with the errors of dream vision. In the unreadable faces of

Vertigo and *North by Northwest*, misinterpretation is strongly associated with attempts to comprehend visual art. The development of this tradition was not original with Hitchcock. Recent studies by Rosalind Krauss and Martin Jay show how surrealist photography and film registered protests against what Jay calls ocularcentrism—the privileged status accorded to the sense of vision as a kind of grail of hermeneutics, the achievement of a true theoretical perspective. For Krauss and Jay, Bataille's enucleated eye, Magritte's *trompe d'oeil* and Dalí's sliced eyeball anticipate the philosophic interrogation of hermeneutics intensified later by deconstruction.[1]

Psycho's extension of this tradition is evident in its shot of Marion Crane's dead eye, which, in a famous dissolve, gradually replaces the image of a bathtub drain. Critics have interpreted the dissolve in many ways, without consensus.[2] Marion's only apparently seeing eye is a synecdoche for *Psycho*'s numerous scenes of illusory vision and interpretation. It emerges from a bathtub drain; both are apertures to nothingness. In this allegory, what the eye takes in, in viewing or reading, is like diluted blood down the drain—a sign only of emptiness or death; what the world calls perception may be no more than mirages that temporarily repress mortality. On this level, what we see in *Psycho* is reducible to the drain-eye image, which subverts psychologies and perceptions as mistakings of absences. No one—not Marion, Norman, Arbogast, Sam, Lila, the psychiatrist, or the critic—ever sees truly; each is condemned to search for a signifying presence—love or money, reason or cause, theme or meaning.

Like *Vertigo*, *Psycho* allegorizes this universal delusion by showing how its characters search for tenable meanings that cannot be grasped. Marion Crane's quest for love necessitates, first, a search for money, as if an advance toward one goal required the substitution of a second goal, a mis-taking. Her embezzlement is a literal misappropriation of signs; the cash becomes *Psycho*'s MacGuffin. Money is the seeming locus of meaning, as it often is in life. Since the necessity to take signs as real is as fundamental to viewing films as it is to financial affairs and love, Marion Crane's misappropriation only repeats as it exposes, belatedly, the viewer's act in taking as real a cinematic play of light and dark. The idea that Marion's substitute goal, cash, consists of new signs momentarily taken as a valued referent is reinforced when she stuffs it into an envelope, like a message in the postal, and then into a newspaper. The cash functions as the object of the viewer's visual curiosity: the camera lingers over it, first in Marion's bedroom, later in her car, finally at the Bates Motel. Camera and viewer follow the cash (or the envelope or newspaper supposedly containing it) until it disappears into the trunk of the Ford; the interminability of circulating signs is established when the car is pulled from the swamp. All of this time the viewer's watching has been an elaborate shell game.

The viewer's expectation of some ground for these signs is rewarded by the psychiatrist's theory of Norman's motivation, personified in "Norman's mother," but aside from her corpse "Mrs. Bates," too, is a sign without a referent—like David Kentley, an impossible anchor for discourse. Death gives the lie to all proper names. Even to name Mrs. Bates or to represent her in the pronoun "her" is to be in error. Like the cash, Norman's mother is a misleading visual sign: Arbogast and Lila think they see her at the window; Marion and a first-time viewer may even see "her" attacking. In the landing scene, when Norman carries his mother's corpse, Hitchcock went to elaborate lengths to show Mrs. Bates in such a way as to pre-empt any objection that viewers had been tricked by film editing.[3] Still, the object of the audience's quest is an optical illusion. Of course, Norman's mother has *some* existence, just as all signs have some material embodiment.[4] This is the effect of the scene with Sheriff Chambers, who exclaims, "If Norman's mother is up there, who is in the grave?" (Since the dead "exist" both as corpses and also as memories, their names may be humankind's first experience of signs that promise but withhold referents.) Put another way, *Psycho* makes no more claims for an interior content for psychological motivation than it does for the referents of names of the dead.

THE PSYCHIATRIST'S SPEECH

Psycho's undermining of psychoanalytic discourses is also not new; *Spellbound* mocked the metaphors that constitute the "white mythologies" of psychiatric hermeneutics.[5] In *Psycho* the cultural critique is more nuanced and the psychiatric authority is given more plausibility because the psychiatrist's explanation delivers the narrative *logos*. His speech is a superb test of the persistence of suspense following plot resolutions. The placement and prominence of the speech suggest a parody of the denouments of genres of crime fiction or Greek tragedy: the long-pursued grail at the end of the hermeneutic quest is announced by the modern world's equivalent of the Delphic oracle or *deus ex machina*.[6] Some critics attack the psychiatrist's personality.[7] Some find his diagnosis incomplete or appeal to realities outside the film. For example, Raymond Bellour's Lacanian reading saw the speech's main shortcoming as its restriction to Norman and blindness to the film's analogy between the two narratives—Marion's neurosis and Norman's psychosis.[8] Adapting Bellour's approach but pursuing a feminist hermeneutic, Barbara Klinger argued that in speaking for society's amalgamation of legal and family values, the psychiatrist perpetuates phallocentrism by excluding the threat to those values posed by Marion and female sexuality.[9] William Rothman indicted the psychiatrist for being unable to appreciate Norman's "triumph," which he saw in the identification with Hitchcock and the camera.[10] Leland Poague thought that the psychiatrist too easily dismissed the importance of money.[11] Robert Corber argued that the psychiatrist illustrates the increasing hegemony of expert opinion in the postwar dispersal of state power."[12]

These critical positions measure the psychiatrist's analysis on new grounds, on new hermeneutics of psychology, aesthetics and politics; however, the idea that the psychiatrist's speech may be invalidated *because* it is an interpretation of an interior—a position that would undermine these responses—can be understood by exchanging hermeneutics for the deconstructive hypothesis that the film narrates *necessary* misinterpretation. As de Man argued, we must question reference in discourses that presuppose reference. The psychiatrist, like Arbogast, Lila, and Marion, must confront "Norman's mother" and frame an interpretation about intention as interior presence out of arbitrary signs. Like *Psycho*'s critics, these characters can no sooner see Norman as motiveless than viewers can see him as an alternation of light and shadow. Attribution of interior cause lies at the heart of hermeneutics.

It is notable that the psychiatrist delivers his explanation as a kind of lecture before a seated audience, in one room, while the presumed object of his discourse sits alone in an adjacent, otherwise empty room; of course, the *true* object of the psychiatrist's discourse—"Norman's mother"—is absent, and her ontological status very much in doubt. The separation between sign and referent is further emphasized when the psychiatrist characterizes his findings as a relay in the postal, as a paraphrase or second hand version: "Now to understand it the way I understood it, hearing it from the mother—that is, from the mother half of Norman's mind . . ." The psychiatrist's figure for the origin of the discourse ("the mother half of Norman's mind") is consistent with his later figure for madness ("when the mind houses two personalities"). This buried metaphor is particularly revelatory in the light of this film's questions about the distinction between exterior and interior. The viewer learns that the Bates mansion conveys only the *illusion* of "housing" two personalities.

As noted in Chapter 4, Hitchcock explored the Cartesian concept of "housing"—the situating of some privileged *res inextensus* within some *res extensus*—in *Rear Window*, where Jeff's position in the wheelchair is doubled by his window view and technological aids to enhanced vision. As noted in Chapter 12, the interior/exterior distinction was subverted in *North by Northwest* by enclosed spaces that produced only an illusion of privacy. In *Psycho* the Cartesian premise is put into question by the succession of anonymous, temporary interiors that define the world Marion inhabits: the bleak hotel room where she meets Sam; her office, where public and private matters are uneasily and vulgarly mixed; her cramped bedroom, which seems only a larger version of her suitcase; her tradable car that promises a protective interior but becomes the object of the patrolman's gaze; the Bates motel, where interior privacy is nonexistent. The situation is little different for Sam Loomis, who foresees his future with Marion in the small room behind the hardware store. Thomas Leitch called *Psycho* Hitchcock's "most annihilating attack on the very concept of human identity";[13] its phony or impoverished interiors give the lie to the psychiatrist's metaphor of exteriors "housing" singular (or even plural) subjectivity. In the interior is emptiness.

The psychiatrist's speech assumes the untenable Cartesian metaphor for the self. Instead of being a private place, *res inextensus*, the self is constructed by language that is instantly readable, like a postcard; in deconstructing the idea of the private or "housed" self, *Psycho* shows the private self supplanted by voices from unfixed or indeterminate sources that transcend inner/outer boundaries. The voices Marion hears in her car are like the voices of Mrs. Bates—disembodied utterances that question any fixed "place of the self." When in Marion's car we hear the voiceovers of the actors who played the parts of George Lowery and Tom Cassidy, we may initially think as the psychiatrist might, that they are "housed" in Marion's head but because they are audible to us, they are also *not* in her head. The effect is even more pronounced when we hear "Mrs. Bates" speaking off-camera—first at the Bates Motel and later at the police station. In neither case have we seen the source of these words. In neither case is it plausible that Tony Perkins was capable of modulating his actual voice to imitate the voice—raspy, screeching, belligerent—of his supposed mother. The audience hears voices that were *not* "housed" in Norman's mind. Far from dramatizing the mind as "housing" interiors, the film figures the self as a continually vulnerable and exposed construct of language.

The psychiatrist uses another metaphor that betrays his ignorance—of "grounds." In the following interchange with Lila and a stationhouse detective, he blithely calls into question his own (and society's) most crucial belief—that words have "grounds"—even as he lamely attempts to make motivation comprehensible:

Lila: Did he kill my sister?

Psychiatrist: Yes . . . and no . . .

Detective: Well now, look, if you're trying to lay some psychiatric groundwork for some sort of plea this fellow would like to cop . . .

Psychiatrist: A psychiatrist doesn't lay the groundwork; he merely tries to explain . . .

The psychiatrist's equivocation about cause subverts his distinction between "explanation" and "groundwork." All along he assumes that his explanation is *grounded* in the ontologically real status of some "Mrs. Bates" inside Norman; however, he also insists that an "explanation" should not provide a "groundwork" for some other discourse. Put another way, the psychiatrist both asserts and denies that verbal explanations can be grounded. If explanations, too, lack "groundwork" and if metaphor is an essential condition of articulation, then it is not surprising that the psychiatrist's monologue leaves his auditors in the same frustrated condition as film audiences—hanging.

DEAD INTERPRETATION

The idea that rational searches for cause or grounds can never escape a world of hanging figures, suspense, and referentless signs is the instruction of Hitchcock's films beginning with *The Lodger* and *Number Seventeen*, whose detectives are shown to bring about disasters—apprehension of the wrong man, train wrecks—through the exercise of reason. In *Vertigo* Scottie's hard work only shows the world as a glamorously dangerous charade. In *Psycho* this tradition is extended in the quests of Arbogast and Lila. Set on Marion's trail by *her* mis-taking of signs, of cash, Arbogast, too, must presuppose the existence of referents—for example, of the photograph of Marion, now dead, that he shows to motel keepers. His deduction that Norman's mother actually exists proceeds from a referentless visual delusion, like film. Arbogast's quest to locate referents results in his death. To speculate on whether he or Marion understood the world as it really was at the time of their deaths—by seeing Norman's mother as unreal—only establishes more clearly the interminability of suspense: if they see "Norman's mother," they die in palpable illusion. But if they see "Norman disguised as his mother," as Sam and Lila do, they are still deluded, just as much as the viewer is, since the hermeneutic question of the meaning of or motive for Norman's attack remains deferred until the psychiatrist's explanation, which only hangs. The fates of Arbogast and Marion show the world as inescapable figuration.

Lila's quest also perpetuates suspense. In her exploration of Mrs. Bates's and Norman's rooms, the camera dwells on portentous, seemingly talismanic images that reveal, after all, only the waywardness of her search. If we understand her journey as a rational quest for true interpretation, we are everywhere reminded of its futility. We see vacant spaces (an empty sink and fireplace; the outline of a body in a bed); we see simulacra of life (the folded hands on the jewelry box, single and double mirror reflections, a stuffed bunny); we see signifiers of signifiers (a phonograph of the Eroica symphony; a book whose contents remain undisclosed). These are hanging figures. George Toles's account of Lila's search admirably captures its fruitless search for significance: "In no other Hitchcock film does the camera close in on so many objects that refuse to disclose their significance. The nearest thing to a penetration of the interior is Lila's exploration of the Bates's house, but here, as before, whatever the inquiring eye approaches seems instantly to escape what it designates."[14] Lila's search vitiates the psychiatrist's analysis in advance, by showing us that no accumulation of biographical signs or details can yield interior motivation. Is the stuffed bear a sign of psychotic regression or of normal sentimentality? Is there any way mute details could interpret themselves? This succession of details "ends" with Lila's confrontation with the corpse of Mrs. Bates, thereby strengthening the sense that signs seem only to occlude, defer, or evade the fact of mortality. These dead representations of life recall Norman's stuffed birds and Marion's dead eye; they suggest the death of theoria, or interpretation. (The etymology of "theory" is inseparable from vision: the words "idea" and "video" proceed from a common ocularcentric root.) The death of interpretation is conveyed in a series of steps: first, *Psycho* shows us the failure of Marion's and Norman's visual quests. Somewhat in the manner of *Rear Window*'s Jeff, their searches are depicted as efforts at visual concentration—Marion's eye-squinting journey down a rainy road looking for a lighted sign; Norman's peering though a peephole. The failures of these visual quests are repeated by the film's theory-builders—Arbogast, Lila, the psychiatrist. Film critics come up lamely behind.

THE DECONSTRUCTION OF THE COUPLE

Raymond Bellour identified *Psycho*'s structural oddness when he observed how little the film's ending constituted a reply to its beginning: nothing in the psychiatrist's speech responds to Marion's initial love dilemma. As we've seen, Bellour like other critics was constrained to discover such a reply, which he accomplished by "completing" the psychiatrist's speech and explaining Norman's psychosis as the intensification of Marion's neurosis. Variants of this thesis comprise the category of what Leland Poague calls the "standard reading" of the film, according to which the viewer is meant to accept complicity in the world of repressed instinct that the psychiatrist endorses. This book has proposed that endings never reply to beginnings but only extend their suspense. Bellour's observation makes it possible to see *Psycho*'s suspense in a new light, as a blatant *dramatization* of a non-reply, especially insofar as this built-in disappointment is manifested in the ironic construction of the couple. The replacement of the expected union between Marion and Sam with first the grim "union" of Marion and Norman and then of the substitute pair, Sam and Lila, dramatizes the deconstruction of the couple that has always been the hallmark of Hitchcock's undecidable endings.

Robert Corber's analysis of Sam and Marion's early motives shows how their future union might always, already have been illusory. Noting Sam's ironic attitude toward respectability and his interest in stories of hotel trysts that enhance marital intensity, Corber suggests that Sam's reason for delaying marriage may be based as much on the prolongation of sexual fantasy as on financial exigency. (His sexual fantasy is taken up in more detail below.) And noting Marion's sly grin at the thought of having defeated Cassidy through her theft, Corber suggests that her motive for the embezzlement may be transgressive and retaliatory as well as affective: she denies to both the old man and his daughter their smug assurance of security.[15] Because these selfish motives coexist with Sam's and Marion's apparently needy love, the true grounds of their relationship are undecidable.

This initial impression is strengthened in Sam's incomplete letter which renders his problematic motivation even less readable: "Dearest right as always Marion, I'm sitting in this tiny back room which isn't big enough for both of us, and suddenly it *looks* big enough for both of us. So what if we're poor and cramped and miserable, at least we'll be happy. If you haven't come back to your senses and still." This representation of Sam's relationship with Marion is self-canceling. For Marion to accept his phrase "right as always" without irony would be possible only if she also saw herself as someone who hasn't come back to her senses. The latter phrase also asks Marion to ignore her recollection of the bitterness against creditors and ex-wife that led Sam to postpone a wedding. In addition, she must decide what degree of irony to extend to Sam's underlining of the word "looks" and to his prediction they will be simultaneously miserable and happy. Did some changed interior self "housed" in Sam's exterior write a letter full of signs more authentic than those we heard during his earlier rationalizing monologue at the hotel? Or is this letter another rationalizing monologue? Might the undecidability of Sam's letter anticipate the rationalizing monologue of that other figure who claims to have achieved new insight—the psychiatrist?

Just as Sam's true feelings for Marion are unreadable, so is the question of her own interior intent. To Norman she announces her decision to return to Phoenix, but even if she had not earlier lied to him about her name, the inscrutability of her interior is narrated when she returns to her room. At her writing desk she subtracts 700 from 40,000. (This simple arithmetical exercise might seem unnecessary for a secretary with ten years' experience; that she is experienced with financial records is clear from the bankbook that lies exposed underneath the paper on which she makes her calculation.) After tearing up these computations, she begins to throw the scraps in the waste-paper basket but instead chooses the toilet. This pantomime seems to narrate "changing one's mind," but it is impossible to know the *content* of that change. Viewers naturally assume that Marion's computations indicate she has stuck with her decision to return, but if so there was hardly a need to subtract 700 from 40,000, since the first figure shows she understands the total amount that she embezzled and must restore. Why does she tear up the paper? The numbers are hanging figures. They acquire meaning only as part of a narrative construct, only if interior motive is attributed to their author, and there is nothing in her actions to prevent the wholly new attribution, *this is the amount I have left to spend.* This possibility would account for Marion's tearing up the scraps: someone else might make such an inference about her motive. On the other hand, since tearing up the scraps might also indicate a *genuine* decision to restore all the money, we can't know if Marion changed her mind *twice.*

Given this display of Marion's unreadable interior, her smile in the shower becomes equally inaccessible to reason. Is she rejoicing in innocence or absolution, as some critics have maintained, or in a renewed determination to see Sam, with $39,300, on the next day? Does the smile denote moral innocence or sexual fantasy? Marion's face is unreadable as Daisy's, Larita's, Nell's, Constance's, Alicia's, Judy's, or Eve's. As in the case of Judy's letter in *Vertigo*, Marion's torn-up writing provides the illusion of a glimpse into her interior but this glimpse reveals, after all, newly canceled signs. When Lila discovers the fragment not yet flushed down the drain, she is like any viewer who must attribute motivation to the arbitrary. Marion's writing is as undecidable as Sam's letter, the psychiatrist's monologue, the film *Psycho*, interpretations of it (like this one) or any text: absent signs temporarily preserved from extinction must be read in terms of a determinable but unknowable interior.

To the extent the unreadable interiors of Marion and Sam suggest that they are masked constructs from the outset, they are not different from other Hitchcock couples—the lodger and Daisy, Jack and Nell, Constance and John, Alicia and Devlin, Scottie and Judy, Roger and Eve. That the expected union of Marion and Sam is a prospect like a combination of ciphers, maybe like Marion's sub-

traction, is evident when the viewer's anticipation of this couple must be satisfied by the surrogate couple, Sam and Lila.

As noted above, Sam's offhand acknowledgment to Marion of the erotic intensity he finds in contemplating sexual trysts in hotel rooms may color our
assessment of the integrity of his commitment to her; however, it becomes impossible to ignore this side of Sam's personality when he and Lila investigate
Marion's disappearance. On their way to the Bates Motel, Lila suggests that
they register as man and wife as a cover for their search of the premises. (One
critic notes that at this remark, "Sam looks at her oddly."[16] More unreadable
looks will ensue.) But when they register at the desk, the story Sam tells Norman
makes it impossible to know if he is acting the part of a married man with his
wife or instead the part of a man checking in with a lover. Glancing at Lila, he
tells Norman that his trip is "90 percent business." To Norman's question, he
replies defiantly that they have no luggage; he flaunts his knowledge that everywhere else, customers like him are expected to pay in advance. Far from acting
the part of a married man with his wife, as Lila had suggested, Sam is here
acting the part of a (perhaps married) man checking into a motel with his lover.
In other words, during the investigation of the disappearance of the woman he
is presumed to love, who for all he knows is still alive, Sam takes time to
indulge his sexual fantasy vicariously, as it were, with Lila. To the extent that
Psycho may have positioned viewers to expect Sam would become one half of
the normative created couple, his obliviousness to the persistence of his sexual
fantasies suggests the way any such "norm" enshrines delusion or hedonism,
not mutual love.

Hitchcock's radical conclusion, reinforced by the many visual parallels between Sam Loomis and Norman Bates, is that there *is* no "norm"—not only no
norm of mutual love in the constructed couple, but also, as the psychiatrist's
speech has taught, no norm for assessing human conduct.[17]

And, what of Lila? As she awaits Sam's return from the Bates motel, her
place at his desk, in the hardware store backroom, positions her in the room
Sam had envisioned for Marion in his letter; she has become Marion's surrogate.
Some critics have seen a physical resemblance between the two characters.[18]
Lila quickly rejects Sheriff Chambers's invitation to continue to work through
legal channels by filing a missing persons report; her impulsive decision to go
to the Bates Motel and pretend to be Sam's wife was based on Arbogast's
unfulfilled promise to be back in touch with her. But in the motel bedroom she
also admits other possible interpretations to Sam: "[Arbogast] lied to me, or he
felt sorry for me and was beginning to feel sorry about you." If Lila realizes
her decision to impersonate Sam's wife may have been ill-conceived, after all,
there is the possibility that it may have proceeded from other motives, of which
she may not be aware. Without fully explaining, Lesley Brill ventured, "Lila's
relationship with Sam becomes increasingly connubial."[19] Before they leave together to find Sheriff Chambers, Lila gives Sam an affectionate pat on the chest.
At the Bates check-in counter, Lila gives Sam an undecidable look—of real or

feigned love. No determination can be made of Lila's interior; like everyone else, she is a figure whose significance "hangs."

At the end, Sam and Lila, the substitute couple, take their seats as members of an audience that listens to the psychiatrist. It adds to the unreadability of their characters that upon hearing for the first time that Norman killed Marion, neither reveals any emotion; instead, both patiently await the conclusion of the psychiatrist's monologue. It is in the attitude of patient, affectless waiting for deferred or hanging meaning that Sam and Lila come to comprise the constructed couple at the end of *Psycho*; as such they signify not some extra-textual norm or template against which the audience should measure itself or the action of the film but instead the waiting audience.

THE VIEWER'S DEAD EYE

In the foregoing *Psycho* was read as the allegory of its characters' mistakings of signs or visual figures for referents. In this extension of Paul de Man's idea, the story illustrates a necessity for redundant misreadings of suspended meaning that are only extinguished by death. The film depicts human seeing or understanding as a delusion, a dead eye. In this regard, *Psycho*'s effect also resembles that of surrealist painting as understood by Jay and Krauss, in impugning human understanding through an assault on ocularcentrism, hermeneutics, theoria, and especially psychoanalytic discourses. At the same time, the film also indicts itself, as a visual spectacle which is helpless to offer any valid alternative to the delusions it dramatizes. The primary means for achieving this simultaneous self-indictment is through its running self-parody, which continually mocks the viewer's necessary efforts to glean meaning.

Psycho's reflexive features—from its titles, opening tracking shot, mirrors, subjective camera, imagery of the eye, to the swinging lightbulb in the root cellar—have received extensive commentary.[20] As Poague suggests, critics frequently assert the extent to which the film makes the viewer morally complicit in Norman's voyeurism and aggression. In a deconstructive analysis, these details function differently, by forcing the viewer to acknowledge, instead, the arbitrary character of all interpretation, even of messages of moral complicity.

The titles may illustrate this difference. The separated letters of the word "Psycho," which momentarily join together, may hint at the popularized understanding of the concept "split personalities"—the very concept endorsed by the psychiatrist. But even before the semantic value of these broken letters can be established, they must first be seen as arbitrary, meaningless marks, which seem to form a referent only in combination. In this way they function just as the credits of *Vertigo* and *North by Northwest* did. Reading the film's title presupposes the imposition of meaning on arbitrary signs—just as the quests of Marion, Norman, and Arbogast require mistakings of absences for presences. Such a mistaking is necessary—as necessary as attributing a name or a voice to a face. So *Psycho* begins with the idea that film viewing and psychoanalytic discourses are first *constructed* from arbitrary signs.

Likewise, the opening tracking shot may well make the viewer an eavesdropper and voyeur. But as Sam and Marion talk, we become conscious of a second aperture—the window, whose shades Sam adjusts and impatiently opens. Thus from the outset there are two windows, two points of view on the affair. (Ultimately, of course, there is an infinite number.) Each point of view is a constructed interpretation of of an interior created by light and shadow. So the viewer as voyeur is no more privileged than anyone else. If the shafts of light here suggest the subject/viewer's self-construction in the filmic analogue of the mirror stage, as Lacanians argue, they also show in retrospect how this identity is created from light and shadow.

The fact that the murder is committed by an impersonator is enough to make viewers aware of the fiction on which cinematic interpretations rest. An even more telling instance of the same subversion is the famous editing of the shower sequence, which (as Paula Marantz Cohen has observed) literalizes the action of *rapid cutting*.[21] That these actions are accompanied by shadows cast upon a screen only further reminds us of the mistakes we cannot help making while viewing. As viewers our quest for some stable referent or end to the suspense of seeing is permanently frustrated. After we understand the shortcomings of hermeneutics, through the psychiatrist's speech, we are returned to the scene of a face dissolved in a skull and to the image of eyes dissociated from words. These images reiterate the idea of the eye/drain dissolve, that all our seeing and theoria may be dead seeing. But interpretation can never rest, and suspense never ends. As noted earlier, the final image of the emergent car promises only that something—something that might finally link signs like the cash and the newspaper with the fact of mortality, Marion's dead body—may someday be brought to light. Art can bring us only to such a threshold of understanding.

14

The Birds: Signs of a World Without Cause or Meaning

Birds hover and hang over Melanie Daniels. Nobody knows why they attack; nobody knows what they mean.

WHAT DO THE BIRDS MEAN?

Robin Wood lucidly explored the logical responses to the question, "What do the birds mean?"[1] He rejected what he called the "cosmological" and "ecological" readings—that the birds are agents of revenge for a deity or for their own species' mistreatment—as leading to absurdity; he also rejected psychological interpretations—that the birds reflect tensions among the characters—on the sensible grounds that this explanation could not account for the birds' attacks on the farmer, Dan Fawcett, and on the innocent schoolchildren. Wood's answer—that the birds don't *mean* but just *are*—dropped the issue of representation. Concurring with Wood's exasperation, Thomas Leitch also rejected both satiric and psychoanalytic readings of the birds in favor of the disturbing conclusion that the bird attacks are "a gag and nothing more."[2] Although both critics' reasons for faulting efforts to understand the birds are sound, their alternatives are difficult to accept and, in any case, have not diminished the critical need to end the suspense.

Two recent attempts to revive psychological interpretations of the birds are those of the Lacanian theorist Slavoj Žižek and Robert Samuels, who modifies Žižek's position in the light of feminism and queer theory.[3] Žižek and Samuels read the birds' attack first as a reflection of the maternal superego—Lydia Brenner's rivalry with Melanie Daniels for the love of Mitch Brenner. For Žižek,

Figure 14.1: *The Birds* (1963). Copyright © 2002 by Universal Studios. Courtesy of Universal Studios Publishing Rights, a Division of Universal Studios Licensing, Inc. All rights reserved.

this correspondence is superseded by the more general understanding of the birds as the irruption of the Lacanian Real into the Symbolic—Lacan's rough equivalents for the Freudian id and ego. Samuels emphasizes the genderless nature of the Real and reads the birds as a rendering of this original psychic undifferentiation. Although Žižek and Samuels eventually conclude that the birds' attack neither has nor needs justification, each arrives at this point after providing one: they ground the birds' ultimate insignificance in their correspondence to the characters' repressed desire.

Thus Lacanianism and queer theory as well as feminism end up like other hermeneutic readings, reinstating the privileged relation between signifier and signified that the film everywhere else challenges. In doing so, none can escape the contradiction that Leitch found in earlier satiric and psychological readings of *The Birds*:

Both [interpretations] agree that the fundamental problem in the film is the disproportion between the relatively inconsequential behavior of the characters and the magnitude of the threat they face, and both attempt to resolve that problem by establishing an intelligible relation between the two. It is the nature of the film, however, to resist any such resolution.[4]

Thus recent readers of the birds have not ended the suspense of what they mean. Viewers still ask *why?* and are still disappointed—a critical experience that, on reflection, was doubtless foreseeable and, in any case, is very likely to persist These observations suggest that suspense may always have been the film's proper subject.

The MacGuffin may provide a way of addressing the problem. In Chapter 2 and in most of Part III, the MacGuffin has been treated as a figure for suspense; thus to interpret the birds as a MacGuffin is to address the problem of suspense. This chapter studies the film's title, credits, and "springboard situation"[5] as indicators of the birds' function as a MacGuffin that induces suspense.

THE TITLE

So far no critics have discussed the title's recollection of Aristophanes' play by the same name—an omission hard to justify with regard to a filmmaker whose work alludes specifically not only to Freud and Nietzsche (in *Rope*) but also to *Hamlet* (in *North by Northwest*) and the Book of Matthew (in *Torn Curtain*). As we've seen in Chapter 12, allusive titles raise the questions of reading and suspense at the outset, before any analysis of plot can begin. Is the true referent of Hitchcock's title an animal or a text? Aristophanes' *The Birds* employed many of the same plot devices as Hitchcock's: the purchase of two birds in the marketplace, as a means of locating someone; the removal of the principal characters from the a city known for its litigation; the enlisting of the help of birds in acquiring a lover; the premise that birds may be capable of some overwhelming, greater than human power; most importantly, the question of the birds' "speech" or, more broadly, meaning. Weary of the empty political rhetoric of Athens, the hero of Aristophanes' play, Pithetaerus, succeeds in leading a rebellion of birds against the Olympian gods. He does so by persuading Tereus, a former king of Thrace who had become a Hoopoe, or bird, to rally others of his species and reclaim the latent power invested in them because their birth preceded that of the Olympians. The birds achieve victory by fortifying the skies in such a way that Iris, the Olympian messenger, can no longer mediate between the immortals and mortals. As the reward for his inspiration, Pithetaerus is given the woman of his dreams, Basibia, and power in the new kingdom. But by the end of the play it is apparent that the newly established city is no freer than Athens. The vanity and futility of human action in each version of *The Birds* is made all the more obvious by its contrast with the seeming omnipotence of the birds.

Part of each work's disillusioning conclusion derives from the question of the birds' speech. In Aristophanes' play, the birds soon manifest the power of speech; Pithetaerus's project can only be realized by *making the birds speak*. Thus, the play's main trope is the making-articulate of formerly cacaphonous sounds, and what is true of bird sounds is easily extendable to human language: meaning is achieved by bestowing semantic reference on arbitrary signs. This idea gives each version of *The Birds* universality. Attributing meaning to birds is in principle no different than discovering it in Greek or English phonemes. Likewise, Hitchcock's characters engage in a suspenseful process of interpretation, of "giving voice to the birds" that, like subsequent criticism, becomes interminable. In this way, Aristophanes' play and Hitchcock's film may be considered allegories of language, of interpretation as a distorted construction of arbitrary sound.

One modern reader of Aristophanes thinks the linguistic theme of *The Birds* deserves pre-eminent position. Noting the play's extended parallel between wings and words, Cedric H. Whitman interprets Peithetaerus's claim, "I will give you wings by talking," to mean "everyone is given wings by words" and that "the whole underlying assumption of the play" is the "Aristophanean gestalt of lunacy and language, the nothingness of things and the power of the word."[6] If Aristophanes' *The Birds* reveals the association between lunacy and language, so does Hitchcock's.

THE CREDITS

Like all of Hitchcock's credits, those of *The Birds* emphasize the way reading, seeing, and hearing are constructions of suspended meaning. The stylized birds appear behind the credits, like shadows on the wall of Plato's cave. Viewers must construe these flapping, flickering black shapes as birds, but they also evoke the *clignotements*—the flickering—of film itself. The superimposition of written language over these shapes invites consideration of both as a series of signifiers. It may be as hard to understand the black shapes as cinematically generated alternations of light and shadow as it is to understand the letters that make up words as mere graphemes. The "pecking away" of verbal figures into meaningless, constituent graphemes is a means of reminding viewers of the way apparent meaning is derived from the arbitrary. Even if these moving shapes "must" be read as birds, their artifice stirs suspense as to how cinematic and linguistic representation arises. By this means the film allegorizes reading as a nearly inevitable mistake that can be understood as such only later, only in retrospect. In previous chapters we've seen this process at work in reading the urgent-insignificant MacGuffin; in *The Birds* Hitchcock uses arbitrarily motivated birds to express the MacGuffin's suspense. This suspense is also induced by the soundtrack of the credits, which blends music, recorded bird calls, and synthetic sound. The blurring of the distinctions between animal and artificial sounds shows not only the way univocal meaning is an abstraction of heterogeneity, but also the sense in which no logical priority can be placed on a "natural" over a "constructed" meaning—neither deserves an ontological privilege. The graphemes and sounds in the credits call into question any natural relation between sign and referent.

THE SPRINGBOARD SITUATION

Everywhere in the springboard situation of *The Birds*, the relation between sign and referent is put in suspense. The story begins with the incoherent squawks of gulls in the streets of San Francisco, followed by the sound of a wolf whistle that makes Melanie Daniels turn in acknowledgment; this vignette repeats the credits' allegory of the way recognizable language is composed of and abstracted from meaningless signs. In such a world, naming and attributions are like wolf whistles, false names, personifications, or catachreses. When Mitch requests lovebirds that are neither too "demonstrative" nor too "aloof," his prosopopoeia reinforces the way meaning is portrayed as a projection of the human onto the mute world; when Melanie says that moulting birds can be identified from their "hangdog" expressions, the pervasiveness of mistaken tropes becomes even more obvious. The question of whether any name is true to its object arises as Mitch and Melanie walk past a cage of small birds and look for the "true referent" of the word "lovebird":

Mitch: Are those lovebirds?

Melanie: Those? Those are red birds.

Mitch: Aren't they strawberry finches?

Melanie: Yes, we call them that, too.

As this exchange indicates, the inability to truly name objects is repeated in the misnaming of subjects as well, since Melanie's "we" is part of her charade as a salesperson. As is always the case in Hitchcock, the true identity of principal characters is unknowable. Melanie and Mitch masquerade from the moment they see each other: she pretends to be a salesperson, and he pretends not to recognize her. These "spontaneous performances" call into question each character's true identity: if masks precede true personalities, the existence of the latter is put in suspense. In Melanie's angry challenges to Mitch ("What are you, a policeman? . . . I think you're a louse") are echoes of the misnaming and prosopopoeia of Mitch's remark to the canary, "Back in your gilded cage, Melanie Daniels." The pet store sequence shows the attribution of names as the suspense of meaning in a world of masks and arbitrary signs, not identities.

The emphasis on arbitrary nomination is insistent. Melanie goes to absurd lengths to determine "the exact name," down to the spelling, of Mitch's sister. Her quest is preceded by dialogue that stresses arbitrariness, as the postal clerk calls to his unseen friend, "What do you call the little Brenner girl? Lois? Alice?" The mistaken reply ("Alice"), cut off from its source, in the spirit of the Derridean postal, highlights the way the misnaming of language is independent of both sender and recipient. The effect of the interchange is duplicated when Melanie hails Annie Hayworth:

Annie: "Who's there?"

Melanie: "Me."

Annie: "Who's me?"

Pronouns, as Benveniste points out, reveal at once the alienability of language from its object and the fallacy of thinking proper names are any less arbitrary.[7] Melanie's interchange with Annie is as potentially endless as the search for the true name of Mitch's sister. There may be a visual suggestion of this idea when the scene concludes with a shot of Annie Hayworth standing next to her name, printed on her mailbox.

The springboard situation's depiction of "spontaneous performances" extends well into the film. Melanie lies when she tells Mitch the reason she is in Bodega Bay; Mitch lies when he tells Lydia that he has already invited Melanie to stay for dinner. Even Cathy Brenner, a supposed innocent, admits a later performance when she says she already knows about her surprise party. The choral recitation and the rote greetings of the schoolchildren exemplify the blend of the seemingly natural with the artificial. Other characters may be said to "perform" through self-deception: Annie Hayworth's insistence that "it's all over between Mitch and me" rings as false as does Lydia's denial of the wish to interfere with Mitch's life. These examples suggest the way self-deception is just as much an impersonation as lies or "spontaneous performances."

The springboard situation also emphasizes suspense in its opening narrative of a *missed delivery*. The mynah bird Melanie ordered has not arrived—the promised "content" of her language is missing from the beginning. To the extent that the plot action is made possible by Melanie's delay in the pet store and by Mitch's inability to find the object of *his* language, too, the film allegorizes the way the events of life proceed irrationally, from language's suspended content. The false intersection of the masks Melanie and Mitch wear is just as accidental as Jeff's first theory about Thorwald in *Rear Window*, or as the challenge to Thornhill's identity in *North by Northwest*, or as Marion's embezzlement in *Psycho*. What unites these Hitchcockian moments is the premise that interpretive decisions are unmotivated. They just happen.

Put another way, the springboard situation of *The Birds* plunges the characters into the vertiginous world of the pursuit of the signified described in Derrida's *Post-Card*: the original deferral of Melanie's delivery leads to an open-ended succession of new relays—to Melanie reading a license plate, then to her phone call to the newspaper office, then to an inquiry to the California Motor Vehicle Department, then to Melanie's writing a note and conveying it first on an elevator ride to Mitch's apartment and later by car (after a detour to determine the true name of the recipient) and then by boat to its destination. Throughout this elaborate tracking of the signifier, the destination of the signifier is also in doubt, since the true recipient of the message has always been Mitch, not Cathy. But before Mitch and Melanie can finally come together, a gull intervenes, swooping down upon Melanie, as if to punctuate the ultimate delivery with the arbitrary. In this way, the bird's function as reminder of the absent referent also marks the separation between desire and its object; Hitchcock invites us to consider a world in which a true coming-together or knowledge of the true destination of the signifier may always be interrupted or suspended.

The bird's function of disclosing the separation between message and destination, sign and referent, has consequences for film criticism. In the absence of any natural or inherent referent, meaning must be bestowed. This seems one implication of Melanie's dialogue with the pet store owner, Mrs. Magruder:

Melanie: Will he talk?

Mrs. Magruder: A full-grown mynah bird won't talk. You'll have to teach him to talk.

Read in the context of the birds as hanging figure and MacGuffin, the dialogue here anticipates the actions of both the characters and critics of *The Birds*: each must "teach the birds to talk." The film's main story consists of looking at birds and speculating as to their meaning. Meaning must be continuously asserted in the light of prior unreadability. This understanding of interpretation is later crystallized in the famous scene in the Tides Café, when the birds are interpreted in three unsatisfactory ways—scientifically, theologically, superstitiously. Each interpretation is discredited, but the necessity to interpret is seen as inevitable. This is the interminable process of "teaching the birds to talk," which extends to film criticism, too, including deconstructive criticism.

MAKING THE MUTE BIRDS SPEAK

The elaborate technical work necessary for the bird scenes, especially the shot of the birds hovering over Bodega Bay in flames, has been documented in several sources.[8] The total effect was created by mechanical birds, real birds, and photographic processes which superimposed bird shadows over the action. Hitchcock's art makes it hard for audiences to distinguish "real" from "constructed" birds. (There are exceptions: the birds that "land" on the shoulders of the fleeing schoolchildren are clearly mechanical props, and the shadows behind the credits are photographic effects; such "pure" rather than "blended" effects temporarily expose for the viewer the constituent parts of the whole, as might individual syllables separated from a word.) This holistic effect of the birds is no different in *kind* from other cinematic effects—for example, back projection. In *The Birds* back projection is obvious as Melanie drives in her Jaguar toward Bodega Bay and later when she motors across it; back projection is present but less noticeable when she and Mitch walk from the dock to the Tides restaurant. Throughout his career, Hitchcock made use of back projection even when other directors had minimized or abandoned the practice in the interests of greater verisimilitude. It is as if—far from seeing back projection as an embarrassment—Hitchcock wanted to call attention to it, to flaunt it subtly, if such a paradox can be allowed. Thus the simplest interpretation of the birds is that they are *constructed visual effects*.

So the birds are visual effects *to which the characters must attribute motivation*. Of course, most characters would be constitutionally unable to endure the bird attacks without asking why, without seeking the cause, without the desire for an inside to explain an outside. This is the whole meaning of the discussion in the Tides restaurant when explanations are shown to be inadequate. But the flawed explanations of science, religion, and superstition are only systematic versions of what analytic philosophers call "ordinary language," such as is exemplified by the characters' spontaneous comments: "It seemed to swoop down on you deliberately" or "It must have lost its way" or "They're massing for an attack." To this degree, the characters behave as do others in Hitchcock's MacGuffin films: they assume the vital significance of the "object" giving rise to the main action and thereby dramatize the necessity for interpretation.

Unlike viewers of earlier MacGuffin films, critics of *The Birds* may now strongly identify with the characters' search for meaning. If it is a matter of indifference what the details of the fighter-jet formula are in *The 39 Steps* or the uranium sand in *Notorious*, critics of *The Birds* are forced to share the characters' obsession with causality. As we have seen, recent critics believe that the mistaken judgements of science, religion, and superstition *must* be replaced by the characters' manifest or repressed sexuality. Critics have been driven to such positions by the hermeneutic enterprise, by an incapacity to endure suspense, by a compulsion to make the birds speak. But if we hold to the definition of the birds as *visual effects to which characters attribute motivation*, we can see that instead of allegorizing sexuality the film allegorizes viewing. The spectacle of the birds in particular only presents more compellingly the spectacle of film in general, in which viewers are asked to attribute motivation to a play of light and shadow, to find an inside for an outside. Re-examining the scene in Davidson's Pet Store will show how reading characters is like reading birds.

We've seen that Mitch and Melanie are undecidable mixtures of the natural and constructed; their dialogue is a tour de force of suspense. Even before we know Mitch's name, before we have any "natural" or "normal" against which to judge his action, he is presented as acting. Is "acting" really normal behavior for a human being? Does his stated motivation—to teach Melanie a lesson—truly represent him? Is it possible that humans cannot represent their *own* motivation? The scene suspends true answers to these questions. As to Melanie, how much of her own "spontaneous acting" is caused by attraction to Mitch and how much is caused by the desire to exact revenge for being mistaken for a salesgirl? Is she capable of interpreting her own motivation? Mitch and Melanie are like *Psycho*'s Sam and Marion—their professed motivations are misrepresentations even to themselves. If neither Mitch nor Melanie can interpret themselves, what of the film critic? Thus before we see even the first "malevolent" bird, questions about the attribution of motivation in human beings permeate the action and stall interpretation as it starts. This stalling process occurs when readers try to precipitate natural from constructed elements in a visual compound—here two human beings instead of birds—in which they have been blended indissolubly.

Suspense is the result of this allegory. The birds are an instance of a visual effect that must be interpreted and given a human construction, despite evidence that no such construction can be true. This is not an ultimate statement or a paradox; instead, it describes two stages of visual interpretation. We first see arbitrary shapes that we then cannot *not* interpret as revealing a valorized "natural" or "interior" within a dispensable "constructed" or "exterior." It is as automatic that "natural" or "interior" motivations be assigned to Mitch and Melanie in Davidson's Pet Store (underneath their supposed "constructed" or "exterior" surfaces) as it will be, later, to assign an interior of "malevolence" to the birds. Making the birds a blend of "real," mechanical, and photographic images—especially in the shot above Bodega Bay—simply duplicates the "normal" treatment of film actors, whom Hitchcock once famously compared to cattle: it is as if Hitchcock could get his audience to reflect fully on the constructed nature of meaning in film only by putting into play an exaggerated parody of the cinematic *mise-en-scène* that reveals the necessity for and the suspense of looking "within" the film image.

In the second half of the film, Hitchcock deconstructs the distinction between interior and exterior, just as he had in *North by Northwest* and *Psycho*. *The Birds* accomplishes this deconstruction in the reversals between humans and birds. In the beginning, humans cage birds, although one happens to make a short lived escape; at the end, birds cage humans, though a few are able to make a tentative (and temporary?) escape.[9] The action sequences erase the distinction between interior and exterior. The attack at the birthday party shows the danger of being outdoors; the attack at Dan Fawcett's farm shows the danger of being indoors. The schoolchildren's outdoor walk/run is as futile as the barricades of the Brenner farmhouse, vulnerable first through its chimney and later through its defenses. The film's conclusion, where humans tiptoe through apparently (temporarily?) quiescent birds, confirms the basic principle of Hitchcockian terror—that there is no safe place. The inside—whether a place or a psyche—is no more privileged or authentic than the outside and is equally vulnerable to catastrophe. In this *The Birds* extends the lessons of *North by Northwest* and *Psycho*. The allegory of the birds is that the meaning bestowed upon them exposes the fictional nature of human distinctions. As soon as we say the birds "really" represent the revenge of a species, a gag, the maternal super-ego or the Lacanian Real, these "inner" signified presences break down as quickly as Mitch Brenner's wooden barricades erected to protect his own indefensible interior.

In defining this deconstruction of interiors, the metaphor of breaking down might be exchanged for the metaphor of *shattering*. Before the movie begins, Melanie has been accused of breaking glass: this is the event which precipitates Mitch's prank. It is as if some primordial shattering precedes even our introduction to the characters, as if the world can't be conceived without a prior shattering. Memorable shatterings include the windows and chinaware of Dan Fawcett's house, the Brenners' china, a child's glasses, the windshield of the car in which Melanie and the schoolchildren hide, the telephone booth, and the windows of the Brenner farmhouse. The film's many instances of shattered glass accompany its process of breaking down its characters' and viewers' fictions of causality. One revered illusion after another is shattered: that people can truly represent their true identities, their inner motives or the meaning of the external world. These illusions are so tenacious, so seemingly impervious to destruction, that they survive in the characters through the end and in criticism's relentless efforts to construct meanings for the birds; it is as if illusions can be shattered but never destroyed, so long as referentless signs, like enigmatic birds, remain.

The metaphor of shattering may be exchanged for the idea of puncturing. To puncture is to pierce through, and the first bird attack on Melanie—which breaks the skin—may be said to be their first instance of puncturing. A second instance is the popping of balloons at Cathy's party. The birds' attacks on the Brenner farmhouse and on Melanie may be understood as visualizations of puncturing glass, wood, clothing, skin—all exterior sheathings of interiors. Roland Barthes thought that the idea of the *punctum* was inherent in photography itself.[10] He argued that the "piercing" of a photograph was one of two structural properties of the art which acted to remind the viewer of the ephemerality, the instant obsolescence of every photographic moment. Hitchcock's birds may accomplish a similar objective; further, they may be said to *dramatize* the puncturing Barthes had in mind. "Puncturing" is also the etymological relative of both "punctuation" and "point," senses of the word that call attention to the rhetorical dimension of the birds as hanging figures. We may say that the film's first sequence was punctuated at its end by the bird attack on Melanie—as if it were a sentence ending with a period. Thereafter the birds' increasingly frequent punctuation of the action resembles repeated exclamation points whose redundancy exposes their arbitrary convention, much as the birds' nibbling at the credit names reduces words to morphemes or phonemes. As the action accelerates and culminates in the horrific assault on Melanie, it may become possible to see life reduced to the alternation of arbitrary sound and nothingness, to the condition of a sentence decomposing into syllables and silence, that is to say, to only the most frantic and futile gesticulations to postpone inevitable death. Marion in the shower or Melanie under attack are synecdoches for humanity caught in a world of incomprehensible figuration.

There can be no question that the birds "bring death into the world," as Miltonic interpretations of the fall would have it; to this extent, the birds link the suspension of truth with human mortality—an association that Heidegger called *Sein-zum-Tode*. In the first fatal attack, on Dan Fawcett, and in the attack on the children, the film insists on the logical separation between death and causality that is plain to intuition: no determination of a "cause" can ever permit an evasion of death. Put another way, the characters' frantic search for causality is allegorized as a denial of mortality: the more obsessive the quest to know and understand, the less reconciled to the inevitability of death. Such a theme paints Western hermeneutics as denial. But of course there is always a footnote in Hitchcock, always an exception that makes it impossible to accept even the plainest theme with certainty; in *The Birds* this function is carried out by the lovebirds that Cathy brings into the car, with the cry, "They haven't hurt anyone!"—a point logic is helpless to refute. Thus in the face of the birds' overwhelming demonstration that human life is only mortality in a world without truth, even this deconstructive conclusion must be withdrawn as soon as it is uttered, as but one more fictional construct which will inevitably be followed by new ones—new attributions of significance, new ways (like this one) of making the mute birds speak.

15

Torn Curtain: The Hanging Figure

At the insistence of a ballerina who thinks an American spy is stowed away inside, the captain of an East German ship docking in Sweden gives orders that a cargo of baskets of theatrical costumes be lifted from the deck to be searched; they now hang from ropes attached to a crane. The ballerina insists so vehemently on the spy's hidden presence that the captain soon orders his men to fire their automatic weapons at the baskets. Because viewers saw the film's protagonists, Michael Armstrong and Sarah Sherman, hide in such baskets before the ship embarked, they see again a hanging figure is suspended at a moment between life and death. After the baskets have been riddled with bullets, we learn that the protagonists had hidden away in a different basket, after all, on the other side of the ship, where under cover of the commotion they jumped overboard and swam to safety. Thus, inside the hanging figure, pictured on the following page, are only theatrical costumes, while a duplicate basket containing human beings, too, is on the other side of the ship. The sequence establishes an uneasy correspondence between the cargos—two bins that are dedicated to the glamorously dangerous charade of life, one with and one without interior content. Forty years after The Lodger, *the hanging figure still suspends a question about the significance of human identity. It is an accident that the crane operator chose to hoist one set of these seemingly interchangeable baskets instead of the other.*

THE MACGUFFIN AS FUTILE TALK

Like its predecessor MacGuffin films, *Torn Curtain* narrates a compulsion to discover and appropriate an urgent-insignificant object; as we've seen, the search

Figure 15.1: *Torn Curtain* (1966). Copyright © 2002 by Universal Studios. Courtesy of Universal Studios Publishing Rights, a Division of Universal Studios Licensing, Inc. All rights reserved.

for the MacGuffin is one of Hitchcock's recurrent allegories of reading—in this case the read object is the formula for an anti-ballistic missile.[1] In *Torn Curtain*, acquiring the formula that is supposed to save the world is dramatized as appropriating knowledge. Armstrong's theft of Lindt's secret is the paradigm for the film's many other acts of supposed knowledge, mutuality, and reading. Understanding Armstrong's theft, with the assistance of Sarah Sherman, as arbitrary and dangerous situates the film in the MacGuffin genre that has included such deluded reader pairs as John and Constance, Devlin and Alicia, Thornhill and Eve, and Melanie and Mitch. In this film, reading, speech, and language are allegorized as torn curtains or as hanging figures. They assume belief in distinctions that prove to be untenable or in apparently sturdy walls that collapse. This chapter studies the film's title, credits, springboard situation,[2] circular structure, and use of foreign languages; it concludes that reading is depicted as an illusory coming-together or an illusory distinction. As in *North by Northwest* and *The Birds*, language in *Torn Curtain* also anticipates Derrida's metaphor of the postal—a world of circulating signs, cut off from origin and destination. This world of empty communication, both frightening and droll, is epitomized when his main characters leave a post office in East Berlin and stand by the shop window of an appliance store where behind them, on a television screen, appears this untranslated line of German: "Gespräche ohne Nutzen" or "futile talk."[3]

UNDECIDABLE CURTAINS

The title *Torn Curtain* may at first seem to announce the destruction of something suspended, perhaps of the hanging figure itself, thereby producing a valedictory resonance, as if anticipating the end of a career given over to such figures. Is there some sense in which the title might be read as Hitchcock's finally being done with hanging figures, as some variant of Prospero's "Lie there, my art"? But any such resonance would be misleading, since—whatever the fate of hanging figures in Hitchcock's last films—suspense was never, and could never be, the signified referent of a hanging figure, only its frequent accompaniment. Suspense continues in the different figures of *Topaz, Frenzy*, and *Family Plot*.

Rhetoricians might classify the phrase "torn curtain" as an example of catachresis, a forced naming and implied metaphor whose "real" referent—some ripped fabric—never appears in the film. The title alludes to "iron curtain," Churchill's neologism for the cold war, though it is important to remember that that phrase is both a metaphor and an oxymoron. This doubling underscores not only the figurative nature of Hitchcock's title but the vexed nature of figuration itself. The referent is absent in both film and life: there is no physical curtain separating Eastern and Western blocs; nothing in the film is actually torn. On a plane from Copenhagen to East Berlin, Armstrong "flies through the iron curtain," and as he swims to safety in Sweden, he must pass through it a second time. Neither boundary is actual; neither is depicted; neither penetration creates a literal tear. And of course an iron curtain *cannot* be torn.

Taking "curtain" figuratively as "iron curtain" makes its "tear" Armstrong's appropriation of Lindt's secrets and successful return to the West. But the very idea of a rip or tear in the "iron" curtain opens the meaning of the curtain as definitive distinction between East and West to question. Are the blocs really so distinguishable after all? The communist scientist Lindt, like Armstrong, is impatient with his country's national security professionals. Karl Manfred's devotion to Sarah is at least as strong and sincere as Armstrong's. Gromek, the stereotypical East German thug, has lived in New York, chews gum, loves pizza but for all we can tell *prefers* the eastern bloc. Lindt loves Viennese waltzes. The East Berlin museum is full of Western art; its opera company performs Western music. As Raymond Durgnat points out, we learn that it is America, not East Germany, that sustains an iron curtain by preventing Countess Kuchinska from emigrating;[4] the contrast with East Germany's willingness to admit Sherman without a visa is instructive. If stereotypes and misrepresentation characterize both sides of the curtain, what does the division signify? *Torn Curtain* clearly continues the deconstruction of twentieth-century political systems already seen in *Notorious* and *North by Northwest*—their sense that political distinctions are specious in a world of moral undecidability and anarchy. From this perspective the title may be a synonym for "destroyed illusion": the curtain is torn because the political distinction it created was never tenable in the first place. Such a reading of the title would comport well with the idea of tearing as figuration already seen in the images of "shattering" and "puncturing" in *The Birds*.

As in the case of *North by Northwest*, the suspense of the title's defective referentiality has prompted critical consideration of other referents—the curtains in Sarah's hotel room, Lindt's blackboard, the stage curtain, etc.[5] These suggest the multiplication of possible referents, though at the outset it should be noted that none is *torn*. In contrast with these, the most famous *truly* torn curtain is the one that immediately follows the crucifixion: "And behold, the curtain of the temple was torn in two, from top to bottom; and the Earth shook, and the rocks were split" (Matthew 27:51). This Biblical curtain surrounded the inner sanctum or Most Holy Place of the Jewish temple; its tear has occasioned much speculation. So the title *Torn Curtain*, like *North by Northwest*, invites comparison between its action and that of a canonical text: according to one allegory, Hitchcock and Matthew narrate the ultimate victory of seemingly self-sacrificing heroes devoted to the salvation of humanity and willing to risk arrest and death at the hands of enemies.[6] The parallel ironically reframes each story and yields only undecidability. Modern audiences in thrall to science and technology might understand the Most Holy Place and its sacred text not as an obsolete ark but as a modern "curtained" blackboard on which equations are written; the hero who promises salvation is not the son of God but a scientist. In this secular reading, Armstrong the physicist might seem, properly, the new savior, who will tear the curtain of ignorance to deliver humanity to a world of peace. On the other hand, the title's allusion allows Christian readers to see a different irony: Armstrong's heroism is an unjustified usurpation of the role of the *true* tearer of the curtain. That a case can be made for each reading is an early measure of the film's suspense.

The Biblical allusion also retroactively illuminates the political import of Matthew's story. Commentaries on Matthew have interpreted the phrase as implying an abrogation of previous religious distinctions. One exegete writes: "Its symbolic significance was probably to emphasize the removal of all religious barriers existing between Jews and Gentiles."[7] Pauline interpretations of this sort explain the tear as affording Jew or Gentile equally unimpeded access to deity; perhaps for Matthew, the "torn curtain" signals the supersession of Judaism and its replacement by a new order. But *Torn Curtain* also unsettles confidence in this kind of interpretation, through its emphasis on the high moral price of the "victory" of Armstrong (and thus by analogy, of Jesus). Both heroic efforts to overcome distinctions—political and religious—entail destruction: Armstrong's victory is won only by putting in jeopardy the lives of many ordinary people who helped him; in this reading, Jesus's victory puts in jeopardy the belief system that nurtured Christianity. The tearing of a curtain, even in some triumphant moment of saving humanity, may also consign some segment of humanity to destruction. In other words, Christian interpreters of the image may read it as both uniting and dividing.

This discussion shows that interpretation of the Biblical torn curtain is already an interpretation of the meaning of the crucifixion or of Christianity: for Christians, the temple's torn curtain cannot *not* be significant. Because it appears immediately after the crucifixion, it seems to offer itself as a commentary on that event. At the same time, it is possible to see the Biblical curtain not so much as a sign to be interpreted in a theological or political sense, but as an example of *the enigma of interpretation itself*—the juxtaposition of portents that cannot interpret themselves.

Among the Biblical synonyms for the word "curtain" are "veil," "tent," and especially "screen," the last of which suggests the reflexive character of the film's title; Hitchcock had often employed curtains in this reflexive way, most notably in *Rear Window* and *Psycho*.[8] As "torn screen," the figure provokes the viewer to consider some rupture inherent in every cinematic experience. (Before the era of the multiplex, theaters often draped curtains in front of screens; these were elaborately raised during the credits. At the beginning of *Rear Window*, Hitchcock mimics this process.) Thus *Torn Curtain* may suggest a commentary on film. To say that film is a torn curtain may mean that it destroys illusions or challenges barriers, divisions, and distinctions—for example, in *Torn Curtain* those between capitalism and communism, Christianity and secularism, love and appropriation. Like all art understood as deconstruction, film destroys illusory distinctions only by creating new fictions. A tear in the curtain of art may promise some revelation, some disclosure of the previously hidden, but it is precisely this promise that the title questions. Instead of bringing the reader or viewer closer into the presence of new truth, "torn curtain" is a hanging figure promising an illumination that never comes.

Put another way, the title *Torn Curtain* provides a way of understanding the film's MacGuffin. Armstrong purloins an equation, or set of signs, which he claims will bring the world closer to peace, but the fact that this rationale is expressed as part of a ruse to fool the East Germans means that there is no way to know its authenticity. This undecidability is brought out at the airport press conference, where one reporter insinuates that Armstrong's motive may simply be scientific hubris. Since viewers learn on two occasions of Armstrong's anger at the American government for refusing further funding, his private act of espionage may well be an emotional response to the withdrawal of recognition. (The fact that Armstrong considers academic life a demotion from Pentagon employment should give pause to viewers who see him as a disinterested champion of science.) The undecidably mixed motives of intellectual attainment, patriotism, and personal revenge make the parallel between Armstrong and the Czechoslovakian ballerina illuminating: after the reporters at the airport prefer to photograph Armstrong, the ballerina's pique leads, eventually, to her seemingly patriotic retribution against her rival. The parallel with Armstrong suggests that the physicist may be just as much a spoiled prima donna as the ballerina, and the patriotic motives of his actions may be just as open to doubt as hers.[9]

That it is the ballerina who attempts to unmask Armstrong on shipboard is another indicator of the parallel.

But even more unsettling than psychological undecidability is the impossibility of predicting or even understanding the political outcome of Armstrong's action. Raymond Durgnat points to the obvious flaw in Armstrong's reasoning: his belief that an anti-missile system will make war impossible only if the Americans have it, too, in fact shows just the opposite—that the weapon may make war more likely.[10] Armstrong's self-contradiction is also caught by a reporter, who asks whether his work may make *defensive* missiles obsolete; the implication is that possessing a reliable anti-missile system might increase a nation's desire to launch a first strike. In this case, Armstrong's "patriotic" motive can't be distinguished from Western aggression against the communist bloc. This detail may have prompted Robin Wood's reaction:

We reflect at once—and the presence of the hostile reporters from the West encourages this—that in fact all the invention will do is make it possible for East to bomb West without fear of retaliation. When we learn the truth, this reflection obviously still stands, not perhaps conscious in the spectator's mind but there to trouble him just below the surface of consciousness: we have merely to reverse the sides.[11]

Wood's inference shows how the motive for peace is indistinguishable from the motive for war or American hegemony; the same set of signs can be interpreted in each way. Defense is offense; peace is war. We begin to surmise the way Armstrong's talk—hardly an exaggeration of normal national security discourses—may be insanely, dangerously useless.

There is no need to assume either hypocrisy or naiveté on Armstrong's part, since consciousness does not affect the outcome. Instead, Armstrong is Hitchcock's version of the inevitable delusion of national security, that scientific inquiry can have a determinable, much less useful, application to war or peace. Armstrong's Enlightenment quest, however "truly" on behalf of peace, requires killing adversaries and endangering allies; as a dangerous catalyst to nuclear holocaust, Armstrong's delusion is now the extension to a global scale of the arrogant blindness of both political sides in *Notorious* and *North by Northwest*; and before them, of the rational detective Barton in *Number Seventeen*, whose work ends in a train wreck or of Joe, the detective in *The Lodger*, who arrested an innocent man; and, before them, of the hanging figure of Enlightenment's Marat, assassinated at a point of relay of undecidable signs. Hitchcock's satire of supposed rationality is only more obvious when the syllables of the hero's name are reversed and the distinction between rationality and power disappears. In the spirit of the MacGuffin, understanding the referent results in endlessly self-canceling interpretation. Like the uranium-sand in *Notorious* or the microfilm in *North by Northwest*, Lindt's equation is an unreadable sign that may betoken, indifferently, salvation or madness.

READING THE CREDITS

The credits' juxtaposition of flames with the faces of the film's characters creates the first visual torn curtain, a vertical division of the screen. Each side is stylized: the flame is apparently the combustion of rocket fuel, though no vehicle can be discerned. The faces, decontextualized from the narrative, embody expression cut off from meaning. Unreadable on first viewing, the juxtaposition may prompt rereaders to interpret, for instance, the film's treatment of the relation between power and human expression. For present purposes, two of the many possible interpretations can be explored. According to the first, which corresponds with the film's popular reception, the film is a narrative of Western triumphalism, and the suffering of the faces on the right side of the screen is undergone in the service of Armstrong's successful, morally benevolent enterprise to extinguish forever the missile flames on the left. The second reading, sketched above, reverses these valences to discover in Armstrong's quest the egomania of the academic-technological establishment that may unwittingly further destabilize the world and fuel its fires.

Like other readings of the credits' torn curtain, these two are possible only after an interpretation of film as a whole. In this respect, the credits of *Torn Curtain* repeat the lesson of the credits of *Vertigo*, where the woman's cosmeticized face can be seen retroactively as predicting the inherent undecidability of all identities. The faces of the credits of *Torn Curtain* are ambiguous, even on rereading. Does Armstrong's contorted face represent a virtuous hero or madman? Does the face of the German farm girl reveal humanitarian commitment or personal fear? Is Sarah's bewilderment the emotion of a love-blinded or unjustly-used woman? In *Torn Curtain* the interpretation of these faces and flames awaits readings of the narrative that follows, readings whose meanings may be suspended indefinitely. Perhaps the world consists only of mute signs (facial expressions) and abstract destruction (fire). Such juxtapositions invite interpretation—in the same way as the Biblical juxtaposition between Jesus's crucifixion and the torn curtain—and that interpretation may be irresistible; nevertheless, interpretation is always a *subsequent* imposition of meaning on signs, arrived at in the light of a previously constructed reading.

FALSE CONGRESSES

This formulation suggests that the film's most crucial "curtain" may be the hanging figure of language itself, the system of signs that appears to distinguish and denominate real entities but which in fact is "torn" by an incapacity to do just that. The film's springboard situation strengthens this hypothesis by emphasizing the curtain effect of foreign languages, the separation between name and identity, and the failure of speech acts. Like the dreamlike vignette that begins *Vertigo* or the scene of dictation that introduces *North by Northwest*, the initial scenes of *Torn Curtain* compress the themes of its later narrative into the synecdochical action of its first few minutes.

Language as curtain is one effect of the mixture of Norwegian and English in the establishing title "Osterfjord, Norway." The priority of the Norwegian word in this phrase is the first challenge to American monoculturalism and to the prejudice of English's privileged or natural status as a language. Norwegian is also the film's first spoken language, overheard in the conversation of the ship's crew. This alienation effect is later conveyed through Hitchcock's frequent use of German dialogue, translated and not. To many in Hitchcock's audience, hearing rapid-fire German may prompt the idea that language can be a curtain, a blockage or barrier to understanding which must be "torn" or seen through in order to arrive at signified meaning. Another Scandinavian language, Swedish, appears at the end, as if to signal the circularity of the film's action or the enclosure of both English and German within a larger frame of language itself as a system of signs. The arbitrary, acoustic property of speech evident in the Norwegian conversation is also given surreal emphasis by the eerie silence of the ship's interior: at this international convention of physicists, no one speaks, not even at meals; it is a mute colloquy, an oxymoron. The ship's cold dining room may satirically equate the meaning of scientific speech with useless talk or silence.

The more unsettling suggestion of the *impossibility* of mutual comprehension is introduced by the film's first line, a startling off-color pun: in bed with Armstrong, Sarah tells him: "I thought this was supposed to be a serious congress of physicists." Of course, the "congress" of Sherman and Armstrong, both physicists, is surely "physical," though it is hardly a meeting of the minds, since the terms of their engagement are being negotiated even as they speak. The intellectual "congress" of physicists on the ship is also a charade, since those scientists are being deceived by Armstrong and since they lack their field's most crucial equation. Their cold silence enacts an irreducible heterogeneity concealed by the ideal of the colloquy. These false congresses are the first of many examples of apparently communicative meetings that collapse into separateness, recrimination, violence. For example, in their Copenhagen hotel room—divided by a shower curtain—Armstrong and Sherman talk but can't agree about picking up Armstrong's book; at their dinner, Armstrong decides to read, making Sarah stalk away in disgust; Armstrong abandons the Copenhagen conference; the meeting arranged for the ballerina arriving in Berlin is late; the airport press conference gives only the appearance of answered questions; the meeting with the peasant girl associated with *pi* is interrupted by Gromek; Armstrong's meeting with the German physicists is interrupted by security; the heroes' meeting with Countess Kuchinska ends in a promise that isn't kept; the heroes' presence on the bus stirs dissent, not solidarity, within the group. And as if to reinforce these scenes of false concurrence, the few times when information transfer does seem to occur are also fatally flawed: the professional spy, on the tractor, ends up questioning Armstrong's motives; the reconciliation between Sherman and

Armstrong leaves the grounds for her change of heart unknowable; Armstrong's yell ("Fire!") unites the ballet audience, but only in pandemonium. Sherman's offhand hope for a "serious congress of physicists" thus anticipates the larger world of *Torn Curtain*, in which similar dreams for a true "coming-together," "congress" or mutual comprehension are thwarted.

This disappointment is the result of the detachability of visual and verbal signs from identity—a tradition visible in Michelangelo's *Santo Spirito Crucifix* as well as in Hitchcock films beginning with *The Lodger*. In *Torn Curtain* the detachability of signs is first evident in the close-ups on the name tags of the conferees; the disjuncture between sign and referent is repeated when Michael denies his own identity to the steward who brings the radiogram. The clothes, name-tags and blankets concealing Armstrong and Sherman may be considered new names, curtains, hanging figures. The blankets also redirect the image of the curtain, from language to film, by exploiting the cinematic convention of "covering" film nudity—a reflexive gesture used with witty and macabre effects from *Murder!* to *Rear Window* and *Psycho*. (In those films, nudity ostentatiously visible to characters was tantalizingly denied to audiences.) In a typically droll interview response, Hitchcock described the parodic effect of the blankets in *Torn Curtain*.[12] The scene mocks film convention not only with regard to the lovers in bed but also in Armstrong's return to bed after rejecting the radiogram: the camera follows his supposedly nude body only from the waist up. The signified objects denied by convention to scopophilia are only local instances of the more general condition of film as an unchanging torn curtain, whose inevitable framing reveals only at the cost of concealing.

In *Torn Curtain*, the initial "curtaining" of Armstrong and Sherman may also arouse suspicions of what may be unseen or incapable of revelation in their characters. The suspicion is deepened when their conversation exposes the disconnect between language and action in speech-acts—in this case Michael's proposal of marriage to Sarah. Sherman's comment that they are "reversing the natural order of things" in having the honeymoon cruise precede their marriage indicates both the arbitrariness of marriage custom and the unreliability of speech-acts. While Michael's procrastination regarding the wedding date may be a function of his concealed mission, this benign interpretation depends on other debatable signs. In this way, the interpretation of Michael's character, as of all characters, follows the same model of belatedness and disappointment as the interpretation of the characters' faces in the credits.

THE CIRCULAR PURSUIT OF THE SIGN

The film's circular structure consists of the journey to the secret, its acquisition, and the return—a structure that may be regarded as an elaborate hermeneutic act, an act of reading understood as the appropriation of signs.[13] Reading's circularity may imply its ultimate uselessness, and within this large circle are smaller acts of appropriation, too. For example, during the journey phase, Armstrong's pursuit of signs requires first that he read a radiogram and then "decode" a new set of signs, a book that instructs him to pursue the sign *pi*; during the return phase, the search for the signs "Friedrichstrasse" and "Herr Albert" requires the intervention and translation of the Countess Kuchinska. These intermediate acts of interpretation temporarily suspend the larger questions as to the meaning of the appropriated signs—is the pursuit of the secret equation ethical? Will it advance the cause of peace or war? It is as if the ultimate goal of reading is assumed and its circularity forgotten in these local acts of reading. Intermediary signs make original signs seem like referents. The meaning of any act of reading (the address of the bookstore or the identity of Albert) gains significance only through the prior conferral of determinable value on signs (Lindt's formula). At the same time, some conferral of meaning seems inevitable—it is as difficult to see "futile talk" in Hitchcock's title as it is in the Biblical "torn curtain." So *Torn Curtain*'s allegory dramatizes a *necessity* for the hermeneutic circle in reading, a theme perhaps hinted at in its central symbol of *pi*, since *pi*, which presupposes circles, is a purely symbolic ratio that mathematicians consider both universal and necessary.

Two crucial scenes advance the allegory of the circular pursuit of the sign. The killing of Gromek and the persuasion of Sarah narrate Armstrong's triumph over their resistance to his reading of the world. Neither confrontation could be foreseen, and each is made necessary by the accomplishment of his foundational interpretation of the importance of the equation. (These demonstrations that specific political results like killing or persuasion are never predictable from signs should unsettle Armstrong's overarching belief in the determinable effects of the formula he is pursuing.) Each confrontation is made necessary by interpretations of signs grounded in patriotism. Gromek's reading of *pi* leads him to defend East Germany, just as Sarah's understanding of Lindt's questions leads her to defend America. Armstrong overcomes both resistances, but he does so not rationally but wordlessly, through brute force or emotional appeal; as a consequence, both scenes deepen doubts as to the moral justification for Armstrong's actions.

Gromek acts lawfully, whereas Armstrong's mission as a wholly private citizen, unsanctioned by his government, gives him no legal justification for his actions; as we've seen, the credibility of Armstrong's stated rationale is very much open to question. In addition, even the morality of the *means* to the end may be put in question here. The farmhouse struggle pits two against one; the peasant girl is able to stab Gromek without risk to herself. In many ways Gromek appears the more sympathetic character. His bilingualism contrasts with his opponents' silent monolingualism, just as his humor contrasts with Armstrong's cold silence. But the scene's moral ambiguity is not simply a matter of the ambivalence of its depiction of Armstrong's or *pi*'s blunt Machiavellianism. In his allusion to gangster films, Gromek reminds the audience that American culture has always glorified the outlaw, the role Paul Newman plays. And the culmination of the long struggle in Gromek's death in the gas oven conveys an unmistakable allusion to Hitler's "final solution."[14] Both allusions recontextualize the killing of Gromek by making it appear, first, part of longstanding American tradition of lawbreaking and, second, morally analogous to Nazism. The unsettling nature of this parallel should come as no surprise to viewers of *Notorious* and *North by Northwest*.

Armstrong's persuasion of Sherman makes his character and purpose questionable in another way. Hitchcock said that one of his interests in the story was in the reaction of the woman to the behavior of her lover as defector.[15] Sarah's refusal to answer Lindt's questions seems to be based on a patriotism no less instinctual than Gromek's. But as Raymond Durgnat suggests, Sarah's motive may also be love for Michael: "It is still possible to hold that Sarah's refusal to divulge America's secrets is motivated less by patriotism than by her sense that Michael is, after all, patriotic, and that to divulge those secrets would lose her his love."[16] Adopting this view of Sarah makes her motives as wholly undecidable as Michael's, and the persuasion scene compounds the suspense. The two converse unheard by both the diegetic and film audiences; both must infer what Michael says. It is assumed that Armstrong finally confides to her his "higher" goal; however, even conceding this unknowable detail, it is also impossible to know the extent to which Sarah may also be persuaded by assurances of his love, of his devotion, even of his commitment to a wedding date. (Certainly the Germans assume this is the *entire* content of the persuasion.) The camera's 360-degree sweep around the embracing lovers has been likened to the famous embrace of Scottie and Judy in *Vertigo*, but as we've seen, that kiss was in fact an elaborate deception that teaches the illusion of tenability. In short, it simply cannot be known to what degree—or even whether—Armstrong appealed to Sarah's patriotism or to her love. The communicated truth in this supposed "serious congress of physicists" remains unknowable.

The center of the film's political circle is also a silently transferred sign—the equation; in this scene, the MacGuffin is revealed to Armstrong on a blackboard that—as soon as Lindt's suspicions are aroused—is "curtained" by a second blackboard. In this way the center of the film dramatizes the title, *Torn Curtain*, not as a political or moral moment, but as a reading moment. Reading apparently tears a curtain, in a moment of revelation. Yet as we have seen throughout, the "revelation" of reading consists only of new signs whose meaning is suspended. The seemingly ultimate revelation comes about only after the physicists' "exchange of equations" at the board. This parody of "dialogue" or of a "serious congress of physicists" reduces human conversation to numerical signs and makes Lindt's equation into a speech-act, signs that seem to force Armstrong to do something—to copy them. There is no doubt that Armstrong believes something has become perspicuous to him; it is equally undeniable that the content of this learning is suspended. The scene dramatizes a dream of linguistic transparency—an illusion sometimes associated with the scientific community— that signs may yield up the same immediate, indubitable meaning that numbers appear to. For scientific readers, this sense of "torn curtain" represents an ideal.

But its fallacy is precisely the dream of finality, the illusion that numbers (or anything else) can pierce figuration once and for all and put an end to suspense.

The film's last phase destroys this illusion and shows again how the appropriation of signs can never determine their meaning—just as the announcement of a speech-act (Armstrong's "We are engaged" or Gromek's "You are under arrest") can never effectuate itself. A torn curtain is, after all, only a metaphor, a hanging figure. The details of Armstrong's escape from the iron curtain reveal, instead, his continuing confinement behind the curtain of figuration that he deludes himself into thinking he has torn open. The university's loudspeaker enjoins students and faculty to search for the spies, but the failure of this speech-act (a command) is reflected in the crowd's chaotic scramble. As in *North by Northwest*, transportation seems an analogue for the defective "conveyance" of meaning—the escapees' feet are replaced by bicycles, which are exchanged for the "simulated" bus and finally by the costume bin hanging in suspense. The vulnerable trajectory of the secret Armstrong bears on its way to its "proper destination" is everywhere apparent; his escape may be regarded as an extended parable of reading understood as the contingency of the sign on its way from sender to recipient, from Lindt's brain to whatever ultimate outcome it will have in the world beyond the film—peace, war, or some distant, unknowable effect. The secret equation is both oral and written; it is enclosed first in Armstrong's head and second on a slip of paper he carries with him. (The writing-down of the formula in Dr. Koska's office is perhaps the first of many examples of the contingency in the transmission of the sign.) The sign's double presence, within Armstrong's brain and pocket, is then doubled again by his enclosure within vehicles.

The simulated bus and the costume bin suggest the lack of any necessary connection between outside and inside, sign and referent—as if these conveyances were the materializations of puns or homonyms. The secret's trajectory passes through a post office—a scene which recalls Melanie's stop at the post office in *The Birds*—proleptic of Derrida's account of the waywardness of the sign in *The Post-Card*; this only further emphasizes the equation's imbrication in a universe of other freely circulating, useless signs, sent on their contingent paths toward termini which become, after all, only unending temporary relays. The arrival of Armstrong and Sarah in Sweden provides the perfect contrast between the ostensibly triumphalist plot and its allegory. As noted in the caption at the outset of this chapter, it becomes immediately apparent that there are *two sets* of theatrical trunks. The double doubling of containers for the secret suggests the open-ended, potentially infinite range of the constructed sign. Armstrong and Sarah are miraculously "transferred" from one set to another between cuts, a "miracle" effected by film art—a droll gesture that acknowledges the artificiality of the entire film. Finally, Armstrong and Sarah's path traces a political shift—from NATO allies Norway and Denmark through the iron curtain twice and then to the neutrality of Sweden. Thus, instead of binaries or the two-sidedness implied by the trope of the curtain (West-East, capitalism-communism), the film ends with the acknowledgment that some third term has "always, already" been available, one which exposes the constructed nature of the title's political allusion, which has always been, after all, only a hanging figure.

THE ILLUSION OF UNDERSTANDING

Torn Curtain continues a longstanding tradition in Hitchcock's films, according to which foreign language dialogue appears sometimes translated and sometimes not, a practice that occurs as early as *The Man Who Knew Too Much* (1934) and is developed with increasing sophistication in *The Lady Vanishes* (1938), *Lifeboat* (1944), and *To Catch a Thief* (1955). As in the decentered modernism of Pound or Hemingway, Hitchcock's heteroglossia does more than simply subvert American monoculturalism; instead, it subordinates the "normal" discourse of American science and national security, which presupposes a referent for every sign, to the frame of language in general. As we've seen, this frame is established at the outset, in the use of Norwegian, and at the end, in the use of Swedish; it situates the binary English/German confrontation—the cold war, the curtain—within the more general context of the arbitrary nature of all political systems and languages. Translation, a transfer from sign to sign, holds forth a dream analogous to that of science—of the transparency of sign and referent.

But the film's actual use of translated and untranslated German dramatizes the illusion of all such true "congress." The first such scene of translation is another physical but not intellectual coming-together—Armstrong's welcome to East Berlin and airport press conference. The translated passages in these scenes convey apparent clarity and faithfulness while concealing not only Michael Armstrong's conscious deception but also, as we've seen, its moral undecidability. The tarmac welcome, first in German, then in English, provides the spurious sense of correspondence between signifier and signified, which is belied by the action of the film: ". . . das Professor Armstrong sich entschlossen hat, in den Volksdemokratien zu leben und für den Frieden zu arbeiten.[17] . . . that Professor Armstrong has decided to live in the people's democracies and to work for peace." The frequent use of cognates ("halt," "Fotografen" "amerikanischen," "Willkommen") also lends the airport sequence a sense of transparency. As the faithful translation of Armstrong's questionable faith, the scene depicts translation as activity that is only seemingly revelatory. (Of course, in retrospect the idea of language as false lure has been implicit from the credits of the film, but in the spirit of the MacGuffin, each translation's seeming promise of extra-linguistic signification temporarily suspends doubt as it renews the hope for meaning.)

Other illusory meetings of the mind occur during the bus ride. The dialogue between the bus driver and first the outlaws, then the German police, is literally translated by Jacobi, the leader of *pi*'s escape effort. The seeming transparency between inside and outside implied by these translations temporarily distracts attention from the lack of moral or political legitimation in either party to this "congress." Armstrong is being spirited out of East Germany in a disguised bus—a subversive bus disguised as "normal." The bus is first stopped and searched by the police. Next, it is stopped by army deserters who rob the passengers, but this robbery is foiled by the military police, who then serve as escorts to guarantee the safety of the simulated bus. An outside observer could not distinguish the legitimacy of the "true" and "false" bus or the "true" and "false" soldiers. This sequence of events raises undecidability to a new level of complexity. The legitimacy of East German state power is subverted first by the existence of *pi* and its bus, and second by its own deserters. The scene thus makes Armstrong and *pi* parallel to the deserter/robbers, who also enter the bus. The translated dialogue of Jacobi, the East German police, and the deserter enacts a coming-together or seeming understanding among parties lacking all legitimacy; the collapse of this false congress into anarchy is dramatized when the East German guards spray the escaping bus passengers with gunfire. When stripped away, the illusion of comprehension created by translation reveals only violence and destruction—a nothingness perhaps prefigured by the abstract fire of the credits.

The relation between illusory understanding and destruction is also evident in untranslated passages of German. For example, after the murder of Gromek the monolingual peasant woman cries out in fearful anxiety to Armstrong: "Blut. Viel Blut. [removes his bloody coat] Ich werde in dem Feuer verbrennen. Fahren Sie nach Berlin zurück. [puts his bloody hand under running water] Ach, Sie müssen das abwaschen. Komm. Komm. Komm hier. Vergraben. [gestures with shovel] Vergraben. Wir vergraben das auch. [indicates motorcycle] Komm, schnell. Auf Wiedersehen." The gestures that accompany this monologue help Armstrong see that his coat must be burned, his hands washed, and the body and motorcycle buried; what he and film viewers may miss is the woman's shift from the formal address ("Sie müssen") to the intimate ("Komm"), a shift no doubt influenced by the enforced proximity of their joint, laborious murder of Gromek.[18] This shift in verb endings as well as Armstrong's seeming comprehension imply a promise of mutuality which is broken, however, by the film's subsequent action. For example, we later learn that—after risking her life for Armstrong—the woman only narrowly avoids arrest and certain death. Like the co-conspirators on the bus or the Countess Kuchinska, she experiences only the illusion of communication with Armstrong. The fact that their supposed solidarity is manifested in a prolonged, brutal murder that ends in a gas oven and destruction by fire makes the morality of *pi*'s cause analogous to that of the totalitarianism it ostensibly opposes; in this respect, *Torn Curtain* tracks the same deconstruction of political binaries already seen in *Notorious* and *North by Northwest*. In any case, the peasant woman's familiar "Komm" resembles the Countess's pathetic cry, "My sponsor!" Armstrong's stony indifference to each woman's plaintive illusion of trust suggests blankness or silence as the ultimate response given to such pleas for mutuality and meaning.

The illusion of communicated common values is illustrated in scenes of untranslated German during Armstrong's escape The post office sequence physically allegorizes the moment of "transfer" or relay that is central to the illusion of referentiality: another curtain or false congress is figured forth in the bar separating the postal clerks from the lines of customers waiting to send or receive messages. Countess Kuchinska's untranslated plea to be allowed to move to the front of the line makes an appeal to common national values: "*Ach bitte, diese Leute sind auf Besuch hier. Zeigen wir ihnen was deutsche Gastfreundschaft ist.* Oh, please, these people are visiting here. Let's show them what German hospitality is." The fact that this appeal to German patriotism facilitates treason against Germany is one more instance of the film's continuing transvaluation of "normal" cold war ethics. The monolingual Armstrong and Sherman remain ignorant of the hospitality that saves their lives.

The Countess's request to speak to "Herr Albert" results in the specter of several multiple referents for the name. By now it should not be surprising that Albert's eventual arrival produces for Armstrong no "significance"—no achievement of safety or national security—but only another sign passed across the bar, the business card of the travel agency to which Armstrong should now report: clearly, the search for the MacGuffin/equation that began in name-tags and radiograms is but an interminable relay, a circulation of messages without signified content in an endless series of new transfers and translations.

But the most telling manifestation of this charade world appears in a nearly subliminal passage of written, untranslated German, legible when Armstrong and Sherman pause before the next relay, the raided travel agency to which they had been referred. While they are speaking to the anonymous "professional" ally of *pi*, they see themselves on televised newscasts in an appliance store's display window. After their images appear on the screen, we are shown a written phrase that lacks any specific context.

Gespräche ohne Nutzen
Useless speech (Literally: conversations without usefulness)

In the plot, this phrase is a sardonic commentary on the East German government's televised efforts to apprehend Armstrong and Sherman. This unexpected self-mockery at first seems at odds with the depiction of the humorless, methodical East German state security apparatus; however, it is not inconsistent with other humanizing features of East German society: its valorization of visual art and ballet; Manfred's earnest pursuit of Sherman; Gromek's engaging Americanisms; Dr. Kozka's daughter's violin practice; Lindt's eccentricities and impatience with state security; the Countess's self-dramatization and willingness to abet spies. Because the East Germany of *Torn Curtain* is depicted as both oppressively communist and individualistic, "Gespräche ohne Nutzen" testifies to the droll but resigned self-criticism of a country conscious of its own limitations. It is worth remarking that self-deprecating humor and an awareness of the limits of language are not Armstrong's pre-eminent traits.

But the sudden, unremarked appearance of the phrase "Gespräche ohne Nutzen" suggests it may also be applicable to the film's allegory of reading, to all "conversations," all "congresses." It is amazing that this enigmatic writing appears in a coming-together of Armstrong, Sherman, the *pi* organization, and the East German authorities behind the televised news—a small "congress" of the film's principals. Nevertheless, at this coming-together there is no response, no understanding of the written message at its center. It is as if human comings-together can take place only on condition of ignoring all evidence of their uselessness. This is an implication of both the film's MacGuffin (Armstrong and Lindt's exchange of equations) and all of the conversations made in promotion of that end. All are "ohne Nutzen" in the sense that they end in no decidable signification and produce instead only the illusion of mutuality, common values, understanding. Useless talk does not or cannot distinguish—heroes from villains, East from West, selfish and selfless. Useless talk is language conceived as torn curtain, as hanging figure.

The film's two concluding scenes strengthen this suspicion. Armstrong's escape stratagem of yelling "Fire!" creates pandemonium. Like the bus ride that puts Germans in increased danger in the supposed cause of peace, this scene makes plain the full anarchic potential of Armstrong's belief in meaning. There is political irony in the fact that his survival depends on breaking the famous legal prohibition articulated by Justice Oliver Wendell Holmes in his establishing the boundary, his putting up of a curtain, defining American free speech—surely a value the patriotic Armstrong should support. Linguistically, Armstrong's flouting of Holmes's famous distinction is itself a "torn curtain," a demonstration that by themselves laws are merely constative signifiers, never performative speech-acts, as the shouting of "Fire!" appears to be. And of course since the fire in the theatre is figurative rather than literal, what we witness is really a false or illusory performative, the demonstration that the effects of speech-acts are in fact independent of signifier and signified.

The film's closing embrace mocks Hollywood endings by being a *photographed* closing embrace, as an intrusive photographer strives to appropriate a cinematic sign; his quest is frustrated by the raising of the film's final curtain, the blanket drawn over Armstrong and Sherman. This demonstration of the camera's inability to capture its apparent object suggests another sense in which the image of the "torn curtain" as broken signification is common to film and language. The closing embrace is the last alleged "congress" or coming-together in the film. Is it, finally and after all, some "Gespräche *mit* Nutzen"? Is it the "serious congress of physicists" that Sherman hoped for in the film's first line? If so, the language of film criticism will be as helpless to grasp it as a camera, and the reader or viewer will be left with only the imagination of its existence, somewhere outside the film or behind the darkness of the blanket, the film's last hanging figure, into which Hitchcock's camera finally moves and blacks out.

Afterword: Figures of Suspense

Hanging figures teach that we cannot know who we are or whether our lives have meaning. This is because language and visual art are never free from figuration. Like the lodger or Roger Thornhill, we live in a world of circulating signs that refer not to reality but to other signs. *North by Northwest*, with its images of figures atop figures, and *The Birds*, with its silence as to cause and referent, depict worlds of signs that aspire to refer beyond themselves but can't. Sometimes it seems as if characters or viewers should be able to cut through the hanging figures to confront what lies behind them, but as in the dream in *Spellbound*, we cut away at eyes hanging on curtains and only find new hanging eyes in their places. At other times we hope something lies "outside" the world of absent referents, but it doesn't: the street beneath the penthouse in *Rope* is a site of empty transfer, like the conversation within. At still other times it seems like some person should be able to rescue us from the "glamorously dangerous charade" of life, but lovers are not exceptions: *The Lodger*, *The Ring*, *Spellbound*, *Notorious*, *North by Northwest*, *The Birds*, and *Torn Curtain* end with the embrace of ciphers or the kiss of unreadable faces; *Easy Virtue* ends with the declaration that identity is nothing; *Vertigo* ends with Scottie embracing the air. Reading a world that may itself be only figuration requires the making of new figures, in the never-ending process that forms the essence of suspense. But what, exactly, are figures?

As promised, the word "figure" has been used throughout this book with deliberate ambiguity: its spatial and rhetorical senses have been conflated, so that the phrase "hanging figure" sometimes seems to denote a visual representation—like Jesus on the cross or the lodger on the wrought-iron fence—and sometimes an incomplete temporal process, as if a figure of speech ("my love is like . . .") had been broken off in mid-sentence before being finished. Both meanings were essential to the argument, which held that a hanging figure (and by implication any visual art) is simultaneously spatial and temporal because its meaning is indefinitely deferred. Still, it is obvious that exploiting the ambiguity of the word "figure" without further justification postponed consideration of fundamental issues. As noted above, I have left open the extent to which the "real" world—whether that is understood empirically or phenomenologically— can itself be considered only a "figure." In other words, if Hitchcock's films reflect the way the world really is, then the world is a sign without a determinable referent. My rationale for delaying consideration of these issues, a weak one, is that readers whose main interests were in suspense or in Hitchcock's films might acquiesce in the postponement of issues that will surely not be resolved here, in any case. It is now necessary to address them. One way of doing so is to examine the history of the word "figure," since from the outset, the coexistence of its rhetorical and visual senses has engaged the world's most intractable problems of belief.

FROM GORGIAS TO DE MAN TO HITCHCOCK

The Latin word *figura* renders the Greek word *schēma*, which most authorities translate as "outward form."[1] The word had two meanings: first, as a visible shape; second, as a term of rhetoric. As Erich Auerbach pointed out, the sophistication of Greek in comparison with Latin is evident in the plethora of related Greek words all having to do with form: *typos* (imprint), *plasis* (plastic shape), *morphē* (ideal form) or *eidos* (the form or idea inherent in matter). Whereas the last two terms, which came to be included in the Latin *forma*, seem to denote proper form or "model," as in Plato, *schēma* refers only to a purely perceptual shape, like an outline.[2] On the other hand, the distinction is unstable. If *eidos* implies a "natural" or "logical" or even "ideal" condition, and *schēma* merely an accidental or detachable outline, on what basis is such a distinction to be determined? It would appear that even in the Greek root of the visible "figure" there is an uncertainty as to the status of the referent—is it necessary or arbitrary? Inherent in or anterior to the object? This uncertainty is later assimilated into the Latin word "figure."

The earliest known use of *schēma* as a rhetorical term carries this incipient uncertainty to dizzying lengths. The fourth-century (BCE) Cynic philosopher Zoilus used the word to apply to "cases when the speaker pretends to say something other than that which he actually does say."[3] George A. Kennedy makes the reasonable observation that Zoilus's definition seems to describe irony.[4] But how could the word for "outward form or shape" have come to imply hypocrisy or even duplicity? There is no way to know for sure, but it would have been natural for Zoilus, like other radical followers of Socrates, to be familiar with his mentor's attack on Gorgias, the founder of rhetoric, in the dialogue *Gorgias*.

According to Harry Caplan, the ancients regarded Gorgias as the inventor of *schemes*.[5] In Plato's dialogue, Gorgias is cross-examined by Socrates in an effort to show the inferior status of rhetoric (he calls it a "knack," not an art) and to make the case that in the absence of any concept of justice or the common good, the study of rhetoric was empty, unethical, and dangerous. At one point Plato mocks Gorgias's interest in rhetoric by attributing to his follower Polus the following ornate speech:

Among mortals, many arts have been discovered empirically from experience. For it is experience which makes our lives proceed by art, but lack of experience which reduces it to chance. Various are the arts of which various men variously partake; but the best partake of the best. Gorgias here is of this company and so has a share in the noblest of arts.[6]

This elaborate speech, which Socrates later refers to as a "jingle," exhibits what Quintilian and later rhetoricians called "schemes," or "figures of language," and it can easily be seen how the passage's blatant singsong (achieved through antithesis, anastrophe, polyptoton, etc.) could well seem "merely external," perhaps bearing out that sense of *schēma*.

But in addition to his reputation as a rhetorician, Gorgias was also known for unusual philosophical positions, the most radical of which appeared in his treatise *On the Nonexistent*, which survives only in outline form.[7] Jeffrey Walker summarizes its argument:

In *On the Nonexistent*, Gorgias argues the surprisingly modernistic thesis that the human mind can neither know nor communicate the true reality of things—if indeed there is any such truth to know—because, in essence, what the human mind can possibly know, believe, or communicate is only a mental representation constructed by means of *logos*, and because *logos* itself has at best a problematic relation to reality (since *logos* existing in human speech and thought, is not the same as the reality it represents).[8]

Behind Socrates's attack on Gorgias and the study of rhetoric may have been an animus against Gorgias's critique of *logos* and his "modernistic" challenge to the efficacy of communication. Socrates's ridicule of the study of rhetoric in *Gorgias* is of a piece with his denunciation of poetry in *Ion* and *The Republic*: in all cases, uses of language that feature its non-referential properties are seen to be threats to the state. Worse, if Gorgias's conception of language was derived from his (proto-Saussurian) insight into the arbitrary nature of the sign, rational knowledge would become impossible, an obvious threat to Socrates's intellectual endeavor. In *Gorgias*, Socrates's solution is to predicate the study of rhetoric on a prior theory of justice; in *The Republic* his solution is to ban poets altogether from the ideal logocentric polity. In other words, the Cynic philosopher Zoilus's intuition that the rhetorical use of *schema* may in fact be ironic may reflect the fear that non-referentiality may endanger justice or virtue; in any case, that inference would be wholly consistent with and perhaps even derivative from the Socratic demonization of both rhetoric and poetry.

For two thousand years, the enormous stakes opened up by the potential fissure in the word "schēma" and its descendent "figure" remained repressed or covered over, although the use of the terms in rhetoric frequently revealed unease. The first move was to distinguish "schemes" from "tropes," with "schemes" being defined as "figures of language" and "tropes" as "figures of thought"; this distinction was first advanced in the anonymous *Rhetorica ad Herennium*.[9] It is obvious that such a distinction is valid only so long as the Socratic/Christian/Cartesian concept of an inner self separate from language is maintained. Quintilian sought to systematize the study of schemes and tropes, but his distinction between the two was only the first in a long series of strained attempts to keep them separate; in fact, and seemingly despite himself, Quintilian re-introduced the problem Zoilus had perceived by saying that "as regards *irony*, I shall show how in some of its forms it is a *trope*, in others a *figure*."[10] In fact, the distinction between tropes and schemes, passed on by medieval and Renaissance authorities like Bede and Puttenham, was never sustainable. In a comprehensive review of sources, Shirley Sharon-Zisser shows how the imminent breakdown of the distinction was accelerated in the nineteenth century and finally accepted in the twentieth.[11] For all practical purposes, in modern rhetoric "scheme" (now rarely used), "figure" and "trope" are synonyms, although synonyms *for what*, of course, remains unsettled. This is the essence of the hanging figure.

Coincidentally, as the rhetorical definition of "figure" broke down, its meaning in Christian hermeneutics also began to show strains. Erich Auerbach has traced the meaning of "figura" to denote events and prophecies in the Hebrew Bible that are construed as predicting future historical events—especially those of the gospels and Revelation; indeed, many such interpretations are already advanced by the gospel writers and Paul. For example, just as it was Joshua and not Moses who actually led the people of Israel to the promised land, so (by this reasoning) Jesus Christ delivers humanity not through the law but through grace. Auerbach believed that the medieval figural tradition was critical to the acceptance of Christianity in Europe, on account of the explanatory power of its appeal to history: figural interpretation read not only texts but *events*. As a result of *figura*, Dante was able to understand not only pagan and sacred history but also the political events of his day and their future providential disposition: Cato and Virgil remained *real people in history* and also pointed beyond themselves to the eschatological Second Coming.[12] Thus the temporal dimension of the word "figure" can be seen in both—in the dawning of the sense of a trope and in the Christian deferral of ultimate meaning to the events predicted in Revelation; in both traditions, "figure" is inherently suspenseful. From the Renaissance to the present, the figural side of Christian hermeneutics has been weakened by scientific understanding not only of the events of history but also of the two principal collections of texts in the Judeo-Christian tradition: in the nineteenth century, Darwin challenged figural history from one side, and the Higher Criticism from the other. The result was further destabilization: by the end of the twentieth century, it became impossible to say with confidence what the word "figure" might mean in either rhetoric or hermeneutics; the result is that at the beginning of the twenty-first century we are left with the word "figure," without knowing what it is a figure *for*—something in a text? Something real? Or does figure *mean* this kind of paralyzed suspense?

Revisiting Socrates's confrontation with Gorgias, where the very possibility of reason seemed to be at stake, may help. To defeat his opponent, Socrates appealed to what he regarded as language that is *not* figural, by which he means language stripped of *schemes*. Socrates says as much when he tells Gorgias that when you strip away the music, rhythm and meter from poetry, you would have "bare prose."[13] It is the possibility of this kind of language *prior* to Gorgias's "jingle," his non-referential *schemes*, that grounds Socrates's position. Such language would be used by the "just man" to speak his case; any use of rhetoric would be secondary, subordinate, detachable from this originary, referential language. From this tradition springs all later views of rhetoric as additive, as detachable ornament or clothes—for example, the views of Puttenham or Neoclassical authorities. Without language conceived in this instrumental way, reason could never define the just man or ideal society. If instead language is ineradicably figural, it may be at the same time ironic—ironic even independently of the speaker's volition. This possibility may have led to the conclusions of the suspicious Zoilus or of the naive Quintilian, both of whom thought schemes might be *inherently* ironic. But again, if this is so, then Gorgias's predictions in *On the Nonexistent*, of a world in which communication was impossible and the existence of the world unprovable, might be more plausible; figures would "hang" in the sense that they would *seem* to refer to the real world while not, in the end, being able to rest in any completed ostensive definition. The "hanging" part of the figure now means the permanent inability to decide whether the referential sense of language is in operation.

Socrates's position is challenged in Nietzsche's early study of rhetoric:

It is not difficult to demonstrate that what is called 'rhetorical,' as the devices of a conscious art, is present as a device of unconscious art in language and its development. We can go so far as to say that rhetoric is an extension [*Fortbildung*] of the devices embedded in language at the clear light of reason. No such thing as an unrhetorical, "natural" language exists that could be used as a point of reference: language is itself the result of purely rhetorical tricks and devices . . . Language is rhetoric, for it only intends to convey a *doxa* (opinion), not an *epistēme* (truth).[14]

In Nietzsche's last sentence we can see an echo of the idea Socrates wanted to combat in Gorgias: if language is rhetorical from the beginning, then we may be left with only opinion, not truth. Paul de Man saw this early theme in Nietzsche as animating his later deconstructions of self and world, moves that led to "the feeling of liberation and weightlessness that characterizes the man freed from the constraints of referential truth."[15] (It may be that such "weightlessness" is another variant of what has here been called "suspense.") But at the same time, this book has already shown that the positions of Gorgias and Nietzsche are dramatized in Hitchcock's films: they were articulated (then disavowed) by Rupert Cadell, in *Rope*, but before that they were implicit in the figure of the lodger and the film of the same name: both character and film are *figures* for this state of undecidability which by definition can never become present (as in a referent) and can never end. The moral and philosophical depth of Hitchcock's films is apparent in their taking the implications of Gorgias and Nietzsche seriously and in delineating their human effects.

From the standpoint of Nietzschean or de Manian deconstruction, the question of whether Hitchcock's hanging figures are apt representations of life—and whether life is also a hanging figure—can only be approached through a study of verbal and visual signs. As to verbal signs, the history of the deconstruction of their referent is familiar. Saussure announced language's arbitrary character but privileged phonologism, holding that in their origin, signs had an acoustic property; Derrida famously amended Saussure's insight to say that signs were independent of any "presence" they might represent and hence *logocentrism* only distorted philosophy by surreptitiously reinstating metaphysics.[16] But what of visual figures, especially those of photography and film? Aren't they inherently, rather than arbitrarily, connected with what they represent? Doesn't the reading of film's figures represent the truth of the referent?

Again we must start from the sign. Throughout this book, discussion of how cinematic signs are composed has been abbreviated: when references to their phenomenality was necessary, appeals were sometimes made to *clignotements*, the flickering of the cinematic image, or to "photons," that wave/particle matrix physicists hypothesize to be a necessary condition of light. The ambiguity of the concept of the photon within physics is not of importance here; instead, "photon" and *clignotement* were invoked only as place-holders for any material embodiment of the visual sign, much as if a literary critic were to allude to "ink." At issue then is deconstruction's unanswered question of the degree to which "photons" or "ink" can be said to be material "presences" independent of their signs. For while the arbitrary nature of the sign seems intuitively plausible in a linguistic world of foreign languages, art historians have resisted the similar treatment of visual representations. For example, writing of the phrase "word and image," W.J.T. Mitchell at first criticizes those who try to shelter the field of visual art from scholars from "text-based academic disciplines"; nevertheless, he himself calls for absolute "resistance to the notion that vision and visual images are completely reducible to language."[17] But if visual images are signs, then they aspire to represent, just as words do. To articulate their representation or lack of it, there is no alternative to the use of language. A portrait may be formed from meaningless colors, just as words may be formed from meaningless alaphones. Whether of not this is the same as saying visual images are "completely reducible" to language depends on how one takes the metaphor of reduction Mitchell employs. In any case, elsewhere in his essay, Mitchell acknowledges the dilemma—he calls the task "hopelessly contradictory"—by admitting that any privileging of the visual over the verbal leaves the art historian "reduced to the repetition of cliches about the ineffability and untranslatability of the visual."[18] Willy-nilly, verbal discourses of art history supplant their visual objects.

We are left with signs—acoustic, inscribed, graphic—which because of their signifying aspirations imply the existence of a phenomenal world. Because the possible existence of a phenomenal world is derived from the sign, not the reverse, it can never be known with certainty. This position is not the same as philosophical idealisms of the Berkeleyan variety, since those assume the most metaphysically weighty presence of all, the self as deity; nor is it the same as skepticism or nihilism, since the inescapability of signs means one can never avoid reading and rest in a position of rejection.

The universe must be read but cannot be known. Such a conclusion is scandalous only to those in the Socratic/Christian/Cartesian/empiricist traditions, for whom the quest for certainty—not to speak of mirages like *security, self-reliance, capitalism*—is predicated on the capacity for representation. In Hinduism the necessity to read a permanently deceiving world—a glamorously dangerous charade—is the occasion for chanting gurus to inveigh against *maya*. In the West, the beckoning signs of the scientific method promise future confirmation of its hypotheses, leading the general public to accept without question the priority of the photon over its sign; in this pursuit they enact the secular version of the medieval Christian's faith in *figura*. But in art—whether that is the speculation of Gorgias, or the intelligence of Hitchcock's films—the physical world continues to present itself and its readers only as hanging figures.

Notes

INTRODUCTION

1. Four accounts of the revolution are the following: Frank Lentricchia, *After the New Criticism* (Chicago: University of Chicago Press, 1980); Art Berman, *From the New Criticism to Deconstruction: The Reception of Structuralism and Post-Structuralism* (Urbana and Chicago: University of Illinois Press, 1988); Vincent B. Leitch, *American Literary Criticism from the Thirties to the Eighties* (New York: Columbia University Press, 1988); J. Hillis Miller, "How We Got from There to Here," in *Black Holes* (Stanford, CA: Stanford University Press, 1999), 59–75. This book is part of a double volume that also includes Manuel Asensi's *J. Hillis Miller; or Boustrophedonic Reading*.

2. The conference featured the first presentations in America by Jacques Lacan and Jacques Derrida; papers delivered were published in Richard Macksey and Eugenio Donato, eds., *The Languages of Criticism and the Sciences of Man: The Structuralist Controversy* (Baltimore: Johns Hopkins University Press, 1970).

3. David H. Richter's *Falling into Theory: Conflicting Views on Reading Literature* (Boston: St. Martin's Press, 1994), which unaccountably omits deconstruction, contains sections titled "Why We Fell into Theory" and "After the Fall." Jay Clayton's *The Pleasures of Babel: Contemporary American Literature and Theory* (New York: Oxford University Press, 1993), despite its title, considers the current state of competing approaches to be healthy. Excellent essays on the many post-1960s schools of criticism are collected in Michael Groden and Martin Kreiswirth, eds., *The Johns Hopkins Guide to Literary Theory and Criticism* (Baltimore: Johns Hopkins University Press, 1994). An updated version is planned for publication in 2002.

4. In literary criticism, the word "hermeneutics" has both a broad and narrow definition. The broad definition in parentheses in the text will be followed in this book. The narrower definition refers to a specifically German tradition of interpretation originating

with the theorists Gotthold Ephraim Lessing and Friedrich Schleiermacher and influenced in part by controversies over Biblical exegesis. This tradition extends through the work of Wilhelm Dilthey to the contemporary Hans-Georg Gadamer; among its contemporary exponents, hermeneutics has affinities with reader-response criticism. For a discussion of hermeneutics in this sense, see Robert C. Holub, "Hermeneutics," in Michael Groden and Martin Kreiswirth, eds., *The Johns Hopkins Guide to Literary Theory and Criticism* (Baltimore: Johns Hopkins University Press, 1994), 375–82. Vincent B. Leitch discusses "hermeneutics old and new," in *American Literary Criticism from the Thirties to the Eighties*, 188–97. My view that hermeneutics in the broad sense may be contrasted with deconstruction has precedents in two earlier works: Gary Shapiro and Alan Sica, eds., *Hermeneutics: Questions and Prospects* (Amherst: University of Massachusetts Press, 1984) and John D. Caputo, *Radical Hermeneutics: Repetition, Deconstruction, and the Hermeneutic Project* (Bloomington: Indiana University Press, 1987).

5. Bill Readings, *The University in Ruins* (Cambridge: Harvard University Press, 1996). Readings's book takes the position that none of the recent critical approaches to literature (especially that of cultural studies) can ground itself or provide an adequate definition of its own object of study, as was the ideal of the Humboldtian university of the nineteenth century. The result is a situation in which neither a return to the Humboldtian paradigm nor the adoption of a different one is possible.

6. Bill Readings maps the contradictions in the attempts of literary and cultural studies to define the object of inquiry. For an account of the arbitrary nature of canon formation, see John Guillory, *Cultural Capital: The Problem of Literary Canon Formation* (Chicago: University of Chicago Press, 1993).

7. J. Hillis Miller, *Reading Narrative* (Norman: University of Oklahoma Press, 1998), 58.

8. For a study of the way never-predictable political effects can ensue from acts of reading, see J. Hillis Miller, *The Ethics of Reading* (New York: Columbia University Press, 1987). Teaching or writing about Hitchcock from a deconstructive perspective always runs the risk that readers will assume the director and his films are *worth* writing about. As we will see from a discussion of the etymology of the word "suspense," this mistaken conclusion may be derived from a failure to appreciate both the arbitrary character and the interminability of the "weighing process" that takes place before words are "meted out." To choose a topic or to begin speaking about it is already to have founded discourse on unprovable intuitions of *worth*. Critical introductions may be elaborate paraphrases of the first words of Beckett's Hamm in *Endgame*: "Me" (*yawn*) "to play."

9. Martin Heidegger, *Nietzsche*, trans. David Farrel Krell, three volumes (San Francisco: Harper and Row, 1984), 2:191.

10. Werner Heisenberg's uncertainty principle held that it was impossible to know both the position and momentum of a sub-atomic particle; it was set forth in the years 1926–27. The English title of his 1930 volume is *The Physical Principles of Quantum Theory*.

11. For most of the details in this paragraph I am indebted to Robert S. Nelson, "At the Place of a Foreword: Someone Looking, Reading, and Writing," in Robert S. Nelson and Richard Shiff, *Critical Terms for Art History* (Chicago: University of Chicago Press, 1996), ix–xvi.

12. Jacques Derrida, *Acts of Literature*, ed. Derek Attridge (New York: Routledge, 1992), 49.

13. My distinction here between "discursive" (or "literal") and "figurative" definitions

of suspense is heuristic—to establish a beginning that will initially separate hermeneutics (which presupposes a "literal" or "discursive" language free from figures) from deconstruction (which accepts the figural nature of language). It could be accurately objected that my use of the distinction here exemplifies Miller's point that beginnings cunningly cover gaps; at the same time, my quick abandonment of the distinction in favor of the consistently ambiguous "figure" in Parts II and III is made clear everywhere else in the text. I return to the use of the word "figure" in the afterword.

14. The use of etymology in deconstructive writing is sometimes criticized as contradictory. For one example, see Christopher Norris, *Deconstruction: Theory and Practice* (London: Methuen, 1983), 93. But discussion of etymology need not imply that early meanings are privileged. Like Hitchcock's indirect definitions of suspense, etymology may add a new or a fresher figure to those already in circulation; the extent of the persuasive appeal of any figure, including those derived from etymology, is unknowable.

15. Roland Barthes, "The Rhetoric of the Image," in *Image-Music-Text*, trans. Stephen Heath (New York: Hill and Wang, 1977), 32–51. In this essay, Barthes' structuralist analysis of painting, photography, and film begins with the way images in advertising may be understood as functioning like the tropes metonymy and asyndeton (49–50).

16. Michael Fried, *Realism, Writing, Disfiguration: On Thomas Eakins and Stephen Crane* (Chicago: University of Chicago Press, 1987).

17. Richard Shiff, "Figuration," in *Critical Terms for Art History*, 323–28, 323.

18. Walter Benjamin, "The Work of Art in the Age of Mechanical Reproduction," from *Illuminations*, trans. Harry Zohn, ed. Hannah Arendt (New York: Schocken Books, 1969), 217–51.

19. Jacques Derrida, *The Truth in Painting*, trans. Geoff Bennington and Ian McLeod (Chicago: University of Chicago Press, 1987).

20. Peter Brunette and David Wills, *Deconstruction and the Visual Arts* (Cambridge: Cambridge University Press, 1994).

21. G. E. Lessing, *Laocoön: An Essay on the Limits of Painting and Poetry* (1766) trans. Edward Allen McCormick (Baltimore: Johns Hopkins University Press, 1984). McCormick's introduction to this edition provides a good survey of the history of the Neoclassical debate over *ut pictora poesis* that had its critical origins in Horace. This essay is the *locus classicus* for the position that literature, the most imaginative art form, is higher than the sense-dependent forms of painting and sculpture. On the other hand, recent commentators, applying semiological approaches to the essay, point to significant similarities in Lessing's view of each art. See David E. Wellerby, *Lessing's Laocoön: Semiotics and Aesthetics in the Age of Reason* (Cambridge: Cambridge University Press, 1984).

22. The five terms in parentheses are a small sample, roughly chronological, of the numerous neologisms Derrida has employed over the course of his career as either *données* or terminal concepts towards which his essays build. "Trace" appeared in "Structure, Sign and Play in the Discourse of the Human Sciences," in Richard Macksey and Eugenio Donato, eds., *The Languages of Criticism and the Sciences of Man: The Structuralist Controversy* (Baltimore: Johns Hopkins University Press, 1970), 247–65. "Différance" appeared in the essay "Différance," trans. David Allison, in *Speech and Phenomena* (Evanston: Northwestern University Press, 1973). "Supplement" appeared in "The Supplement of Copula," trans. James S. Creech and Josue Harrari, *The Georgia Review* 30 (1976). "The call" is the operation of the *à-Dieu*, Derrida's adaptation of Levinas's idea of the "illeity" of the Other; it appears in *Adieu to Emmanuel Levinas*, trans. Pascale-

Anne Brault and Michael Naas (Stanford: Stanford University Press, 1997), 59–62 and 142–43. "Chora" appears in Jacques Derrida and Peter Eisenman, *Chora L Works* (New York: The Monacelli Press, Inc., 1997), beginning on p. 9.

23. Rodolphe Gasché, *The Tain of the Mirror: Derrida and the Philosophy of Reflection* (Cambridge: Harvard University Press, 1986).

24. For one of Derrida's many claims that deconstruction is within the Enlightenment tradition, see "The University in the Eyes of Its Students," *diacritics* (fall, 1983), 3–19. For one of Derrida's recent statements that deconstruction is not a negative but an affirmative, a discourse that is not incompatible with the quest for the *archē*, see *Chora L Works*, 105ff.

25. For de Man's speculations on language as automaton, see "On the Marionette Theatre" in *The Rhetoric of Romanticism* (New York: Columbia University Press, 1984).

26. Further discussion of the "ultimate" boundaries of my subject are taken up in the afterword's discussion of the word "figure."

27. In twentieth-century criticism, an important source of hermeneutic evaluations of endings is Northrop Frye's *Anatomy of Criticism: Four Essays* (Princeton: Princeton University Press, 1957).

28. Virginia Wright Wexman, *Creating the Couple: Love, Marriage, and Hollywood Performance* (Princeton: Princeton University Press, 1993), 14–16.

29. Robin Wood, *Hitchcock's Films Revisited* (New York: Columbia University Press, 1989), 106.

30. Paula Marantz Cohen, *Alfred Hitchcock and the Legacy of Victorianism* (Lexington: University Press of Kentucky, 1995), 113.

31. Thomas Leitch, *Find the Director and Other Hitchcock Games* (Athens: University of Georgia Press, 1991), 173.

32. Jacques Derrida, *The Post-Card: From Socrates to Freud and Beyond*, trans. Alan Bass (Chicago: University of Chicago Press, 1987).

33. Slavoj Žižek, " 'In His Bold Gaze My Ruin Is Writ Large,' " in Slavoj Žižek, ed., *Everything You Always Wanted to Know about Lacan (But Were Afraid to Ask Hitchcock)* (New York: Verso, 1992), 211–16.

34. Alfred Hitchcock, "Master of Suspense: Being a Self-Analysis by Alfred Hitchcock," in Sidney Gottlieb, *Hitchcock on Hitchcock: Selected Writings and Interviews* (Berkeley: University of California Press, 1995), 123.

35. Paul de Man, *Allegories of Reading: Figural Language in Rousseau, Nietzsche, Rilke and Proust* (New Haven: Yale University Press, 1979), 205. In his " 'Reading' Part of a Paragraph in *Allegories of Reading*," in Lindsay Waters and Wlad Godzich, eds., *Reading de Man Reading* (Minneapolis: University of Minnesota Press, 1989), 155–70, J. Hillis Miller rigorously analyzes this passage in connection with de Man's views of "ethicity" and of language. It is difficult to escape Miller's conclusion that the passage's personifications betray de Man's inability to establish the definition of reading he is proposing. As a result, my citing this definition as a parallel to the process of viewing films already suggests that my analogy will break down. On the other hand, this book accepts the prospect of the groundlessness of all analogies and seeks to derive whatever new knowledge is possible merely from the tracing of parallel figures.

36. Dominique Paini and Guy Cogeval, eds., *Hitchcock and Art: Fatal Coincidences* (Montreal: Mazzotta, 2000)

37. Jean-Luc Godard, *Histoire(s) du cinema*, trans. John Howe, 4 vols. (New York: ECM New Series, 1998), 4:43.

38. *Hitchcock and Art*, 18.

39. Francois Truffaut, *Hitchcock*, revised edition (New York: Simon and Schuster, 1984), 183.

CHAPTER 1

1. Minet de Wied, "The role of temporal expectations in the production of film suspense," *Poetics* 23: 1–2 (1995), 107–23.

2. Peter Vorderer, Hans J. Wulff, and Mike Friedrichsen, editors, *Suspense: Conceptualizations, Theoretical Analyses, and Empirical Explorations* (Mahweh, NJ: L. Erlbaum Associates, 1996).

3. de Wied, "The role of temporal expectations," 111.

4. Bordwell, *Narration in the Fiction Film*, 39. Bordwell's note for this passage refers the reader to Leonard B. Meyer, *Emotion and Meaning in Music* (Chicago: University of Chicago Press, 1956), 13–42, and George Mandler, *Mind and Emotion* (New York: John Wiley, 1975), 65–172. For a classification of the emotions from a cognitive perspective, see Andrew Ortony, Gerald L. Clore, and Allan Collins, *The Cognitive Structure of Emotions* (New York: Cambridge University Press, 1988). The authors envision their study as the description of the "grammar" of human emotion, which they define as follows: "valenced reactions to events, agents, or objects, with their particular nature being determined by the way in which the eliciting situation is construed" (13). Such a definition makes emotion practically synonymous with reading or interpretation. Further evidence of the cognitivists' assimilation of affect into cognition is David Bordwell's unaccountable speculation that psychoanalytic models "may be well suited for explaining emotional aspects of film viewing" (30), without acknowledging that any such psychoanalytic interpretation would render cognitive explanations untenable. Bordwell's assumption that cognition can be understood independently of affect has been challenged from a different perspective, that of historical reception studies, by Janet Staigler, in *Interpreting Films: Studies in the Historical Reception of American Cinema* (Princeton: Princeton University Press, 1992), 66–68.

5. Peter Ohler and Gerhild Nieding, "Cognitive Modeling of Suspense-Inducing Structures in Narrative Films," in *Suspense*, 129–48, 129–30.

6. Among cognitivists, the acceptablity of behavioral and physiological evidence has been a matter of controversy. Classical cognitivism, established in opposition to behaviorism and in sympathy with Chomsky's view of innate linguistic competencies, devises information-processing models of the human subject that are theoretically distinct from the physiology of the brain; this is the basic orientation taken by Ortony, Clore, and Collins in *The Cognitive Structure of Emotions*. In cognitivist psychology as in structural linguistics, evidence is derived from intuition and logic. (Recently this orientation in cognitivism has been challenged by the movement known as connectivism associated with the work of James McClelland and David Rumelhart.) The anthology *Suspense* includes contributions from both cognitive and behavioral psychologists; as is indicated by the editors, the main division within the research field cuts across the distinction between cognitive and behavioral psychology and, instead, concerns the amount of determination either school gives to text or recipient. For a synopsis of some controversies within cognitivism, see John R. Anderson, *Cognitive Psychology and Its Implications* (New York: W. H. Freeman and Company, 1995), 10–18.

7. In "The Psychology of Suspense in Dramatic Exposition," in *Suspense*, 199–232, Dolf Zillmann discusses the cognition arousal theory. For discussions of the physiological measurements, see Axel Mattenklott, "On the Methodology of Empirical Research on Suspense," in *Suspense*, 283–300, 287; for studies of expressive behavior and self-reports, see ibid., 289–95.

8. In "The Paradox of Suspense," in *Suspense*, 71–92, Noel Carroll, for example, justifies his argument that mere thoughts (as distinct from beliefs) may induce the emotions of suspense with the speculation as to the "overall adaptive advantage this delivers to humans in terms of educating the emotions in the response to situations and situation types not already at hand" (86).

9. Ibid., 83.

10. David Bordwell, *Narration in the Fiction Film* (Madison: University of Wisconsin Press, 1985), 37–38, 40–47.

11. For a clear statement of these disciplinary foundations, see Ortony, Clore and Collins, *The Cognitive Structure of Emotions*, 176–78.

12. William F. Brewer, "The Nature of Narrative Suspense and the Problem of Rereading," in *Suspense*, 107–27, 119.

13. Carroll, "The Paradox of Suspense," in *Suspense*, 72. In Carroll's introduction to his essay there is the suggestion that the existence of anomalous suspense exposes a weakness in cognitivism that makes it potentially vulnerable to psychoanalytic criticism, which of course assumes not only the existence of unconscious affect but an intellectual superstructure with which to account for it; however, I am not aware of any psychoanalytic critic who has used this "opening" in cognitivism for polemical purposes.

14. Richard J. Gerrig, "The Resiliency of Suspense," in *Suspense*, 93–105, 101.

15. Ibid., 102–105.

16. Brewer rejected Gerrig's hypothesis on the grounds that it should predict no reduction in affect on rereading, and experimental results found some reduction; he rejected the pure cognitivism of Ortony, Clore, and Collins, according to which suspense was synonymous with uncertainty, on the grounds that it was incapable of accounting for any affect in rereading; he rejected the view of the literary critics who distinguished serious literature (reread, in their view) from popular literature (not reread) on the grounds that the rereading of popular literature actually took place. Brewer found more explanatory power in Lipsky's theory of vicarious doubt, according to which doubt shared between reader and protagonist remained on rereading, and in theories of forgetting. See E. Lipsky, "Suspense," in H. Brean, ed., *The Mystery Writer's Handbook* (New York: Harper, 1956), 103–112. Of course, the latter class of theories can account only for reductions in affect; the implications of Lipsky's theory are taken up in the next note.

17. Lipsky's hypothesis of the existence of a "vicarious doubt" is really just another effort to invent an entity that would circumvent the cognitive determination of affect. Lipsky defines the concept as "doubt shared by the reader with the fictional actor as to the outcome of the fictional intention. This sharing of doubt arises through emotional identification of the reader with the fictional actor" ("Suspense," 107–108). Many questions could be asked about the meaning of the phrase "fictional actor"; many more could be asked about this actor's doubt as to "fictional intention." But it is unnecessary to pursue either of these weaknesses, since Lipsky's new category makes "emotional identification" rather than consciousness the origin of affect, hence violating the foundation of cognitivism. Carroll argued that recidivist suspense was understandable as the result of readers' rapt *thoughts* about the unfolding events, which override their *beliefs* about

outcomes. But the degree to which Carroll's distinction can account for the way rereading blocks access to memory was challenged by Gerrig, "The Resilience of Suspense," in *Suspense*, 103–104.

18. Brewer uses the term "resolution." See "The Nature of Narrative Suspense and the Problem of Rereading," in *Suspense*, 107–27, 116. Zillmann, "The Psychology of Suspense," in *Suspense*, 226.

19. Zillmann writes: "It is further proposed that, because of humoral mediation of excitatory processes, elevated sympathetic activity decays comparatively slowly. Portions of it persist for some time after the termination of the arousing stimulus condition." Ibid., 225. On the other hand, William F. Brewer, in "The Nature of Narrative Suspense," in *Suspense*, 107–27, reports experiments in which suspense ratings fall to the "original base level" after the outcome event (118).

20. Among reader-response critics, Wolfgang Iser distinguishes the "text" from the "work" (generated in reading) and both from its "realization"—the phenomenological "realization" of the reading. ("The Reading Process" in Davis, 376–77). In a later essay, Iser makes intertextuality inseparable from reading: "Each text is a rewriting of other texts, which are incorporated and stored in the text concerned." See Iser's "What Is Literary Anthropology? The Difference between Explanatory and Exploratory Fictions," in Michael P. Clark, ed., *Revenge of the Aesthetic: The Place of Literature in Theory Today* (Berkeley: University of California Press, 2000), 157–79, 174. Of course, reader-response critics are not the only theorists who question the formalist assumption of an autonomous text. For a deconstructive analysis of the problem, see J. Hillis Miller, "Stevens' Rock and Criticism as Cure, II," *Georgia Review* (1976): 330–48, and "The Critic as Host," *Critical Inquiry* 3 (1977): 439–47. The gnostic critic Harold Bloom has fully developed the implications of his early insight, "Any poem is an inter-poem," by tracing the way predecessor texts are misread in subsequent texts that seek to displace them. For this argument see Bloom's *A Map of Misreading* (New York: Oxford University Press, 1975), *Poetry and Repression* (New Haven: Yale University Press, 1976) and other works.

21. It is true that some cognitive theorists accept the importance of extra-diegetic material in the composition of suspense. David Bordwell's calls this the viewer's "transtextual motivation," by which he means the viewer's knowledge brought to the cinematic experience—including expectations of genre, director, actor, etc., which assist the viewer in making "suspense-hypotheses" or predictions of plot outcomes. Still, Bordwell's formalist, Aristotelian assumptions are clear in his position that meaning of a film is readable only in its diegetic outcome. See *Narration in the Fiction Film*, 36. Among the researchers represented in *Suspense*, two note the work of Wolfgang Iser. In "Suspense and Disorientation: Two Poles of Emotionally Charged Literary Uncertainty," in *Suspense*, 189–98, Gerald Cupchik affirms the value of Iser's concept of "blanks," or narrative lacunae that demand a reader's active participation and interpretation (191). On the other hand, Ohler and Nieding reject reader-response criticism; they claim that Iser overemphasizes the ambiguous parts of a text and neglects the interdependence of textual precision and imprecision, which ensures that there will be "internal coherence" within the mental models formed by each viewer; see their "Cognitive Modeling," in *Suspense*, 129–48, 130. To this degree, Ohler and Nieding concur with Bordwell's Aristotelianism, against reader-response theory.

22. Zillmann, "The Psychology of Suspense," in *Suspense*, 205. The examples of the caper film and *Zulu* in this paragraph are from Carroll, 79.

23. Robin Wood, *Hitchcock's Films Revisited* (New York: Columbia University Press, 1989), 351–52. Deborah Knight and George McKnight also point out the way Wood's reaction to *Strangers on a Train* poses problems for Carroll's thesis. See their "Suspense and Its Master," in Richard Allen and S. Ishii-Gonzales, editors, *Alfred Hitchcock: Centenary Essays* (London: British Film Institute, 1999), 107–21, 115.

24. Ohler and Nieding, "Cognitive Modeling," in *Suspense*, 129–47, 139.

25. Zillmann, "The Psychology of Suspense," *Suspense* 199–231, 205.

26. The editors of *Suspense* make this broad distinction between two approaches within the prevailing Cartesian/empiricist/psychological paradigm governing the studies in their collection, claiming that text-centered and reception-centered approaches constitute "two opposite ends within the research fields" and that "correspondence between the two seems to be quite difficult." See their preface, vii.

27. Wolfgang Iser, "Indeterminacy and the Reader's Response in Prose Fiction," in *Aspects of Narrative*, ed. J. Hillis Miller (New York: Columbia University Press, 1971), 16.

28. Peter Ohler and Gerhild Nieding, "Cognitive Modeling of Suspense-Inducing Structures in Narrative Films," in *Suspense*, 129–47, 130.

29. David Bordwell, "Happily Ever After, Part Two," *The Velvet Light-Trap* 19, 2 (1982), 2–7, 6. For another view of Hollywood endings, see Virginia Wright Wexman's *Creating the Couple: Love, Marriage, and Hollywood Performance* (Princeton: Princeton University Press, 1993), touched on in my introduction.

30. Richard Neupert, *The End: Narration and Closure in the Cinema* (Detroit: Wayne State University Press, 1995).

31. Frank Kermode, *The Sense of an Ending* (New York: Oxford University Press, 1967); D. A. Miller, *Narrative and Its Discontents: Problems of Closure in the Traditional Novel* (Princeton: Princeton University Press, 1981). A third study is Barbara Herrnstein Smith's *Poetic Closure* (Chicago: University of Chicago Press, 1968), a rhetorical study of the syntax and language with which poets end their work. Smith's interest is in the way poets build on and sometimes undercut expectations of traditional forms, for example the Shakespearean sonnet, and in the way newly created forms generate their own expectations. Another book-length study is John Gerlach's *Toward the End: Closure and Structure in the American Short Story* (Tuscaloosa: University of Alabama Press, 1985). Gerlach's thesis is that nineteenth-century short story writers predominantly practiced variations of "closed" form, whereas their twentieth-century counterparts adopted new varieties of "open" form. A practicing short story writer, Gerlach makes clear that his interests are not of a theoretical nature. Although he finds much to admire in the reader-response theories of Wolfgang Iser and Stanley Fish, Gerlach favors the use of certain terms—"the problem level, natural termination, the antithetical level, the moral or thematic level, encapsulation" (162)—which to date have not been adopted by other writers on the subject.

32. Another term for the illuminative concordance of time provided by great literature is "aevum" (80–82, 169); at other times Kermode praises an "extraordinary moment" in which "we are by our own spirits defied" (171).

33. D. A. Miller takes the terms "bound" and "free" closure from the Russian formalist critic Boris Tomashevsky's essay, "Thematics," in Lee T. Lemon and Marion J. Reis, eds., *Russian Formalist Criticism: Four Essays* (Lincoln: University of Nebraska Press, 1965).

34. Sigmund Freud, *Introductory Lectures on Psycho-analysis*, in *The Standard Edi-*

tion of the Complete Psychological Works of Sigmund Freud, vol. 16, trans. James Strachey (London: The Hogarth Press, 1963), 410.

35. Ibid., 403–404.

36. The critic who first studied the way texts could elicit readers' unconscious anxieties was Simon O. Lesser, in *Fiction and the Unconscious* (Boston: Beacon Press, 1957) and *The Whispered Meanings* (Amherst: University of Massachusetts Press, 1977).

37. E. Ann Kaplan, "Introduction: From Plato's Cave to Freud's Screen," in E. Ann Kaplan, ed., *Psychoanalysis and Cinema* (New York: Routledge, 1990), 1–23, 12–13.

38. Christian Metz, *The Imaginary Signifier: Psychoanalysis and the Cinema*, trans. Cecelia Britton, Annwyl Williams, Ben Brewster and Alfred Guzzetti (Bloomington: Indiana University Press, 1982); Slavoj Žižek, *Everything You Always Wanted to Know about Lacan (But Were Afraid to Ask Hitchcock)* (London: Verso, 1992). For "suture theory" see Steven Heath, *Questions of Cinema* (Bloomington: Indiana University Press, 1982); a good summary is provided by Garry Leonard, in "Keeping Our Selves in Suspense: The Imagined Gaze and Fictional Constructions of the Self in Alfred Hitchcock and Edgar Allan Poe," in *Suspense*, 19–35. Noel Carroll's attack on suture theory is part of his *Mystifying Movies Fads and Fallacies in Film Theory* (New York: Columbia, 1988). A good collection of feminist responses to Lacanian film theory is available in E. Ann Kaplan's *Psychoanalysis and Cinema* (New York: Routledge, 1989).

39. See E. Ann Kaplan's "Introduction," ibid.

40. For discussions of the Lacanian "cure," see Lacan, "The Direction of the Cure," in *Ecrits* (Paris: Editions du Seuil, 1966).

41. Carroll, *Mystifying Movies*, 62–73.

42. Jacques Lacan, *The Four Fundamental Concepts of Psychoanalysis*, trans. Alan Sheridan (New York: Norton, 1978), 73.

43. Pascal Bonitzer, "Hitchcockian Suspense" in Žižek, *Everything*, 15–30, 26.

44. This is the thesis of Christian Metz in *The Imaginary Signifier*.

45. Bonitzer, 28.

46. Lothar Mikos, "The Experience of Suspense: Between Fear and Pleasure," in *Suspense*, 37–49.

47. Žižek, " 'In His Bold Gaze My Ruin Is Writ Large,' " in Žižek, *Everything*, 211–72, 222–23, 245.

48. Ibid., 244. For deconstructive responses to Zizek's articulation of the meaning of the unconscious, see Tom Cohen, *Anti-Mimesis from Plato to Hitchcock* (New York: Cambridge University Press, 1994), 229–37, and "Beyond 'The Gaze': Žižek, Hitchcock, and the American Sublime," *American Literary History* 7 (1995), 350–79. Alluding to a concept valorized in Lacan's late writing, Cohen faults Žižek for arguing that in *Psycho* the viewer experiences "the hoary epiphany of the Thing" (*Anti-Mimesis*, 231).

49. Leonard, "Keeping Our Selves in Suspense," in *Suspense*, 23–24.

50. In "Some Ruminations around the Cinematic Antidotes to the Oedipal Net(les) while Playing with DeLauraedipus Mulvey, or, He May Be Off Screen, but . . . ," in Kaplan, *Psychoanalysis and Cinema*, the feminist filmmaker Yvonne Rainer took the psychoanalytic critics Teresa de Lauretis and Laura Mulvey to task, complaining that through the continued use of Freudian and Lacanian vocabulary, women only implicated themselves more deeply into its operations (195).

51. Robert Samuels, *Hitchcock's Bi-Textuality* (Albany: SUNY Press, 1998), 143. For the most part, Samuels interprets Hitchcock as himself anxious before the spectacle of lack and castration suggested by the feminine and eager to contain it; nevertheless, in

certain films, like *Marnie*, Samuels argues that Hitchcock should be identified with the multidimensional representation of sexuality associated with the unconscious (101).

52. *Hitchcock's Bi-Textuality*, 124. In fact, for Samuels, the readability of the unconscious is not rare; neither is it confined to closures. He writes: "In Hitchcock's works, we often find the representation of a straight heterosexual narrative that is coupled with a visual bi-textual discourse" (122). On the other hand, the fact that the critic is able to read the unconscious raises the familiar contradiction of psychoanalysis, of how the unconscious can become conscious. Žižek's equivocations about closure in Hitchock are one manifestation of this dilemma. Samuels makes a call for "cultural workers" to become agents who battle against containment and repression; nevertheless, even for these critics, there must be an acknowledgement that "the truth can only be half-said" (134).

53. *In the Name of National Security: Hitchcock, Homophobia, and the Political Construction of Gender in Postwar America* (Durham: Duke University Press, 1993). Samuels's book, with very similar aims, unaccountably takes no notice of Corber's. While Corber never invokes queer theory, his thesis is compatible with the idea that the social construction of gender is an arbitrary process with which the discourses of traditional psychoanalysis collude. As in the case of feminist writers and Samuels, Corber's use of Lacan allows him a vocabulary to represent affect in the diegesis and analysis of film; thereafter, psychoanalytic categories (even Lacan's) are interpreted as reinforcements of dominant and oppressive cultural discourses.

54. *In the Name of National Security*, 60, 66, 77, 210.

55. For an account of the extension of catharsis to genres other than tragedy, see Baxter Hathaway, *The Age of Criticism: The Late Renaissance in Italy* (Ithaca: Cornell University Press, 1962), 298–300. For the extension of catharsis to comedy, see Gene Fendt, "Resolution, Catharsis, Culture: *As You Like It*," *Philosophy and Literature* 19 (1995), 248–60.

56. G. F. Else, *Aristotle's Poetics: The Argument* (Cambridge: Harvard University Press, 1967), 439. My review of the literary interpretations of catharsis in this paragraph is indebted to Donald Keesey, "On Some Recent Interpretations of Catharsis," *Classical World* 72 (1978), 193–205. For a semiotic interpretation of catharsis, see Thomas O. Beebee, "Cathartic Thinking: Tragic Theory from a Semiotic Point of View," in Roberta Kevelson, editor, *Hi-Fives: A Trip to Semiotics* (New York: Peter Lang, 1998), 173–90.

57. The first position is that of I. A. Richards and Kenneth Burke; the second, of G. F. Else and H.D.F. Kitto; the third, of I. A. Post and Leon Golden. For details of their positions, see Keesey, "On Some Recent Interpretations of Catharsis."

58. Sextus Empiricus, *Outlines of Pyrrhonism*, trans. R. G. Bury (Buffalo: Prometheus Books, 1990).

59. For Nietzsche's discussion of the ephectic drive, see *On the Geneology of Morality*, trans. Carol Diethe (New York: Cambridge University Press, 1994), 86.

60. Søren Kierkegaard, *The Concept of Dread*, trans. Walter Lowrie (Princeton: Princeton University Press, 1957), 86.

61. Edmund Husserl, *Ideas: General Introduction to Pure Phenomenology*, trans. W. R. Boyce Gibson (New York: Colier Books, 1962), 99–100.

62. Martin Heidegger, *Being and Time*, trans. John Macquarrie and Edward Robinson (New York: Harper and Row, 1962), 228–35.

63. Jacques Derrida, *Speech and Phenomena and Other Essays on Husserl's Theory of Signs*, trans. David B. Allison (Evanston: Northwestern University Press, 1973); "Differance," in *Margins of Philosophy*, trans. Alan Bass (Chicago: University of Chicago

Press, 1982), 1–28; *The Post-Card: From Socrates to Freud and Beyond*, trans. Alan Bass (Chicago, University of Chicago Press, 1987).

64. Ludwig Wittgenstein, *Philosophical Investigations*, trans. G.E.M. Anscombe, third edition (New York: The Macmillan Company, 1968), 193–229. In *The World and Language in Wittgenstein's Philosophy* (Albany: State University of New York Press, 1988), Gordon Hunnings explains the distinction as another of Wittgenstein's refutations of the "inner picture" theory of concept-formation. He concludes that whatever else a concept may be—aside from a word in a language game—can be known only through grammatical investigation (218). In *Wittgenstein: A Way of Seeing* (New York: Routledge, 1995), Judith Genova concedes that "seeing may be as interpretative as seeing-as." She defends Wittgenstein's distinction as necessary bulwark against skepticism and appeals for its resolution to the notion of the *Weltbild*. At the same time, she holds that any ultimate collapse of Wittgenstein's distinction may be understandable in the light of Wittgenstein's idea of philosophy as a kind of action (77–83). In *Clear and Queer Thinking: Wittgenstein's Development and His Relevance to Modern Thought* (New York: Rowman and Littlefield, 1999), Laurence Goldstein calls Wittgenstein's seeming resolution of the problem—as "experienced meaning"—"unWittgensteinian" and "utterly different from anything he says in the first part of *Philosophical Investigations*" (112, 113).

65. For de Man's discussion of irony, see his *Blindness and Insight: Essays in the Rhetoric of Contemporary Criticism* (Minneapolis: University of Minnesota Press, 1983), 208–28. For the idea that literary and philosophical texts could be read as allegories of their own incapacity to represent, see *Allegories of Reading: Figural Language in Rousseau, Nietzsche, Rilke, and Proust* (New Haven: Yale University Press, 1979).

CHAPTER 2

1. Deborah Knight and George McKnight, "Suspense and Its Master," in Richard Allen and S. Ishii Gonzales, eds., *Alfred Hitchcock: Centenary Essays* (London: BFI Publishing, 1999), 107–21, 107. The authors adopt a Cartesian model of suspense based on the work of William F. Brewer and Hans J. Wulff. Brewer's definition of suspense is very similar to Minet de Wied's, analyzed in Chapter 1. Wulff argued that suspense proceeded through the use of "cataphors," or cinematic foreshadowings. Brewer's essay, "The Nature of Narrative Suspense and the Problem of Rereading," is in Peter Vorderer, Hans J. Wulff, and Mike Friedrichsen, eds., *Suspense: Conceptualizations, Theoretical Analyses, and Empirical Explorations* (Mahwah: Lawrence Erlbaum Associates, 1996), 107–27; Wulff's essay, "Suspense and the Influence of Cataphora on Viewer's Expectations," is at 1–17 in the same volume.

2. Alfred Hitchcock, "Let 'Em Play God," in Sidney Gottlieb, editor, *Hitchcock on Hitchcock* (Berkeley: University of California Press, 1995), 113–15, and Francois Truffaut, *Hitchcock*, rev. ed. (New York: Simon and Schuster, 1984): "In the usual form of suspense it is indispensable that the public be made perfectly aware of all of the facts involved. Otherwise, there is no suspense" (72).

3. For Hitchcock's remarks in "Lecture at Columbia University" on informing the audience, see Gottlieb, *Hitchcock on Hitchcock*, 273. For the distinctions between suspense and terror or surprise, see "The Enjoyment of Fear," in Gottlieb, *Hitchcock on Hitchcock*, 118–19.

4. Knight and McKnight, "Suspense and Its Master," in *Suspense*, 117–20.

5. The undecidable endings of Hitchcock's films are discussed in Part III.

6. "Lecture at Columbia University," in Gottlieb, *Hitchcock on Hitchcock*, 272–73.

7. Hitchcock further blurs his own distinction by conceding it deals only "with the treatment of what is the convention of suspense" (272). Later he refers to an earlier passage where he claims that suspense can be elicited from titles. He asks the reader to contrast the effect of the titles *Mutiny on the Bounty* and *The Good Ship Bounty*: "With its real title, however, the audience in the cinema is waiting from the moment the picture starts, wondering when the mutiny is gong to start" (272). This point assumes that a greater or lesser amount of uncertainty may reside in particular words; thus, it is odd that the number of Hitchcock's titles that resemble *The Good Ship Bounty* is unexpectedly high—almost half, by my count. On the other hand, the assumption that words contain varying degrees of uncertainty, independently of context, is surely open to doubt. The suspense seemingly engendered by prosaic titles like *Rope* or *The Birds* could be reckoned as two entirely different amounts, depending on whether the intertextual dimensions provided by Hitchcock's persona, studio publicity, etc., are taken into account.

8. Truffaut, *Hitchcock*, rev. ed. (New York: Simon and Schuster, 1984) 73, 272.

9. Ibid., 72.

10. A survey of five recent studies leads Dolf Zillmann to conclude, "Suspense in drama is predominantly created through the suggestion of negative outcomes." See his "The Logic of Suspense and Mystery," in Jennings Bryant and Dolf Zillmann, eds. *Responding to the Screen: Reception and Reaction Processes* (Hillsdale: Lawrence Erlbaum Associates, 1991), 281–303, 284. Most of the contributors to *Suspense* concentrate on fear and consider "hope" only in de Wied's negative sense of a desire to see liked characters avoid a "harmful outcome event." In *The Cognitive Structure of Emotions* (New York: Cambridge University Press, 1988), the cognitive psychologists Ortony, Clore, and Collins define suspense as "involving a Hope emotion and a Fear emotion coupled with the cognitive state of uncertainty;" both are examples of "Prospect-based" emotions (131). Hitchcock's example of the telephone operator has the effect of assimilating her altruistic form of hope into the hope/fear dyad that forms the basis of traditional discussions of suspense.

11. "Lecture at Columbia University," in Gottlieb, *Hitchcock on Hitchcock*, 271–72.

12. "Master of Suspense," in Gottlieb, *Hitchcock on Hitchcock*, 123.

13. Truffaut, *Hitchcock*, 111. This passage gains resonance when read in the light of Hitchcock's obesity. For discussions of misleading faces in Hitchcock, see the chapters on *Vertigo, North by Northwest*, and *Torn Curtain*.

14. For Spoto's attribution of the source, see *The Dark Side of Genius: The Life of Alfred Hitchcock* (New York: Ballantine Books, 1983), 159–60. Gottlieb reports that Hitchcock used the concept in a question-and-answer period following his Columbia University lecture in 1939. See Gottlieb, *Hitchcock on Hitchcock*, 267. The version of the story paraphrased here is from Hitchcock's essay, "Rear Window," first published in 1968 and reprinted in Albert J. LaValley, editor, *Focus on Hitchcock* (Englewood Cliffs: Prentice-Hall, 1972), 40–46, 43–44.

15. Ibid., 43.

16. Critics who define the MacGuffin as plot pretext include Spoto, *The Dark Side of Genius*, 160; Thomas Leitch, *Find the Director and Other Hitchcock Games* (Athens: University of Georgia Press, 278); Lesley Brill, *The Hitchcock Romance: Love and Irony*

in Hitchcock's Films (Princeton: Princeton University Press, 1988), 7–8. The quotation from Hitchcock is from Gottlieb, *Hitchcock on Hitchcock*, 124, emphasis added.

17. Ibid., 123–24. The quotation is from the 1950 essay, "Master of Suspense." In his 1967 interview with Truffaut and in his article "Rear Window," Hitchcock expanded on the definition of the MacGuffin; portions of both later discussions are analyzed later in this chapter. In the sentences deleted from this passage quoted here, Hitchcock predicts that the gravity of international espionage in the postwar era—a clear allusion to nuclear weapons—should make it less likely that the MacGuffin will succeed in espionage films. Of course, Hitchcock violated his own prediction in *North by Northwest* and *Torn Curtain*. For critics who may want to see Hitchcock's remarks as theoretically consistent, it remains unaccountable why he made no retroactive correction to this prediction in his comments on the MacGuffin in 1967 or 1968. On the other hand, this chapter argues that Hitchcock's theoretical comments, like his films, often *dramatize* the breakdown of theory.

18. Thomas Elsaesser, "The Dandy in Hitchcock," in Allen and Ishii-Gonzales, eds., *Alfred Hitchcock: Centenary Essays*, 7. Elsaesser's essay appeared in Italian in 1981 and in English translation, in the journal *The McGuffin*, in 1994.

19. Tom Cohen, *Anti-Mimesis from Plato to Hitchcock* (New York: Cambridge University Press, 1994), 240.

20. In "Allegory and Referentiality: *Vertigo* and Feminist Criticism," *MLN* 106, No. 5 (1991), 910–32, Susan White invoked the work of Paul de Man as part of her proposal that *Vertigo* be understood at least in part as challenging referentiality.

21. Doubts as to the validity of the concept of the "proper name" have been expressed by Jacques Derrida throughout his career. See his essay "Différance," trans. David Allison, in *Speech and Phenomena* (Evanston: Northwestern University Press, 1973). A later treatment of the subject is included in *The Ear of the Other: Otobiography, Transference, Translation*, trans. Peggy Kamuf (Lincoln: University of Nebraska Press, 1985), 98–103.

22. Of course, whether the absence of referentiality of the word "MacGuffin" is demonstrated "empirically" depends on the assessment of the interlocuter's protest ("But there *are* no lions in the Scottish highlands"), in other words, on his word alone.

23. Cohen, *Anti-Mimesis*, 239–40.

24. In "The Psychology of Suspense in Dramatic Exposition," Dolf Zillmann argues that the drama can produce a euphoric "grand resolution" at "curtain fall," though such conclusions may at times even understate the amount of pleasure derived from intermittent experiences of suspense arousal. His article is included in *Suspense*, 199–231.

25. The three versions I am aware of are in Spoto, *The Dark Side of Genius*, 299–300; in Truffaut's *Hitchcock*, 138; and in the essay on "Rear Window," in LaValley, *Focus on Hitchcock*, 44. The version paraphrased here is from LaValley.

26. Spoto, *The Dark Side of Genius*, 300.

27. LaValley, *Focus on Hitchcock*, 43.

28. Truffaut, *Hitchcock*, 139.

29. Gottlieb, *Hitchcock on Hitchcock*, 122

30. To analyze all of the instances of irony in this passage (and to relate them to the essay as a whole) would require an extensive digression. Among the more salient are the following: (1) the use of the word "juicy" to describe the cameo—does this indicate or mock the value of the scene? (2) Hitchcock's comparison between himself and a worm that intrudes into a narrative in progress—the echoes of Genesis here (especially in the

context of a film whose main character is named Eve) perhaps points to some gnostic or Manichean conception of the artist; (3) another comparison, between the director and a spy, inverts the normal relation of the actors and MacGuffin in espionage films; (4) the antithetical senses of the word "shoot" when used to mean to record or preserve on film.

31. The term "enunciation" was introduced by the structural linguist Emile Benveniste, who distinguished the *enonce*, roughly the story or diegesis, from the *enonciation*, roughly the set of competencies which makes an *enonce* possible; in the work of later theorists this distinction sometimes becomes *histoire* and *discours*. The distinction is fundamental to the semiology of Roland Barthes and the film criticism of Christian Metz and Marie-Claire Ropars-Wuilleumier. For a critique of the influence of Benveniste's distinction on film studies, see David Bordwell, *Narration in the Fiction Film* (Madison: University of Wisconsin Press, 1985), 21–26.

32. A thoughtful analysis of the cameos is included as an appendix in Maurice Yacowar's *Hitchcock's British Films* (Hamden, CT: Archon Books, 1977), 270–78. Yacowar sees the cameos as providing thematic comment and instantiating the figure of the director as maker. Thomas Leitch sees the cameos as establishing an anticipatory contract between the filmmaker and the viewers. Lesley Brill, in "Redemptive Comedy in the Films of Alfred Hitchcock and Preston Sturges: 'Are Snakes Necessary?' " in Richard Allen and S. Ishii-Gonzalès, eds., *Alfred Hitchcock: Centenary Essays* (London: British Film Institute, 1999), 205–20, argues that the cameos have primarily a comic effect.

33. For a discussion of "parabasis" as the momentary suspension of the dramatic illusion, see J. Hillis Miller, *Reading Narrative* (Norman: University of Oklahoma Press, 1998), 37. Miller adapts the term from Paul de Man's discussion in *Blindness and Insight* (Minneapolis: University of Minnesota Press, 1983), 218–22. There de Man defined irony as a moment of permanent incapacity to know whether a passage is ironic. The connection with personal identity arises in his discussion of "the self-conscious narrator" in prose fiction: at the moment readers understand a difference between the author and the fictional persona, "there is no way back from his fictional self to his actual self" (219).

34. Miller, *Reading Narrative*, 37.

35. Wittgenstein, *Philosophical Investigations*, trans. G.E.M. Anscombe, third edition (New York: The Macmillan Company, 1968), 197.

36. Truffaut, *Hitchcock*, 190–91.

37. In *The Dark Side of Genius*, Donald Spoto narrates occasions on which Hitchcock may have deliberately fabricated in order to enhance his persona. An example is his alleged prescience in using uranium as a plot device in *Notorious*, which Hitchcock reinforces in his interview with Truffaut (300). For an excellent account of Hitchcock's persona-building during his television series, see Thomas Leitch, "The Outer Circle: Hitchcock on Television," in Allen and Ishii-Gonzalès, *Alfred Hitchcock: Centenary Essays*, 59–71.

INTRODUCTION TO PART II

1. Ludwig Wittgenstein, *Philosophical Investigations*, trans. G.E.M. Anscombe (New York: The Macmillan Company, 1958), 194–205. Wittgenstein questions whether the meaning of a sign can be said to be identical with itself. Beginning with familiar optical illusions that seem to represent two images, he asks a series of questions that imply a

human inability to say that *any* visual image discloses its meaning in some way other than as a *taking* of it, as one thing or another. For an extended treatment of Wittgenstein's challenge to the principle of self-identity, see Harry Staten, *Wittgenstein and Derrida* (Lincoln: University of Nebraska Press, 1984), 131–49.

2. Jacques Derrida, *The Truth in Painting*, trans. Geoff Bennington and Ian McLeod (Chicago: University of Chicago Press, 1987). Derrida's theory of the frame in this work represents an expansion of earlier comments made in the essay "Tympan," Derrida's introduction to the volume *Margins of Philosophy* (Chicago: University of Chicago Press, 1982), ix–xxix. Marie-Claire Ropars-Wuilleumier discusses Derrida's theory of the frame in "The Dissimulation of Painting," in Peter Brunette and David Wills, eds., *Deconstruction and the Visual Arts* (Cambridge: Cambridge University Press, 1994), 65–79.

3. Brunette and Wills, "The Spatial Arts: An Interview with Jacques Derrida," in *Deconstruction and the Visual Arts*, 15.

4. Sir James Frazer, *The Golden Bough*. 12 vols. (New York: The Macmillan Company, 1935). Frazer's comments on the hanged god are contained in chap. 5 of the second book of vol. 1, *Attis and Adonis*, 288–97; his discussion of the crucifixion is added as a note at the end of vol. 11, *The Scapegoat*, 412–23.

5. Michel Foucault, *Discipline and Punish: The Birth of the Prison*, trans. Alan Sheridan (New York: Pantheon Books, 1977). Chapter 2 is "The Spectacle of the Scaffold."

6. Lionelli Puppi, *Torment in Art: Pain Violence and Martyrdom*, trans. Jeremy Scott (New York: Rizzoli, 1991). Puppi cites Camus' analysis of the way Christianity reinforced capital punishment, in "Réflexion sur la guillotine," in Albert Camus and A. Kostler, *Réflexions sur la peine de mort* (Paris: Calmann-Levy, 1957).

CHAPTER 3

1. Paul G. Bahn, *The Cambridge Illustrated History of Prehistoric Art* (Cambridge: Cambridge University Press, 1998), 92. In this section, the word "pendant" will be taken to mean any object that hangs from a string, throng, cord or other flexible material. A technical distinction between "beads" and "pendants" is not observed in this section, as it is a matter of extreme nuance among archeologists; for a discussion, see Horace C. Beck, *Classification and Nomenclature of Beads and Pendants* (1925; rpt. York: Liberty Cap Books, 1973), 1.

2. Robert A. Lunsingh Scheurleer, "From Statue to Pendant: Roman Harpocrates Pendants in Gold, Silver, and Bronze," in Adriana Calinescu, ed., *Ancient Jewelry and Archaeology* (Bloomington: Indiana University Press, 1996), 152–71, 160.

3. Alexander Marshack, "Olmec Mosaic Pendant," in *Archaeoastronomy in Pre-Columbian America*, edited by Anthony F. Aventi (Austin: University of Texas Press, 1975), 341–77.

4. Holly Pittman, "The 'Shell' Pendant in the States Museum in Berlin: Egypt or the Ancient Near East?" *Source* 13 (1994), 28–35, 33.

5. For a discussion of the iterative essence of signs see Jacques Derrida, "Signature/Event/Context," in *Margins of Philosophy*, trans. Alan Bass (Chicago: University of Chicago Press, 1982), 315, and "Différance," in the same volume, 1–28.

6. Rosalind Krauss, "Sculpture in the Expanded Field," in Hal Foster, ed., *The Anti-Aesthetic: Essays on Postmodern Culture* (Seattle: Bay Press, 1983), 31–42.

7. In *Speech and Phenomena*, trans. David B. Allison (Evanston: Northwestern University Press, 1973), Jacques Derrida argues that neither speech nor writing is a privileged or originary representation of presence; on the contrary, they attest only to a "breakup of presence" that is older than logocentric truth or history. For a sample of some pendants from the proto-literate period of Mesopatamia, see Jeanny Vorys Canby, "Ancient Near Eastern Jewelry," in *Objects of Adornment: Five Thousand Years of Jewelry from the Walters Art Gallery* (Baltimore: The Walters Art Gallery, 1984), 29–34.

8. Uwe Sievertsen, "Das Messer vom Gebel el-Arak," *Baghdader Mitteilungen* 23 (1992), 1–76. My thanks to my colleague David Ward for confirming Sievertsen's point about the reflexivity of the pendant.

9. For de Man's account of narrative as a means of arresting or halting "infinite" or "dissolving" irony, see "The Concept of Irony," in *Aesthetic Ideology*, ed. Andrzej Warminski (Minneapolis: University of Minnesota Press, 1983), 166, 176.

10. Richard Erdoes, in *The Sun Dance People* (New York: Knopf, 1972) reproduces a "picture, painted in 1832" that purports to represent the sun dance (107), but I have been unable to establish its provenance.

11. This account of the sun dance is synthesized from Peter J. Powell, *Sweet Medicine: The Continuing Role of the Sacred Arrow, the Sun Dance, and the Sacred Buffalo Hat in Northern Cheyenne History* (Norman: University of Oklahoma Press, 1969), 319–20; Joseph G. Jorgensen, *The Sun Dance Religion: Power for the Powerless* (Chicago: University of Chicago Press, 1972); Phillip M. White, *The Native American Sun Dance Religion and Ceremony: An Annotated Bibliography* (Westport: Greenwood, 1998), xix–xxii.

12. This image can be found in Walter Wreszinski, *Atlas zur altägyptischen Kulturgeschichte*, vol. 2 (Leipzig: Verlag der J. C. Hinrichschen, 1935), Plate 36. It is discussed in Anthony J. Spalinger, "A Canaanite Ritual Found in Egyptian Reliefs," *SSEA Journal* 8 (1977–78), 47–59. My thanks to Ellen Morris for alerting me to this article.

13. Roland de Vaux, *Studies in Old Testament Sacrifice* (Cardiff: University of Wales Press, 1964).

14. The *Santo Spirito Crucifix* is attributed to Michelangelo by Casa Buonarroti and included in *Michelangelo: The Complete Works* (New York: Morrow, 1966) but not in William E. Wallace's *Michelangelo: The Complete Sculpture, Painting, Architecture* (Hong Kong: Hugh Lauter Levin Associates, 1998). Wallace's collection includes three drawings of the crucifixion by Michelangelo. Jesus does not wear a crown of thorns in any of the three, and in one he appears entirely nude, without a loincloth. It is interesting that on the ceiling of the Sistine Chapel there is only one crucifixion, in a lunette, seen from the rear. Meanwhile the *signs* of the crucifixion—the crown of thorns, the shroud, etc., are being borne toward heaven, perhaps signifying the transcending of the Passion in the Day of Judgement; on the other hand, the separation of the signs of the crucifixion from the figure of the crucified Jesus may bear out the implications of the Santo Spirito statue—that the representation of the Passion depends on arbitrary and alienable signs. Of course, if this interpretation is allowed, new questions will arise about the representability of all other elements of the Christian narrative depicted on the ceiling of the Sistine Chapel, from the account of creation in Genesis to the Day of Judgment in Revelation.

15. For a summary of scholarly discussions of the sources of the identity of the Beloved Disciple, see D. Moody Smith, *Johannine Christianity: Essays on Its Setting, Sources, and Theology* (Columbia: University of South Carolina Press, 1984), 20.

16. Renewed attention to the *Gospel of Thomas* leads many scholars to refer to five instead of four gospels, but since *Thomas* recounts no Passion narrative, visual details of the crucifixion story must still be drawn from the four canonical gospels. In Mark and Matthew, the title "The King of the Jews" is also said to be the "charge against" Jesus, whereas in Luke and John the title appears without that legal stipulation; clearly the latter versions leave open other possibilities for interpreting the juridical proceedings against Jesus. Luke's version, "This is the King of the Jews," may be read as both genuine (Jesus, even if Christ, is certainly at least the king of the Jews) and ironic (Jesus is much more than merely the king of the Jews); these two readings might be favored by one or another segment of Luke's audience.

17. Jacques Derrida, *The Ear of the Other: Otobiography, Transference, Translation*, trans. Peggy Kamuf (Lincoln: University of Nebraska Press, 1985), 98–103. The question of the existence of the "proper noun" or the "unique name" has preoccupied Derrida since the essay "Différance." It was the subject of a famous dialogue with Jean-Francois Lyotard, summarized in Lyotard's "Discussions, or Phrasing 'after Auschwitz' " (1980; rpt. trans. George Van Den Abbeele, University of Wisconsin Center for Twentieth-Century Studies, 1986).

18. *Aporias*, trans. Thomas Dutoit (Stanford: Stanford University Press, 1993), 10.

19. After Pilate writes the title in three languages, the chief priests of the Jews say to him, "Do not write 'The King of the Jews' but, 'This man said, 'I am King of the Jews.' " Pilate answered, "What I have written I have written." The priests' anxieties may indicate an awareness of the performative potential of language, which they hope to eliminate with a constative version. Pilate's refusal may be read as preventing an *ex post facto* reinterpretation of the charge against Jesus. (Of course, the exact nature of the charge against Jesus was and continues to be a matter of dispute among theologians.) From the Roman perspective, Pilate's refusal of the priests' request allows him to maintain neutrality on the question of Jesus's *actual* role. while he may have been the king of the Jews, neither that fact nor Jesus's assertion of it could prevent the punishment called for by the Jews. Of course, from John's perspective, Pilate's effort to maintain deniability on behalf of the Roman governor is in itself ironic, since in allowing the interpretation that Jesus *was* the king of the Jews, Pilate still fails to anticipate the later spread of Christianity to the Gentiles. On the other hand, John's depiction of these ironies of misrecognition—first by the Jewish priests, then by Pilate—is made possible only by his own construction of the identity of Jesus, a construction which *he* fails to recognize in the scene of translation he has just narrated. In this way, John's narrative repeats Paul de Man's two-stage process of deconstruction.

20. Israel Knohl, *The Messiah before Jesus: The Suffering Servant of the Dead Sea Scrolls*, trans. David Maisel (Berkeley: University of California Press, 2000).

21. Gertrud Schiller, *Iconography of Christian Art*, vol. 2, trans. Janet Seligman (Greenwich: New York Graphic Society Ltd., 1972), 91. Of the hundreds of depictions of the Passion analyzed in this volume, only one—a Wolf Huber painting from 1523–30—depicts Jesus as crucified naked, and even in this painting the genitalia of Jesus are obscured by his leg.

22. The logical possibility remains that someone—the Roman soldiers or Joseph of Arimathea—unwound and removed the loincloth after the crucifixion but before the removal of the body from the cross; this possibility is depicted in certain scenes of the deposition in which the loincloth cannot be seen. In this possibility, Michelangelo's statue represents a moment of deliberate human unveiling that could on the one hand be un-

derstood as malicious, in the case of the Roman soldiers, or on the other as reverent, in the case of Joseph of Arimathea. It is consistent with everything else about Michelangelo's sculpture that the *motives* for the physical revelation of Jesus's body cannot be read from the statue itself. In duplicating the action of either the soldiers or Joseph, Michelangelo the sculptor may imply that the artist's motivation for creation is just as undecidable, just as open to the indeterminable imputations of reverence or desecration, as those of the people who unveiled the body of Jesus.

23. For a discussion of medieval and renaissance representations of the circumcision of Jesus—in painting, theology, and poetry—see David L. Gollaher, *Circumcision: A History of the World's Most Controversial Surgery* (New York: Basic Books, 2000), chap. 2. Gollaher summarizes the tradition of Christian speculation as to the fate of the foreskin of Jesus, which at times was held to be an authentic relic with healing powers; he also explains that in Christian theology, the fact that Jesus was circumcised and his followers were not posed conceptual problems for the tradition of the *imitatio Christi* and for the doctrine of the perfection of the body in resurrection (35–37).

24. In his *Problems in Titian, Mostly Iconographic* (New York: New York University Press, 1969), Erwin Panofsky expressed doubts about the attribution to Titian (171). According to a recent survey of opinion, the painting is now generally accepted as Titian's. See Paolo Rossi, "The Flaying of Marsyas," in *Titian: Prince of Painters* (Munich: Prestel-Verlag, 1990), 370–72.

25. Sister Wendy Beckett, *Sister Wendy's 1000 Masterpieces* (New York: DK Publishing, 1999), 461.

26. Katya Berger Andreadakis and John Berger, *Titian: Nymph and Shepherd* (Munich: Prestel, 1996), 49.

27. For a review of the vexed interpretation of this figure, see Rossi, 370–72. One critic holds that the youth with the violin is a second Apollo; another that it is Olympus, Marsyas' pupil. Others believe that the figure was added by a different painter. Rossi calls his instrument a *lira da braccio*, although its resemblance to the *viola da bracchio*, the instrument first made in 1510 that transformed Western music, is unmistakable.

28. This old man with the crown has sometimes been identified as King Midas. Rossi claims the figure has an ass's ears, "the sign of his punishment by Apollo for failing to achieve victory in his musical contest with Pan" (370), though I confess those details are not easy to discern; see also Sister Wendy Beckett (461). Rossi also recounts the tradition of seeing the crowned figure as Titian's self-portrait.

29. Avigdor W. G. Posèq, "The Hanging Carcass Motif and Jewish Artists," *Jewish Art* 16/17 (1990–91), 139–56. Even the formalist critic Sir Kenneth Clark thought that the details of the painting "set off new trains of association. The flayed ox has become a tragic—one might almost say a religious picture." See Kenneth Clark, *An Introduction to Rembrandt* (New York: Harper and Row, 1978), 114. In *Reading "Rembrandt": Beyond the Word-Image Opposition* (Cambridge: Cambridge University Press, 1991), Mieke Bal argues that the nonfunctional nails in the carcass "bring the work one step closer to a crucifixion" (387).

30. Posèq, 139. For a discussion of Israelite sacrifices to Moloch, see de Vaux, *Studies in Old Testament Sacrifice*, 73–90. In "A Canaanite Ritual," Spalinger takes note of this controversy and endorses de Vaux's thesis (52).

31. Posèq cites St. Jerome's letter to Damascus as recorded in *Patrologia Latina* XCII, 388; St. Ambrose's commentary on Luke (*PL*, XV, 1761); and other references in the Venerable Bede, Haymo of Halberstadt and Peter Chrysologus.

32. *The Anatomy Lesson of Dr. Tulp* works just as *The Flayed Ox* does to define but transcend the paradox it depicts. In the former painting we are shown ostensible healers who are supposedly learning from a "master healer." And yet the corpse, which might be read intertextually in terms of Lazarus, is irrevocably dead. Most of the supposed healers cannot regard the corpse directly. What they read, perhaps all that their naturalism makes them capable of reading, is a list of their own names; the meaningless signs are tautological. The self-blinded and narcissistic character of seventeenth-century science is presented as inevitable, like a self-portrait, but it is also mocked; this is the theme of *The Flayed Ox*, too. But *The Anatomy Lesson* does not end in paradox, either. Instead, the cadaver's role as model for both science and painting links Rembrandt with the physicians, showing that art's satirical or paradoxical achievement is inseparable from the science it condemns: the master doctor's scissors, like Rembrandt's brushes, is the laid-on or "applied" prosthetic device that cannot avoid "coloring" the body, every time, anew. So Dr. Tulp is like Rembrandt in "opening up" an unanswerable question.

33. According to the four canonical gospel-writers, many women "looked on from afar" at the crucifixion; Luke also includes "all" the acquaintances of Jesus. Mark, Matthew, and John specify that Mary Magdalene witnessed the crucifixion. Mark also adds Mary the mother of James the younger and of Joses, and Salome; Matthew also adds Mary the mother of James and Joseph, and the mother of the sons of Zebedee; John also adds Mary, the mother of Jesus, Mary, the wife of Clopas, and the anonymous "Beloved Disciple." If we accept that Mary Magdalene was one of the "acquaintances" of Jesus in Luke's account, then she is the only person that all four gospel writers agree witnessed the crucifixion. All four also include her among the women who subsequently visited the tomb.

34. "Surfmen" is the name given to the crew members of the life-saving stations that were administered by the civilian U.S. Life-Saving Service, the predecessor organization of the U.S. Coast Guard. A "breeches buoy" is the name of the device depicted in the painting. If the shipwreck lay close enough to shore to permit its use, the breeches buoy was made operational by shooting a projectile with attached ropes at the ship from a Lyle gun (a small cannon); once secured to ship and land, the principal rope became a hawser on which a pulley carrying the breeches buoy rode. Sewn inside the buoy was a pair of leggings into which the surfman put his legs; this position permitted him to hold onto the rescued passenger. The buoy was moved to and from the wreck by means of a second rope. In Homer's painting, the second rope is taut to the right, as the breeches buoy is being pulled toward the shore, and limp at the left. Breeches buoys were introduced in the early 1870s and continued to be used until they were replaced by helicopters in the twentieth century. For further details concerning the history and operation of the breeches buoy, see Ralph Shanks et al., eds., *The U.S. Life-Saving Service: Heroes Rescues and Architecture of the Early Coast Guard* (Petaluma, CA: Castano Books, 1996), 31–33 and 207–208.

35. J. H. Merryman, "The United States Life-Saving Service," *Scribner's Monthly* 19 (January 1880), 327. Quoted in Nicolai Cikovsky, Jr., and Franklin Kelly, *Winslow Homer* (New Haven: Yale University Press, 1995), 224.

36. Ibid., 224.

37. "The Spring Academy," *The New York Times*, 5 April 1884, quoted in Cikovsky and Kelly, 224.

38. Jules D. Prown, "Winslow Homer in His Art," *Smithsonian Studies in American Art* (Spring, 1987), 31–44, 39–40.

39. Cikovsky and Kelly, *Winslow Homer*, 224.

40. Prown, "Winslow Homer in His Art," 39.

41. "Fine Art Notes," *New York Evening Telegram*, 21 April 1884. Quoted in Cikovsky and Kelly, 225.

42. Prown, "Winslow Homer in His Art," 38.

43. Julia Frey, *Toulouse-Lautrec: A Life* (New York: Viking, 1994), 327.

44. Ibid., 328.

45. For discussions of the way avant-garde art may be regarded as both antithetical to and compatible with mass art, see Renato Poggioli, *The Theory of the Avant-Garde* (Cambridge: Harvard University Press, 1983), and Richard Murphy, *Theorizing the Avant-Garde: Modernism, Expressionism, and the Problem of Postmodernity* (Cambridge: Cambridge University Press, 1998).

46. The literature on the Calas affair is enormous. Two studies that take the side of Voltaire and Calas are Alex Coutet, *Jean Calas, roué vif et innocent* (Toulouse: Musée du desert an Cevennes, 1933) and Edna Nixon, *Voltaire and the Calas Case* (New York: Vanguard Press, 1961); two studies that side with the parlement's original verdict are the Abbe Salvan's *Histoire du proces de Jean Calas* (Toulouse, 1863) and Marc Chassaigne, *The Calas Case*, trans. Raglan Somerset (London: Hutchinson, 1930). David D. Bien's *The Calas Affair: Persecution, Toleration, and Heresy in Eighteenth-Century Toulouse* (Princeton: Princeton University Press, 1960) takes a neutral position; the author reviews the political climate that formed the ideological context for the scandal. The popular and intellectual impact of this inflammatory incident may be gauged from W. D. Howarth's study of numerous stage adaptations of the event published between 1767 and 1832, "Tragedy into melodrama: the fortunes of the Calas affair on the stage," *Studies in Voltaire and the Eighteenth Century* 174 (1978), 121–50.

47. In eighteenth-century France, the official legislation concerning the treatment of suicides was extremely harsh; it included dragging the body in the streets and throwing it on the town's dumping ground; on the other hand, the extent to which these measures were enforced is the subject of debate. See Bien, *The Calas Affair*, 8–10.

48. In its depiction of the possibly murderous death of a human being by hanging, Toulouse-Lautrec's *Le Pendu* raises the issue of the artistic status of representations of lynching. These issues have been given new prominence with the publications of Leon F. Litwack's *Without Sanctuary: Lynching Photography in America* (Santa Fe, NM: Twin Palms, 2000). The appalling photographs collected in this volume bear testimony to a violence of racial bigotry on a scale at least as devastating as that of the Protestant-Catholic hatred Voltaire condemned. Artistic representations of actual hanging corpses, whether painted or photographed, may open their creators to charges of the exploitation of the sordid no matter how long the interval between the depicted death and its subsequent representation. It seems inevitable that in both cases the corpse's claim on the viewer must be conveyed, however minimally, within the constraints of representation itself: for example, the distribution of color and light, in the case of *Le Pendu*, or the composition of the frame, in the case of the photographs collected by Litwack.

49. In her book *A History of Playing Cards and a Bibliography of Cards and Gaming* (Boston: Houghton Mifflin, 1930), Catherine Perry Hargrave cites the year 1392 as the first European record of the existence of Tarot cards; however, like other writers on the subject, she speculates that their appearance in Europe came after long traditions in India, Persia, Arabia, etc.

50. Kathleen Raine's *Yeats, the Tarot and the Golden Dawn* (Dublin: The Dolmen

Press, 1972) surveys the poet's interest in these subjects and makes a case for the relevance of the Tarot in the poem "Vacillation." Interest in Eliot's use of the Tarot cards in *The Waste Land* has continued over the years. See Tom Gibbons, "*The Waste Land* Tarot Identified," *Journal of Modern Literature* (1972), 560–65; Robert Currie, "Eliot and the Tarot," *ELH* 46 (1979), 722–33; Max Nanny, " 'Cards Are Queer': A New Reading of the Tarot in *The Waste Land*," *English Studies* 62 (1981), 335–47; Betsey B. Creekmore, "The Tarot Fortune in *The Waste Land*," *ELH* 49 (1982), 908–28; Julie Nall Knowles, "London Bridge and the Hanged Man of *The Waste Land*," *Renascence* 39 (1987), 374–82.

51. On the sense in which human language and interpretation is already a distortion of the truth of Kabbalah, see Gershom Scholem, *On the Kabbalah and Its Symbolism*, trans. Ralph Mannheim (New York: Schocken Books, 1969), 30–31. In his *The Painted Caravan: A Penetration into the Secrets of the Tarot Cards* (The Hague: L.J.C. Boucher, 1954), Basil Ivan Rakoczi explains that a magus or writer on the Tarot is bound by oaths of inner and outer secrecy that constrain him to set down "only the intelligible definitions of the symbols themselves," leaving their higher meanings for moments of mystical apprehension. In a similar vein, Papus [M. Gerard Encausse], in *The Tarot of the Bohemians*, trans. A. P. Morton (No. Hollywood, CA: Melvin Powers Wilshire Book Company, n. d.), claims that full communication of the truth of the Tarot is available only to certain initiates: "The Word will only reach those who should be touched thereby" (13).

52. Rakoczi, *The Painted Caravan*, 69.

53. Arthur Edward Waite, *The Pictorial Key to the Tarot* (1910; rpt. New Hyde Park: University Books, 1959). Waite also wrote a preface to the English translation of Papus's *The Tarot of the Bohemians*. For a scholarly account of the history of the Tarot, see Catherine Perry Hargrave, *A History of Playing Cards and a Bibliography of Cards and Gaming* (Boston: Houghton Mifflin, 1930).

54. *The Tarot of the Bohemians*, 317, 318.

55. Rakoczi, *The Painted Caravan*, 49.

56. For one description of Prometheus as hanging, see Catherine B. Avery, *The New Century Classical Handbook* (New York: Appleton-Century Crofts, 1962), 935.

57. In other accounts, Prometheus's role with regard to humanity was even more profound. Some claimed that Prometheus created the human race from clay and the breath of Athena; others said Prometheus's theft prevented Zeus from annihilating the race of mortals. The iconographic tradition of Prometheus the "animator" is discussed in Olga Raggio's "The Myth of Prometheus," *Journal of the Warburg and Courtauld Institutes* 21 (1958), 44–62. Analogies between Prometheus and Jesus are discussed below; a lengthier treatment is Justin Glenn's "Prometheus and Christ," *Classical Bulletin* 62 (1986), 1–5. The name "Prometheus" means "forethought" or "foresight."

58. For the references to Prometheus by the early Church fathers, I am indebted to Justin Glenn, "Prometheus and Christ," *Classical Bulletin* 62 (1986), 1–5. Raggio also refers to representations of Prometheus as "crucified" as early as the second century B.C. (46).

59. In *Transformations in Late Eighteenth Century Art* (Princeton: Princeton University Press, 1967), Robert Rosenblum claims that the painting evokes a "clandestine Christianity" (82–84). Tony Halliday, in "David's *Marat* as Posthumous Portrait," in William Vaughan and Helen Weston, eds., *Jacques-Louis David's* Marat (Cambridge: Cambridge University Press, 2000), 56–76, declares that the "quasi-Christian character of the Marat-cult" has in fact been overemphasized (56). The connection between David's painting

and Rembrandt is made by David Lomas, in "Staging Sacrifice: Munch, Picasso, and *Marat*," in *Jacques-Louis David's* Marat, 153–78, 160.

60. For an analysis of these paintings, see Lomas, "Staging Sacrifice." Lomas offers a Lacanian reading of the icon in the work of each painter, associating the absent Charlotte Corday with the castration threat and the death of Marat himself with the Oedipal scene.

61. For a formalist discussion of the painting in terms of genre and David's career, see Robert Rosenblum's book. An excellent study of David's public role in the revolution is David Lloyd Dowd's "Pageant-Master of the Republic: Jacques-Louis David and the French Revolution," *University of Nebraska Studies*, New Series, No. 5 (June, 1948).

62. Six recent articles appear in Vaughan and Weston's collection; another excellent study is Jean-Remy Mantion, "Enveloppes à Marat David," in Jean-Claude Bonnet, editor, *La Mort de Marat* (Paris: Flammarion, 1986), 203–32. Lomas calls attention to the parallels between David's painting and both the crucifixion and Rembrandt's hanging carcass. Among other arguments, Mantion sees David's painting as propagating an "undecidable contamination" between history and art (214).

63. In "Enveloppes à Marat David," Mantion cites "le *Marat* de David," "*Marat assassine*," "*Marat expirant*," "*Marat mourant dans son bain*," "*Le Mort de Marat*," and "*Marat à son dernier soupir*." The different titles come from catalogues, public exhibitions, David's letters, and the critical tradition (206).

64. Paul de Man, "Autobiography as De-Facement," in *The Rhetoric of Romanticism* (New York: Columbia, 1984), 80.

65. The letters may be translated as follows: (1) Corday's, held by Marat: "It is enough that I am quite unfortunate that I might have the right to your benevolence." (2) Marat's, left on the table: "Give this *assignat* to this mother of five children, whose husband died defending his country."

66. Weston, *Jacques-Louis David's* Marat, 135. Weston argues that David deliberately effaced the figure of Charlotte Corday from the scene, the better to ennoble Marat. Corday's threat to Jacobinism, her independence, and her own moral agency are all evident from the painting's historical context. According to Weston, David endowed the figure of Marat with attributes that counterbalance and ultimately prevail over Corday's threat. Weston's reading of the painting sees it as a "paradoxical expression," both of David's Jacobite sympathies and his acknowledgment of Corday's otherness. On the other hand, to take such a view is to see David's brush as exempt from the undecidability that accompanies his depiction of the quill (can writing be believed?) and the knife (when is assassination just?).

67. Foucault's thesis is set forth in *The Birth of the Clinic: An Archaeology of Medical Perception*, trans. A. M. Sheridan Smith (New York: Pantheon Books, 1973) and *Discipline and Punish: The Birth of the Prison*, trans. Alan Sheridan (New York: Pantheon Books, 1977).

68. Mantion, "Enveloppes à Marat David," 219; Lomas, "Staging Sacrifice," 173.

69. For Roland Barthes' famous discussion of the death of the author, see his essay, "The Death of the Author," trans. Stephen Heath, in Roland Barthes, *Image Music Text* (New York: Hill and Wang, 1977), 142–48. Barthes found the death of the author in the multivalences of language and not in the arbitrary nature of the sign.

70. For an account of the construction of the tanks, see Christopher Flacke, "Held in Suspense," *Art and Antiques* (Summer, 1987), 25; for analysis of the "Equilibrium Series" in the context of Koons's developing career, see Roberta Smith, "Rituals of Consumption," *Art in America* (May, 1988), 164–71.

71. Moral and political interpretations of Koons's "Equilibrium Series," especially with regard to issues of race, class, the media, and consumerism, are developed in Smith's article and in Dan Cameron, "Pretty as a Product," *Arts Magazine* 60 (1986), 22–25; Gary Indiana, "Jeff Koons at International with Monument," *Art in America* 73 (1985), 163–64; Robert Pincus-Witten, "Entries: Concentrated Juice and Kitschy Kitschy Koons," *Arts Magazine* 63 (1989), 34–39. For Koons's concern to maintain the integrity of the object or not "infringe" on it, see his interview with Jeanne Siegel, "Jeff Koons: Unachievable States of Being," *Arts Magazine* 61 (1986), 66–71.

72. Ibid., 68.

73. Jacques Derrida, "Parergon," *The Truth in Painting*, trans. Geoff Bennington and Ian McLeod (Chicago: University of Chicago Press, 1987). Derrida also discusses the frame in relation to the "Tympan," in *Margins of Philosophy*, trans. Alan Bass (Chicago: University of Chicago Press, 1982), ix–xxix.

74. "Starting out from the Frame (Vignettes)," in Peter Brunette and David Wills, eds., *Deconstruction and the Visual Arts: Art, Media, Architecture* (New York: Cambridge University Press, 1994), 118–40.

75. Paul de Man, "Phenomenality and Materiality in Kant," in *Aesthetic Ideology*, ed. Andrzej Warminski (Minneapolis: University of Minnesota Press, 1996), 90. De Man's more general use of the concept of "materiality" has mystified and stimulated his readers. A volume of essays exploring these other usages is Tom Cohen's *Material Events* (Minneapolis: University of Minnesota Press, 2001).

CHAPTER 4

1. The application of a rhetorical term like "metonymy" to visual media is clearly itself a figure or "white mythology" of criticism. This subject is taken up in the afterword.

2. In *Hitchcock's British Films* (Hamden, CT: Archon Books, 1977), Maurice Yacowar sees the film's moral center as Sir John, the actor who maintains balance and control (124, 127). In *Find the Director and Other Hitchcock Games* (Athens: University of Georgia Press, 1991), Thomas Leitch agrees with Yacowar's assessment and concludes that the implication of the theatre metaphor is "the assumption that everyone hides a secret self under a public disguise" (69). William Rothman, in *Hitchcock: The Murderous Gaze* (Cambridge: Harvard University Press, 1982), argues that the essence of the film is its "declaration of its own decisive separation from theatre" (60). Critics who find authenticity in Fane include Rothman, Modleski, and Zupancic; their views are discussed later in this section.

3. Yacowar defends Sir John from the charges of Raymond Durgnat, in *The Strange Case of Alfred Hitchcock* (Cambridge: MIT Press, 1974), and of early reviewers of *Murder!* who found Sir John dilettantish or classist (134–36); Leitch claims that in a world divided between public and private, "the greatest power belongs to those who are most aware of the inveterateness of acting" and that the audience's point of view comes to coincide with Hitchcock's in seeing the stage metaphor "from above" (*Find the Director*, 68). Rothman interprets Sir John as having a special bond with the camera and as acting, until just before the very end, as "Hitchcock's agent and surrogate" (*Hitchcock: The Murderous Gaze*, 61); with Fane's suicide, Hitchcock's view is identified with that of the camera and with the persona of the director as a violent avenger on the viewer.

4. Marc Vernet, "Blinking, Flickering, and Flashing of the Black and White Film,"

trans. Lee Hildreth, in Theresa Hak Kyung Cha, ed., *Cinematographic Apparatus: Selected Writings* (New York: Tanam Press, 1980), 357–69.

5. Slavoj Žižek, " 'In His Bold Gaze My Ruin Is Writ Large,' " in Slavoj Žižek, ed., *Everything You Always Wanted to Know About Lacan . . . (But Were Afraid to Ask Hitchcock)* (London: Verso, 1992), 211–72, 246.

6. The subject of Fane's homosexuality was first broached in 1966 by Truffaut, who told Hitchcock he considered *Murder!* a thinly disguised story about Fane as homosexual; Hitchcock neither confirmed nor denied Truffaut's interpretation. However, in 1972, forty-two years after making the film, Hitchcock told Charles Thomas Samuels that Fane was a "half-caste homosexual." See Samuels's *Encountering Directors* (New York: G. P. Putnam's Sons, 1972), 241. In *The Strange Case of Alfred Hitchcock*, Durgnat, apparently unaware of the Samuels interview, proposed Fane be considered a homosexual on the basis of his effeminacy and transvestite performances (112–13), reasoning that is obviously open to question. In 1982, William Rothman, also apparently unaware of the Samuels interview, claimed that Hitchcock contested Truffaut's claim that the film was about homosexuality, although I can find no such denial in the interview. In 1988, Tania Modleski, also apparently unaware of the Samuels interview, interpreted Fane's character as embodying a "feminizing potential" that threatens Sir John's patriarchal values. See *The Women Who Knew Too Much* (New York: Routledge, 1988). The intertextual history of this issue suggests the way the designation "homosexual" for Handel Fane is curiously suspended.

7. *The Women Who Knew Too Much*, 36

8. Alenka Zupančič, "A Perfect Place to Die: Theatre in Hitchcock's Films," in Slavoj Žižek, ed., *Everything You Always Wanted to Know About Lacan . . . (But Were Afraid to Ask Hitchcock)* (London: Verson, 1992), 73–105, 98.

9. For some of the action of *The 39 Steps*, Hannay and Pamela are handcuffed together in scenes that directly parody the concept of the construction of the couple. In *Shadow of a Doubt*, Charlie and her murderous uncle of the same name wrestle on the coupling of a moving train; their postures enact undecidability—repressed eroticism and murderous rage—at a physical site of coupling. In *To Catch a Thief*, the wrongly accused cat burglar Robie wrestles the real burglar, Danielle, who always loved him, on a rooftop. In *Vertigo* Scottie and Judy repeat these movements atop a bell tower. Thornhill and the undecidable Eve dangle together from Mount Rushmore in *North by Northwest*, while Armstrong and Sarah hide in hanging cargo in *Torn Curtain*. From Hitchcock's early uses, it would appear that the artificiality of the yoke that harnesses or joins dangling couples is a visual figure for the undecidability of their "natural affections." The implications of the "hanging couple" in last three films is taken up in detail in Part III.

10. The truck driver's rooting for Kane may be an analogue for the audience's, one that may anticipate the later spectacle of a film audience enthralled by the spectacle of *film noir*, the genre notorious for its reversals of sympathy between criminals and law enforcement agents.

11. Patricia softens toward Kane despite the fact that he disables her car. Her first reason for reversing her opposition to Kane is fear for her own safety—Kane reminds her of the snakes in the desert to which she'll be vulnerable without him; later, she claims to believe in him because she is shamed by the greater charity shown to him by the members of the carnival troupe, especially Esmeralda. But both her original suspicion of Kane and her changes of heart are based not on exculpatory evidence but on her interpretation of his appearance. It is instructive that Patricia reverses course on two

further occasions—once after she overhears Kane's "impersonation" of a saboteur in Soda City; later, she decides she can trust Kane after he kisses her. These changes in Patricia's perception of Kane are another instance of character conceived as parabasis: that is, Hitchcock depicts the issue of Kane's guilt not as a matter of inner character but as the interpretation of particular performances.

12. Martin's isolated existence deep in the interior of the woods is made possible by his seeing-eye dog and by his niece's regular visits; that even this hermit-like existence is no utopian sanctuary is suggested by the ease with which the police penetrate it. The Martin episode shares many of the ironies as the DeLacey episode in Shelley's *Frankenstein*. The seemingly guilty outsider is treated with compassion by a blind man, until the return of younger relations implicated in the world of desire. The intolerance of the younger generation becomes an ironic commentary on the alienating effects of vision; the fact that both Frankenstein's creature and Barry Kane first learn love in bucolic situations is made ironic in both works. The creature's subsequent desire for a mate inspires his obsessional quest, and Kane's winning of Patricia can take place only after the destruction of the author of his alienation, Fry/Frankenstein.

13. Guy DeBord, *Society of the Spectacle* (Detroit: Black and Red, 1970).

14. Ludwig Wittgenstein, *Philosophical Investigations*, trans. G.E.M. Anscombe, third edition (New York: The Macmillan Company, 1968), 193–229. Wittgenstein's discussions of aspect dawning as a philosophical analogue for suspense is discussed at the end of chapter 1.

15. In "Hitchcock's *Rear Window*: Reflexivity and the Critique of Voyeurism," in Marshall Deutelbaum and Leland Poague, eds., *A Hitchcock Reader* (Ames: Iowa State University Press, 1986), 193–206, Robert Stam and Roberta Pearson argue that over the course of the film, Jeff and Lisa narrow their differences and they are thereby "rendered ready for marriage" (204). That Lisa and Jeff misinterpret the characters across the courtyard is the position of Virginia Wright Wexman in *Creating the Couple: Love, Marriage, and Hollywood Performance* (Princeton: Princeton University Press, 1993), 15. But as pointed out in the introduction, Wexman also brings to her study of constructed couples a template of how normative couples *ought* to be figured.

CHAPTER 5

1. In *The Dark Side of Genius: The Life of Alfred Hitchcock* (New York: Ballantine Books, 1983), Donald Spoto claims that the credits of some prints, following the novel adapted by Hitchcock, identify the lodger as "Jonathan Drew" (94); however, my print identifies Ivor Novello's character only as "the Lodger," and the name "Jonathan Drew" is never used in the diegesis. Critical practice varies; most identify the character as "the Lodger." The fact that it is impossible to refer correctly to the title figure furthers the film's subversion of identity.

2. Francois Truffaut, *Hitchcock*, revised edition (New York: Simon and Schuster, 1983), 43. The effect of Hitchcock's putting the phrase "Hitchcock movie" in quotation marks after the word "true" is difficult to gauge. The quotation marks may distinguish *The Lodger* from earlier films which were not memorable or in which he did not exercise full directorial authority; on the other hand, the quotation marks unsettle the adjective "true," as if the referent "Hitchcock movie" itself was not wholly decidable.

3. Rothman, *Hitchcock: The Murderous Gaze* (Cambridge: Harvard University Press, 1982), 46.

4. Ken Mogg, "Hitchcock's *The Lodger*: A Theory," *Hitchcock Annual* (1992), 115–27.

5. Truffaut, *Hitchcock*, 43–44.

6. Spoto, *The Dark Side of Genius*, 95.

7. In the present study, the title character is referred to as "the lodger," in lower case, in contrast to critical convention, as a means of leaving open the question of other referents of the title.

8. Truffaut, *Hitchcock*, 47.

9. Lesley Brill is alone in arguing that the allusion unambiguously lends moral stature to the lodger; he claims the allusion is appropriate because the lodger suffers not on his own behalf but on behalf of "the society that gave rise to the Avenger and that is implicated in his crimes." See his *The Hitchcock Romance: Love and Irony in Hitchcock's Films* (Princeton: Princeton University Press, 1988), 91. In *Hitchcock's British Films* (Hamden, CT: Archon, 1977), Maurice Yacowar argues that the lodger shares the Avenger's instincts (40). In *The Art of Alfred Hitchcock* (New York: Hopkinson and Blake, 1976), Donald Spoto claims that the lodger's murderous intentions are even worse than the Avenger's because they are coldly premeditated rather than instinctual (7).

10. Truffaut, *Hitchcock*, 34

11. Richard Allen, "Hitchcock, or the Pleasures of Metaskepticism," in *Alfred Hitchcock: Centenary Essays*, edited by Richard Allen and S. Ishi-Gonzalès (London: British Film Institute, 1999), 221–37, 224.

12. Truffaut, *Hitchcock*, 45.

13. In "Hitchcock and Bunuel: Authority, Desire, and the Absurd," in *Hitchcock's Rereleased Films: From Rope to Vertigo*, eds. Walter Raubicheck and Walter Srebnik (Detroit: Wayne State University Press, 1991), Robert Stam draws attention to this aspect of *The Lodger* in his discussion of its "theme of ambiguous gender identity," which he sees as "taking the form of hints at possible homosexuality in the protagonist" (122).

14. Yacowar was the first to notice the "shutter effect" of the opening credits (33).

15. Ludwig Wittgenstein, *The Blue and Brown Books* (New York: Barnes and Noble, 1969, 162–63.

16. Truffaut, *Hitchcock*, 183.

17. For a discussion of the way surrealist film foregrounds the arbitrary attribution of presence to cinematic montage, see Linda Williams, *Figures of Desire: A Theory and Analysis of Surrealist Films* (Berkeley: Univ. of California Press, 1981). For the affinities between Hitchcock's films and those of the surrealists, see Robert Stam, "Hitchcock and Buñuel: Authority, Desire, and the Absurd," in Walter Raubicheck and Walter Srebnik, eds., 116–46, and Harry Ringel, "*Blackmail*: The Opening of Hitchcock's Surrealist Eye," *Film Heritage* 9.2 (1974), 17–23.

18. René Girard, *Deceit, Desire, and the Novel*, trans. Yvonne Freccero (Baltimore: Johns Hopkins University Press, 1965). For an account of triangulation in Hitchcock's films that makes use of the work of Eve Kosofsky Sedgwick, see Paula Marantz Cohen, *Alfred Hitchcock and the Legacy of Victorianism* (Lexington: Univ. of Kentucky Press, 1995), 87.

CHAPTER 6

1. Following Edward Said, Tania Modleski in *The Women Who Knew Too Much: Hitchcock and Feminist Theory* (New York: Methuen, 1988), describes her approach as

a "frankly inventive" (13–15) way of giving voice to previously unheard women in Hitchcock; she does not mention *Easy Virtue*.

2. In *The Dark Side of Genius: The Life of Alfred Hitchcock* (New York: Ballantine Books, 1983), Donald Spoto describes Hitchcock as on occasion exhibiting a sadistic personality and abusing women; he believes Hitchcock's films sometimes reflect and rationalize these traits. In "Visual Pleasure and Narrative Cinema," in Constance Penlye, ed., *Feminism and Film Theory* (New York: Routledge, 1988), Laura Mulvey argues that in Hitchcock's heroes, the "power to subject another person to the will sadistically or to the gaze voyeuristically is turned on to the woman as the object of both" (66–67). In *Hitchcock on Hitchcock: Selected Writings and Interviews* (Berkeley: University of California Press, 1995), Sidney Gottlieb argues that Hitchcock rationalizes, rather than denies, the charge that he is a misogynist (70); he finds Hitchcock's writings about women "more than a little troubling" (71).

3. For commentary on Hitchcock's films that uses the idea of reflexivity in these ways, see for example Robert Stam, *Reflexivity in Film and Literature: From Don Quixote to Jean-Luc Godard* (New York: Columbia University Press, 1992), on *Rear Window*, and Edward Recchia, "Through a Shower Curtain Darkly: Reflexivity as a Dramatic Component of *Psycho*," *Literature/Film Quarterly* 19 (1991), 258–66, on *Psycho*.

4. Yacowar argues that the cameras suggest "voyeuristic intrusion" as part of Hitchcock's social satire leveled against both the upper class and the stigma of divorce (56, 57). In *Alfred Hitchcock* (Boston: Twayne Publishers, 1984), Gene D. Phillips sees in the photographers Hitchcock's satire of a "scandal-mongering press" (40).

5. The technical virtuosity of the scene is praised by Yacowar (55) and Philips (40). For Derrida's concept of the postal, see his *The Post-Card: From Socrates to Freud and After*, trans. Alan Bass (Chicago: University of Chicago Press, 1987).

CHAPTER 7

1. See Eric Rohmer and Claude Chabrol, *Hitchcock: The First Forty-Four Films*, trans. Stanley Hochman (New York: Frederick Ungar,1979), 13–14; and the next note.

2. In his *The Art of Alfred Hitchcock: Fifty Years of His Motion Pictures* (New York: Hopkinson and Blake, 1976) Donald Spoto noted three of these referents (12). Gene D. Phillips in *Alfred Hitchcock* (Boston: Twayne Publishers, 1984) links the title with the plot's circular structure (42). Ivan Butler in *Silent Magic: Rediscovering the Silent Film Era* (New York: Ungar, 1988), also notes the title's multiple meanings (161).

3. In the work of Mikhail Bakhtin, the "carnivalesque" is understood as an ontologically real condition somewhat analogous to Nietzsche's "Dionysian," though with a democratic emphasis: all discourses have an equivalent truth claim in an egalitarian condition of "heteroglossia." This anarchic state of affairs is reproduced best in the novel, which can accept into its loose structure many conflicting voices while privileging none. As it is used in this chapter, the idea of the carnival or the "carnivalesque" implies no such ontologically real state; instead it is only a metaphor for a leveling of undecidable narratives or discourses whose referent is always in doubt, closer in spirit to Derrida's "postal."

4. The problem of naming in this film is especially vexed. Critics refer to "the girl" in the film as "Nelly Hall," though there is no evidence for this view. In the film the character is introduced with the name of the actress: "The girl . . . Lilian Hall Davis." I

will follow the critical practice of misnaming this character. Another character, Corby's promoter, is named in the film by his calling card, which identifies him as "James Ware." However, he is never referred to by this name either within the diegesis or in the credits. Finally, it is noteworthy that the name "One Round Jack" appears in the diegesis first on a placard which is held upside-down in front of the tent where Jack fights. For each of these characters, even the visual representation of the name is depicted as arbitrary. The silent film's separation of name from voice is doubled by a second, visual separation.

5. Jacques Derrida, "Signature/Event/Context," in *Margins of Philosophy*, trans. Alan Bass (Chicago: University of Chicago Press, 1982), 307–30.

6. Donald Spoto, *The Art of Alfred Hitchcock* (New York: Hopkinson and Blake, 1976), argued that the film's "psychological maturity lies in its refusal to smooth things out" and that despite Nelly's eventual loyalty to Jack, "the implication is that emotions are tentative, shifting and basically superficial" (12).

7. Tom Gunning, " 'Now You See It, Now You Don't': The Temporality of the Cinema of Attractions," in Richard Abel, editor, *Silent Film* (New Brunswick: Rutgers University Press, 1996), 71–84, 75.

8. In *Aporias* (Stanford: Stanford University Press, 2000), Jacques Derrida interprets Martin Heidegger's concept of *Sein-zum-Tode* as equiprimordial with the existence of boundaries that make reading possible. But since Dasein can never define itself in language, the "Da" of Dasein presupposes its death.

CHAPTER 8

1. Andrew Britton, "Hitchcock's *Spellbound*: Text and Counter-Text," *Cineaction* 3/4 (1985), 72–83. Britton points out that Cassius is making a plea to Brutus to join in a revolution (72).

2. Brulov disparages Edwardes's interest in "outdoor therapy"—swimming and skiing—from what at first might seem the orthodox Freudian position that only the talking cure can adapt patients to the reality principle. But Britton points out that Brulov's own orthodoxy is called into question by his willingness to entertain a pre-Freudian interpretation of dreams—that "wish fulfillment" may simply be conscious lust or that dreams may unravel the mystery of the past (80). Constance praises Edwardes's "unorthodox" intellect and supports his interest in physical exercise. Her own assumption that the source of traumatic amnesia can be rediscovered and mastered through controlled re-enactment is also a fugitive therapy; it reappears in *Vertigo* in the advice given by Scotty Ferguson's analyst. Murchison's differences with Edwardes suggest that professional differences may be inseparable from resentment over inferior status—precisely the point of Cassius's incitement to Brutus.

3. There is the hint of a paradox in the idea that a "locked" door can simply be "opened" without first having been unlocked; to this extent, the epigraph suggests the contradiction of conceptualizing both an unconscious that can *never* become conscious but that can, nevertheless, be read in such surface symptoms as jokes, phobic behavior, slips of the tongue, dreams, etc.

4. Britton, "Hitchcock's *Spellbound*," 72. There is another contradiction between the scrolled tribute and the rest of the film—its representation of gender ("to induce the patient to talk about his hidden problems"). The uneasy implication of this passage is that neurosis is restricted to males. This inference can then give rise to a reading of the

film in which Mary Carmichael's incarceration and all of the psychiatric treatments of it—including Dr. Peterson's—are unjust.

5. Britton is able to reconcile the differences between psychoanalysis and love only by evaluating the action on the basis of a more rigorous Freudianism than the film itself employs. A different attempt to reconcile these discourses is Thomas Hyde's "The Moral Universe of Hitchcock's *Spellbound*," in Marshall Deutelbaum and Leland Poague, eds, *A Hitchcock Reader* (Ames: Iowa State University Press, 1986), 153–61. Hyde argues that the film narrates a process by which the lead characters lose their alienating features: Constance exchanges the intellect for emotion and John overcomes his instinctual aggression. Hyde's thesis finds in the ending a normative paradigm that defines what constitutes a moral couple.

6. Potential contradictions between epigraph and narrative occur as early as *Easy Virtue*, which began with the title, "Virtue is its own reward, they say, but 'Easy Virtue' is society's reward for a slandered reputation." Conflating phrase and title lends a reflexive dimension to the epigraph that makes its applicability to the narrative uncertain. *The Manxman* begins with a quotation from the Sermon on the Mount, "What shall it profiteth a man to gain the whole world if he loseth his soul." Although the sentence ostensibly applies to Philip, the guilty deemster, it might also apply to Peter, who earns a fortune *without* losing his soul. In the latter case, the epigraph questions the purpose of all morality. *The Man Who Knew Too Much* (1956) begins with the epigraph, "A single clash of the cymbals and how it rocked the lives of an American family." As others have noted, the reflexivity derived from reading the epigraph's homonym ("symbols") makes the epigraph apply to the film medium as well as the diegesis. The inherent reflexivity of epigraphs, at the liminal position inside and outside the narrative, makes their referentiality always suspect.

7. As we shall see in chapter 9, the undecidability of a kiss that is "enacted" as passionate is also central to the action of *Notorious*. In Alex Sebastian's wine cellar, Devlin grabs Alicia and "pretends" to be kissing her passionately, as a lover, in order to prevent Alex, who discovers them, from suspecting his national security motive for being where he is. Yet throughout the film, Devlin's feelings for Alicia are precisely at issue and still generate critical controversy. As in the case of the kiss between Constance and John at the train station, the visual spectacle of the kiss is helpless to convey motive; these kisses are like hanging figures in being only more noticeable forms of undecidability.

8. Lloyd Michaels, *The Phantom of the Cinema: Character in Modern Film* (Albany: State University of New York Press, 1998). Adapting the title of De Chirico's painting, Michaels persuasively shows that character in film frequently calls its own authenticity into question, resulting in phantoms that exhibit a residual "mystery and melancholy of a self." This formulation comes close to the idea of character I develop here, but Michaels argues that these characters retain the representational function of conveying the disillusionment he discovers in them, whereas in my approach that function, too, is the momentary illusion born in the act of reading the film.

9. Britton argues that the "counter-text" of *Spellbound* continually subverts its text of apparent endorsement of psychoanalysis, and to this degree his conclusions and mine agree. At the same time, the condition for discovering the "countertext" is that both of us construe the black lines on white of Hitchcock's text, the *clignotements*, as signifying "real" characters. Both of us commit this error, which can be understood only after having committed it and which the film *narrates* as fundamental to reading the hanging figure.

CHAPTER 9

1. Robin Wood, *Hitchcock's Films Revisited* (New York: Columbia University Press, 1989); Tania Modleski, *The Women Who Knew Too Much: Hitchcock and Feminist Theory* (New York: Routledge, 1988); Robert Corber, *In the Name of National Security: Hitchcock, Homophobia, and the Political Construction of Gender in Postwar America* (Durham: Duke University Press, 1993); Andrew Britton, "Cary Grant: The Comedy of Male Desire," *CineAction!* 7 (1987); Laura Mulvey, *Visual and Other Pleasures* (Bloomington: Indiana University Press, 1989).

2. For a critique of the organicist assumptions of Romanticism, see Paul de Man, *Allegories of Reading: Figural Language in Rousseau, Nietzsche, Rilke, and Proust* (New Haven: Yale University Press, 1979), Chapter 4.

3. Donald Spoto, *The Dark Side of Genius: The Life of Alfred Hitchcock* (New York: Ballantine, 1983).

4. Maurice Yacowar, *Hitchcock's British Films* (Hamden, CT: Archon Books, 1977), 258–59; Pascal Bonitzer, "*Notorious,*" in Slavoj Žižek, *Everything You Always Wanted to Know about Lacan . . . But Were Afraid to Ask Hitchcock* (London: Verso, 1992), 151–54, 153.

5. For an account of the cinematic figure of the castrating mother, see Barbara Creed, *The Monstrous-Feminine: Film, Feminism, Psychoanalysis* (London: Routledge, 1993).

6. Paul de Man, *Aesthetic Ideology*, ed. Andrzej Warminski (Minneapolis: University of Minnesota, 1996), 166, 176.

7. Robin Wood is representative of critics who demonize Alex as masculinist murderer, in contrast to Devlin. See his *Hitchcock's Films Revisited*, 323. In *The Women Who Knew Too Much*, Tania Modleski sees in Alex the failure of Oedipal development (64); in *In the Name of National Security*, Robert Corber concurs, seeing him as wholly manipulated by his mother and hence incapable of entry into the Symbolic order (204). In his "*Notorious*: Perversion par Excellence," in Marshall Deutelbaum and Leland Poague's *A Hitchcock Reader* (Ames: Iowa State University Press, 1986), 162–69, Richard Abel defends Alex, noting that his love for Alicia may be stronger than Devlin's and that he is victimized at least as much as Alicia is (167). Alex's vulnerability and humanity are also recognized by Spoto, in *The Art of Alfred Hitchcock* (New York: Hopkinson and Blake, 1976), 168–69.

8. Spoto, *The Art of Alfred Hitchcock*, 173.

9. Wood, *Hitchcock's Films Revisited*. 325.

10. Modleski, *The Women Who Knew Too Much*, 68–71.

11. Corber, *In the Name of National Security*, 208.

12. Andrew Britton, "Cary Grant: Comedy and Male Desire," *CineAction* 7 (1987), 36–51, 46.

13. Abel, "*Notorious*: Perversion par Excellence,"168.

14. Spoto, *The Dark Side of Genius*, 307.

CHAPTER 10

1. Truffaut, *Hitchcock*, revised edition (New York: Simon and Schuster, 1983), 139. The MacGuffin is discussed in chapter 2.

2. In his "Life with(out) Father: the Ideological Masculine in *Rope* and Other Hitch-

cock Films," in Walter Raubicheck and Walter Srebnik, eds., *Hitchcock's Rereleased Films: From Rope to Vertigo* (Detroit: Wayne State University Press, 1991), 240–52, Robert G. Goulet examines Rupert as the embodiment of Lacan's Law of the Father, whose ambiguous triumph exemplifies a textual rupture in Hitchcock's films reflective of a tension between heterosexual patriarchy and a decadent skepticism that threatens it. In his "Anal *Rope*," *Representations* 22 (1990), 114–33, D. A. Miller demonstrates the relevance of the film's construction of homosexuality for Hitchcock's technical experiment of making an "uncut" film; he concludes that the cuts thematized both castration anxiety and its negation as the spurious gender boundary that Rupert Cadell and Hitchcock's camera police. Thomas Hemmeter, in "Twisted Writing: *Rope* as an Experimental Film," in *Hitchcock's Rereleased Films*, 253–65, adopts a Derridean perspective to argue that Brandon's deconstructive position exposes as illusory Rupert Cadell's seemingly altruistic appeals to "something" independent of language, which otherwise would imprison everyone in the penthouse.

3. Paul de Man, *Allegories of Reading: Figural Language in Rousseau, Nietzsche, Rilke and Proust* (New Haven: Yale University Press, 1979), 205. The relevance of de Man's idea for reading or viewing films in general is discussed in the introduction; its relevance for specific Hitchcock films is discussed in individual chapters of this book.

4. J. Hillis Miller, *Reading Narrative* (Norman: University of Oklahoma Press, 1998).

5. The classic case for film's artistic purity as derivative from that of the photograph is Sigfried Kracauer's *Theory of Film: The Redemption of Physical Reality* (New York: Oxford University Press, 1960). A more recent statement of the privileged position of photography within visual representation is Kendall L. Walton's "Transparent Pictures," *Critical Inquiry* 11:2 (1984), 246–77. This article inspired rejoinders by Noel Carroll and Gregory Currie; these are considered in Walton's "On Pictures and Photographs: Objections Answered," in Richard Allen and Murray Smith, eds., *Film Theory and Philosophy* (Oxford: Oxford University Press, 1997), 60–75. Like Hitchcock's *Rope*, Andy Warhol's minimally edited films, *Sleep* (1963) and *Empire* (1964), may also be contributions to the critical debates over the privileged ontological status of film and photography: one critic has described them as "an investigation into the presence and character of film." See Gregory Battock, "Four Films by Andy Warhol," in Michael O'Pray, ed., *Andy Warhol: Film Factory* (London: British Film Institute, 1989), 45.

6. Miller, *Reading Narrative*, 55.

7. For a discussion of the abstract grid that precedes *North by Northwest*, see chapter 12.

8. Of course, since viewers of the film never see the "signified referent" of David Kentley's corpse revealed in the cassone, they must base their certainty on visual and verbal signs. The point is not a quibble, since as D. A. Miller points out, the *condition* of the corpse—especially the question of whether it manifests an erection—is a crux for interpretation. See his "Anal *Rope*," 130. On one level, the film's withholding of the revelation of the corpse only underscores the larger truth of cinematic representation: that "signification" is a circular process, inseparable from artificial signifiers. On another level, the presence or absence of the corpse's erection only repeats the film's demonstration that gender "essence" is undecidable and wholly constructed from signs.

9. The undermining of essential character identity by reflexive allusions is discussed later in the chapter. The end credits begin by identifying all characters through their relation with David: i.e., "David's father," "David's aunt," etc. To imply that specific

human identities are to be formally acknowledged with regard to the film's example of the "absent signified" is already to sow doubt as to any essentialism of character. The doubt may be compounded by the irony of the credit, "His friends" for Brandon and Phillip.

10. Hitchcock's career-long preference for depicting the depraved in the trappings of the civilized (as Brandon, in this case) should caution viewers in concluding that the uniformed figure in the credits is in fact a policeman and not a criminal or psychopath *disguised* as a policeman. The opening view from on high, very much like a view from a window, may recall the scene of Descartes' self-questioning, as to how he could be sure the people below him in the streets really were what they appeared to be to his senses.

11. For a discussion of other parallels between Hitchcock and Brandon, see Thomas M. Bauso, "*Rope*: Hitchcock's Unkindest Cut," in *Hitchcock's Rereleased Films*, 226–39.

12. Hemmeter, "Twisted Writing," 263.

13. For de Man's account of narrative as a means of arresting or halting "infinite" or "dissolving" irony, see his "The Concept of Irony," in *Aesthetic Ideology*, ed. Andrzej Warminski (Minneapolis: University of Minnesota Press, 1996), 163–84, especially 166, 176.

14. In *Find the Director and Other Hitchcock Games* (Athens: University of Georgia Press, 1991). Thomas Leitch writes that the "film's dialogue is filled with jokes that establish a prevailing mode of black comedy" (143). In *The Dark Side of Genius: The Life of Alfred Hitchcock* (New York: Ballantine Books, 1983), Donald Spoto calls the jokes "savagely unfunny" (325). Both descriptions seem apt. Phrases like "black comedy" or "unfunny jokes" help suggest the undecidable character of Hitchcock's irony, or irony in general, as it is understood here.

15. D. A. Miller, "Anal *Rope*," 119. Miller, following Roland Barthes, calls Hitchcock's practice linguistic "connotation" as opposed to "denotation." Of course, for Miller and for queer theory generally, language retains an unmistakable denotative property that connects human identity, now matter how thoroughly constructed by culture, with human sexuality.

16. As he brings champagne from the kitchen, Brandon tells Phillip, "Murder can be a work of art. We've killed for the sake of danger and for the sake of killing." As Brandon sets the candelabra on the cassone, he tells Philip he is "making our work of art a masterpiece."

17. Hemmeter, "Twisted Writing," 258.

18. I've been unable to locate a source for the story, "The Mistletoe Bough." In the diegesis, the title of Mr. Kentley's story refers to neither mistletoe nor bough.

19. D. A. Miller, "Anal *Rope*," 119.

20. Of course, "The Mistletoe Bough" is a fairy tale whose original "sender" is unknowable in any case.

21. This perspective on Borges's parable has been adopted by Jacques Derrida in *The Ear of the Other: Otobiography, Transference, Translation*. Trans. Peggy Kamuf (Lincoln: University of Nebraska Press, 1988), 99.

22. Hitchcock's interest in and use of foreign languages in his films is well known. For further discussion of the way they undermine "normal" referentiality, see Chapter 15. In *Rope* some uncertainty may attend the characters' national affiliations. Brandon and Phillip appear to be Americans who attended the prep school at which Rupert was

"housemaster of Somerville"; however, Brandon's mockery of "American undergraduates" raises a question as to the nature of his irony. David's father and aunt are clearly English. This residual ambiguity about the characters' nationalities may have been brought about by traces of the original play (by the English playwright Patrick Hamilton) which are oddly unexpunged in the adaptation by the American screenwriter Arthur Laurentis.

23. For the classic post-structuralist argument that determination of the "author" can longer be considered the goal of criticism, see Roland Barthes, "The Death of the Author," in *Image-Music-Text*, trans. Stephen Heath (New York: Hill and Wang, 1977). Paul de Man's concept of "parabasis," discussed in chapter 2, makes the same argument in a different way.

24. The term "idle talk" comes from Martin Heidegger, *Being and Time*, trans. John Macquarrie and Edward Robinson (New York: Harper and Row, 1962), 211. It is not used disparagingly in Heidegger; instead, it refers to the everyday use of language in which a stance toward representation is already presupposed. I use the term here to distinguish the characters' ordinary conversation in *Rope* from interpolated narratives.

25. Hemmeter, "Twisted Writing," 258–59.

26. Hitchcock's awareness of the pun on "strand" is apparent in his jokes about the film's publicity: "One press agent suggested that we have a world premiere in the Philippines because hemp comes from there. Another wanted us to hang it on New York's Strand Theatre. I thought it best to let the boys have their fun. Their work was just beginning; mine was done. You see, I had come to the end of *my Rope*." *Hitchcock on Hitchcock: Selected Writings and Interviews* (Berkeley: University of California Press, 1995), 284.

27. The destabilization of character identity was discussed earlier in the chapter and again in note 9, with regard to the end credits. In *Find the Director*, Thomas Leitch has commented on the "unnatural intimacy" among the characters created by these credits (141). To the extent they may be regarded as humorous, the second set of credits extends the diagetic irony—the many unresolvable instances of "funny or unfunny" talk—intertextually, beyond the diegesis; Hitchcock's ironic essay on *Rope* (see note 26) effects such an extension, too.

CHAPTER 11

1. For background to the controversy over gender essentialism, see Judith Butler, *Gender Trouble: Feminism and the Subversion of Identity* (New York: Routledge, 1990) and *Bodies that Matter: On the Discursive Limits of "Sex"* (New York: Routledge, 1993). In both works Butler explores the dilemma of formulating constructed definitions of gender in discursive practices that do not presuppose language as speech-act and that do not relapse into essentialism; the first book explores this problem with regard to feminism; the second, with regard to queer theory. Critics of *Vertigo* who exemplify this controversy are taken up elsewhere in the notes.

2. Laura Mulvey, "Visual Pleasure and Narrative Cinema," *Screen* 16, No. 3 (1975), 6–18, and "Afterthoughts on 'Visual Pleasure and Narrative Cinema' Inspired by *Duel in the Sun*," *Framework* 15–17 (1981), 12–15.

3. Susan White, "Allegory and Referentiality: *Vertigo* and Feminist Criticism," *MLN* 106, No. 5 (1991), 910–32; Deborah Linderman, "The Mise-en-Abime in Hitchcock's

Vertigo," Cinema Journal 30, No. 4 (1991), 51–74. White's thesis is summarized in note 5. Eight years later, White published "*Vertigo* and Problems of Knowledge in Feminist Film Theory," in Richard Allen and S. Ishii-Gonzales, eds., *Alfred Hitchcock: Centenary Essays* (London: British Film Institute, 1999), 279–98. Although she calls this essay "to some extent a revision" of her earlier article (296), she does not amplify the thesis of "Allegory and Referentiality." Instead, she analyzes the feminist, Lacanian, and deconstructive readings of *Vertigo* at greater length; as a part of that survey, she accurately summarizes the argument of this chapter as it first was first advanced in a journal article, "Feminism, Deconstruction, and the Pursuit of the Tenable in *Vertigo*," *Hitchcock Annual* (1996–97), 3–25. White concludes that my work continues "the oscillation between an 'untenable' essentialism and a politically ineffective anti-essentialism characteristic of *Vertigo* criticism and of feminist theory in general" (292). I am pleased that White borrowed my (or *Vertigo*'s) metaphor to describe the current state of criticism. Her characterization of my argument is fair; I acknowledge that it is politically ineffective.

4. Laura Hinton, "A Woman's View: The *Vertigo* Frame-Up," *Film Criticism* 19 (1994), 2–22.

5. In "Allegory and Referentiality," White discusses not only feminist but also Marxist and other materialist studies of the film, in part from the vantage point of Paul de Man's understanding of allegory. Her essay brilliantly shows that in their attempt to excavate a "single dominating reality" behind *Vertigo*, these critical approaches elide their own storytelling amid nostalgia for a "content proper" (931). At the same time, White reinscribes feminist essentialism in arguing that "woman's desire for a (perhaps impossible) reconciliation with the mother" (917) is thematized as the object of the quest in *Vertigo*. Despite her demonstration of the allegory of criticism, White's ultimate recourse to essentialism is also suggested by her view that a different line of analysis (born of the work of Chodorow, Scheman, and Spivak) might indeed capture in the film a tenable "maternal realm" that is not an "object of knowing" (930, 926, 927).

6. Linderman, "The Mise-en-Abime in Hitchcock's *Vertigo*," 60.

7. Hinton, "A Woman's View," 10.

8. Hinton reads the face in the credits sequence as Medusa and links it with Midge. For Hinton, both figures communicate "an astounding acknowledgment" of women's subjectivity, despite its "frame-up," to the female spectator ("A Woman's View," 21).

9. Robin Wood, *Hitchcock's Films Revisited* (New York: Columbia University Press, 1989), 122. Despite Wood's nuanced discussion of Judy's undecidability, he finds her character is, after all, readable. See the opening of Part III and note 12.

10. The allusion to Eurydice is discussed by Walter Poznar, "Orpheus Descending: Love in *Vertigo*," *Literature/Film Quarterly* 17 (1989), 59–65; see esp. 62. The allusions to Proust's madeleine and to the Hebrew *migdal* are discussed by Richard Goodkin, "Film and Fiction: Hitchcock's *Vertigo* and Proust's 'Vertigo,' " *MLN* 102, No. 5 (1987), 1171–81, see esp. 1180. In "Delusions and Dreams in Hitchcock's *Vertigo*," *Hitchcock Annual* (1993), 28–40, Donald O. Chankin compares Madeleine and Mary Magdalene (32). For the allusion to Pygmalion/Galatea, see David Sterritt, *The Films of Alfred Hitchcock* (Cambridge: Cambridge University Press, 1993), 97. For the allusion to Melasine, see Stanley R. Palumbro, "Hitchcock's *Vertigo*: The Dream Function in Film," in Joseph H. Smith and William Kerrigan, eds., *Images in Our Souls: Cavell, Psychoanalysis, and Cinema* (Baltimore: Johns Hopkins University Press, 1987), 50. For the allusion to Lamia, see Wood, *Hitchcock's Films Revisited*, 114; for the connection between vertigo and madness, see White, "Allegory and Referentiality," 931.

11. Nietzsche formulates this famous doctrine first as an afterthought to *The Gay Science* (1882) and later in *Thus Spake Zarathustra* (1884) and *Ecce Homo* (1888). The interpretation of it advanced here is influenced by Martin Heidegger's, in his *Nietzsche*, trans. David Farrell Krell (San Francisco: Harper and Row, 1984) II, 191: "[Nietzsche's doctrine] expresses the way in which the one who poses the guiding question remains enmeshed in the structures of that question, which is not explicitly unfolded; thus enmeshed, the questioner comes to stand within being as a whole, adopting a stance toward it." For other interpretations of Nietzsche's doctrine that emphasize its articulation of an interpretive dilemma, see David B. Allison's introduction to the volume he edited, *The New Nietzsche: Contemporary Styles of Interpretation* (Cambridge: MIT Press, 1985), xi–xxviii, and Pierre Klossowski's essay, "Nietzsche's Experience of the Eternal Return," in the same volume, 107–33. This understanding of the eternal return is developed in my book, *Models of Misrepresentation: On the Fiction of E. L. Doctorow* (Jackson and London: University Press of Mississippi, 1991). I return to Nietzsche's idea at the end of this essay.

12. Wood writes: "Yet Judy, we feel (the Judy of the last third of the film), is not a girl who would ever allow herself to become explicit about, perhaps even conscious of, such fears: she hasn't the intelligence, the self-awareness, or (despite her evident capacity for suffering) the depth" (122–23). Virginia Wright Wexman, in "The Critic as Consumer: Film Study in the University, *Vertigo*, and the Film Canon," *Film Quarterly* 39 (Spring, 1986), 32–41, believes Judy's character is definable: she "represents not a projective fantasy but an actual woman" (40). Walter Poznar sees Judy as an emissary of the banal normal world and its "inability to love" (62). In *In the Name of National Security: Hitchcock, Homophobia, and the Political Construction of Gender in Postwar America* (Durham: Duke University Press, 1993), Robert J. Corber sees Judy exclusively as a victim and never mentions her complicity in Elster's plot. The film offers no independent corroboration for these generalizations about Judy's character, even when she is alone. In *The Hitchcock Romance: Love and Irony in Hitchcock's Films* (Princeton: Princeton University Press, 1988), Lesley Brill argues that when Judy writes to Scottie, "she is undoubtedly sincere" (216); if so, this scene's depiction of a message composed and canceled equates the "authenticity of the subject" with the undecidability of its representation.

13. In "The Mise-en-Abime in Hitchock's *Vertigo*," Linderman argues that Midge is "the point of balance" in a film that is otherwise wholly destabilized by the representation of patriarchal systems of gender difference in imminent danger of collapse (70). Hinton grants that Midge is no "female role model," but sees her portrait as a confrontational joke that invokes the figure of Medusa, which conveys the film's larger truths about the position of women ("A Woman's View," 18–19).

14. Wood, *Hitchcock's Films Revisited*, 111.

15. Goodkin sees in Midge's surname ("Wood") evidence of her availability to Scottie ("Film and Fiction," 1180), a point also emphasized by Thomas Leitch in his *Find the Director and Other Hitchcock Games* (Athens: University of Georgia Press, 1991), 198. Against these assessments should be weighed equally compelling accounts of Midge's autonomy and independence from Scottie. For example, Wexman (38) interprets Midge's painting as a parodic demystification. This view is seconded by Karen Hollinger, "The Look, Narrativity, and the Female Spectator in *Vertigo*," *Journal of Film and Video* 39 (Fall, 1987), 18–27, see esp. 24; by Tania Modleski, *The Women Who Knew Too Much:*

Hitchcock and Feminist Theory (New York: Methuen, 1988), 90; by Linderman, 70; and by Hinton, 17–18.

16. Modleski, *The Women Who Knew Too Much*, 94.

17. Leitch agrees with Modleski's position, seeing Scottie as in psychological possession of Madeleine (*Find the Director*, 199). Mulvey sees Scottie's behavior in the second part of the film as exhibiting "active sadistic voyeurism" ("Visual Pleasure and Narrative Cinema," 14). For a challenge to this thesis, see Marian Keane, "A Closer Look at Scopophilia: Mulvey, Hitchcock, and *Vertigo*," in Marshall Deutelbaum and Leland Poague, eds., *A Hitchcock Reader* (Ames: Iowa State University Press, 1986), 231–48.

18. Wood, *Hitchcock's Films Revisited*, 128.

19. Sterritt, *The Films of Alfred Hitchcock*, 98.

20. Keane, "A Closer Look at Scopophilia," 244.

21. White, "Allegory and Referentiality," 931–32.

22. William Rothman, "*Vertigo*: The Unknown Woman in Hitchcock," in Smith and Kerrigan, *Images in Our Souls*, 77.

23. In *The Postmodern Condition: A Report on Knowledge*, trans. Geoff Bennington and Brian Massumi (Minneapolis: University of Minnesota Press, 1984), Jean-Francois Lyotard discusses the *grand recit* or master narratives of the West, by which he means narratives used for the legitimation of knowledge, especially in the political realm. My application of Lyotard's term to the political narrative in *Vertigo* implies a way that it may legitimize knowledge in film criticism, too. For another account of the film's commentary on American industrial power and expansionist aspirations, see Wexman, "The Critic as Consumer," 39.

24. Foucault's argument that the Kantian Enlightenment contained the seeds of its atavistic, irrational other is set forth in "What Is Enlightenment?" in Paul Rabinow, ed., *The Foucault Reader* (New York: Pantheon, 1984). The argument provides an interesting gloss on the way Scottie's irrationality is exploited by the *Ubermensch* Elster. Stephen Greenblatt's thesis that the European Renaissance harbored a project of imperialist subjugation of the other is outlined in *New World Encounters* (Berkeley: University of California Press, 1993); it may be brought to mind by the film's reminders of the Spanish as California's first conquerors and later as the victims of Anglo migration. Gayatri Chakravorty Spivak's indictment of the colonizing West as marginalizing the other is presented in *In Other Worlds: Essays in Cultural Politics* (New York: Methuen, 1987); this argument could be invoked in a discussion of Carlotta's fate. But at the same time, *Vertigo* seems to suggest critical approaches like these, it also challenges them as untenable allegories.

25. White, "Allegory and Referentiality," 931, 930.

26. In *Allegories of Reading: Figural Language in Rousseau, Nietzsche, Rilke and Proust* (New Haven: Yale University Press, 1979), de Man posited a potentially infinite series of errors arising from allegorical interpretation (205). For an extended discussion of this passage, see J. Hillis Miller, " 'Reading' Part of a Paragraph in *Allegories of Reading*," in Lindsay Waters and Wlad Godzich, eds., *Reading de Man Reading* (Minneapolis: University of Minnesota Press, 1989), 155–70. White's use of "Madeleine" to designate the entity Scottie pursues and is tormented by ("Allegory and Referentiality," 928, 930) is a local example of the inevitable error common to criticism of *Vertigo*: it is not possible to name this entity—and of course, the word "entity" conceals metaphor, too—without error. The errors in the present essay begin in the allegory of tenability

announced in its title and thesis; these continue throughout. In *"Vertigo* and Problems of Knowledge in Feminist Film Theory," White responded forthrightly to my claim that she had elided the full implications of de Man's idea of allegory: "My 'elision' of de Man's most radically deconstructive implications—for indeed such an elision takes place—speaks of my divided loyalties to the political agenda of feminist theory and the epistemic project of deconstructivism" (291).

27. The colorlessness of the ambience may be noted in the white modern churches and the gray of the Elsters' apartment building or the McKittrick Hotel; like the latter, Ernie's Restaurant is furnished in subdued tones. The colors of the streets are weak, washed-out, blanched; Midge's studio-cum-apartment is similarly devoid of color, and her workspace crowds out living space. Her exterior vistas are ignored or shut out by blinds; venetian blinds are also emphasized in Scottie's beige apartment. Color is drained even from Gavin Elster's office: though he complains of the modern world's colorlessness, his windows shut out the day, and the paintings on his walls repudiate color. Little wonder that Scottie puzzles over them in cognitive dissonance as Elster bemoans the loss of color in the modern world.

28. J. Hillis Miller, *The Ethics of Reading: Kant, de Man, Eliot, Trollope, James, and Benjamin* (New York: Columbia University Press, 1987), 21.

29. This conclusion agrees with Chankin's: "We are also forced to acknowledge that Scottie's quest, call it mad if you will, is ours" (38). However, Chankin's conclusion is derived from a Freudian account of Scottie's delusion, according to which its source lies in his near-death experience in the opening chase sequence, rather than in the act of reading.

30. The colonnades of the Mission San Juan Bautista are reminiscent of the signature element of de Chirico's early "metaphysical" paintings, as are the film's many extremes of perspective. Hitchcock's admiration for de Chirico's work is noted by Donald Spoto, *The Dark Side of Genius: The Life of Alfred Hitchcock* (New York: Ballantine Books, 1983), 292. This essay has argued that the empty signifiers and untenable points of view of visual art constitute the true subject matter of *Vertigo,* perhaps as they do of de Chirico's work, too.

CHAPTER 12

1. An important exception to this generalization is Frederic Jameson's essay, "Spatial Systems in *North by Northwest"* in *Everything You Always Wanted to Know about Lacan (But Were Afraid to Ask Hitchcock),* ed. Slavoj Žižek (London: Verso, 1992), 47–72. Jameson condemns such readings as "form-intrinsic," which in the case of *North by Northwest* lead only to the trivial "pop-psychological" message of "maturity" (48).

2. Lesley Brill, *The Hitchcock Romance: Love and Irony in Hitchcock's Films* (Princeton: Princeton University Press, 1988). Brill devotes the first chapter of his book to a reading of *North by Northwest* as an example of Frye's paradigm of romance.

3. Thomas Leitch, *Find the Director and Other Hitchcock Games* (Athens: University of Georgia Press, 1991).

4. Richard H. Millington, "Hitchcock and American Character: The Comedy of Self-Construction in *North by Northwest,"* in Jonathan Freedman and Richard Millington, eds., *Hitchcock's America* (New York: Oxford University Press, 1999), 135–54.

5. Robert J. Corber, *In the Name of National Security: Hitchcock, Homophobia, and*

the Political Construction of Gender in Postwar America (Durham: Duke University Press, 1993).

6. Brill sees Thornhill as "maturing"; however, he observes of the ending that "we may pause to hope that the new Mrs. Thornhill will fare better than her predecessors" (*The Hitchcock Romance*, 8, 21). Leitch qualifies his description of Thornhill's maturation with the proviso: "Thornhill's progress is arduous; for every step forward, he seems to take two steps back" (*Find the Director*, 213). Corber's argument for the culminating importance of Thornhill's complicity with the American government is modified by the acknowledgment that in disobeying the Professor, he also breaks with it (*In the Name of National Security*, 201).

7. George M. Wilson, *Narration in Light: Studies in Cinematic Point of View* (Baltimore: The Johns Hopkins University Press, 1986), 74, 80. Wilson's hesitation on this point is especially marked in this passage: "Probably the chief mark of Thornhill's self-reform is that he, through his love of Eve, breaks out of this network of skin-trade valuation. And yet, the irony remains that it is only as the embodiment of the fictional Kaplan that he achieves this breaking out. Certainly *something* has to change in him . . ." (74).

8. Geoffrey Hartman, "Plenty of Nothing: Hitchcock's *North by Northwest*," *Yale Review* 71 (1981), 21.

9. The phrase *grand recit* (or "master narrative") comes from Jean-Francois Lyotard in *The Postmodern Condition: A Report on Knowledge*, trans. Geoff Bennington and Brian Massumi (Minneapolis: University of Minnesota Press, 1984). Lyotard means by this phrase the narratives used for the legitimation of knowledge, especially in the political realm. My application of Lyotard's term to the narrative of growth or maturation in *North by Northwest* implies a way that this narrative strives to legitimate knowledge in film criticism, too.

10. "Alfred Hitchcock Talking," *Films and Filming* 5 (July, 1959), 7.

11. Of course, another way of taking the title is to see it as referring to "the direction of the plot"—that is, to the fact that Thornhill's movements take him north-northwest, from New York to Chicago to Sioux Falls, North Dakota, and that on his last journey he takes Northwest Airlines. It may be observed in passing that because this movement is not *truly* "north northwest" (closer to west northwest), the title is already a mis-naming. No one has argued that the film's plot-direction is of any significance. The idea of naming a work after such compass points implies that the film's major issues—identity, love, national security—are of as little consequence as random movement. Another way of putting this is to say that the viewer's choice in construing the title is between the mis-naming/tautology of the "direction of the plot" and the undecidability of the allusion to *Hamlet*. The first critic to argue for the acceptance of that allusion was Marian Keane, in "The Designs of Authorship," *Wide Angle* 4 (1980), 44–52. (Like some other critics, Keane mistakenly thinks Hamlet's speech welcomes the players; however, it is addressed to Rosencrantz and Guildenstern.) Stanley Cavell, in *Themes out of School: Effects and Causes* (San Francisco: North Point Press, 1984), 156–58, makes the most extended case for the allusion. His position is seconded by William Rothman, "*North by Northwest*: Hitchcock's Monument to the Hitchcock Film," *North Dakota Quarterly* 51 (1984), 11–23; by George M. Wilson; and by Brill. On the other hand, several critics remain silent on this subject, including Geoffrey Hartman, "Plenty of Nothing"; Robin Wood, *Hitchcock's Films Revisited* (New York: Columbia University Press, 1989); Thomas Leitch; Richard H. Millington; Robert J. Corber.

12. Michel Foucault explores the question of the source of the definitions of madness in *Madness and Civilization: A History of Insanity in the Age of Reason*, trans. Richard Howard (London: Tavistock, 1967), and in *The Birth of the Clinic: An Archeology of Medical Perception*, trans. A. M. Sheridan Smith (New York: Pantheon Books, 1973).

13. Oscar James Campbell's gloss on "hawk from a handsaw" is as follows: "There are three interpretations of this phrase: (1) takes the words in their literal modern meaning; i.e., two objects so unlike that anyone could distinguish between them; (2) takes "handsaw" as a corruption of "hernshaw," a kind of heron; (3) takes "hawk" in the sense of a tool like a pickaxe." William Shakespeare, *Hamlet*, eds. Oscar James Campbell, Alfred Rothschild, and Stuart Vaughan (New York: Bantam Books, 1961), 285.

14. Stanley Cavell lists these affinities between *North by Northwest* and *Hamlet* in *Themes out of School*. For the critics who explore the analogy and those who don't, see note 9.

15. Derrida discusses this aspect of the postal in *The Post-Card: From Socrates to Freud and Beyond*, trans. Alan Bass (Chicago: University of Chicago Press, 1987), 29–33.

16. For a discussion of distancing, see *The Post-Card*, 29.

17. Ibid., 53.

18. Ibid., 33.

19. Ibid., 51.

20. Thomas Cohen, *Anti-Mimesis from Plato to Hitchcock* (New York: Cambridge University Press, 1994), 257.

21. Andrew Britton also calls attention to the way Thornhill's renaming of Eve constitutes a reinstatement of male authority at the end of the film. See his "Cary Grant: Comedy and Male Desire," *CineAction* 7 (1987), 36–51.

22. For the argument that Thornhill's character defects grow out of his urban life, his vocation as an advertising executive, and his relationships with women, see Wood, *Hitchcock's Films Revisited*; Leitch, *Find the Director*; Brill, *The Hitchcock Romance*; and Millington, "Hitchcock and American Character."

23. The temptation to interpret this scene as somehow representing originary or elemental existence comes from its stripped-down character—only a human being, nature, and strangers. But of course, this makes the scene no less a metaphor than any other in the film, no matter how apparently complex.

24. The argument that prosopopoeia is a constitutive trope of fiction is made by J. Hillis Miller in *Ariadne's Thread: Story Lines* (New Haven: Yale University Press, 1992).

25. It was Hitchcock himself who playfully interpreted the scene in this way: "There are no symbols in *North by Northwest*. Oh yes! One. The last shot, the train entering the tunnel after the love scene between Grant and Eva-Marie Saint. It's a phallic symbol. But don't tell anyone." Quoted in Wood, *Hitchcock's Films Revisited*, 131. Hitchcock repeats the interpretation in Francois Truffaut's *Hitchcock* (New York: Simon and Schuster, 1967), 108.

26. Others have noticed this link in the film. For example, Hartman writes of the moment Thornhill is confused with Kaplan: "He is immediately divested of his identity, one that sits on him as easily as his suit" ("Plenty of Nothing," 15).

27. Ibid., 16.

28. Even though the Professor refers to the "cold war," we don't know that Vandamm is a communist, *pace* Corber's assertion that communists and homosexuals are coded as the same.

29. For a useful discussion of the parallels between the Professor and Vandamm that suggest they are surrogate *auteurs*, see Keane, "The Designs of Authorship," 45–46.

30. In *Narration in Light*, Wilson's admirable demonstration that *North by Northwest* questions the reliability of individual perception is not extended to his own essay, which both uneasily follows the *grand recit* of maturation in Thornhill and questions it. In "Plenty of Nothing," Hartman's astute thesis—that the film undermines the "solidity" of understanding—is never extended to his own argument's traditional assumption of film as mimesis.

CHAPTER 13

1. Martin Jay, *Downcast Eyes: The Denigration of Vision in Twentieth-Century French Thought* (Berkeley: University of California Press, 1993), chapter 4. Rosalind Krauss, "The Photographic Conditions of Surrealism," in *The Originality of the Avant-Garde and Other Modernist Myths* (Cambridge: Harvard University Press, 1985).

2. In *Hitchcock: The Murderous Gaze* (Cambridge: Harvard University Press, 1982), William Rothman interprets the dissolve as an image of birth (308). In *The Hitchcock Romance: Love and Irony in Hitchcock's Films* (Princeton: Princeton University Press, 1988), Lesley Brill sees the dissolve as the failure of hopes for renewal and regeneration (221, 227). In *Find the Director and Other Hitchcock Games* (Athens: University of Georgia Press, 1991), Thomas Leitch says the dissolve marks the moment when the film's mode "switches decisively from psychological drama to black comedy" (217). In " 'In His Bold Gaze My Ruin Is Writ Large,' " in *Everything You Always Wanted to Know About Lacan (But Were Afraid to Ask Hitchcock)*, ed. Slavoj Žižek (London, Verso, 1992), 211–72, Slavoj Žižek interprets the dissolve as a movement through a "zero point," analogous to the twist in a Moebius strip, through which the viewer may understand the continuity between the film's two main narratives as illustrative of the unconscious as defined by Jacques Lacan.

3. Francois Truffaut, *Hitchcock*, rev. ed. (New York: Simon and Schuster, 1983), 276. In "The Impossible Embodiment," Michel Chion analyzes the landing scene at length as part of his argument that Mrs. Bates embodies the concept of *acousmetre*, a being who presents himself or herself as a disembodied voice. His essay is collected in Slavoj Žižek's *Everything You Always Wanted to Know about Lacan (But Were Afraid to Ask Hitchcock)* (New York and London: Verso, 1992), 195–207.

4. In his late work, Paul de Man argued for the existence of something he called the "materiality" of the sign, but also of the "event"; for a variety of perspectives on the latter idea, see Tom Cohen, ed., *Material Events: Paul de Man and the Afterlife of Theory* (Minneapolis: University of Minnesota Press, 2001). This book makes no claims for the materiality of the event and assumes only that signs have some material expression (ink, celluloid, photons, and the like). The existence of the material world apart from its expression in signs is not addressed in this book.

5. "White mythologies" is Derrida's famous phrase for the unacknowledged metaphors at the "basis" or "heart" of all philosophy. See his "White Mythology: Metaphor in the Text of Philosophy," in *Margins of Philosophy*, trans. Alan Bass (Chicago: University of Chicago Press,1982), 207–72.

6. In "Deus Ex Animo, or Why a Doc?" *Journal of Popular Film and Television* 18 (1990), 36–39, Irving Schneider uses the analogy to Greek tragedy to argue that the

psychiatrist's presence reassures viewers of both the legitimacy of their presence in the theatre and the superiority of their insight.

7. In *The Art of Alfred Hitchcock* (New York: Hopkinson and Blake, 1976), Donald Spoto calls the psychiatrist "pompous and unattractive" (380). In *Hitchcock's Films Revisited* (New York: Columbia University Press, 1989), Robin Wood calls him "glib" and "complacent" (149). In *Alfred Hitchcock: The Legacy of Victorianism*, Paula Marantz Cohen calls the psychiatrist "posturing" and "paternal" (150).

8. Raymond Bellour, "Psychosis, Neurosis, Perversion," *Camera Obscura* no. 3–4 (1979); rpt. in Marshall Deutelbaum and Leland Poague, *A Hitchcock Reader* (Ames: Iowa State University Press, 1986), 311–31. In Bellour's account, Norman's psychosis is born of fetishism and scopophilia; this supplement maintains Freudian and Lacanian categories. Bellour describes his intention as "to complete the psychiatrist's speech" (324).

9. Barbara Klinger, "*Psycho*: The Institutionalization of Female Sexuality," *Wide Angle* 5:1 (1982); rpt. *A Hitchcock Reader*, 332–39.

10. William Rothman, *Hitchcock: The Murderous Gaze* (Cambridge: Harvard University Press, 1982) makes other challenges to the psychiatrist's speech, too (332–40).

11. Leland Poague, "Links in a Chain: *Psycho* and Film Classicism," *A Hitchcock Reader*, 340–49.

12. Robert Corber, *In the Name of National Security: Hitchcock, Homophobia, and the Political Construction of Gender in Postwar America* (Durham: Duke University Press, 1993), 186–92.

13. Leitch, *Find the Director*, 218.

14. George Toles, " 'If Thine Eye Offend Thee . . . ': *Psycho* and the Art of Infection," in Richard Allen and S. Ishii-Gonzales, eds., *Alfred Hitchcock: Centenary Essays* (London: British Film Institute, 1999), 159–74, 173.

15. Corber, 211–12. Corber maintains that despite these mixed motives, Sam genuinely loves Marion. But consider this "assurance"—as Corber calls it—that Sam gives Marion: "Whenever it's possible, I want to see you, and under any circumstances, even respectability." Certainly his initial qualification goes far to undermine the apparent assurance, just as his "even" sustains his preference for the illicit.

16. Donald Spoto, *The Art of Alfred Hitchcock*, 378.

17. For the physical resemblance between Sam and Norman, see Robin Wood, *Hitchcock's Films Revisited*, 147, and Corber, *In the Name of National Security*, 215. For other parallels between Sam Loomis and Norman Bates, see Toles, "If Thine Eye Offend Thee," 168–69.

18. The physical resemblance between Marion (Vivian Leigh) and Lila (Vera Miles) is noted by Wood, *Hitchcock's Films Revisited*, 147.

19. Brill, *The Hitchcock Romance*, 228.

20. In *The Dark Side of Genius: The Life of Alfred Hitchcock* (New York: Ballantine Books, 1983), Donald Spoto reviewed the film's mirror and cutting imagery to show the viewer's implication in the psychological instinct of attraction/repulsion that is narrated; in "Through a Shower Curtain Darkly: Reflexivity as a Dramatic Component of Psycho," *Literature/Film Quarterly* 19 (1991), 258–66, John Recchia extends Spoto's thesis in an analysis of subjective camera and soundtrack. William Rothman's study of the reflexivity of *Psycho* identified the camera with Hitchcock.

21. Cohen, *Alfred Hitchcock*, 150.

CHAPTER 14

1. Robin Wood, *Hitchcock's Films Revisited* (New York: Columbia University Press, 1989), 153.

2. Thomas Leitch, *Find the Director and Other Hitchcock Games* (Athens: University of Georgia Press, 1991), 229. One of the psychological interpretations with which Leitch takes issue is Margaret M. Horwitz's "*The Birds*: A Mother's Love," in Marshall Deutelbaum and Leland Poague, eds., *A Hitchcock Reader* (Ames, Iowa: Iowa State University Press, 1986), 279–87. For another psychological interpretation, indebted to Horwitz's article, see Camille Paglia, *The Birds* (London: The British Film Institute, 1998).

3. Slavoj Žižek, *Looking Awry: An Introduction to Jacques Lacan Through Popular Culture* (Cambridge: MIT Press, 1991); Robert Samuels, *Hitchcock's Bi-Textuality: Lacan, Feminisms, and Queer Theory* (Albany: SUNY Press, 1997).

4. Leitch, *Find the Director*, 230.

5. Hitchcock used the term "springboard situation" to refer to the expository section of the film, usually the first reel, in which the basic dilemma confronting the hero was set forth. See Sidney Gottlieb, *Hitchcock on Hitchcock* (Berkeley: University of California Press, 1995), 273.

6. Cedric H. Whitman, *Aristophanes and the Comic Hero* (Cambridge: Harvard University Press, 1964), 193–94.

7. Emilo Benveniste, *Problèmes de linguistic générale*, trans. Mary Elizabeth Meek, Miami Linguistics Series, No. 8 (1966; rpt. Coral Gables: University of Miami Press, 1971), 217–23.

8. See Kyle B. Counts, "The Making of Alfred Hitchcock's *The Birds*," *Cinefantastique* 10 (Fall, 1980), 15–35 and Robert Boyle, "Designed for Film," *Film Comment* 14 (1978), 33–35.

9. Hitchcock's original ending—in which the Brenners arrived at the Golden Gate Bridge only to find it teeming with birds—suggests an apocalypticism that is not necessary, since the imagination can well extrapolate the effect of *billions* of birds, in the ornithologist's reckoning, massing against the human race. In any case, Hitchcock's open ending continues the undecidability of the birds. In the final analysis the film refuses to make them "mean" either the death or the freedom of the human race.

10. Roland Barthes, *Camera Lucida: Reflections on Photography*, trans. Richard Howard (New York: Hill and Wang, 1981).

CHAPTER 15

1. In *The Art of Alfred Hitchcock* (New York: Hopkinson and Blake, 1976), Donald Spoto classified *Torn Curtain* with earlier MacGuffin films but reads their collective theme as the idea that "relationships matter, not political secrets" (418). My discussion of the MacGuffin as the sign that puts meaning in doubt is in chapter 2.

2. Hitchcock used the term "springboard situation" to denote the general plot problem, established in the first reel, for which the remainder of the film provided the resolution. See Sidney Gottlieb, ed., *Hitchcock on Hitchcock* (Berkeley: University of California Press,1995), 273. I use the term slightly more broadly, to denote the early scene which first encapsulates the film's allegory.

3. For Derrida's account of "the postal," see his *The Post-Card: From Socrates to Freud and Beyond*, trans. Alan Bass (Chicago: University of Chicago Press, 1987).

4. Raymond Durgnat, *The Strange Case of Alfred Hitchcock* (Cambridge: MIT Press, 1974), 374.

5. See Spoto, *The Art of Alfred Hitchcock*, 416.

6. I am preceded in the identification of the title's allusion to Matthew by James M. Vest, in his excellent essay, "Hitchcock's Cameo in *Torn Curtain*," *Hitchcock Annual* 1998–99, 3–19. Other aspects of the film suggest a religious dimension to the allegory. After Sherman leaves the bookstore with the volume that contains Armstrong's coded instructions, the bookseller tells his assistant to "pray for him." Encouraging her to tidy up, he then says, "Them religious books is in a hell of a shambles, Magda." There is no way to tell from these remarks whether the bookseller speaks from a religious or secular perspective; this indeterminacy echoes the moral undecidability of Armstrong's actions. The bookseller's expletive is one that is also invoked by Armstrong to Sherman on the plane ("What in hell are you doing here?"). Both references may have contributed to Donald Spoto's idea that Armstrong's journey is a descent into hell; see *The Art of Alfred Hitchcock*, 418–21. Armstrong's role as harrower of hell may be enhanced by the fact that he briefly rides on a plow and digs in the ground with his toe or that he successfully emerges from the Inferno of the stage production of *Francesca da Rimini*.

7. *New Catholic Encyclopedia* (New York: McGraw-Hill, 1967), 590. This interpretation is echoed in *The Interpreter's Bible* (New York: Abingdon Press, 1951): "The division between Jew and Gentile now is gone: the Gentile now can go beyond the outer court into the holy place, yes, and into the 'holiest' " (III, 610). One difficulty in understanding the torn curtain in its relation to the Jewish people is reflected in the claim of *The Interpreter's Bible* that the torn curtain is also a signal of the displeasure of God (610); if so, it is unclear whether the torn curtain is meant to obliterate a distinction or to establish a new one.

8. The connection between curtains and theatrical drapes in *Rear Window* is made by Robert Stam in "Hitchcock's *Rear Window*: Reflexivity and the Critique of Voyeurism," in Marshall Deutelbaum and Leland Poague, eds., *A Hitchcock Reader* (Ames: Iowa State University Press, 1986), 193–206. For the connection between *Psycho*'s shower curtain and a cinematic screen, see John Recchia, "Through a Shower Curtain Darkly: Reflexivity as a Dramatic Component of *Psycho*," *Literature/Film Quarterly* 19 (1991), 258–66.

9. The ambiguity of Armstrong's character is only deepened when understood in the context of the film persona of Paul Newman. In *Torn Curtain*, Hitchcock's practice of casting actors in parts that manifested something contradictory but latent in their personae—beginning with Cary Grant in *Notorious* and *Suspicion*—is extended to the actor whose stoic athleticism had been colored, in such films as *Cat on a Hot Tin Roof* (1958) and *The Left-Handed Gun* (1958), with a strain of homoeroticism. The mixed message of Newman's coldness toward women may be exploited in the opening bedroom scene and in the final scene, both of which play with the effects of merely apparent warmth; the extent of Newman's physical prowess may be "made ironic" in his long struggle with Gromek, which succeeds only because of the farm girl. The innocence of the Julie Andrews persona, inherited from *Mary Poppins* (1964) and *The Sound of Music* (1965), is dispelled in the bedroom scene and in her willingness to use flirtation as a means of helping Armstrong purloin the secret of the formula from Lindt. I thank one of the

anonymous readers for *Cinema Journal*, where the original version of this chapter first appeared, for drawing my attention to this point.

10. Durgnat, *The Strange Case of Alfred Hitchcock*, 372.

11. Robin Wood, *Hitchcock's Films Revisited* (New York: Columbia University Press, 1989), 202.

12. "I got so bored with seeing those English films with the nude couple in bed and that constant shot over the bare shoulder of the man, which is just covering the breasts of the girl ... I wanted all the people in the dining room to be wrapped in coats and freezing to death having their lunch. And then I go down below and show our couple in bed, covered with blankets, covered in topcoats, and you barely see them at all. For some inexplicable reason, my sense of propriety in this matter didn't seem to meet the approval of the Legion of Decency; they complained that there were premarital occupations going on, and I don't understand why they said that because I can't see a thing." Budge Crawley, Fletcher Markle, and Gerald Pratley, "I Wish We Didn't Have to Shoot the Picture: An Interview with Alfred Hitchcock," in Albert J. LaValley, editor, *Focus on Hitchcock* (Englewood Cliffs, NJ: Prentice-Hall, Inc., 1972), 25.

13. In "Beyond 'The Gaze': Žižek, Hitchcock, and the American Sublime," in *American Literary History* 7 (1995), 350–78, Tom Cohen notes a similar connection between the MacGuffin and the circularity of the plot in *To Catch a Thief*, a film in which "theft itself is also to be conceived as the act of representation or of language" (368). Cohen's illuminating reading of *To Catch a Thief* suggests ways in which that film's metaphor for language may anticipate Armstrong's theft as reading or as "false congress" in *Torn Curtain*.

14. This association was first noticed by Gene D. Phillips, *Alfred Hitchcock* (Boston: Twayne Publishers, 1984), 169.

15. Francois Truffaut, *Hitchcock*, rev. ed. (New York: Simon and Schuster, 1983), 309.

16. Durgnat, *The Strange Case of Alfred Hitchcock*, 373.

17. For the transcription and translation of German-language portions of *Torn Curtain*, I am indebted to my brother Michael and to my colleague David Ward, Department of Modern Languages, Norwich University.

18. I am grateful to David Ward for calling my attention to this detail.

AFTERWORD

1. The *OED* gives "form, figure."

2. Eric Auerbach, *Scenes from the Drama of European Literature* (New York: Meridian Books, 1959), 14–15.

3. *The Institutio Oratoria of Quintilian*, trans. H. E. Butler, four volumes (Cambridge: Harvard University Press, 1953), III, 355.

4. George A. Kennedy, *A New History of Classical Rhetoric* (Princeton: Princeton University Press, 1994), 86.

5. Harry Caplan, trans. [Cicero], *Rhetorica ad Herennium* (Cambridge: Harvard University Press, 1954), 275.

6. Plato, *Gorgias*, trans. W. C. Helmbold (Indianapolis: Bobbs-Merrill, 1952), 5.

7. The outline of Gorgias's *On the Nonexistent* can be read in Kathleen Freeman's *Ancilla to the Pre-Socratic Philosophers* (Cambridge: Harvard University Press, 1983).

8. Jeffrey Walker, *Rhetoric and Poetics in Antiquity* (New York: Oxford University Press, 2000), 27.

9. In fact the author of *Rhetorica ad Herennium* uses the phrases "verborum exornatio" and "sententiarum exornation" rather than "figura," although Harry Caplan follows scholarly tradition by translating the phrases as "figures of diction" and "figures of thought" and by regarding this passage as the first Latin appearance of the distinction between schemes and tropes (274). Quintilian was the first to use "figura" for "scheme"; it is unclear whether he knew *Rhetorca ad Herennium*.

10. In Book IX of *The Institutio Oratio* Quntilian struggles to assert a distinction between figures and tropes. His main idea is that in tropes there is a "transference of expression from a natural and principal signification to another," whereas in a figure "we give our language a conformation other than the obvious and ordinary" (351). Quintilian's comments on irony are also on this page. It can easily be seen how many questions are begged by this distinction.

11. Shirley Sharon-Zisser, "A Distinction No Longer of Use: Evolutionary Discourse and the Disappearance of the Trope/Figure Binarism," *Rhetorica* 11:3 (1993), 321–42. Sharon-Zisser attributes the breakdown of the distinction to nineteenth-century discourses on evolution and utilitarianism. On the other hand, as I suggest here, the untenability of the distinction may have been present from the start.

12. Auerbach's discussion of Dante, especially his depictions of Cato and Virgil, occupies most of the fourth section of his essay, 60–76.

13. *Gorgias*, 76.

14. Friedrich Nietzsche, *Gesammelte Werke* (Munich: Musarion Verlag, 1922), 5:300, quoted in Paul de Man, *Allegories of Reading* (New Haven: Yale University Press,1979), 105.

15. Paul de Man, *Allegories of Reading Proust* (New Haven: Yale University Press, 114.

16. Ferdinand de Saussure, *Course in General Linguistics*, trans. Wade Baskin (New York: Philosophical Library, 1959); Jacques Derrida, *Speech and Phenomena*, trans. David B. Allison (Evanston: Northwestern University Press, 1973).

17. W.J.T. Mitchell, "Word and Image," in Robert S. Nelson and Richard Shiff, eds., *Critical Terms for Art History* (Chicago: University of Chicago Press, 1996), 47–57, 49.

18. Mitchell's claim is as follows: "The task may seem hopelessly contradictory: if, on the one hand, art history turns the image into a verbal message or a 'discourse,' the image disappears from sight. If on the other hand, art history refuses language, or reduces language to a mere servant of the visual image, the image remains mute and inarticulate, and the art historian is reduced to the repetition of cliches about the ineffability and untranslatability of the visual. The choice is between linguistic imperialism and defensive reflexes of the visual" (56). The figures in this passage include hyperbole ("the image disappears from sight") and metaphor ("a mere servant," "imperialism"); these call for analysis. But the passage as a whole also exemplifies the fallacy of the false alternative.

Index

Titles not otherwise attributed refer to works by Alfred Hitchcock.

About the Author

Christopher D. Morris is the Charles A. Dana Professor of English at Norwich University in Northfield, Vermont. He is the author of *Models of Misrepresentation: On the Fiction of E. L. Doctorow*, as well as many articles on English and American literature.

AEF- 1381

WITHDRAWN